ROLE OF PANCHAYATI RAJ INSTITUTIONS IN 60 YEARS OF INDEPENDENT INDIA

Vision of the Future

About the Academy of Grassroots Studies and Research of India

The Academy of Grassroots Studies and Research of India (AGRASRI) is an autonomous, non-profit and Non-Governmental Professional Organisation, Registered under the Societies Registration Act xxi of 1860 in the year 2001, being headquartered at Tirupati (A.P.), a World renowned Hindu pilgrim centre. The Academy was formally inaugurated by Shri Mani Shankar Aiyar, a champion of democratic decentralisation movement in India, on 20th August, 2001 at Tirupati.

The Academy works to provide an environment suitable for the study and promotion of academic research, training, education and consultancy in grassroots democratic institutions for self-sufficient Village Republics in India. The Grassroots Governance Journal (Bi-annual) and Grama Sabha Magazine (Monthly) are the official publications of Academy, besides books, working papers, occasional papers and monographs.

In pursuance of the aims and objectives, the AGRASRI is organising the Bharat Ratna Rajiv Gandhi Memorial Lecture and presenting the Bharat Ratna Rajiv Gandhi Outstanding Leadership and Bharat Ratna Rajiv Gandhi Best Panchayat Awards at three levels—District, Taluk and Gram Panchayats—on 20th August every year since 2002, in recognition of Shri Rajiv Gandhi's significant achievements and services to the nation, as Seventh Prime Minister of India.

About the Editor

Dr. D. Sundar Ram is a Founder and Director of Academy of Grassroots Studies and Research of India (AGRASRI), being headquartered at Tirupati (A.P.). He is heading the Rajiv Rural Development Foundation (RRDF), Tirupati. He is Editor of The Grassroots Governance Journal (Bi-annual) and Grama Sabha Magazine (Monthy). He is a prolific writer, author, researcher and analyst. He has written extensively on Indian governance, parliamentary studies, electoral reforms, decentralisation, federalism and state politics, with over 20 books and 150 research papers to his credit. He was earlier Reader in Public Administration, Sri Subbaraya and Narayana College P.G. Centre (Acharya Nagarjuna University), Narasaraopet, Guntur District (A.P.); UGC Research Associate in Political Science at Sri Venkateswara University, Tirupati; and Parliamentary Fellow at the Institute of Constitutional and Parliamentary Studies, New Delhi.

He is a Member in many professional bodies and organisations of national repute. He is actively involved in imparting Capacity Building Training for the elected representatives of PRI's and SHG's in Andhra Pradesh state, under the aegis AGRASRI, Tirupati. He is conferred the Man of the Year Award-2004; Man of the Achievement Award-2005 and Man of the Year Commemorative Medal for the Year-2006, by the American Biographical Institute, USA.

Presently, he is the Chief Organiser of the Bharat Ratna Rajiv Gandhi Memorial Lecture programme and Convener of the Bharat Ratna Rajiv Gandhi Outstanding Leadership and Best Panchayat Awards Jury, under the aegis of AGRASRI and Rajiv Rural Development Foundation, Tirupati (A.P.).

Role of Panchayati Raj Institutions in 60 Years of Independent India

Vision of the Future

Edited by

D. Sundar Ram

Director, AGRASRI
Tirupati (A.P.)

Academy of Grassroots Studies and Research of India, Tirupati (A.P.)

in association with

KANISHKA PUBLISHERS, DISTRIBUTORS
NEW DELHI-110 002

KANISHKA PUBLISHERS, DISTRIBUTORS
4697/5-21A, Ansari Road, Daryaganj
New Delhi-110 002
Phones : 2327 0497, 2328 8285
Fax : 011-2328 8285
E-mail : kanishka_publishing@yahoo.co.in

First Published 2008

ISBN 978-81-8457-087-8

PRINTED IN INDIA

Published by Madan Sachdeva for Kanishka Publishers, Distributors, 4697/5-21A, Ansari Road, Daryaganj, New Delhi-110 002. Typeset by Sunshine Graphics, Delhi, and Printed at Nice Printing Press, Delhi.

Preface

Ever since India's Independence, the Panchayati Raj Institutions have been played a significant role in providing basic services to the people and strengthen democracy at the grassroots level. Pandit Jawaharlal Nehru, the first Prime Minister of India, was of the opinion that India would maker real progress only when people living in villages became politically conscious and said that the *'progress of our country is bound up with the progress in our villages'*. This vision was given a Constitutional shape and sanction by late Shri Rajiv Gandhi, by empowering Panchayati Raj Institutions to function as *'Institutions of Self-government'* to plan and implement programmes of economic development and social justice. The 73rd and 74th Amendments to the Constitution aimed at the empowerment of Panchayati Raj and Nagar Palika Institutions as a progressive step towards democratic decentralization, generating hopes that these would result in the realisation of Mahatma Gandhi's dream of *'Gram Swaraj'*. It is a fortunate that the present Union Minister for Panchayati Raj Shri Mani Shankar Aiyar has taken many remarkable initiatives to get closer to the realisation of Shri Rajiv Gandhi's unfinished agenda and dreams towards Panchayati Raj.

As a basic unit of Local Self-government, the effective functioning of Gram Panchayat is vital for good governance. Today, in our country, there are 2,50,000 elected bodes with 32 lakh elected representatives at three levels of Panchayati Raj Institutions, out of which 10 lakhs are women. After enactment of 73rd Constitution Amendment Act, every attempt has been made to constitutionalise grassroots democratic institutions and make them as effective instruments of people's participation which will ultimately prove to be the torch bearer of social change and development at the grassroots level. When we look at the signal achievements of the Sixty Years of Independent India, it is clear that the country has made tremendous progress over the years in all sectors. Unfortunately, Mahatma Gandhi's Gram Swaraj concept has still not reached the millions of the under privileged sections of the society. No doubt that after an enactment of 73rd Constitution Amendment, the decentralisation of power and the role of Panchayati Raj Institutions (PRIs) is not only empowering the people at the grassroots but also enhancing the democratic functioning. However, India has failed to create the Panchayati Raj Institutions (PRIs) as a true constitutional bodies for social transformation even after 60 Years of India's Independence and 15 Years of the gazeting and entry into force of the 73rd Amendment (Part IX-The Panchayats) of the Constitution.

In view of significance and importance of the Panchayati Raj Institutions in the nation's progress and development, one has to take a fresh perception at the delivery of good governance at the grassroots level to the Indian citizens with the following questions: What is wrong with the working of our Panchayati Raj system? Why so much of poverty even now after Sixty Years of Independence? Why illiteracy continues to plague the villages? Why basic civic amenities are not available at many places in Indian villages? Why many people do not participate and raise their voice in an era of decentralised governance? Finding answers to these questions, the need of the hour is to ensure that our Panchayats can function as true institutions of Local Self-government, with full fledged 3 F's – Finances, Functions and Functionaries, as stipulated in the 73rd Constitution Amendment Act.

This publication is outcome of the proceedings of the National Conference of the Academy of Grassroots Studies and Research of India (AGRASRI), funded by the Union Ministry of Panchayati Raj, Government of India, held at Tirupati (Andhra Pradesh) during 19 and 20 August, 2007.

The present volume aims at looking the pros and cons of the working of the Panchayati Raj Institutions over a period of Six decades of India's Independence and 15 Years of the gazeting and entry into force of the 73rd Amendment (Part IX-The Panchayats) of the Constitution and draw out a blue print for the vision in the context of further reforms and delivering a good governance at the grassroots.

The Twenty-five Chapters in the present volume, written by distinguished policy makers, scientists, administrators and scholars provide a comprehensive review of the initiatives of various governments at the federal as well as state levels in bringing out a revolutionary Panchayati Raj reforms, through 73rd Constitutional Amendment Act of 1992 and various State Panchayati Raj Acts, for transformation of rural India. The distinguished panel of contributors of the volume identifies the strengths and weaknesses of the Panchayati Raj Institutions over a period of 60 Years of Independent India and suggests a holistic reforms package for efficient functioning of the grassroots democratic institutions for delivering good governance.

I take this opportunity, as Director of the National Conference, to thank *Dr. A.Chakrapani,* Hon'ble Chairman, Andhra Pradesh Legislative Council, Hyderabad; *Shri R.L. Bhatia,* His Excellency, the Governor of Kerala, Thiruvananthapuram(Kerala); *Dr. R.A. Mashelkar,* President of the Indian National Science Academy and CSIR Bhatnagar Fellow, National Chemical Laboratory, Pune; *Dr. Agarala Easwara Reddy,* former Speaker, Andhra Pradesh Legislative Assembly, Hyderabad; *Shri Manoranjan Bhakta,* Hon'ble Member of Parliament (Lok Sabha), Andaman and Nicobar Islands, Port Blair; *Shri Solipeta Ramachandra Reddy,* former Member of Parliament (Rajya Sabha), Hyderabad; and *Shri R. Dileep Reddy,* State Information Commissioner (RTI), Government of Andhra Pradesh, Hyderabad, for their august presence and academic contributions in the Inaugural as well as Valedictory Sessions of the National Conference at Tirupati during 19 and 20 August, 2007. I am grateful to the distinguished panel of Resource Persons, Delegates and Participants of the Conference, for their enriched academic inputs and research papers.

I am very much thankful to the Board of Governors, my colleagues and well-wishers at AGRASRI, for their valuable support and encouragement extended to the National Conference as well as the Sixth Bharat Ratna Rajiv Gandhi Memorial Lecture programme. The financial support to the National Conference provided by the Ministry of Panchayati Raj, Government of India, New Delhi, is greatly acknowledged.

I am grateful to Shri Madan Sachdeva of Kanishka Publishers, Distributors, New Delhi, for bringing out the present volume very promptly in a such a short period.

D. SUNDAR RAM

Director, AGRASRI

Contents

List of Contributors

Dr. A. Chakrapani is the Chairman, Andhra Pradesh Legislative Council, Government of Andhra Pradesh, Hyderabad (Andhra Pradesh).

Shri R.L. Bhatia is the Governor of Kerala, Raj Bhavan, Thiruvananthapuram (Kerala).

Dr. R.A. Mashelkar is the President, Indian National Science Academy and CSIR Bhatnagar Fellow, National Chemical Laboratory, Pune (Maharashtra). He has earlier been the Director-General of the Council of Scientific and Industrial Research (CSIR), New Delhi.

Dr. N.C. Saxena, *IAS (Retd.)* is Member, National Advisory Council, Government of India, New Delhi. He has earlier been the Secretary to Government of India and Member-Secretary to the Planning Commission of India, New Delhi.

Dr. (Mrs.) V. Mohini Giri is the Chairperson, Guild of Service, New Delhi. She has earlier been the Chairperson, National Commission for Women, New Delhi.

Shri K. Karunakar Patnaik, *IAS (Retd.)* is Senior Fellow, Institute of Social Science, Bhubaneswar. He has earlier been the Director, Panchayati Raj Department, Government of Orissa, Bhubaneswar (Orissa).

Dr. B.S. Bhargava is Senior Fellow, Institute of Social Sciences, Bangalore (Karnataka).

Dr. K. Subha is Regional Co-ordinator, Institute of Social Sciences, Bangalore (Karnataka).

Mr. D.S. Hanumantha Rao is Programme Co-ordinator, Institute of Social Sciences, Bangalore (Karnataka).

Dr. G. Palanithurai is Rajiv Gandhi Chair Professor for Panchayati Raj Studies, Gandhigram Rural University, Gandhigram (Tamil Nadu).

Dr. (Mrs.) Snehalata Panda is Professor of Political Science, Berhampur University, Berhampur (Orissa).

Dr. N.S. Gehlot is Professor of Political Science, Maharshi Dayanand Saraswathi University, Ajmer (Rajasthan).

Dr. Damodar Rout is Member of Legislative Assembly, Orissa State Legislative Assembly, Bhubaneswar. He has earlier been the Minister for Panchayati Raj, Government of Orissa, Bhubaneswar (Orissa).

Dr. Mohanan Bhaskaran Pillai is Professor, Department of Politics and International Studies, Pondicherry Central University, Pondicherry.

Dr. M.L. Santhanam is Rural Development Consultant and Guest Faculty, Management Studies, Chennai. He has earlier been the Director, National Institute of Rural Development, Hyderabad (Andhra Pradesh).

Dr. I. Satya Sundaram is Visiting Faculty Member in the Department of Rural Development, Acharya Nagarjuna University, Guntur (Andhra Pradesh).

Dr. Pramod K. Mishra is Reader in Political Science, University of Delhi, Delhi and Hon. Director, Academy for Asia and Pacific Studies, New Delhi.

Dr. Jos Chathukulam is Director, Centre for Rural Management, Kottayam (Kerala).

Dr. K. Gireesan is Senior Fellow, Centre for Rural Management, Kottayam (Kerala).

Dr. M. Gopinath Reddy is Associate Professor in Economic, Centre for Economic and Social Studies, Hyderabad (Andhra Pradesh).

Dr. N. Sivanna is Associate Professor, Centre for Political Institutions, Governance and Development, Institute for Social and Economic Change, Bangalore (Karnataka).

Dr. Veerashekharappa is Associate Professor, Post-Graduate Department of Management Studies and Research, Siddaganga Institute of Technology, Tumkur (Karnataka).

Dr. V. Raghupathy is Associate Professor, Department of Political Science and Development Administration, Gandhigram Rural University, Gandhigram (Tamil Nadu).

Dr. D. Krishnamoorthy is Associate Professor in Econometrics, Sri Venkateswara University, Tirupati (Andhra Pradesh).

Dr. M. Devendra Babu is Senior Assistant Professor, Centre for Economic Studies and Policy, Institute for Social and Economic Change, Bangalore (Karnataka).

Shri S. Viswanathan is Special Correspondent, Frontline, The Hindu Group of Publications, Chennai (Tamil Nadu).

Ms. K.C. Smitha is Research Scholar, Centre for Political Institutions, Governance and Development, Institute for Social and Economic Change, Bangalore (Karnataka).

Dr. D. Sundar Ram is Founder and Director, Academy of Grassroots Studies and Research of India (AGRASRI); Secretary-General, Rajiv Rural Development Foundation (RRDF); Editor, The Grassroots Governance Journal (TGGJ) and Grama Sabha (GS) Telugu Magazine, Tirupati (Andhra Pradesh).

Introduction

THE VITALITY OF PANCHAYATI RAJ INSTITUTIONS AFTER 60 YEARS OF INDEPENDENT INDIA: FUTURE VISION

D. SUNDAR RAM

Panchayat as an 'Institution of Local Self-Government' at the village level had its own origin in ancient India. A sort of Village Council or an association of the residents of the village often consisting of the village elders, Panchayat or Gram Sangha performed administrative and judicial functions. Sometimes, the Gram Sanghas or Panchayats were elected from among the villagers who regulated their own lives through these bodies. We find reference to Gram Sanghas in the Manusmriti (code of Manu), Kautilya's Arthashastra (400 B.C.) and the Mahabharata. Valimiki's Ramayana speaks of the Ganapada which was a sort of federation of village republics. Later, village commonwealths are mentioned in Sukra Niti (Sukracharya's Nitisara). In fact, the institution of Village Panchayats in one form or the other, has had an unbroken continuity almost all over India and throughout her long history.

After India's Independence, the statesmen and political leaders have been advocating adoption of Panchayati Raj system as a panacea for overcoming economic, social, political and other problems of rural India. However, the decentralisation was the essence of the Mahatma Gandhi's concept of Gram Swaraj. For Mahatma Gandhi, the village was the appropriate organisational level for direct democracy. Recognising the importance of democratic institutions at the grassroots level at the insistence of Mahatma Gandhi, the Panchayats were included in the Constitution of India, under its Directive Principles of State Policy (Article 40). Following the recommendations of various committees, Pandit Jawaharlal Nehru established the institutions of Panchayati Raj as the primary instrument for bringing development to the doorstep of rural India in 1959. Later, Smt. Indira Gandhi stressed the need for people's participation in the process of economic and social transformation. However, it was only in 1989- under the leadership of Shri Rajiv Gandhi that Panchayats were sought to be given a constitutional status, through 64th and 65th Constitutional Bills. No wonder, these two bills were lost in the Rajya Sabha by 3 votes only. But, Shri P.V. Narasimha Rao as Prime Minister succeeded in seeing through Parliament the two Bills in a somewhat diluted form through 73rd and 74th Constitutional Amendments in 1993.

No doubt that after enactment of 73rd Constitutional Amendment Act the decentralisation of power and the role of Panchayati Raj Institutions (PRIs) are not only empowering the people at the grassroots but also enhancing the democratic functioning, as true institutions of people. In recent years, the initiatives of Union Ministry of Panchayati Raj towards strengthening the Panchayati Raj Institutions (PRIs) have been made consummate at the grassroots. However, India has failed to create the Panchayati Raj Institutions (PRIs) as a true constitutional bodies for social transformation even after 60 Years of India's Independence and 15 Years of the gazetting and entry into force of the 73rd Amendment (Part IX—The Panchayats) of the Constitution. For this, one has to take a fresh look at the delivery of good governance at the grassroots to the Indian citizens with the following questions. What is wrong with the panchayati raj system in India? Why so much of poverty even now after 60 Years of Independent India? Why illiteracy continues to plague the villages? Why civic amenities are not available at many places in Indian villages? Why many people do not participate and raise their voice in an era of decentralised governance? Why the devolution of funds, functions and functionaries to the PRIs are getting delayed by the State Governments? Seeking answers to these questions, the need of the hour is to ensure that panchayats can function as true institutions of local self-governments.

Keeping in view the background of the Second Generation of Panchayati Raj reforms initiatives by the United Progressive Alliance Government led by Dr. Manmohan Singh, the Academy of Grassroots Studies and Research of India (AGRASRI) has organised a two-day National Conference on 'Role of Panchayati Raj Institutions after 60 Years of Independent India : A Vision of the Future', during 19 and 20 August, 2007 at Tirupati, Andhra Pradesh, to formulate a new vision for good governance at the grassroots by the PRIs after Six decades of India's Independence, with financial support of the Ministry of Panchayati Raj, Government of India, New Delhi.

In order to stock-taking situation of the Panchayati Raj Institutions status and position for the last six decades in Independent India, the present volume explore the following objects: *(i)* To analyse the concerted efforts and initiatives of the successive Governments both at the Centre as well as States in the implementation of the provisions of the 73rd Constitution Amendment Act over a period of 15 years in respect of Panchayati Raj Institutions, as Constitutional bodies; *(ii)* To probe the areas of conflicts and consensus in light of the available experiences and experiments of various State Governments towards the devolution of 3 F's—Functions, Finances and Functionaries—to the Panchayati Raj Institutions; *(iii)* To outline the popular participation of people for rural transformation through Panchayati Raj Institutions, after the 73rd Constitution Amendment Act, with reference to Gram Sabha; *(iv)* To evaluate the role of women and youth in Panchayati Raj activities and programmes ushering in a new development culture; *(v)* To visualise the future of Panchayati Raj Institutions as a basic instruments for service delivery in contemporary India.

The present volume aims at looking the pros and cons of the working of the Panchayati Raj Institutions over a period of six decades of India's Independence and 15 Years of the gazetting and entry into force of the 73rd Amendment (Part IX—The Panchayats) of the Constitution and drawout a blue print for the vision in the context of further reforms and delivering a good governance at the grassroots. To find out the ways and means in strengthening the Panchayati Raj Institutions further as local self-government bodies in contemporary India, scholars are invited to submit papers and experts are requested to address one or more relevant aspects of the theme of the volume, with the significant role of PRIs in the implementation of multiple welfare and developmental programmes at the national as well as state level. In this context, the following sub-themes were discussed at length in two-day National Conference with useful output. Panel-I: Devolution of 3 F's—Functions, Functionaries and Finances—to the Panchayati Raj Institutions: A Myth or Reality; Panel-II: Panchayati Raj and Right to Information Act: A Way Forward for Transparent Administration; Panel-III : Capacity Building and Decentralised Governance:

Strategies and Challenges; Panel-IV : Panchayati Mahila Shakthi and Yuva Shakthi Abhiyans : From Unrest to Prosperity and Panel-V : Role of Panchayati Raj Institutions towards Good Governance: A Vision of the Future.

D. Sundar Ram, editor of the volume, outlines the vitality of Panchayati Raj Institutions after 60 Years of Independent India, in an Introductory Chapter. After presenting the general view of the working of the Panchayati Raj Institutions in India, he advocates that the need of the hour is to revamp the existing system of Panchayati Raj, as the real basic unit of Local Self-government in all respects, with devolution of powers and sufficient financial resources at the disposal of the elected representatives of Panchayati Raj Institutions.

A. Chakrapani, in Chapter-1, provides a comprehensive assessment of the signal role of Panchayati Raj Institutions in contemporary India. Examining the implementation of the provisions of the 73rd Constitutional Amendment Act, especially the devolution of powers to the Panchayati Raj Institutions, he said that they must be included in the Constitutional Schedule so that they become mandatory and insulated against judicial or any other external intervention. Realising the role of people in the development of Village Panchayats, he opines that the Gandhian dream of Gram Swaraj has fully realised only when the powers have delegated to Panchayati Raj Institutions. They should be given powers of 'Nyaya Panchayat' to the Village Panchayat with right to appeal to the civil and criminal court. Some minimum police powers must also be given for the Village Panchayat for maintaining peace and tranquility in rural areas. Its involvement and report to local police station once in a week will establish a better link between the people and state of police and helps to reduce law and order problems in rural areas. Government officials should act like facilitators in the system but not masters for power, decision-making and implementing the programmes in the Village Panchayats. While evaluating the real picture of the Panchayati Raj Institutions in contemporary India, A. Chakrapani suggests that the Functional Committees consisting among all caste groups may be formed at the village level providing sufficient funds basing on the population, reservation policy for women and scheduled caste, scheduled tribes, Backward Communities be continued further. Training for women to develop leadership and administrative skills, promoting participation of community and NGO's encouraging non-party basis .elections to Panchayati Raj Institutions to avoid the interference of politicians in the functioning, elected representatives, particularly at the Village Panchayat level be given need based regular training are some of the important ingredients to strengthen the Panchayati Raj Institutions.

R.L. Bhatia explores that Shri Rajiv Gandhi as one of the finest Prime Ministers of India who aspired a lot, dreamt a lot about making India strong, modern and self-reliant. India was at the threshold of a transition in several spheres when his life was snatched away leaving many glorious dreams unfulfilled in Chapter-2. Surveying the perspectives and initiatives of Shri Rajiv Gandhi in respect of human development, he outlines that it was indeed Shri Rajiv Gandhi who set afoot India's modernisation process, equipping our country for its historic launch in to the 21st century. It was his insight and initiative that enabled us to be a major partner in the technological revolution sweeping the world over. It was Rajivji's far-reaching steps that led to the decentralisation of power through the Panchayati Raj. It was again Rajivji who realised the immense potential of computerisation and took initiative for harnessing it for the rapid progress of our country. In every sense, Shri Rajiv Gandhi was an architect of modern India. Praising the uncompromised determination, zeal and sacrifice to the national unity and integrity, Bhatia asserts that Shri Rajiv Gandhi has always stressed on the relevance and significance of National, and urged that it should be cultivated at the grassroots level. Different faiths and beliefs coexist in our country in perfect harmony. In spite of varied customs and lifestyles, we share a deep-rooted spirit of oneness cutting across rigid barriers of region, language or religion. He firmly held that only on such a firm foundation of National Integration can India build up its strong and stable future. Complimenting the lofty values of Shri Rajiv Gandhi, who preached and practiced in public life, Bhatia feels that it is our bounden duty to strive for the realisation of the hopes and aspirations for which he lived and sacrificed his life. What is so unique about Shri Rajiv Gandhi was that he could instill a profound sense of confidence among the youth on the creation of a better tomorrow for the entire nation. He has often reminded us that no religion worth its name would ever promote enmity, hatred or intolerance. He reiterated that the social fabric of our country is woven with the strands of mutual love, trust and respect. It was not as a mere slogan he held aloft the message of National Integration, but as the very life-breath of every Indian.

R. A. Mashelkar, in Chapter-3, presents a perspective of New Indian Knowledge and Innovation Systems. Tracing roots of concern for the commitment and determination of late Prime Minister Shri Rajiv Gandhi towards science and technology policy in 21st century in India, he opines that handsome and charming with a steely determination and vision to see that India enters the 21st century with head held high with pride of achievement, Shri Rajiv Gandhi, as a person who blended beautifully three qualities of innovation, compassion and passion. Recollecting his memories with late Prime Prime Minister Shri Rajiv Gandhi, Mashelkar, who was a Member of Scientific Advisory Committee (SAC) at that time reveals that it was Rajiv Gandhi's dream to see that rural India does not suffer for lack of water and quoted the Rajiv Gandhi's own words that 'I have a dream equivalent to John F. Kennedy's dream to take a man on the moon and that equivalent dream is to take drinking water to 1,86,000 villages'. This is how the water mission began, which was a forerunner for a number of other missions that followed. Shri Rajiv Gandhi's commitment to Science and Technology was total. Praising the Shri Rajiv Gandhi's innovative initiatives and commitment to India's forward march and its subsequent significant growth and development in various fields, Mashelkar feels that India has changed dramatically after it opened up in 1991. The changes have been particularly spectacular in the last five years or so. I wish he was alive today. He would have loved to see the emergence of knowledge economy, which he championed, when he sowed the seeds of information and telecommunication revolution. After all C-DOT and C-DAC were his creations. He would have enjoyed India's march towards becoming a true knowledge society. In its true integrative culture, India has opportunity of creating new knowledge systems. Emphasising the need for more focused research in Universities and Institutes, Mashelkar, who is also President of Global Research Alliance, a network of publicly funded R & D Institutes from Asia-Pacific, Europe and USA, with over 60,000 scientists, outlines that the indigenous knowledge system must be sustained through active support to the societies that are keepers of this knowledge, be they villagers or tribes, their ways of life, their languages, their social organisation and the environment in which they live. We need innovative ways of preventing the erosion of such knowledge, which usually vanishes with people. Equally importantly, we need an in-depth analysis of the parallelism of insights between the indigenous knowledge systems, on the other hand, and certain areas of modern science concerned with fundamental aspects, on the other. Our university education and research needs to shift the search light on this important issue, which it has neglected so far. Finding a solutions and alternative approaches for using traditional knowledge digital library to demonstrate our power to the rest of the world, Mashelkar believes that India has to show the way to synthesise a new Indian knowledge and Innovative Systems, which has the confluence of the old and the new, the traditional and the modern and those who work in modern laboratories and those, who work in laboratories of life.

N.C. Saxena traces the real potential of the Indian Panchayati Raj system in Chapter-4. Discussing basic components of democratic decentalisation and service delivery system in India, he argues that though providing a framework for decentralised rural development trends so far suggest that the panchayati raj system has not been able to enhance participation and empowerment PRI's operate as extension of government line departments rather than as local governance institutions. Emphasising the need for political and civil service reforms along with empowerment of Panchayats, Saxena opines that these reforms would of course need political support both at the federal and state levels.

V. Mohini Giri, in Chapter-5, describes the future vision of the Panchayati Raj system, particularly empowerment of women in grassroots governance. Emphasising the significance of participatory governance as a hall mark of a true democracy in India, she reveals that the advantages of Panchayati Raj Institutions are manifold, particularly for women and other hitherto marginalised and oppressed groups. It gives the population in small villages and areas a sense of selfhood, self-esteem, dignity, power and importance. It enables them to find their key role in the machinery of the government, thereby finding their role in shaping the future of their own families, communities and country. It also provides a boost to their self-confidence, especially the women, that if they set their minds to something there is no end to what can be achieved.

K. Karunakar Patnaik outlines the devolution of 3 F's—Finances, Functions and Functionaries—to the Panchayati Raj Institutions, in Chapter-6. Providing a comprehensive reforms package towards the devolution of powers to the Panchayati Raj Institutions in India, he feels that the concept of performance of decentralised institutions depends on three major dimensions: effectiveness, responsiveness and process. If these indicators are addressed positively, Panchayati Raj Institutions can continue to play a major role in the development paradigm of the country. For strengthening the financial position of various state governments, Sri Karunakar Patnaik suggests that there is an urgent need to review the operation of the system governing center-state fiscal relations. The fiscal position of almost all states is under stress mainly on account of the competitive populism practiced by the State Governments. But at the same time the central government cannot absolve of its responsibility in contributing to the fiscal mess in the states due to several actions including hefty salary revision in the wake of the fifth pay commission putting pressure on state governments to carryout similar pay revisions for state government employees. It is necessary, therefore, to have transparent fiscal practices and rule-based transfer of funds to states. In this connection, the terms of reference of the thirteenth finance commission may be sufficiently comprehensive to address some of the issues raised above.

K. Subha B.S. Bhargava, and D.S. Hanumantha Rao bring out the innovative initiative model of Gram Panchayat Libraries in Karnataka state in Chapter-7. While discussing the growth and development of the public library system in Karnataka, they opine that the Department of Public Libraries in Karnataka state has rendered salutary service by installing a network of libraries through out the state and is, by way of offering library facilities, striding fast from the capital towards the villages in the direction of evoking an intellectual revolution among the people by instilling in the common man an active interest for reading. Highlighting the advantages of the rural libraries in all respects, the authors advocate that since libraries serve as a centre for a wide variety of educational media, immediate steps should be taken to establish gram panchayat libraries in all the gram panchayats of the nation.

G. Palanithurai, in Chapter-8, attempts the conflict areas between the Constitutional and Community Laws in India.

Discussing the radical transformation of rural society through grassroots institutions, Palanithurai believes that the constitutional institutions created at the grassroots should be made vibrant and they have to shed their present character of unresponsiveness to the demands of the people. A constant drive should be maintained from the upper level governments to strengthen the constitutional structures for which mobilisation of the people is imperative. The elected leaders have to be equipped to carryout the roles and responsibilities of the grassroots institutions. Equally the traditional institutions have to be democratic and they are to be integrated with constitutional Panchayats. A meaningful synergy between the constitutional structures and the traditional structures will produce needed results from the grassroots institutions.

Snehalata Panda provides an overview of intricacies and hurdles in the implementation of Universalisation of Education in Chapter-9. Projecting the drastic changes in rural India through new education policy, she points out that the Education is fundamental to children for their optimum growth and development in all areas like health and hygiene, language and communication, physical, emotional and intellectual development, personality building and adjustment with their immediate environment as well as the larger community. Surveying the challenges and threats posed by the societal problems, Snehalata Panda argues that the main obstacles to education for children are, rural poverty, increased population, lack of financial resources, attitude of parents and low official priority. Education for children in our country suffers from lack of quality, high dropout rate, and perception of its irrelevance for economic benefits.

N.S. Gehlot dwells the importance of a participatory democracy in India for strengthening the Panchayati Raj Institutions in Chapter-10. Surveying different hurdles and problems with the parliamentary democracy in India over a period of six decades, he observes that the democracy in India has to move from elections to development and the same has to be extended to all organisations and institutions. Our family, religious institutions, political parties, educational institutions and development organisations have to be democratised. As there is no democratic spirit in our institutions, the organisations have to be democratic, accountable and responsive in its functioning. Following a discussion on the reforms and initiatives towards empowerment of grassroots democratic institutions, he feels that with the active participation of stakeholders delivery of services will be done effectively. Grassroots empowerment is more important than grassroots development. By doing so the self-dignity of the poor, marginalised, women and dalit will be restored. They should have a feeling that they can decide their destiny on their own. While discussion the causes for failure of Panchayati Raj Institutions in India, Gehlot observes that all major changes in the electoral politics came after Shri Rajiv Gandhi through the Panchayati Raj Institutions have created revolutionary changes, but this new arrangement is yet not properly shaped to function with autonomy. Today, forces are working against the devolution of powers, inclusion of women and dalits in governance.

Damodar Rout, in Chapter-11, explores the E-governance advantages in maintaining the Public Accountability and Community Empowerment in India. Examining the approaches and policies of the local self-government institutions towards poverty eradication, he postulates that the role of local self-government, as an instrument of poverty reduction must be given a re-look. Many government institutions and project managers are reluctant to carryout impact evaluation because they are deemed to be expensive, time consuming, technically complex, and because the findings can be politically sensitive, particularly if they are negative. Focussing on select institutional arrangements in the Indian Panchayati Raj system, he outlines that the revitalised local government is essential if many of the government's aims are to succeed. Public faith in politicians and their institutions are in fragile. The need to restore the link in people's minds between their vote and the services that their lives is urgent. Local democracy is the place to start. The open question still remains why Panchayati Raj as an instrument and mechanism of poverty reduction. It is the panchayat that can reduce the distance of poor from power.

Mohanan Bhaskaran Pillai postulates the participatory planning through democratic decentralisation in Kerala in Chapter-12. Assessing the transformation of the state as the location of innovations in local democracy and participatory development, in the age of globalisation, he argues that the Kerala's political culture of inflated consciousness about one's own rights that got shaped through a hundred years social history and that stood in the way of economic growth started showing signs of melting out. Thus a new culture of development rooted very well in the dynamics of parliamentary democracy is in the making, thanks to democratic decentralisation initiative. Analysing the initiatives taken by the successive governments in Kerala, Mohanan concludes that it is quite clear that the politics of democratic decentralisation and campaign for people's planning initiated in Kerala is the outcome of the quest for a new agenda for action in response to the development challenges of the state political demography and the contextual compulsions.

M.L. Santhanam, in Chapter-13, assessing the Capacity Building for Rural Development Personnel and Panchayati Raj Functionaries in India. Understanding the concept of capacity building, he considers that the capacity building encompasses the country's human, scientific, technological, organisational, institutional and resource capabilities. A fundamental goal of capacity is to enhance the ability to evaluate and address the crucial questions related to policy choices and modes of implementation among development options, based on an understanding of environment potentials and limits and of needs perceived by the people of the country concerned.

I. Satya Sundaram provides a vivid picture of Right to Information in India in Chapter-14. Exploring various dimensions of the multi-faceted advantages, he outlines that in spite of its limitations and shortcomings, the Right to Information Act has come as a boon. It is a powerful tool to hold the state accountable and secure the service to which he/she is entitled. In India, there are endless irregularities—delays in the execution of projects costing crores of rupees, misuse of funds, malpractices in administration etc. The officers, under the Act, will have to play a proactive role in guiding the public to access information and in ensuring that the public authorities adopt a positive attitude in dealing with citizens and in disseminating information.

Pramod K. Mishra highlights the women empowerment in Panchayati Raj Institutions and emerging challenges on their reservations in Chapter-15. Giving a vitality of the participation of women in decision-making at the grassroots, he asserts that when the 73rd Constitutional Amendment was passed by the Indian Parliament in order to inject new life to the decadent Panchayati Raj Institutions in India, it was expected that most of the state governments will implement them in letter and spirit. Particularly it was believed that with 33 per cent reservations given to women in the three-tier system of Panchayati Raj Institutions and adequate reservation to other minority groups one could expect that the situation will substantially improve in these institutions over the years. But what has happened during the last decade and half in the real working of the Panchayati Raj Institutions is really painful.

Jos Chathukulam and K. Gireesan, in Chapter-16, visualise the role of the Panchayati Raj Institutions in total sanitation in Four Indian States. Highlight the growing importance and significance of Nirmal Gram Puraskar during the Total Sanitation Campaign in four states of West Bengal, Uttar Pradesh, Tamil Nadu and Kerala, the authors spell out that the initiation of Nirmal Gram Puraskar for the PRIs has definitely given a positive boost to the sanitation drive at every nook and corner of the country. It is believed that this is a crucial move to make India open defecation free by 2012, much ahead of the UN timeframe for achieving the Milliennium Development Goal target for drinking water and sanitation. Only then we can hope to make a 'Swaraj without foul stench' as visualised by Gandhiji. Bringing out the real picture towards the Total Sanitation Campaign after a thorough field analyses in four major states, they find that the interactions with the campaign managers and analysing the activities carried out, it is realised that Mahatma's perspectives and comments on sanitation have not been properly taken into account during the implementation at different States, though he can be called as 'the greatest proponent' of sanitation and hygiene. It is dismal to note that Gandhian activists and academicians did not give the desired attention to the campaign.

M. Gopinath Reddy dwells the future vision for decentralisation and good governance in Andhra Pradesh in Chapter-17. Portraying the unique experiments in Panchayati Raj administration of Andhra Pradesh State, he considers that the interface has become an important part of the Government of Andhra Pradesh agenda in order to help make the numerous CBOs become more effective, sustainable and to strengthen the Panchayati Raj Institutions. A word of caution here is to accept that the inter-linkages would have limited role and effect in the process of decentralisation and good governance unless definitive measures are taken up by the Government to devolve functions, funds and functionaries to the PRIs, ensuring decentralised planning and convergence.

Empowering the Panchayati Raj Institutions would necessitate the higher authorities to neutralise themselves. Devolution of power and authority from the State Government to the three-tier Panchayati Raj Institutions would create space and opportunity to ensure closer measures of accountability.

N. Sivanna, in Chapter-18, highlights the pragmatic vision of good governance through panchayati raj in Karnataka state. While attempting the journey of Panchayati Raj system in Karnataka State towards good governance, he explores that various policy initiatives and amendments that Karnataka state is certainly moving towards a 'progressive state' as far as promoting decentralised planning and development is concerned. Discussing the ground realities in Karnataka Panchayati Raj system, Sivanna feels that it is significant to note in this context that this achievement is being made possible irrespective of political regimes governing at the state level. The subject of decentralised governance has never been neglected, but the quantum of reforms depended on politico-administrative dynamics at a given point of time. Many of the recent reforms for empowering panchayats, no doubt, are taking time. But efforts are being made that the appropriate messages reach the common man in rural areas, development administration and panchayats. On the whole, the Government of Karnataka has made sincere efforts to move towards the attainment of the spirit of Article 243 G of the 73rd Amendment for making its panchayats as real centres of institutions of self-government engaged in promoting economic development in the rural areas and also to ensure social justice in distributing the benefits of development to all the sections of society, including the vulnerable ones.

Veerashekharappa narrates various approaches of Social Marketing in respect of Drinking Water Supply and Sanitation in Karnataka State in Chapter-19. Giving the backdrop of the new economic reforms in India and its impact over the Panchayati Raj Institutions especially in Karnataka, he contends that it is anticipated that involvement of PRIs was to help correct the imbalance in provision of water and sanitation services. For this, each tier is specified particular function in provision of potable drinking water and sanitation services. However, in recent years these bodies are outsourcing some functions under pretext of reforms. The outsourcing is done through social marketing. Tracing the hurdles and challenges in respect of implementation of various developmental programmes by the Panchayati Raj Institutions under the dispensation of World Bank reforms, Veerashekharappa reveals that based on the experience, it can be stated that the Gram Panchayats are unable effectively involve themselves in social marketing due to non-availability of funds and required manpower. The bilateral and multilateral agencies approach for social marketing by community participation neither helped to save public expenditure nor social marketing sustained. Thus, both the approaches have their own limitation in the effective delivery of services. In the process, the household economy is affected due to increased health expenditure.

V. Raghupathy gives the outlook of various stages and struggles in the process of empowerment in Panchayats in Tamil Nadu in Chapter-20. Discussing the status of the process of empowerment of scheduled caste people in Panchayats in Tamil Nadu state, he asserts that empowerment process is affected by the domains in which it takes place social and economic domains in rural areas are not still conducive for empowerment of SC leaders in Panchayats. In Tamil Nadu, state has not taken significant steps in bringing changes in the social and economic domains in Tamil Nadu. The status of SC Panchayat Presidents are much more better in Kerala and West Bengal because of the favourable climate in the political, social and economic domains. State policies and powerful social and political movements for change have created such a climate in these states. In Tamil Nadu and in many other states, state and civil society have not taken effective steps in this direction. In the absence of such powerful social and political movement reservation policy cannot achieve desired outcomes.

D. Krishnamoorthy, in Chapter-21, presents a comprehensive roots of Self-Helf Group movement in Andhra Pradesh panchayati raj administration. Tracing briefly the undergone changes in the context of Women empowerment through Self-Helf Groups in Andhra Pradesh, he reveals that the DWCRA women in the two study mandals have performed extremely well by fostering savings, by pursuing a diversified structure of occupations, by earning income to achieve economic independence. The study also made it clear that a substantial number of stakeholders in the programme were women belonged to weaker sections of the society who were socially and economically oppressed by the society at large. These women now do not depend on their husbands or sons or wards for their needs. They do not also depend on the local money-lenders whenever they need any money to meet the education, medical or other emergency expenditures in the family or to meet their personal needs. They simply use their pooled savings or SHG loans from banks. This according to them is a remarkable achievement of DWCRA programme.

M. Devendre Babu brings out the existing decentralised planning in the context of post-73rd Constitution Amendment period in Chapter-22. Visualising the importance of planning at the grassroots, Devendra Babu considers that the success of grassroots level planning depends not merely on the working of DPCs but largely on the provision of supportive facilities to decentralised bodies. This, results in empowering people, promoting public participation and increasing efficiency. The prerequisites such as powers, responsibilities, functionaries, finances, space for public participation are crucial for the success of local democratic institutions and the plans they prepare and implement. Analysing the status of district planning in the post-73rd Amendment period in India, he opines that the foregoing analysis of the working of DPCs and the enabling inputs provided to PRIs to undertake what may be called bottom-up planning still remains a mirage. It is of no use in talking and analysing the working of the DPCs without the provision of powers, functions, finances and functionaries to PRIs. The states, by and large, have shown interest only in transferring some functions but it should be complemented by the devolution of funds and functionaries to implement those functions. This should get precedence before the setting up of DPCs and making them functional.

K.C. Smitha focuses an emerging Women Leadership at the Grassroots in Andhra Pradesh, in Chapter-23. Examining the question of emerging women leadership in Panchayati Raj Institutions and their leadership potentials with special reference to the Chittoor District of Andhra Pradesh, she outlines that the representation of women at Gram Panchayat, Mandal (Taluk) Panchayat and Zilla Panchayat levels were increased in a satisfactory manner. This has contributed for the enhancement of women leadership especially in Panchayati Raj Institutions to get access to decision-making process concerning to vital problems of economic development, social reconstruction and distribution of scarce resources. Exploring various dimension of women leadership abilities in Panchayati Raj, she argues that the political empowerment is not an end in itself. It is a means to achieve something, which is nothing but socio-economic empowerment. Another positive symptom of reservation is the growing political socialization of women. We can understand this by comparing the twin situations of pre-reservation and post-reservation period. In the former case the women had option to join or not to join the politics and as the socio-economic situation plays a decisive role in the participation, a few women entered into the arena of politics. But after reservation came into force, a lot of women are coming to politics notwithstanding the fact that women politics has been a thrust on them, because of the magnitude of pressure exerted over them for the purpose. By compulsorily coming to politics, the representatives are now creating an atmosphere where female mentality is getting socialised politically. Women are gradually learning how to articulate their demands, thus enabling them to act upon their visions of a better society and to make a meaningful contribution to national and societal development.

S. Viswanathan, in Chapter-24, portrays the dissent voice of dalit Women panchayat elected representatives in Tamil Nadu . Explaining the parameters of the reservation system and treatment of the successive governments in Tamil Nadu, he feels that the most glaring flaw in the working of the system was the failure of the state machinery for 10 long years to conduct elections to four village panchayats in which the posts of president had been reserved for Dalits, owing to resistance from caste forces. The four defiant villages were Pappapatti, Keerippatti, and Nattarmangalam in southern district of Madurai and Kottakachiyendal in the neighbouring Virudhunagar district. Sections of caste Hindu people, who had been enjoying power all along, were in no mood to yield to those at the bottom of or outside the caste hierarchy even on the basis of a system of rotation, as provided in the Act. Finding a solution to the long-pending social evil in Tamil Nadu, Shri Viswanathan advocates that the ill-treatment of Dalits by the upper castes is only highlights the need for the government not only to restrain the oppressive caste forces but also to sensitise the bureaucrats about the plight of a substantial section of the people who have been victims of prejudice and social injustice for long.

D. Sundar Ram, Editor of the Volume, provides a vivid picture of panchati raj set up and its working towards good governance in

Independent India over a period of 60 years in Chapter-25. While evaluating the initiatives and reforms package towards Panchayati Raj Institutions over a period of six decades in India, he reveals that today, a need of the hour is to look at the devolution of powers to the Panchayati Raj Institutions to achieve vibrant development at the grassroots. For this, the major issue of the devolution of powers to PRI's is to be reviewed, policies are to be redesigned and grassroots level realities are to be recognised. What is now needed, in this 15th anniversary year of Constitutionally obligated Panchayati Raj, is a stock-taking of the experience of all states which will enable us to review and appraisal for the time-bound implementation of the devolution of 3 F's—Functions, Finances and Functionaries to the Panchayati Raj Institutions. Providing a good governance at the grassroots through Panchayati Raj Institutions in India, Sundar Ram emphasises that the issue to be examined is whether the 73rd Constitutional Amendment Act make the Panchayati Raj Institutions as constitutional bodies? Will these institutions reflect the aspirations of the people at the grassroots? Why is that Panchayati Raj Institutions do not receive adequate powers to its potential, even after 15 years of the enactment of the 73rd Constitutional Amendment? What are the factors contributing to the disempowerment of Panchayati Raj Institutions in contemporary India?

The twenty-five chapters in the present volume, written by distinguished policy-makers, scientists, administrators and scholars, outline the pros and cons of the working of the Panchayati Raj Institutions after 60 Years of Independent India in a holistic way. This volume provides a comprehensive review of the initiatives of various governments at the federal as well as state levels in bringing out a revolutionary panchayati raj reforms, through 73rd Constitutional Amendment Act of 1992 and various State Panchayati Raj Acts, for transformation of rural India. The distinguished panel of contributors of the volume identify the strengths and weaknesses of the Panchayati Raj Institutions over a period of 60 years of Independent India and suggest a holistic reforms package for efficient functioning of the grassroots democratic institutions for delivering good governance. Let us hope that the Panchayati Raj Institutions would be flourished as a real local self-government institutions with full fledged 3 F's—Finances, Functions and Functionaries—for fulfilling the people's expectations and aspirations at the grassroots level at the time of the 60th Anniversary of India's Independence and 15th Anniversary of the gazetting and entry into force of the 73rd Amendment (Part IX – The Panchayats) of the Constitution.

1

Panchayati Raj Institutions in India: An Instrument of Participatory Democracy

A. CHAKRAPANI

I am delighted to be amidst you today here to Inaugurates the National Conference on one of the very vital subjects like the Role of Panchayati Raj in India. I am also congratulates the organisers for choosing an appropriate and very relevant theme for two-days Conference on the auspicious occasion of the 60th Years of India's Independence. The Academy of Grassroots Studies and Research of India (AGRASRI) is richly deserves our appreciation and support for its initiatives and commendable work in strengthening a sound and efficient grassroots democratic system through its manifold rèsearch and training programmes, for the past 6 years or so.

Today you have organised the present Conference as part of celebrating the 60 Years of India's Independence as well as the Sixth Bharat Ratna Rajiv Gandhi Memorial Lecture and Bharat Ratna Rajiv Gandhi Outstanding Leadership and Best District, Taluk and Gram Panchayat Awards presentation programmes. I do hope that the proceedings of two-days Conference would go a long way in making Panchayati Raj Institutions more and more helpful in devleopment of our rural India.

The history of the local bodies began with the Constitution of the Municipal Corporation of Madras State in the year 1688 followed by the similar Corporations in Calcutta and Bombay in the year 1726. Later on, number of Town Municipalities and City Municipal Corporations have come into existence and their number increased manifold over the years. The problems of these Municipalities have become more complex but the structure of these bodies has remained the same to a greater extent.

The leaders of our freedom movement nurtured these civic bodies in many ways. Popular leaders like Dadabhai Nauroji, Feroze Shah Mehta, Bala Gangadhar Tilak, Gopala Krishna Gokhale, Chittaranjan Das, Subhash Chandra Bose, Motilal Nehru, Pandit Jawaharlal Nehru and many others played a significant role in serving the people through these civic bodies. It is interesting to note that these leaders started their political career through the civic bodies and this laid the foundation for the development of the country. Till we achieved the freedom of our country in the year 1947, it was only 10 per cent of the population that resided urban areas and the remaining India lived in its villages. So, Gandhiji concentrated his attention on democratic local bodies (self-government) in Rural India.

Democracy is involving the people in the process of decision - making. Participation of the people in the lower units of the administrative through Panchayati Raj Institutions is the sine quo non of the success of development programmes.

Article 243-G of the Constitution, which is the heart of the entire scheme of decentralisation through Panchayati Raj system says that the Legislature of a State may, by Law, endow the Panchayats with powers and authority as may necessary to enable those to function as institution of the self-government and such law may contain provisions for the devolution of powers and responsibilities upon Panchayats at appropriate levels including preparation and implementation of plans for economic development and social justice including the matters listed in the 11th Schedule of the Constitution, which contains a list of 29 subjects.

In India, Panchayati Raj Institutions, which commenced functioning in the year 1959, have been increasingly perceived as important institutions and regarded as an instrument of participatory democracy for national development. Participatory democracy or grassroots democracy or democratic decentralisation for development through Panchayati Raj has drawn the attention of policy makers, programme planners, programme implementing authorities, researchers, sociologists and other professional workers.

The Government of India Act, 1935, Malaviya Committee (1956), Balwant Rai Mehta Committee (1957), Ashok Mehta Committee (1978), Hanumantha Rao Committee (1983), G.V.K. Rao Committee (1985), Singhvi Committee (1986) etc, have dealt with the development, functioning, autonomy and freedom, weaknesses, and remedial measures for strengthening of the Panchayati Raj system.

The Panchayati Raj movement started with the Balwantrai Mehta Committee's report suggesting streamlining the administrative and democratic decentralisation process. The Committee was of the opinion that the Community Development Projects launched in 1952 did not make any satisfactory headway towards Rural Development. Mahatma Gandhiji's vision of Community Development concept, aimed at a major devolution of resources and administrative and political authority to the people through people's representative bodies. This kind of self-government would evoke people's participation to help implement the programmes and schemes of the Government at District, Block and Village levels and accelerate the process of social and economic development. It was expected to encourage an egalitarian perspective in rural areas. However, encroachments on the jurisdiction of the Panchayati Raj system, lack of financial resources, greater centralisation or creation of parallel structure of authority at the local level, which curbed the development role of the Panchayati Raj system.

In the year 1977, the Janata Government at the Centre had appointed the Ashoka Mehta Committee which was of the view that the system was surely meant for the decentralisation of power and people's participation. Further, the Committee felt that it was more important to develop it as means for supporting rural development and strengthening the planning process at the grassroots level. The Committee saw a wider development role for such bodies in number of spheres like agriculture, forestry, cottage industries and welfare activities. Recognising the value of women's contribution to these areas, it suggested a greater representation for women in Panchayati Raj bodies to influence both planning and implementation. The Committee suggestions included:

1. Two tier system of Panchayati Raj.
2. Party based elections to these institutions.
3. Regular elections to these institutions.
4. Establishment of Nyay Panchayat.

The Hanumantha Rao Working Group on Planning, the G.V.K. Rao Committee and the Singhvi Committee suggested that in order to strengthen the Panchayati Raj Institutions, District-level Rural

Development Agencies and similar other organisations at lower level should be formed to undertake poverty alleviation programmes.

The 73rd Constitution Amendment Act, 1992 aimed at the Panchayati Raj Institutions brought far reaching changes in these local bodies.

The main objectives of 73rd Constitution Amendment are:

1. Constitution of Autonomous State Election Commissions.
2. Constitution of State Finance Commission similar to the one existing at the Centre.
3. Gram Sabha should play a primary role in the Gram Panchayat set up. All the voters in the Panchayat will become members of Gram Sabha.
4. Election should be conducted for every 5 years to Panchayati Raj Institutions on par with Parliament and State Elections.
5. All Offices in the Panchayati Raj set up would be filled only with elected representatives.
6. Sarpanchas of Gram Panchayats should be elected through direct elections, irrespective of party affiliations. Similar procedures should be adopted in the case of ward members.
7. The most important feature of this Act is to allocate separate seats to women and Weaker Sections of society, in the ratio-SCs 17.5 per cent, STs 7.5 per cent, 34 per cent of the total seats to BCs and 33.3 per cent to Women.
8. As mentioned in Article 243-G and Schedule 11 of the Constitution of India, powers should be delegated to Local Bodies on 29 items.
9. In consonance with the same, AP Panchayati Raj Act came into force in May 1994 choosing elections to various levels such members to Gram Panchayat, MPTs to Mandal and ZPTs to Zilla Parishad and at the same time three tier Administrative system was adopted by local bodies throughout the country.

Recommendations Made by Various Finance Commissions

In tune with the 73rd and 74th Constitution Amendments, First State Finance Commission was constituted in Andhra Pradesh under the Chairmanship of Shri G. Lakshmana Swamy on 24th June, 1994. Its objective was to study the economic condition of Gram Panchayats and other Local Bodies and suggest ways as to how the State Government would transfer a part of its accrued income to Local Bodies. But, the State Government had not revealed how far the recommendations of the First State Finance Commission were implemented. There is every need to include the recommendations made by the First State Finance Commission in the Panchayati Raj Act.

Apart from that, a Monitoring Cell should be constituted in the State, similar to the one existing at the Union level, to monitor and to supervise the implementation of the recommendations made by the State Finance Commissions.

List of 29 items (subjects) to be transferred to Panchayati Raj Institutions as per the 73rd Constitution Amendment Act, 1992 are indicated below:

1. Agriculture and its extension.
2. Development of Land, Implementation of Land Reforms, Integration of Land Holdings, Soil Conservation.
3. Minor Irrigation, Water Management and Development of Watersheds.
4. Animal Husbandry, Poultry.
5. Fisheries.
6. Social Forestry and Horticulture.
7. Small Scale Industries.
8. All Small Scale Industries, including Food Processing Industries.
9. Khadi and Village Industries.
10. Rural Housing.
11. Drinking Water.
12. Fuel and Fodder.
13. Roads, Culverts, Bridges, Canals, Waterways and Communication net works.
14. Rural Electrification and Distribution of Power.
15. Non-conventional Energy.
16. Poverty Alleviation.
17. Technical Training and Vocational Education.
18. Education, including Primary and Secondary Education.
19. Adult and Non-Formal Education.
20. Libraries.
21. Cultural Affairs.
22. Markets and Shandies.

23. Hospitals, Primary Health Centers, Dispensaries, Health and Sanitation.
24. Family Welfare.
25. Women and Child Welfare.
26. Social Welfare, Welfare of handicapped including Mentally Handicapped.
27. Welfare of Weaker Sections, including the Welfare of SCs and STs.
28. Public Distribution System.
29. Maintenance of Social Assets.

The State Government has yet to transfer certain subjects to Local Bodies out of the above 29 items. The officers were given umpteen powers to divert the funds earmarked for rural development to other Departments. This has greatly diluted and weakened the role of the people's representatives in the entire set of things.

10th Finance Commission

The 10th Central Finance Commission was constituted under the Chairmanship of Shri K.C. Pant and was operational from 1st April, 1995 to 31st March, 2000. It had implemented certain recommendations. Firstly, it had allocate Rs. 5,380.93 crore to the Gram Panchayats throughout the country and the State of Andhra Pradesh had received Rs. 424.94 crore as its share. The amount so received has to be distributed among the Local Bodies throughout the State within span of 5 years. But, the State Government had transferred only Rs. 227.50 crore to Local Bodies in two phases.

Now the questions to be addressed are:

1. How many of these aims have been translated into reality?
2. What has been the impact of 33 per cent reservation of seats for women?
3. Do women play a meaningful role as Panchayat functionaries?
4. Has there been devolution of funds for these bodies?
5. Has training of Panchayat functionaries made them more effective?
6. What has been the impact of Information Technology on PRIs?
7. Has the recently passed Right to Information Act (RTI) empowered PRIs?

8. Is the PRIs taking the advantage of the Rural Employment Act and implementing successfully in the creation of employment for the unemployed youth in the villages ?

These are the few among many issues that needed to be examined, since these institutions are working at the grossroots level.

The Panchayati Raj has provided a common forum for social, economic, political and legal advancement of rural women. Now women are more than nominal in the political bodies and this is an epoch-making step in the women's empowerment and political participation.

Women are now involved in the local political process and are confronted with complex situations while carrying out their tasks as local leaders. One of the important issues plaguing the country is widespread corruption and grassroots level is no exception to corruption, nepotism and malpractices. Studies reveal that during elections there were many malpractices. The political parties do not follow any standard nor do they maintain records. Money and muscle still rule the elections. This is an extremely difficult situation for women to enter present politics.

To curb this, local electoral system has to be further reformed so that money and muscle power is eradicated. 'Ombudsman Institution' could be introduced so that the role of the middleman is reduced and there is direct link between citizens and the local body.

As the decisions of the local government have a profound effect on the problems that concern women, effective participation in decision making is the direct implication. Effective participation demands skill knowledge and attitude which is at a large extent conspicuously absent in a majority women. The need for systematic training and orientation is therefore necessary to empower the women members to exercise their authority and to access the resources available to transform the existing conditions of existence to a better one. The political parties have to take a major responsibility in facilitating women's participation. Deliberate efforts should be made to place women members within and outside party organisation. Electroal system, which is based on money and muscle power, should be changed. State funding of elections by creation of a separate election fund is a possibility. Least, but not the least, is the role of mass media in building awareness.

The women being the members of the local authorities can play a better and effective role in attending the civic amenities.

It was seen that all the political parties are represented in the local bodies. But the predominant political culture, which is masculine, is reflected in the political parties as women were put up as candidates only in the reserved seats. The women's wing of political parties does not play a decisive role. This is common in respect of all political parties including regional as well as national parties.

Experience shows that reservation alone cannot deliver the goods, the members need education and information to handle their responsibilities in the right way. The role of mass media in building awareness cannot be ignored. Equipping girls and women with the knowledge and skills to facilitate participation in the development process should be among the major concerns of mass media.

Transparency in the government functions, effective electoral machinery and above all, sensitive and a responsive public together, matter the most. This will go a long way in political mobilisation of women and thereby promote participation.

The local women leaders who form a crucial part of the government and manage the institution should be empowered in the light of the new developments. The need for training and orientation, therefore, cannot be undermined as an important part of "human capital formation." Increasing emphasis has to be laid on the role of human capital in development.

Being the political force at the grassroots that shape policy, women especially have to be trained to be a different kind of leaders unlike the leaders that political parties usually throw up.

Reservation in local bodies has provided tremendous opportunity to women for their entry into the political arena. Being a step towards equality, the most striking participation of women in politics is found at this level. But numbers alone cannot indicate the adoption of gender sensitive policies. However, eventually it will lead to a gender perspective on issues and policies.

It is to be noted that historically Panchayats have played a significant role in the country. Today, PRIs are the only institutions to facilitate planning, participation, mobilisation of resources and to evoke people's initiative. These institutions have brought governance to the people in general, women and B.Cs in particular. Decentralisation has therefore facilitated empowerment and not only changed women to suit political situation but also recent developments render gender justice as Mrs. Pratibha Patil elected to the highest constitutional position and a minority leader Sri Hamid Ansari has been elected to the post of Vice-President of India.

Thus, the women and minorities in India moved from 'general places' to the highest 'elevated positions'.

The Gandhian dream of Gram Raj has fully realised only when the powers have been delegated to Panchayati Raj Institutions. They should be given the power of 'Nyaya Panchayat' to the Village Panchayat with right to appeal to the civil and criminal court. Some minimum police powers must also be given for the Village Panchayat for maintaining peace and tranquility in rural areas. Its involvement and report to local police station once in a week will establish a better link between the people and State police and helps to reduce law and order problems in rural areas. Government officials should act like facilitators in the system but not masters for power, decision-making and implementing the programmes in the Village Panchayats.

The real powers must be given to the Gram Sabha to control the village Panchayat and people of the Panchayat should be educated and trained on the system, because they are not participating in planning, implementation and monitoring the programmes. Avoid caste and party politics in the elections to Panchayati Raj Institutions, which led to groupism causing obstacles in the process of development in rural areas. Functional committees consisting among all caste groups may be formed at the village level providing sufficient funds basing on the population, reservation policy for women and scheduled caste, tribes and B.Cs be continued further. Training for women to develop leadership and administrative skills, promoting participation of community and NGO's encouraging non-party basis elections to Panchayat Raj Institutions to avoid the interference of politicians in the functioning, elected representatives, particularly at the Village Panchayat level be given need based regular training are some of the important suggestions to strengthen the Panchayati Raj Institutions in our country.

2

Rajiv Gandhi: An Architect of Modern India

R.L. BHATIA

I have immense pleasure to be here at this august function that has been convened to present the Bharat Ratna Rajiv Gandhi Outstanding Leadership and Best District, Taluk and Gram Panchayat Awards for the year 2007 to distinguished individuals and institutions in recognition of the remarkable contributions they have made in their respective fields.

Let me, at the outset, compliment Dr. D. Sundar Ram, Founder and Director, Academy of Grassroots Studies and Research of India and the activists of Rajiv Rural Development Foundation on their initiative to perpetuate the memory of Rajivji in such a betting manner. I would like to avail of this opportunity to congratulate the award winners on having been honoured today in the name of a leader so beloved to all of us. It is indeed appropriate and laudable that a Rajiv Gandhi Memorial Lecture is being held every year as part of Rajiv Gandhi's birth anniversary celebrations at Tirupati, under the aegis of Academy of Grassroots Studies and Research of India, in collaboration with the Rajiv Rural Development Foundation.

Shri Rajiv Gandhi, as we all known, was one of our finest Prime Ministers and definitely, the most dynamic. He aspired a lot, dreamt a lot, about making India strong, modern and self-reliant. He initiated many scheme so as to translate his dreams into reality. He was a man of action who used his tenure as Prime Minister to attain the goals he imposed on himself, the goals of building a better nation where people will live in mutual trust and social amity. Our country was on the threshold of a transition in several spheres, when his precious life was snatched away, that too in the prime of youth, by the forces of evil, having many a glorious dream unfulfilled.

Having been able to observe him from close quarters and appreciate the lofty values he preached and practiced in public life, I ardently feel that it is our bounden duty to strive for the realisation of the hopes and aspirations for which he lived and sacrificed his life.

It was indeed Shri Rajiv Gandhi who set afoot India's modernisation process, equipping our country for its historic launch in to the 21st century. It was his insight and initiative that enabled us to be a major partner in the technological revolution sweeping the world over. It was Rajivji's far-reaching steps that led to the decentralisation of power through the Panchayati Raj. It was again Rajivji who realised the immense potential of computerisation and took initiative for harnessing it for the rapid progress of our country. In every sense, Shri Rajiv Gandhi was an architect of modern India.

What is so unique about Rajvjji was that he could instill a profound sense of confidence among the youth on the creation of a better tomorrow for the entire nation. He has often reminded us that no religion worth its name would ever promote enmity, hatred or intolerance. He reiterated that the social fabric of our country is woven with the strands of mutual love, trust and respect. It was not as a mere slogan he held aloft the message of National Integration, but as the very life-breath of every Indian.

Rajivji has always stressed on the relevance and significance of national, and urged that it should be cultivated at the grassroots level. Differenct faiths and beliefs coexist in our country in perfect harmony. In spite of varied customs and lifestyles, we share a deep-rooted spirit of oneness cutting across rigid barriers of region, language or religion. He firmly held that only on such a firm foundation of National Integration can India build up its strong and stable future.

Let me congratulate Dr. R.A. Mashelkar, recipient of 2007 year's Bharat Ratna Rajiv Gandhi Outstanding Leadership Award and wish him long years of fruitful service to the nation. The other awards, I am sure, will serve as a great impetus for better performance in the future.

3

Synthesising New Indian Knowledge and Innovation Systems: Future Agenda

R.A. MASHELKAR

I am beholden to *Academy of Grassroots Studies and Research of India and Rajiv Rural Development Foundation* for conferring the Sixth Bharat Ratna Rajiv Gandhi Outstanding Leadership Award for the year 2007 on me.

I am especially happy that last year's award winner was Dr. M.S. Swaminathan, whom, not only I, but the whole nation holds in the highest esteem. He is truly an iconic figure. He was not only the architect of our very own green revolution, but he has also provided a pioneering leadership to the world in promoting the idea of a sustainable global society.

Rajiv Gandhi's Legacy

I am particularly honoured and privileged that the award has been named after Shri Rajiv Gandhi, who was our youngest Prime Minister. He was a great leader and had a unique vision for the 21st century India.

I was fortunate to serve as the Member of Rajiv Gandhi's Scientific Advisory Committee to the Prime Minister (SAC-PM) in mid-80's. I vividly remember my first meeting with him. His handsome profile and a charming affectionate smile made an immediate impression on me. He was a thorough gentleman and very courteous. On the other hand, he had a steely determination and a great vision for India's entry into the 21st century. Many initiatives that were taken during his time have made a lasting impact on Indian Science and Technology.

He blended beautifully three qualities of innovation, compassion and passion. He gave a great push to technological innovation. His passion for modern India of the twenty-first century was unquestionable. His compassion showed up time and again. I remember his commenting in one of our earlier meetings of SAC to PM about the problem of drinking water in villages. He said "I have a dream equivalent to John Kennedy's dream to take a man on the moon and that equivalent dream is to take drinking water to 186,000 villages." This is how the water mission began, which was a forerunner for a number of other missions that followed. His commitment to S&T was total.

Indeed, one remembers the immortal words of Pandit Jawaharlal Nehru, who had once said "It is an inherent obligation of a great country like India with its traditions of scholarship and original thinking and its great cultural heritage to participate fully in the march of science, which is probably mankind's greatest enterprise today."

Rajiv Gandhi was fully committed to India's forward march of science. I still remember the last SAC-PM meeting that was held at his residence in late 1991. Little did we know that the following day the elections will be announced. With his usual enthusiasm he asked all of us as to what should be the goal for S&T in the next five years? What is that the Government should invest? When we were speaking about the investment in S&T as a percentage of GDP, it had stood at around 1 per cent then. He said this must be raised to 2 per cent in line with the advanced nations. Someone from the Government was participating in the meeting. He pointed out the constraints on resources. Rajiv Gandhi smiled and in his own charming way he said, "we will keep aside 2 per cent of GDP for S&T. We will then give the rest to the nation. There is no future to India without S&T. It has to have a priority."

I must say that it is India's fortune that successive Prime Ministers have repeated this pledge to raise the S&T expenditure to 2 per cent of GDP. I remember Shri Atal Bihari Vajpayee announcing this in the Science Congress that was held in Pune in the year 2000. I also remember our current Prime Minister Dr. Man Mohan Singh reaffirming his commitment about raising the Indian S&T expenditure to 2 per cent of GDP in the last Science Congress. For India to be globally competitive, we have to achieve this target and that too sooner rather than later.

India has changed dramatically after it opened up in 1991. The changes have been particularly spectacular in the last five years or so. I wish he was alive today. He would have loved to see the emergence of knowledge economy, which he championed, when he sowed the seeds of information and telecommunication revolution. After all C-DOT and C-DAC were his creations. He would have enjoyed India's march towards becoming a true knowledge society. In its true integrative culture, India has opportunity of creating new knowledge systems. It is this new emerging paradigm on which I am going to focus in this lecture.

Synthesising a New Knowledge and Innovation System

While building the Indian knowledge society, we will have to worry about three different domains of knowledge. We as scientists, have focused rather narrowly only on S&T based knowledge, which is established through the rigorous methodology of science. But there are two other domains of knowledge, which we have kept away from. One is the so-called 'parallel', indigenous', 'traditional' or 'civilizational' knowledge system. These systems belong to societies in the developing world, that have nurtured and refined systems of knowledge of their own, relating to such diverse domains as geology, ecology, agriculture and health etc., our Ayurvedic medicinal systems being one such domain.

Indigenous knowledge systems must be sustained through active support to the societies that are keepers of this knowledge, be they villagers or tribes, their ways of life, their languages, their social organization and the environments in which they live. We need innovative ways of preventing the erosion of such knowledge, which usually vanishes with people. Equally importantly, we need an in-depth analysis of the parallelism of insights between the indigenous knowledge systems, on the one hand, and certain areas of modern science concerned with fundamental aspects, on the other. Our university education and research needs to shift the search light on this important issue, which it has neglected so far.

The third is the knowledge systems of the spiritual world. Here again, the tools of modern science are giving us deep insights. For example, quantum physics is leading to inquiry into consciousness, computational advances are leading to inquiry into human intelligence, advances in neuro-sciences are leading to inquiry into the working of a human mind.

The new knowledge system will have to be a beautiful confluence of these three knowledge systems. I feel confident that India will lead in interpreting, creating, synergising and enhancing these knowledge systems. As a first step towards this journey, I will like to give you a perspective of how we can build bridges between the traditional and modern by illustrating what we can do with specific reference to Ayurveda, which follows from our ancient wisdom.

Leveraging India's Wisdom

I was attending a meeting of the Third World Academy of Sciences in Trieste a few years ago. Frederico Mayor, the then Director General of UNESCO made an interesting statement. He said "Knowledge flows from north to south and wisdom flows from south to north." I remember making a small correction: 'knowledge' may flow from north to south but 'usable knowledge' does not flow that easily from north to south, since usable knowledge has the potential to create wealth. No country, no corporation gives a competitive advantage to another, excepting at a price. India itself has realized this in the post liberalization era. However, the flow of wisdom from India to the rest of the world has been rather free. People are just realizing this value of our wisdom now. Let us take one specific example of India's great wisdom, the example of Ayurveda.

New Interest in Ayurveda

There are winds of change now. First and foremost, a number of our country's leading scientists and doctors are now getting persuaded about the real value of Ayurveda. This has stimulated a major support from the Central Government, in addition to the large patronage from our country's various states. Major organisations in world's health system all now recognize Ayurveda. These include organisations in developed and developing countries. US National Institute of Health's NCCAM, as well as the great international organisations like WHO, can be cited as examples. Following the lead of the Commonwealth, the UK and several European countries recognize Ayurveda as a form of complementary medicine.

In India, there are half a million registered practitioners of Ayurveda. Indian Government has created a department for AYUSH, which is actively promoting every aspect of its development. Ayush means life, and Ayurveda means "Science of Life." It is a beautiful terminology. Our educational system includes two dedicated Ayurveda universities with both undergraduate and post-graduate studies. There are also 200 Ayurvedic colleges training practitioners of all aspects of Ayurveda.

Also, if you look at the way things are marketed today in many countries, be it diet, cosmetics, you will find they are marketed with Ayurvedic nuances.

Building the "Golden Triangle"

As I said earlier, Ayurveda literally means, "science of life". It dates long before the emergence of life sciences, which have now become so fashionable with the students, who now-a-days make a beeline towards courses in life sciences. But Ayurveda was the original science of life itself. It encompasses the total sweep of life sciences, pursuing its quest for understanding life in all its ramifications. It is truly holistic.

Ayurveda is possibly the earliest formal system of health care. It is not a mere compendium of therapeutic recipes as many other systems tend to be; nor was it the first one to use herbs. Herbs have been used from time immemorial. Ayurveda is one of the earliest frameworks which systematized knowledge of health and healthcare. Its framework is not only self-consistent, but also uses cause and effect arguments to correlate manifestations of sickness, its causes and its treatments. When this framework was developed in ancient India - and I am very proud of this - the notion of a molecule did not exist, nor was the cell and the role it plays in the life process known. The discoveries of DNA and functional genomics lay more the 3000 years in the future, yet in spite of all this Ayurveda offered effective treatments for many disorders, particularly those with multiple causes. For some degenerative diseases, most Indians consider it to be the treatment of last resort. There is a general belief that when all other treatments fail, Ayurveda may still succeed, and it often does! We should be proud of this.

Ayurveda and Modern Science

The 20th century has revealed some of the greatest insights into our understanding of life at successively higher levels of organization: molecules, sub-cellular organelles, cells, tissues, organs, organisms, species and ecosystems. A remarkable feature of modern medicine is its close integration with basic sciences, like physics, chemistry and biology. For example, that new frontier of modern medicine, gene therapy, would not have been possible if the structure of DNA had not been known. That itself was made possible by structural elucidation achieved by x-ray diffraction, that means physics. The contribution of modern physics to the elucidation of the structure of DNA - and then gene therapy is obvious.

This example illustrates how the connection between modern medicine and modern science has always been strong, whereas that between modern science and traditional medicine has been poor. This has resulted in a poor connection between modern medicine and traditional medicine. That is why India can benefit enormously if we can build a Golden Triangle between Modern Science, Modern Medicine and Traditional Medicine. I used the term, 'Golden Triangle', for the first time at a meeting in Chitrakut, where I gave the valedictory address. I am very happy the term has become so popular. Indeed, triangles are a popular concept in complementary medicine, but for AYUSH, the Golden Triangle project is not merely a triangle, but a 'Golden Triangle' because it presents a golden opportunity to bring these different systems together.

During the colonial period of world history, which was also a time of phenomenal growth in science and technology, science was projected and accepted as an essential feature of western civilization. An unfortunate, retrograde corollary was that modern scientific knowledge was seen as an adversary of traditional wisdom and traditional knowledge: the two were considered mutually exclusive. This was a regrettable syndrome, because it had the effect of belittling the intellect and wisdom of the vast proportion of the world's population, the heritage of the whole human race.

I believe we need to remind ourselves of a profound statement made by Mahatma Gandhi. He said "I do not want my house to be walled in on all sides and my windows to be stuffed, I want the cultures of all the lands to be blown about my house as freely as possible. Gandhiji implied that our minds should be open and uninhibited. We should be open to new ideas and new thinking. There should be no artificial boundaries, no walls or borders between different domains of knowledge or their practitioners. That is why I am so happy to see the present confluence of these different domains of knowledge, and their adherents.

Ayurvedic Research: Scientific Questions to Address

At the Science Congress that was at the Pune University Campus in 2000, I happened to be the President. Nobel Laureate Professor Richard Ernst lectured on his work using the latest advances and tools in high-resolution solid-state NMR. He gave indications on how an understanding of the Chinese system of acupuncture at the molecular level was being reached. He referred to papers in the Proceedings of the US National Academy of Science. You see, while western scientists are scientifically probing the ancient practices of the East, our own Indian research is invariably focused on the West's left-over problems. That is unfortunate. It is a great pity indeed. We need to change our ways.

As I have said, Ayurveda is the "Science of Life". The period 600 B.C. to 800 A.D. has been called the 'Ayurvedic period'. At that time, developments in Ayurveda led to fundamental advances in chemistry, and in our ancient forms of botany and zoology, as well as its own discipline of medicine. Today, however, Ayurveda gets equated only with herbal products. That is not only unfortunate, it is just plain wrong. It presents a vision of Ayurveda through the spectacles of molecular medicine and pharmacology, and excludes the greater proportion of its substantial scientific value. Dravyaguna, Ayurvedic knowledge of herbs, forms only a small part of the whole system.

Similar to the way that Nobel Laureate Richard Ernst was looking at Acupuncture and the science behind it by probing with high resolution solid-state NMR, much of Ayurveda requires fundamental physical investigation. For example, Ayurvedic etiology is couched in terms of the concept of Dosha Prakriti, as are physician's strategies of treatment. It is scientifically very important to decide whether Prakriti has a genomic basis or if they are only phenotypes. We are only beginning to address this question, and future developments may be very important, since establishing a full scientific basis for Tridosha would be of utmost significance.

As Prof. Valiathan had so thoughtfully suggested, if we investigate Panchakarma, that powerful tool to detoxify the body, does it alter the patient's biological and immunological profiles? This has not yet been investigated. Then there are the Rasayanas. What do they do? Do they accelerate the repair of damaged DNA? Can any show improvements in mouse models of Alzheimer's, such as inhibition of beta-amyloid accumulation? These questions have not been addressed. There have not been any studies on them; they are virgin territories, where the Indian scientists can make major advances.

I would go as far as saying that just as we have cellular biology, molecular biology, and structural biology, there must be an "Ayurvedic biology" that we should start talking about. I must give credit to Dr. Valiathan for coining out with this phrase. The more I think about it, the more I believe in it. What has India given to the rest of the world? Did we give cellular biology, molecular biology, or structural biology? Did we give structural genomics, functional genomics, or pharmacogenomics? No, but we can give 'Ayurvedic biology' and 'Ayugenomics' to the world.

CSIR Involvement : The New Initiatives

It makes me very happy to see that formal scientific systems that used to be averse to traditional medicine, are getting integrated nicely with it. When I was the Director-General of CSIR, I was very happy that we had instigated major programmes of research, which partner traditional medicine, modern medicine and modern science. Getting the programme going was very tough.

I still remember my visit to Arya Vaidya Shala, Kottakal, where I went with Dr. Warrier to sign our Memorandum of Understanding with CSIR, of which I was then the Director-General. It took us almost an year to get together. Dr. Warrier is a very great visionary and Dr. Valiathan managed to bring us together. I well remember how, when we had signed the memorandum, Dr Valiathan said, "This is a holy place for me, because there are two rivers meeting here. One is the river of traditional knowledge, Arya Vaidya Shala, and the other is the river of modern knowledge represented by CSIR." "Sangam" is the word he used.

I only wondered why it had taken so long for this "Sangam" to take place, but now that it has done so, an unbelievable programme has developed.

There are 19 CSIR laboratories, 21 universities, Arya Vaidya Shala and a whole range of people working together. It has evolved into a great programme. Prof. R. Kumar, a legendary scholar and leader from Indian Institute of Science is providing a leadership for this 'Team India' effort. The CSIR programmes include identification of target therapeutic areas, discovery of active fractions, molecular description of active fractions, understanding mechanisms of action, toxicological studies, clinical trials, etc.

A whole range of promising leads for new therapeutics are beginning to emerge.

Science Based Ayurveda Products

We now have an opportunity to create new products that are science-based Ayurvedic products, see four different types of use. Firstly, those to be used for minor ailments like dysphagia, unpleasant taste, anorexia, etc. Secondly, the other ones that are more specific products like detoxifiers, toners, resistance builders, and rejuvenators for longevity. Both these sets of preparations are likely to be available over-the-counter, OTC.

Thirdly, those for support therapy where the therapeutics may be administered together with allopathic preparations. Traditional medicines may even partially replace allopathic ones.

These will most probably be prescribed by existing medical practitioners, who will be using combo-therapy tc take advantage of the synergy between the two sets of preparations for patients' overall benefit. In combo-therapy, use can be made of bio-enhancers, detoxifiers, toners, and specific therapeutic agents to accelerate recovery. Similar use may also be made of them at hospitals based on the existing systems. With time, such combo-therapy may become acceptable not just in India, but universally.

Questions of Toxicity and Mechanism

In addition to molecularly defined, and mechanistically understood, non-toxic herbal fractions containing only a few molecules, there are other important preparations, which are unique to Ayurveda: the bhasmas, which are made from mixtures of metals or minerals. Most are traditionally calcined in sealed earthen containers by burning cow dung cakes, or else in furnaces. The final products are fine powders about 50 microns, or less in diameter. They use elements like lead, tin, iron, arsenic etc. Nearly 10 per cent of Ayurvedic products are bhasmas, I understand.

Most of the elements used in these preparations have been classified in standard scientific textbooks as toxic. For example, lead in any concentration is described as toxic; not only that, it is known to accumulate in various tissues. Bhasmas, however, are considered fast acting healing agents and are used quite freely, particularly Siddha preparations. No toxic effects have apparently been reported from them; but to make them internationally acceptable, it will not only be necessary to show that they are efficacious and non-toxic, but also to define their physico-chemical characteristics by accurate scientific measures. In this regard, the work being done at the National Chemical Laboratory by Dr. Rajiv Kumar is pioneering. He is looking at what is happening in bhasmas at the atomic and molecular levels. Very interesting findings are coming out.

My last question is: How do we get more and more outstanding scientists such as Dr. Rajiv Kumar interested in this? Let me remind you that Dr. Rajiv Kumar, till the other day, was busy developing catalysts for Indian and international companies. Today, his mind is engaged in these issues that interface the tradition and the modernity. Therefore, the first need is to expose our best minds and our best scientists to the accumulated wisdom of Indian systems of medicine, including Ayurveda. There is no doubt that there are enormous opportunities for doing focused, basic-cum-applied research. Mechanisms need to be elucidated in such areas as actions of bhasmas, detoxification, reversal of ageing and bio-enhancers and how molecular synergism occurs.

All these offer great scientific challenges. All are going to be very valuable.

Traditional Knowledge Digital Library

It is also important to protect our traditional knowledge. I remember fighting the turmeric battle and Basmati battle. Wrong patents were given by the patent office in United States. We fought these battles and won them. But we do not have to fight them again and again, if we use modern technology to digitise traditional knowledge. This is the effort that CSIR has launched in partnership with the Department of Ayush in Central Ministry of Health and Family Welfare. We have created a Traditional

Knowledge Digital Library. This is a knowledge repository of the traditional knowledge. The objective of this library is to protect the ancient and traditional knowledge of the country. The idea is to avoid bio-piracy and unethical patents.

Data on 65,000 formulations in Ayurveda, 70,000 in Unani and 3,000 Siddha have been put in the TKDL. TKDL is available in five languages - English, German, French, Spanish and Japanese. Some more Unani and Sidha formulations and 1,500 postures in yoga remain to be included. The entire process is expected to be completed by December, 2008.

Conditional access to international patent offices of TKDL will ensure that they become aware of our knowledge base, realise that this is prior art, and not grant wrong patents anymore. We do not have to fight turmeric and Basmati type of battles anymore.

Future Agenda

Great visionaries such as Dr. Valiathan and Prof. Kumar, who really represented modern medicine and modern science, are helping us to build a bridge of these with traditional medicine. They are laying an ambitious agenda.

What should be the new agenda? First, encourage clinical research in Ayurvedic institutions. Second, create a complete Ayurvedic pharmacopoeia thousands of products. Third, create an effective surveillance system like the post market surveillance systems. This would include providing support from modern laboratories spread all over India. Fourth, we must carry out multi-centric trials of Ayurvedic biology. Fifth and the last, we must establish a presence in international scientific journals. We must have a very strong presence in the world's scientific journals.

Then there is another challenge linked with new Institution building. We first built IIT's i.e. Indian Institutes of Technology. We already have IIM's i.e. Indian Institutes of Management. Then we built IIIT's i.e. International Institutes of Information Technology. We have heard recently about building several more IITs, IIMs and IIITs. What else should we be building? What we should now focus on are IIIM's? What is an IIIM? An International Institute of Integrative Medicine: that is where our great strength is? We should create and demonstrate to the rest of the world our own power, what it is, and where it lies.

Final Challenge

The bigger battles of integrating knowledge and innovation systems must be continuously fought. Prof. Anil Gupta is leading a great movement of National Innovation Foundation to give a voice to the grassroots innovators such as local artisans, craftsmen, farmers, etc. His Honeybee network experiment is a great movement today. The problem is that their technologies and innovations are never included in the fabric of modern technology. Again a change of mindset and value systems is required. I tried an experiment in Pune during the Indian Science Congress in January 2000. As President of the Science Congress, I said let this Science Congress be 'knowledge congress'. Let it be 'people's congress'. We will show that we value people's knowledge.

We had several grassroot innovators participate in our science exhibition. They demonstrated their technologies. None of them spoke English. We had a session, where they made a presentation on their technologies in local languages to around 2000 scientists. They stood on the same platform from which the Nobel Laureates spoke. I must say that they got a bigger applause than even the Nobel Laureates. I believe the scientists, for the first time, realised the power of innovation that takes place in the field. They also saw the innovative and creative abilities of those, who were unadulterated by the modern day educational system.

Can this realisation now turn to respect and then to meaningful partnership? I believe it can. India has to show the way to synthesise a new Indian Knowledge and Innovation Systems, which has the confluence of the old and the new, the traditional and the modern and those who work in modern laboratories and those, who work in laboratories of life.

4

Democratic Decentralisation Through Panchayati Raj Institutions: The Indian Experiences

N.C. SAXENA, IAS (Retd.)

Introduction

This paper discusses the experience of democratic decentralisation in India through panchayats, so that appropriate lessons may be drawn by the Ministry of Panchayati Raj as how to involve the panchayats and other local groups for achieving its goal of equitable rural development. Obviously the objective of achieving convergence of services will be more effective if there is strong beneficiary participation. Programmes of poverty alleviation, child survival, health, nutrition, primary education, water, and sanitation undertaken by development organisations with local participation would perform much better than those without beneficiary involvement.

There is now substantial evidence that basic public services and programmes meant for the poor and the weaker sections function inefficiently in India, especially in the poorer states. This is due to low capacity of the local implementing organisations caused by poor accountability, lack of motivation, absence of performance appraisal, absence of system of incentives and penalties, poor working conditions, and large-scale leakage due to corruption. At the receiving end, the poor are disempowered, and are not included in the decision-making processes. Delivery will not improve in India unless the process simultaneously empowers the common person.

Economic well-being of the marginalised people can be achieved in several ways. Growth, successful development project in health, education, or water can all mitigate their misery without empowering them, at least directly. Therefore empowerment can be conceptualised as a strategy as well as a goal. It is desirable in itself, as it improves the confidence of the women and other marginalised groups in themselves, but also

- makes bureaucracy more accountable and hence improves the efficiency and effectiveness of government programmes.
- improves their awareness and hence makes them better recipients of aid.
- reduces repression and exploitation.

We need empowerment in India because much of development effort in India is supply driven, top-down, does not involve people, non-transparent, and hence full of leakages and not sustainable.

Panchayats – Empirical Evidence

This has been sought to be achieved through democratic decentralisation in India, by creating institutions of self-governance at the district, block and village levels. Creation of panchayats raised hopes initially, as decentralisation was expected to achieve higher economic efficiency, better accountability, larger resource mobilisation, lower cost of service provision and higher satisfaction of local preferences. But despite their potential and promise, have they delivered? Are the PRIs inclusive and participative? Whereas village panchayats in Kerala and Karnataka seem to be working well, what is their record in empowering the excluded people in other states? We discuss the evidence on these issues below, particularly from the poorer states, where delivery through officials is also weak.

The mid-term appraisal of the 9th Plan discusses a study from UP which analyses the extent to which the village panchayats are accountable to the common people and look after their interests. The study concluded that there is no evidence that "the Gram Sabhas have been involved in any of the roles assigned to it, even though on occasion the rare meeting has been held under some external compulsion. For practical purposes, the panchayat is identified with the office of the Pradhan and the role of the Pradhan is itself subsidiary to the bureaucratic functionaries. The poor respondents mention periods when enlightened Pradhans or even bureaucrats have been able to accelerate the implementation of these programmes or have been able to steer them more firmly in the direction of the poor." Generally, however, this is not the case. Benefits from programmes accrue to a group of people who are close to the Pradhan or the official machinery. Some of them acquire multiple benefits.

Devolution, as it has been implemented, in the opinion of the villagers, may not have brought about development, but it has on the other hand reinforced the unequal access to power. References to the works are often accompanied by sneering remarks about the money which has gone down the drain, or has disappeared into the pocket of the Pradhan and the block officials. Much of what comes from the government, they feel, is snatched away by the important people.'

Results of a Field Study from Rajasthan and MP

In a World Bank study, respondents were asked to rank the village organisations. The results are described below:

From the small sample, it can be inferred that the Panchayat is not perceived as a very valuable organisation by villagers; the main reason being lack of individual benefits, but also lack of transparency, lack of influence and corruption. People place much higher value on other development activities that bring a larger number of individual benefits and are more transparent.

Table–1
Ranking the Value of Different Development Activities in a Panchayat in Ujjain District, MP

Activity	*Score*	*Most Common Explanation*
Rajiv Gandhi Watershed Mission—Land Development	44	Many people got labour. Private land and Village tanks were developed. Transparency in high. People can take part of decision-making.
Farmer's Cooperative Society	65	Provides loans at a crucial time when crops inputs needs to be purchased.
Gram Panchayat	90	Few individuals benefits. It is for the benefit of the elected representatives. There is no justice in selection of beneficiaries or prioritisation of community works.

A ranking exercise was carried out in the Panchayats in Dungarpur district, Rajasthan in order to understand the value people attribute to the Panchayat as a local development body when compared with other development activities in the villages. A cross-section of twenty villagers in each Panchayat were asked individually to rank the existing development activities in their village based. The outcome of the exercise is presented below:

Table–2
Ranking the Value of Different Development Activities in a Panchayat in Dungarpur District, Rajasthan

Activity	*Score*	*Most Common Explanation*
Participatorty Approach to Human and Land Resource Development (PAHAL)	33	All villages get benefits in terms of labour. Land is developed to become more productive. Few people also mentioned that the transparency is high compared to other development activities.
Shiksha Karmi and Lok Jumbish – Education	47	Education is perceived to be the gate-way to the future, Uneducated people have fewer possibilities.
Women's savings group	66	Savings enable productive investments in assets of own choice (e.g., wells, land-levelling, livestock
Farmer's Cooperative Society	8	Loans are provided that enable investments in crops. (Members are mostly large landholders).
Gram Panchayat	92	Individual benefits are few. Little transparency and corruption is high. Exception: One man said that it is a permanent strucuture and therefore valuable whereas other development activities are temporary.

In tribal Dungarpur district (Rajasthan) two women described the difference between participating in the women's savings group and the Panchayat:

> "The savings group has a purpose. All women meet to deposit money and to decide on who can take loans. We will get benefits. There is no work for the individual in the Panchayat, and especially not for women. What will we gain from participating there? Whether we go or not does not make a difference."

This study by Alsop, Krishna and Sjoblom (2000) on villages of Rajasthan and Madhya Pradesh demonstrates that in general it is difficult to make PRI representatives accountable in India.

Limited benefits distributed by the Panchayat, pre-occupation with managing daily sustenance, local dependency relationships (both social and economic), corruption and fear of social exclusion from the community more generally hamper the use of the existing accountability mechanism. When people complain against any elected representative, it is difficult to get the complaint enquired into or get justice, as the officials have not shown adequate responsiveness to their complaints or may be aligned with the Sarpanch. It has been found that livelihood-secure households are often included in benefits of different developmental schemes at the expense of more vulnerable households.

In all 53 villages in the extensive study, the vast majority of villagers did not attend a single gram sabha meeting during the previous year and barely seven per cent of villagers attended meetings regularly. The 10 per cent quorum requirement stipulated by law in both states for gram sabha meetings is very often hard to meet in many villages, and sarpanchas resort to diverse stratagems in order to record a quorum on paper.

Ranking in UP

In UP, a study (Srivastava, 2004) evolved some criteria for ranking twenty panchayats. Points were given to panchayats along three dimensions – democratic functioning, efficiency, and transparency and the total marks obtained by each panchayat was used to rank each of the panchayats. The criteria used are summarised below:

Table–3
Ranking of Panchayats

Dimension Scale

Participation

1. *Regularity of Gram Panchayat Meetings:* Regular-03, Irregular 02, Not held 01.
2. *Participation in Gram Panchayat Meetings:* All sections 05, Some sections 03, On Paper/Nil 01.
3. *Regularity of Gram Sabha Meetings:* Regular-05, Irregular 03, Not held 01.
4. *Participation in Gram Sabha Meetings:* All sections 05, Some sections 03, On Paper/Nil 01.

Transparency

1. *Selection of Beneficiaries:* Open Meeting 05, Open Meeting but tampered-03, Outside Meeting-01.

2. *Selection of Schemes:* Open Meeting-05, Open Meeting but tampered-03, Outside Meeting-01.
3. *Publicity of Funds and Expenditure:* Well advertised-05, Selectively known-03, Not known to anyone-01.

Implementation

1. *Level of Activity:* Active 03, Less Active 02, Inactive 01.
2. *Supervision of Works:* Collective Involvement 03, Pradhan or Relative 02, Contractor 01.
3. *Quality of Works:* Good-05, Medium 03, Poor/v. poor 01.
4. *Corruption:* Honest 05, Relatively honest 03, v. Corrupt 01.

Grades for Panchayats: V. Good 40-49, Good 30-39 and Unsatisfactory 21-29

Very Unsatisfactory 11-20

Out of the 20 studied panchayats, 15 (75%) rank in the 'Unsatisfactory' (12) or 'Very Unsatisfactory' (3) category. But two achieve a 'Good' rank while three achieve a 'Very Good' rank. Of the five well functioning panchayats, two were in the Hill region, and one each were in the Western, Central and Eastern regions. Notably, two of the best functioning panchayats in the sample were headed by women Pradhans. These two successful women Pradhans had significantly different profiles, yet they performed reasonably well as leaders of their respective panchayats.[1]

Other States

In Himachal Pradesh, 75 per cent of Gram Sabha meetings had to be adjourned in 2002-03, despite the fact that quorum for the meeting is only 10 per cent. In the four Southern states, only 20 per cent of the people had ever attended a Gram Sabha meeting.

A detailed study of panchayats in MP was done by the ODI, London, given in its Working Paper 226, called, 'Grounding the State: Poverty, Inequality and the Politics of Governance in India's Panchayats'. According to the study, MP's decentralisation process has failed to challenge the well-entrenched power of the village chiefs, the Sarpanches. In practice, the committees and the Gram Sabha in the MP villages appeared largely dysfunctional. The selection process of beneficiaries was dominated by the Sarpanch, often in collaboration with the line ministry officials whose projects were being implemented in the village. 'Selection' here was essentially a matter of compiling a list of names, and submitting them to the relevant line departments. In one village, for instance, a forest committee was formed on the basis of a 20 minute meeting between the Mantri and the Gram Sabha, whereby the former instructed the latter to form a committee, documented eight names and then left the village. In many cases, committee members were completely unaware that they were even on a committee.

In the household surveys, the number of respondents who said they were members of a village committee was less than 2 per cent. Finally, the committees in question appear to have been highly ineffectual. Forest committees, for instance, showed no resistance to illegal logging around the village; water conservation committees had no powers to curtail the extraction of groundwater and the sinking of borewells. Sarpanches in the Tikamgarh villages told the researchers that they 'were forced' to decide matters outside the Gram Sabha (GS) because it 'takes too long' to reach consensus and to achieve the 20 per cent quorum, as the legislation requires. In the best case scenarios, the GS served as a 'final stamp of approval' for decisions about the location of projects, the selection of beneficiaries, and the distribution of state resources.

However, the 'vote' or voice of the GS had little power to alter or challenge the decisions presented within this village forum. Interviews with the villagers in question reveal an opaque process in which the Sarpanch would accept the relevant documentation, providing little information about whether and how the claim would be processed. Many respondents told us that their claims were still outstanding, and that they had received no follow-up information about their status. Moreover, Sarpanches were highly adept at manipulating the Gram Sabha to meet the requirements of Gram Swaraj. Signatures of villagers and ward members were commonly added to the register; Gram Sabhas were arranged with very little time or notice for ward members to organise opinion or support on a particular issue. Indeed, the researchers encountered many responses to suggest that ward members and villagers were completely unaware that Gram Sabhas had in fact been held.

A study of Andhra Pradesh panchayats (available at panchayats.org) observed that the non-devolution of funds and functions combined with the upscaling of departmental programmes have meant an increased focus on departmental initiatives at the cost of the PRIs in Andhra Pradesh. The subjectivity of beneficiary selection criteria and the presence of higher level political representation (MLA, MP, Minister) in the final decision-making bodies (DDRC, ZP) are indicators of the influence that the state level political system bears on issues of economic and social development. The NGO networks that have managed to articulate and force consultations at the state level are also vehicles that indicate a preference for the non-PRI route for local management of natural resources.

From these studies, it appears that though the ordinary village people feel optimistic about the potential of panchayats, they think that it has not brought the fruits of development to them. Corruption is singled out as the most important cause for the ineffective functioning of these institutions. Control which is exercised by the sarpanch and Block Level officials over the village panchayats and gram sabhas has not only buttressed corruption, but it has also led to pessimism that villagers at their own level cannot change and improve performance because of heavy dependence on elected functionaries and Block officials. The present system is, therefore, seen as to have actually reinforced dominance and unequal access to power, besides rendering the villagers helpless and alienated.

The experience of West Bengal under the panchayat system stands in sharp contrast with that of other states and, together with land reform, it has been credited for playing an important role in the impressive economic turnaround of the state since the mid-1980s. West Bengal is the first and the only major state to have had timely panchayat elections on a party basis regularly every five years since 1978. However, despite its pioneering status in terms of reforms of the panchayat system, West Bengal lags behind several other states today in terms of devolution of power, finances and functions to the panchayat. Also, the extent of people's participation in the planning process is significantly less compared to that in Kerala.

Another distinguishing feature of West Bengal panchayats is that many people from the lower and middle rungs of the rural society, poor peasants, sharecroppers, agricultural labourers and school teachers for the first time came to hold seats of power and resource distribution in the rural areas. Sample surveys conducted after the 1978 elections suggested that 75 per cent of the elected representatives of village councils came from households owning less than two acres of land. A distinct feature of the village constituency meetings is that those who participated were largely members or supporters of some political party or the other. Those who do not belong to any political party kept away from the meetings. Second, without any exception, in each of the 20 constituencies, a majority of the voters who were present belonged to the party of the elected member, which was the Left Front in 65 per cent of the constituencies. Indeed, the simple correlation coefficient between the party of the elected member and the percentage of voters participating who belong to the same party is 0.95.

Still, it would not be fair to conclude that there were no voices of opposition in these meetings. The average percentage of participants who did not belong to the party of the elected representative among all the twenty constituencies was approximately 20 per cent. The relatively affluent individuals do not attend these meetings because they do not see any immediate benefits as they are not eligible for financial support under the various poverty alleviation programmes. Political minorities and those not directly associated with political parties stay away as they feel their opinion would have little effect. They feel that the dominant party would do whatever they want to do anyway. Members of backward groups (SC/ST) felt that they did not have much voice in their own party where the leadership consists largely of members of higher castes. Women, too, felt that they are not encouraged to participate. To summarise, there is some evidence that participation rates are particularly low for the relatively affluent, people belonging to opposition parties, women and minority groups. The negative wealth bias has to do with the fact that these meetings deal mainly with welfare programmes for the poor and not enough with investment in infrastructure. However, one has to remember that these patterns of participation reflect existing social and gender inequalities, which have a long history, and are present in even sharper forms in most other Indian states. One hopes that the process of decentralisation itself, and the reservation of seats for women and lower caste groups will lead to some progress on this count.

The village council chief in West Bengal and the local representatives are questioned on the progress of implementation of projects, and often face allegations about misuse of funds and selection of beneficiaries. The response of the elected officials to these criticisms showed that they could not take the voters present in the meeting for granted. This represents a marked improvement over the previous situation where the power of the village council (gram panchayat) was totally concentrated in the hands of the Pradhan. He was the sole authority to take decisions on how and where resources sanctioned for the village council area were to be utilised.

From the studies discussed above, it appears that although some village level panchayat leaders have done commendable work, on the whole they have not benefited the people to the extent of funds provided by government. The performance of the block and district level PRIs is even more disappointing.

Analysis

Several empirical studies on the working of panchayats have brought out the following features about their functioning:

- Gram Sabha meetings were regularly held only in a few places, and in most cases, participation in gram sabha meetings was low. Often such meetings were only on paper.
- There was little knowledge in the villages of the amounts of funds received by the panchayats and the heads under which expenditure had been incurred.
- The criterion for the selection or rejection of beneficiaries was not clear to the poor. In many cases, it was obvious that lists were manipulated by the village chief and/or officials, and that only those who had the ability to pay bribes were selected as beneficiaries.
- Elected village sarpanches have spent huge amounts, often up to several lakhs in elections.
- Heterogeneous and unequal village societies often throw up leaders who have little concern for the poor.
- Factional fights at the local levels divert the energies of the elected officials from working for public welfare to consolidating the power of their group.
- The quality of delivery of benefits to the poor was low and leakages ranged from 20 to 70 per cent. Most elected officials had the propensity to make money, and almost in all cases, panchayat sarpanch/beneficiaries paid

'commissions' to officials. In effect, there were only a small proportion of cases—perhaps 25-30 per cent where the delivery of programmes had improved after the recent spell of decentralisation.

- Picture is worse at the taluk and district level. The elected members of the PRIs at these levels behave more or less as contractors, with no institution of the gram sabhas at that level to put moral pressure on them. ZP and panchayat samiti members look upon devolved funds as equivalent to MP or MLA quota funds, and the Adhyakhsha and the block President distribute these funds equally between all members. They in turn choose the contractor and the nature of schemes. Obviously schemes that offer maximum commission and least risk of verification (such as earth work, which of course is often done by machines but shown to be performed by fake labourers) are preferred.
- Panchayats at all levels are mostly busy implementing construction oriented schemes, which promote contractor-wage labour relationship. These do not require participation of the poor as equals, on the other hand these foster dependency of the poor on Sarpanch and block staff. In such a situation panchayat activities get reduced to collusion between Sarpanch and block engineers. Panchayats are not active in education, health, SHGs, watershed, nutrition, pastures and forestry programmes, which require people to come together as equals and work through consensus.

Moreover many government programmes are implemented either departmentally or through parallel bodies. The sole exception has been the SGRY (Sampoorna Gramin Rozgar Yojana-previously called Jawahar Rozgar Yojana), which is implemented through the village panchayat. But even under SGRY there is no social control by the people. Most often the Pradhan/Sarpanch selects the project which suits his needs or for which he is pressured by the dominant castes/clans. Participation of the poor especially women is missing.

Elite capture is a major drawback of decentralization and for providing services that are in line with the preferences of the poor. As observed by Pardhan (Decentralization of Governance and Development, Journal of Economic Perspectives, Volume 16, 2002, pp. 185-205), the extent of local elite capture depends on the levels of social and economic inequality within communities , traditions of political participation , voter awareness, fairness and regularity of elections, transparency in local decision-making processes, government accounts, media, etc. The extent of elite capture may be more at the local level under conditions of high inequality between different sections of society. Local governance is more successful in states like West Bengal, which have experienced a greater degree of land reforms and Kerala which has benefited from a higher degree of literacy resulting in a higher number of newspaper readers and a vigilant press that exposes corruption in local governments. Elite capture also arises out of the lack of a system of checks and balances which exist at higher government levels that include: seperation of powers, independent adjudicatory mechanisms, regular auditing of public funds and vigilance by the national media.

Many panchayat elected leaders as well as the block/district level officials saw in these programmes an opportunity to loot. Panchayati Raj is not about helping people as it should be, in reality it is about access to state power, driven by a desire to personal gain, not by a genuine commitment to serving people. A client patron relationship has emerged out of this impulse, between district bureaucracy and the panchayati raj non-officials.

Though providing a framework for decentralised rural development, trends so far suggest that the panchayati raj system has not been able to enhance participation and empowerment. PRIs operate as extensions of government line departments rather than as local governance institutions.

Why are Panchayats not Delivering?

Some of the reasons for their lacklustre performance (especially of the taluk and district panchayats) are discussed below:

Lack of adequate devolution: So far the progress on fiscal and functional decentralisation has been disappointing. The primary function of Panchayats in all the three tiers is "the preparation of plans for economic development and social justice" (Art. 243-G). Excepting Kerala and Karnataka, no other State has taken any positive step to devolve funds, functions and functionaries to the PRIs to enable the Panchayats to discharge this constitutionally mandated function properly. Further, it is imperative that the PRIs have resources to match the responsibilities placed on them. While State Finance Commissions have submitted their recommendations, very few States have implemented these or taken the necessary steps to ensure fiscal viability of the PRIs.

Too much control by bureaucracy: Under the State laws, wide powers of suspension and dismissal have been vested in the State bureaucracy. This straightaway places PRIs in a position of disadvantage vis-a-vis even middle rung functionaries of the State Governments. It also takes away the essential characteristic of PRIs as elected representative bodies. In some states, even Gram Panchayats have been placed in a position of subordination vis-a-vis Intermediate Panchayats and so on. However, these provisions have in-built limitations because they directly affect the concept of democratic decentralisation on the one hand and the autonomy of the PRIs on the other.

Instances have been reported where the Gram Panchayat Sarpanches have to spend extraordinary amount of time visiting Block Offices. There are also instances of harassment by Block level officials. Systems which require Gram Panchayat Pradhan / Sarpanch to approach block office for funds and/or technical approval need to be drastically changed. Village bodies should be able to spend funds on their own without having to take technical approval from government officials. These interactions with the Block staff distort the role of Sarpanch as elected representatives of the Gram Sabha and induct them into the bad old ways of officialdom, besides encouraging corruption.

Another factor limiting initiative is the tied nature of funds disbursed to these institutions. They generally prescribe activities and target groups for the scheme as a whole. This has two implications. The activities stated under a certain scheme are not always appropriate for all parts of the district. This results in unsuitable activities being promoted or an under-spend of the funds, and hence loss of funds. Secondly, tied funds are inflexible, giving little scope for tailoring to local needs and conditions.

Overwhelming dependency on government funding: A review of money received and Own Source funds shows the overwhelming dependency (often more than 95%) of Panchayats on government funding. How these funds are used is not properly audited. These funds are a soft option and discourage any effort to generate local revenue. When Panchayats do not raise internal resources and instead receive funds from outside, people are less likely to request a social audit (i.e., accountability of PRI) if they are not asked to pay taxes. The tables below show the actual funds received by the Panchayats in Narsimhapur district (MP).

Table–3

Funds Available to Gram Panchayats in MP, by Block

Receipts	*Jhoteshwar (1988-99)*	*Manegaon (2000-01)*	*Thalwada (2000-01)*	*Batesara (2000-01)*
Owns Source	Nil	Nil	Nil	2594 (1%)
Funds from SFC, Centrally and State sponsored Schemes, etc.	497,027	211,844	487,851	229172
Total	497,027 (100%)	211,844 (100%)	487,851 (100%)	231,766 (100%)

Table–4

Fund Available to Block Panchayats and Zilla Panchayat in Narsimhapur District

Receipts	*Block Panchayat Chichli Block (2000-01)*	*Block Panchayat Gotegaon Block (2000-00)*	*Zilla Panchayat Narsimhapur District (1999-00)*
Owns Source	2,30,356 (2%)	390,034 (3%)	1,615,192 (0.71%)
Funds from SFC, Centrally and State sponsored Schemes, etc.	11,541,621 (98%)	14,229,292 (97%)	212,500,040 (99.29%)
Total	13,891,977 (100%)	14,619,326 (100%)	228,652,324 (100%)

Reluctance to use fiscal powers: At the village level, an important power devolved to GP is the right to levy tax on property, business, markets, fairs and for the service provided, like street lighting or public toilets, among other. Only a small number of village people are aware of this fiscal power, as it is in disuse. Very few panchayats use their fiscal power to levy new taxes. The argument pushed by the Panchayat heads is that it is difficult to levy tax on your own constituency, especially when you live in the community.

Status of gram sabha: Empowering Gram Sabhas could have been a powerful weapon towards transparency, and involvement of the poor and marginalised people. However, most of the State Acts have not spelt the powers of Gram Sabhas nor have any procedures been laid down for the functioning of these bodies.

Neglect of PESA: The Provisions of the Panchayats (Extension to the Scheduled Areas) Act, 1996 (PESA) applies to the tribal areas of nine States namely, Andhra Pradesh, Jharkhand, Gujarat, Himachal Pradesh, Maharashtra, Madhya Pradesh, Chattisgarh, Orissa and Rajasthan, which intends to enable tribal society to assume control over their own destiny to preserve and conserve their traditional rights over natural resources. PESA is unprecedented in that it gives radical self-governance powers to the tribal community and recognises its traditional community rights over natural resources. In reality, however, since its passage it has almost been forgotten and has not become part of mainstream political or policy discourse. Many state governments have passed laws not fully in conformity with the central law.

Academics, administrators, policy makers and even parliamentarians remain unaware of it. The tribal communities informed about the provisions of the law greeted it with enthusiasm but found themselves progressively handicapped by the lack of actual preparedness to negotiate development and democratisation in the manner envisaged by the law.

We summarise below some of the lacuna in the state laws, and how they violate the PESA provisions.

Section 4 (m) (ii) of this Act provides that—"while endowing panchayats in the Scheduled Areas with such powers and authority as may be necessary to enable them to function as institutions of self-government, a state legislature shall ensure that the Panchayats at the appropriate level and the Gram Sabha are endowed specifically with the ownership of minor forest produce."

Further, PESA required that state government would change its existing laws wherever these were not in consistent with the central legislation. Following the Central PESA Act, the Orissa Act has tried to circumscribe the constitutional provisions of the

Central Act by adding a clause[2] 'consistent with relevant laws in force' while incorporating the constitutional provision concerning the competence of the Gram Sabha to manage community resources and dispute resolution as per the customs and traditions of the people. Thus, tribals can have ownership rights over Minor Forest Produce, but only if the relevant laws in force allow that. This is clear violation of the Constitutional Provision of the Central Act since in case of any inconsistency the relevant state laws have to be changed instead of negating the rights granted to Gram Sabha as per the Central Act in this regard.

In Andhra Pradesh too, there is a clear contradiction between PESA and GOMs. 173 dt. 7/12/96 of the Environment, Forest, Science and Technology Department. The Usufructory Rights of Vana Samrakshana Samitis prescribed therein include, 'All Non-timber Forest Produce except those for which GCC holds monopoly rights. However, the right to collection shall remain with the VSS members, if they so desire. The members shall be paid the collection charges upon delivery of the produce as per the rates fixed by the Government.' It can also be seen that there is a contradiction between the 'ownership' vesting in Gram Panchayats/Sabhas clause and the monopoly rights vested in GCC. Whether bamboo constitutes major or minor forest produce is also an unsettled question.

Secondly, MFP has been defined to exclude cane and bamboo. This is contrary to the commonsense definition of MFP which is 'that part of a tree that can be sustainably harvested without damage to the survival of the tree.' MFP is a product of the living tree, as opposed to timber which is product of the dead tree. More significantly, the state governments deny access to poor tribal artisans to two types of MFP, bamboo and cane, on which their livelihoods are most critically dependent. On the other hand, many state policies have subsidised bamboo for private industry.

Lastly, Government should not lease out forest lands to industries even though local institutions like Vana Samrakshana Samithis, particularly in the Scheduled Areas (as attempted by the Government of A.P. under G.O.112).

According to PESA, prior consultation with Gram Sabha or Panchayats at the appropriate level shall be made mandatory before acquisition of land for development projects. Here again the states have diluted PESA provisions. In Andhra Pradesh, Gram Sabhas have no role. Gujarat assigned this power to Taluka Panchayat. Orissa assigned the power to Zilla Panchayat with no role for the Gram Sabha/Gram Panchayat.

Similarly PESA lays down that recommendations of Gram Sabha or the Panchayats at the appropriate level shall be made mandatory before grant of prospecting licence or mining lease for minor minerals. Here again Andhra Pradesh gives no role to Gram Sabha. Gujarat does not make any mention of it. Himachal Pradesh retained primacy of Gram Sabha but the term 'shall be made mandatory' has been replaced by `shall be taken into consideration'. Maharashtra assigns powers to Gram Panchayat, and Gram Sabha has no role in the matter. Orissa gives powers to Zilla Parishad, with no role for the Gram Sabha or the village panchayat.

Another PESA clause lays down that Panchayats at appropriate level and the Gram Sabha to be endowed with power to prevent and restore tribal alienated land. Gujarat, Himachal Pradesh, Madhya Pradesh Panchayati Raj Amendment Act do not make provisions for this. Only in Madhya Pradesh, the Land Revenue Code, 1959 has been amended to give power to Gram Sabha. However, the Code should have also laid down that no new entry in the ownership register will be permitted through sale or gift in favour of a non-tribal, unless it is approved by a resolution of the Gram Sabha.

These interpretations have almost killed the concept of ownership and control of local resources by Gram Sabha. The irony is that while PESA remains unimplemented, Ministry of Mines in GoI has proposed amending Schedule V of the Constitution itself to open up tribal areas for commercial exploitation by national and multi-national corporate interests. The secret document of the Ministry of Mines, Government of India, No.16/48/97-M.VI, dated 10th July, 2000 which contained the legal advice of the Attorney General suggesting amendment of the Fifth Schedule to overcome the Samatha Judgment, is shocking evidence of the shift in the mindset of the political powers and the bureaucracy with regard to Scheduled Tribes and tribal areas. Such moves only reflect that the state is looking for justification for opening up these areas to global market forces and not to fulfil its constitutional/social responsibility. At no cost should the Fifth and Sixth Schedule laws of the Constitution be amended to open up the areas for control or ownership by private non-tribal individuals, industries or institutions.

In order to make the Central Act effective, it is necessary for the State Governments to make appropriate amendments in their State Laws/Acts which impinge on specific provisions contained in the Central Act namely *(i)* Land Acquisition Act; *(ii)* Excise Act; *(iii)* State Irrigation Act; *(iv)* Minor Forest Produce Act; *(v)* Mines and Minerals Acts; *(vi)* Land Revenue Code/Act; *(vii)* SC/ST Land Alienation Act; *(viii)* Money Lenders Act; and *(ix)* Regulated Market Act. No doubt, some State Governments (MP) have already amended some of the relevant Acts, others are yet to follow suit.

Sustainability: The 73rd and 74th Constitutional Amendments Act itself has certain provisions, which adversely affect the sustainability of these institutions. Most importantly, while there are reservations for women and scheduled castes/scheduled tribes, these seats are to be allotted by rotation to different constituencies. In practice, this implies that a woman or a scheduled caste/tribal elected to a panchayat will normally have a term of five years, with no prospect of re-election (In Karnataka the term used to be only for 20 months). This goes against the spirit of democracy, as people work hard for their constituencies in the expectation that they would be returned to power in the next elections. The existing provisions provide no incentive for the elected persons to deliver on their promises; on the contrary, self-interest would dominate, with little concern for the community at large.

Interference by MLAs with executive and neglect of legislative and functions: There is a nebulous domain of executive powers into which MPs, MLAs, PRI and the judiciary all foray, each one working in this space by legitimate or illegitimate means. Along with this, there is no accountability for taking on the role of other wings of Government, having the necessary powers and authority for back-door influencing in decision-making. One school of thought is to legitimize this by the MLA being made TP (taluk panchayat) president in a configuration wherein the constituency is co-terminus with the TP. Today many Assemblies meet only for 10 to 20 days in a year, as MLAs are not interested in legislative functions, they all want a share in the executive! By giving a role to MLAs in the panchayat system, one would make them strong supporters of delegation of functions and funds to the panchayats.

Suggested Reforms

Rural decentralisation and PRIs are a profound change in the Indian rural institutional scene. They may ultimately offer a better option for rural development and poverty alleviation. Disadvantaged jurisdictions could then be the main winners. It is an important opportunity. However, it was a mistake to think that PRIs will emerge as caring institutions in an environment of rent-seeking politics and unresponsive and inefficient bureaucracy. If district level civil servants and politicians are indifferent to public welfare, it is too much to expect that village and block level politicians will be any different. To hold that the directly elected MLA is wily, corrupt, and irresponsible, while the indirectly elected Adhyaksha or Taluk President can be trusted with crores, is honest, and committed to public welfare is neither good theory, nor is empirical valid.

Thus, there are big risks in premature promotion of PRIs. Past attempts at decentralisation failed in India, in part because of resistance of the vested interests of the bureaucracy and state level politicians. These vested interests remain. Steep deterioration in political morality as well as in governance has further distorted the scene. If not carefully designed, sequenced and implemented, decentralisation can increase the fiscal burden on the states and lead to a break-down in service delivery[3], in particular to the poor. Effective panchayats/user groups would also require effective district and block level administration. Hence efforts towards better accountability and performance from local bureaucracy should go simultaneously along with building local PRI capabilities, otherwise the elected PRI leaders would not change their perception of the state being an 'open treasury'.

Thus political and civil service reforms must go hand in hand with empowerment of panchayats. We describe below the reforms that are specific to panchayats and decentralisation.

Change Financing System

Considerable amount of funds flow to the Panchayats from the governments. Panchayats hardly raise internal resources such as taxes, revenue from common pool resources, etc., and instead depend upon funds from outside. The current system of funding is reinforcing the dependency on government funding and is the source of much corruption in local institutions. It is necessary to reconsider the current funding system. More emphasis should be put on Panchayats generating more internal revenue at all the three levels with matched funding from the government. This would also introduce more flexibility in the way the Panchayats use their resource.

One such area, which has high tax potential and tax buoyancy and remains untapped by many states, is the utilisation of common property resources (CPRs) of PRIs. The state finance commission reports of Haryana and Punjab have shown that around 70 per cent of "own tax resources" of the panchayats in these states are obtained through leasing common or "shamlat" land only. Panchayats in several other states also exploit their common property land and water resources to earn taxes, duties, tolls and fees. Utilising these resources in a planned manner with long-term perspectives may be the key for many of the panchayats to strengthen themselves, today and for days to come (Tapping Local Resources to Increase Panchayat Incomes SUBROTO DHAR Economic and Political Weekly April 8, 2006).

Rather than receiving a share in taxes and central grants the panchayats should have the right to levy and collect taxes on their own in order to reduce their dependence on state and central governments. For instance, Tamil Nadu collects land tax through government machinery and then transfers 85 per cent to the panchayats. It will be more cost effective if the entire burden of collection is shifted to the village panchayats. Today the PRIs hesitate to levy and collect taxes, as they prefer the soft option of receiving grants from GoI. This must be discouraged and the local bodies be encouraged to raise local resources for development and then receive matching grants from the Centre/States. The more dependent a PRI is on the mass of its citizens for financial resources, the more likely it is to use scarce material resources to promote human development and reduce poverty. External funds with no commitment to raise internal funds make PRIs irresponsible and corrupt.

While participatory governance of the kind being experimented with in West Bengal and Kerala have undoubtedly improved the accountability of government officials and elected representatives, it has brought about an accountability problem of a different kind.

Panchayats depend almost completely on the central and state governments for funds and raises a negligible amount of revenue themselves. Even if there is no leakage in the form of corruption, the village councils as a whole have less incentives to focus on the social returns from how they have spent these funds (or to assess their performance in this regard) as they do not have to raise even a fraction of these funds. The negative incentive effects of such a soft budget constraint is well-known from the literature on public sector enterprises and socialist economies.

An innovative approach is needed for taxation and fund mobilization for Panchayats. There is an urgent need to transfer the task/function of levying of taxes to LSGI. Strengthening of funding and tax collection, with an emphasis on taxes collectable from within the geographical spread of the LSGI like the land revenue, irrigation cess etc., unlike those from outside the LSGI's area such as Octroi. A system of fixing the tax rates for different areas and provision of a basket of taxes from which the LSGI could choose the appropriate ones for themselves. Similarly, there is a need to rationalize taxes by looking at differential taxes for large holdings (vertical relation to be changed to horizontal relation). Therefore, panchayats should not only collect taxes on land, irrigation drinking water, power, and houses, but also be given the authority to levy taxes on politically unpopular subjects such as agricultural income tax on large holdings. Even if one percent panchayats start doing it, the fear that collecting such taxes is a political liability will disappear.

Untied Grants

In addition, panchayats would need a share in state revenues. States need to increase the share of transfers to PRIs from state governments as untied grants, by *(i)* consolidating state schemes with broad rural development objectives into untied grants, as Kerala has done; *(ii)* making these grants a share of state revenues; *(iii)* explicitly defining through state legislation a formula to allocate grants to jurisdictions and PRI levels; and *(iv)* transfer collection of village taxes, such as land revenue, irrigation tax to PRIs.

The formula of transfer should no doubt give weightage to population and poverty, but also to efficiency, so that there is incentive to them for increasing the sources of own revenues of

PRIs through own and assigned taxes and increasing their capacity to collect. State grants should be given to them only when the PRIs are able to collect a minimum percentage of the taxes assigned to them. Flow of funds from the State/GoI should also be dependent on good work or mobilization done by them. For instance these could be linked to the efforts made by panchayats in population and disease control, cleanliness, school attendance of females and their performance, and negatively with hunger deaths, crime, and civil and revenue suits.

Therefore, the additional allocations recommended by the Union Finance Commission to States, and in particular the supplementary sources to local governments, should be contingent upon the States fully implementing the suggestions given above.

Link Devolution with Performance

A "Devolution Index" may be prepared for all States and at least 1/3rd allocation of Centrally sponsored schemes in the Panchayat functional domain or block grant (when introduced) may be allocated to the State Governments on the basis of this index. It is emphasized that the Devolution Index will be prepared by the States themselves on the basis of self-assessment but would be available for further evaluation and assessment by academic bodies. A mechanism for calculating the index has been suggested at the Round Tables of the PRI Ministry, which could be adopted. This may be implemented after giving due notice to the States, say from Eleventh Five Year Plan (2007-12).

Audit of Panchayats

Increasing the finances and authority of panchayat bodies is of course likely to lead to corresponding abuses of power. Accordingly there is a need for more intensive and independent monitoring and auditing of the spending and assessment of panchayat performance, involving a combination of citizen bodies, representatives of higher levels of government, and NGOs. At the moment the auditing process is very weak (and much too delayed) at best. The mandatory meetings of the gram sabha, where major policies and items of expenditure are to be discussed can provide some salutary checks. But in many areas the attendance in the gram sabha meetings is rather thin and the requisite quorum is barely managed. One idea is to replicate at the panchayat level the model of the public accounts committee system that exists in the Lok

Sabha: appointment of opposition party members can be mandated to key local committees with some measure of veto power over large spending programmes.

Large expenditures are now being incurred by PRIs. Their accounts are to be audited by Local Fund Audit, but there are several problems. First, there are huge arrears, and in some cases accounts have not been audited for more than ten years. Secondly, the quality of their reports is very poor, therefore, the utility of such audits is doubtful, the impact it makes on improving systems is at best marginal, perhaps negative. Thirdly, there are complaints of corruption, and the general impression is that audit reports can be bought. Lastly, elected officials are not held accountable for any lapses noticed in their reports, only officials are, which breeds irresponsible behaviour on the part of non-officials.

The quality of work done by panchayats should be closely monitored by a team of journalists, civil society members, panchayat leaders from the neighbouring districts (who have already done excellent work), and stakeholders. Based on these reports, panchayats should be graded, and future funds should be linked with their grade. Strengthening financial management and audit procedures will also strengthen accountability of the local bodies, their standing committees and its representatives to the people as well as to government.

Connecting the Three-tiers

In the structure of Gram Panchayats, Taluka Panchayats and Zilla Panchayats, there is a disconnect between the Gram Panchayat President and Taluka Panchayat. There ought to be a system of representation of Gram Panchayat Presidents in the Taluka Panchayat with direct election of Taluka Panchayat President. A similar system ought to be in place for the Zilla Panchayats too. The indirect election of ZP/TP President leads to malpractices and undesirable compromises motivated by money, muscle and power.

Gender Empowerment

The empowerment of women through reservations in the panchayats is a necessary first step but needs to be reinforced by a number of other measures such as:

- the provision of Women Component Plans in the budgets of the PRIs;

- linkages with Self-Help Groups (SHGs);
- adequate training and capacity building;
- encouragement to political parties to put up women candidates;
- the opportunity to women to serve a full term when they are elected to posts in the PR system;
- Mahila Sabhas (or equivalent) to facilitate women's concerns and priorities being raised in meetings of Gram Sabhas and Ward Sabhas (or equivalent sub-Gram Sabha forums); and
- separate quorum for women's participation in Gram Sabhas and sub-Gram Sabha forums.

Encourage Outside Involvement

The situation in villages scattered across India indicates that there is a real need to build the human capital there and channelize it towards all round development and excellence. An initiative which may be attempted, could be, to invite persons or organizations from the village or other parts of the country or even NRIs and other organizations of 'Indians' to any village of their choice in India. These village 'architects' are not to be given any remuneration or grant or subsidy. They would have to present their credentials before the Gram Sabha and Gram Panchayat and, if the LSGI chooses to, they may be given the task of architecting the GP for a period of not less than 1 year. They would have no legal status or authority but, if there is commitment and sincerity, they can win over the villagers and play the role of a guide, mentor and architect, who harnesses the human energies of the village and channelizes it, giving the village the 'hand holding' it needs to formulate its own strategy for development and all round excellence. Typically, the architect comes with his knowledge, ideas, experiences and networks to be able to really make a difference, developing leadership in the village, imparting confidence and faith by being there and actively participating. This may be tried out on a pilot basis and if it succeeds, this can be documented and disseminated widely for covering nearly all villages which require this intervention. A similar variant at TP and ZP level may be formulated too.

This innovation is very much within the existing legal framework, as the State Governments, in accordance with the provisions of Article 243ZD (3)(b), may specify institutions, organizations and individuals, who may assist the Panchayats, Municipalities and DPCs in preparing plans of a technically acceptable nature.

Do we Really Require Three-tiers?

In most states one of these two-tiers is weak, district unit is weak in Tamil Nadu and Rajasthan, whereas the block unit is weak in Maharashtra and Gujarat. Some people have suggested that the states should be given the option of doing away with one of the levels, in case they so desire. Its implication for efficiency, equity and participation should be studied.

Increase the Use of IT

IT as tool can be very effectively used in the area of implementation by the PRIs. Several transactions can be carried out using on-line applications. This has been sufficiently demonstrated in various pilot projects carried out across the country such as Mahitishakti in Gujarat, Gyandoot in Madhya Pradesh, Bhoomi in Karnataka and FRIENDS in Kerala. All these initiatives help disseminate information to the public at large and also help carrying out of on-line transactions using ICT. It is proposed that in every Gram Panchayat, just as there are ISD/STD/PCO booths, a series of similar booths for disseminating information and making available various forms, services and transactions to people are set up by encouraging Public-Private Partnership (PPP). The booths/kiosks should operate more on the basis of principle of entrepreneurship than merely to be looked upon as extensions of state machinery. A combination of variety of services for the consumption of both government and public through these units would make them commercially and socially viable.

For instance, land records can be put on the web, and then disseminated through the private kiosks. This can be done on a basis wherein the revenue accrued from these transactions is taken by the operators while he pays a flat enrolment fee to the Panchayats to ensure that various forms and data is regularly put up and he pays for the information that is available to him.

This would need backend support by parallel ICT efforts for computerization of various services at the Gram Panchayats, taluka panchayats, Zilla Panchayats, which could, in turn be networked to the Panchayat Department and the Office of the Development Commissioner at the State Headquarters.

Linkages with MPLAD

Presently, moneys earmarked for Local Area Development of MPs are spent solely at the discretion of individual MPs. The implementation of MPLAD schemes is through the Collectors and not through the network of Panchayat institutions. This must be altered and PRIs made the principal agency instead of the Collectors. The MPLAD funds should be deposited with the Zilla Parishad as untied funds. MPs may indicate their preferences for schemes/programmes to the Zilla Parishad or/Block Panchayats/ Gram Panchayats which should be implemented by Panchayats as a part of the overall village/area /district plan.

It is suggested that MPs and MLAs declare the specific details of the work done under the MPLADS and MLA Fund, if these are not scrapped, while completing his term. In addition, s(he) should declare these details at the time of filling his nomination forms and at the completion of his term, in the form of an affidavit and these details may also be declared in the District Planning Committee Meeting and be open to questions. Similarly, in Parliament, it is suggested that these details be shared with a full discussion with questions raised on this, which the concerned member has to defend.

CBOs and PRIs

In some sectors, there is people's involvement through parallel institutions like the Joint Forest Management Committees, Village Education Committees, Water User Groups, etc. In such development projects, government has relied upon committees that are independent of panchayats. Often in the same region, such as UP hills, the World Bank has promoted different committees, one for forests, the second for drinking water, and the third for education, and these may be all distinct from panchayats!

Difficulties tend to arise in the *inter-relationship* between multi-purpose elected bodies and single-purpose user committees. The two types of bodies often exist at slightly different levels - with, for example, one covering a single village and the other a cluster of villages—which makes synergy between them difficult. There is often confusion about which of the two types of bodies has jurisdiction over a particular topic—water use, education, etc. Such confusion is sometimes deliberately sown by politicians and/or bureaucrats at higher levels, to weaken bottom-up development processes.

Most or all members of user committees are often chosen by nomination from above rather than by elections (through which members of most multi-purpose councils are selected). Bureaucrats may nominate pliable locals as user committee members, or politicians may pack them with loyalists of the ruling party. This difference in modes of selection often produces dissonance between the two types of bodies - and sometimes politicians set these bodies against one another, again to weaken bottom-up development processes.

The overwhelming evidence on user committee managed natural resource projects, such as forests and watershed management, is that the benefits are not sustainable in the long term. After the source of funds from the project dries up, plantations disappear, committees are disbanded or abandoned, and the livelihood base of the poor remains only marginally improved, if at all. Perhaps in some cases they create some sustainable social capital by raising awareness amongst the poor. However, the evidence suggests that most of the social capital which projects with CBO involvement create is held by the rich, and that in fact most projects have contributed to a further entrenchment of their powers.

Finally and crucially, user committees often have far more funds than do multi-purpose bodies - and sometimes far more funds than they can manage effectively. This can create a doubly invidious situation - feast and famine, cheek by jowl. It can mean that user committees struggle to manage *excessively funded mandates,* while in the same place, multi-purpose bodies groan under the weight of *unfunded mandates.*

Thus the institutional links between political decentralisation, in the form of Panchayati Raj (PRIs), and administrative decentralisation, in the form of user committees promoted by the external donor projects needs to be strengthened. Linkages between these two institutions will also reinforce the voice of the weaker sections of the society. Panchayat representatives are strong, first, because they are democratically elected; second, they have better reach both horizontally and vertically among the bureaucracy as compared to any other people's institution; and third, they have the support of other forums. It is needless to mention that these forums have a much wider say in shaping up the policies and for advocating their cause.

However, it is not being advocated that PRIs replace CBOs. It needs to be clearly understood that while panchayats are institutions of local self-government, CBOs will have to function as one of their implementing organs. Often panchayats are too big, Kerala panchayats cover a population of 23,000 people, Orissa and West Bengal panchayats cover 15 to 20 villages, and therefore smaller bodies need to be formed for operational purpose. For instance, school committees work much better when they consist of the parents of the actual school going children. Giving the authority over the school to the Sarpanch or panchayat often results in weakening accountability. All such parallel bodies should be required to report periodically to the Gram Sabha(s) so that the community as a whole is kept informed of the activities of parallel bodies.

While parallel structures are not to be encouraged, the multiplicity and enormity of tasks at the village requires that more and more villagers take up ownership of various activities, developmental programmes and functions in the village. It is suggested that for each function of the GP, the Gram Sabha be a Forum where people can volunteer or be selected to be a part of the Committee looking after a specific function, e.g. MDM, PDS, FFW, Health, Anganwadi, lights, water etc. In addition to the villagers, a member of the GP can be identified for each of these Committees to ensure good quality service delivery leading to development and overall excellence. This will help at the time of the Panchayat Metric Grid (PMG) grading and also bring in better right to information, participation with checks and balances.

To sum up, effective panchayats would also require effective district and block level administration, hence one should promote reforms at all levels. These reforms would of course need political support both at the federal and state levels.

REFERENCES

1. The score was arrived at by calculating the average of the 20 informants. The lower the score, the higher the value of the activity. No differences were found in ranking on the basis of gender, social group etc.
2. Many other states have also diluted the GoI Act. Both the Gujarat and Maharashtra Acts make ownership subject to the relevant state acts on NTFPs. The Maharashtra State Act leaves bamboo and cane out of the list of NTFPs over which ownership is granted to the panchayats.
3. A cynic remark is that PRIs have only succeeded in decentralisation of corruption.

5

Panchayati Raj in India: A Vision for the Future

V. MOHINI GIRI

Sudhamani, a former President, of a Panchayat in the Mysore district, was being threatened by a police constable, who came from a clan whose tradition was committing murders, threatening and extorting money. Her family members told her that she being a woman could not change age-old traditions. But she did not care for the threats she received. She mustered her Panchayats support and had him sent to jail for two months. Later he became a changed person and is now working for her.

India is a poor because the villages of India are poor. India will be rich if the villages of India are rich. Panchayats should be given greater power; for we want the villagers to have a greater measure of real swaraj [self-government] in their own villages.

– *Jawaharlal Nehru, first Prime Minister of India*

There is a growing feeling of awakening in India these past few years. There is a pulsating, energetic wave that rouses people from their sleep, demanding that steps be taken towards betterment of this great nation of great people. It would be an enormous step forward if this pulse found its way to the grassroots level.

Mahatma Gandhi first introduced the notion that he coined 'Gram Swaraj' which referred to Panchayat Raj with the idea of self-sufficient and self-reliant villages functioning as Republics. He had a dream that all villages within the country should be characterized by direct and participating democracy, endowed with all the powers that enable it to function as a government in the true sense of the term.

Rajiv Gandhi has ensured Mahatma Gandhi's vision of Gram Swaraj. This has become a reality after the 33 per cent elected members have joined Panchayats. In a nation of over 6 lakh villages, this means that villages are now able to experience the joys of independence and self-governance instead of restricting this privilege to a select few in the higher reaches of the administrative hierarchy.

Only in 1993, after the adoption of the 73rd Amendment to the constitution that was championed by the Late Shri Rajiv Gandhi, did India begin a process with the potential to create genuine democracy at the village level. This Amendment represented a historic opportunity to transform the face of rural India, as the amendment gave mandate to the transfer of decision-making power and resources in rural areas to local democratic councils known as panchayats. The Amendment mandates that resources, responsibility and decision-making power be devolved from central government and placed in the hands of rural grassrocts people, with elections every five years.

The most innovative aspect of the amendment is that one-third of all panchayat seats are reserved for women. Rural women - who for centuries have lived under oppressive conditions of malnutrition, illiteracy, ill-health and powerlessness - are now taking leadership roles in addressing these very issues.

Since India is a patriarchal society, social and political elites in many regions of the country are seeking to undermine and nullify the benefit of panchayati raj. Men so far have held monopoly in this area and they oppose women's induction and leadership. But this mindset is gradually changing which can be seen with the establishment of Smt. Pratibha Patil as the first woman President of India, this year.

In order for any country to progress it is necessary that all her children find their place in its governance. Panchayati Raj provides administrative powers to villagers, strengthening their belief in the overall central government, and in themselves. It allows villagers to be heard, and their grievances to be addressed. Until and unless the policies made at the top take into account life as it is at the lower rungs, true progress cannot be said to occur. This would lead to a government in which villages do not feel represented, making policies and strategies that are tailor made to all others but them. Panchayti Raj assures that corruption is minimized, the views of minorities are taken into account and that the voices of the most vulnerable in society are heard in decision-making. Thus the Government of India comes closer to fulfilling all these characteristics by virtue of the Panchayati Raj system.

Thus good governance through Panchayti Raj Institutions thus has the following characteristics:

- *Participatory:* All adult persons, male or female, of the village shall have a say in the village administration in order to make it truly participatory, as wide as the community.
- *Consensus oriented*: All decisions in the village Panchayat shall be on the basis of consensus, which steer clear of out divisive approaches arising from consideration of party politics, religion, caste, creed, class or culture.
- *Governance should be accountable, transparent and responsive:* They should be accountable, approachable and should make the people aware of their functioning.
- *Effective and efficient:* Good governance should be efficient.
- *Equitable:* "Antodaya" or unto the last, should be the philosophy behind distribution of resources so that an equitable distribution of scarce resources can be ensured.
- *Inclusive*: All village disputes have to be settled within the four corners of the village and not to be taken outside it so that the curse of litigation may not shatter the rural economy.
- And last by not the least good governance should follows the rule of law.

Shri Rajiv Gandhi, through the 73rd and 74th Constitutional amendments made local government a reality in India. Panchayats have become an important cornerstone for empowerment of people and for building the grassroots' most crucial process for people to assert their community identity and fulfill their basic needs of democracy.

A democracy works when all citizens, including the most marginalized people have the capability to ask questions, seek accountability from the state and participate in the process of governance.

Panchayats and urban local institutions, under the new scheme are one of the crucial processes to fight exploitation, and unequal and oppressive power relations, so as to promote human rights and protect community assets for the goal of self-reliance and sovereignty.

Shri Rajiv Gandhi's amendment to the Panchayati Raj institution allowed women an opportunity to prove that if given a chance, they would be able to achieve great success in any endeavour. By bringing the women and dalits to the process of governance and development, many of the development issues pertinent to them are brought to light for discussion, deliberation and decision-making. The issues of children, water, environment, and other vital subjects related to livelihood are being brought into focus. This amendment provides scope for planning from below for achieving economic development and social justice. By activating grassroots democracy, not only is our society democratized but good governance is being established at the grassroots; where it is needed the most. The goal for India is not simply to be the largest democracy, but the most participatory and representative democracy.

Elected Panchayats and local bodies can play a dynamic role in the information, knowledge and skill empowerment of rural women and men if they are empowered to do so. Panchayati Raj Institutions (PRI) cover more than 96 per cent of India's rural population, where Gram Sabhas Act as platforms for people's participation, to raise demands and to ensure transparency and accountability in the responses of panchayats.

Various training programmes have made women empowered in India, there have been many success stories of women in Panchayats.

- Kamalamma, Mandal Panchayat member from Siddalingapura Gram Panchayat, Mysore Taluk spoke of the obstacles facing her and how they were overcome. "One male Gram Panchayat member was jealous of my ability to get things done and was harassing me. I told him, 'If you hit me, I will hit you back.' Once he abused me at the work spot. So I hit him." This act has earned her the nicknames of 'Chamundeshwari', 'Onake Obawa' among others from the officials and the police in her Panchayat.

Kamalamma says, "Officials are happy with the work of the women Gram Panchayat members. Male GP members want the seat, power and contracts only to make money. We women have shown that we can also take contracts and get roads and houses built." Kamalamma has fought with the men in her GP for toilets for women and obtained them free through an Asian Development Bank scheme.

- Ambujamma, a member of another Panchayat, gathered funds and signatures from women for a Rajiv Gandhi Water Supply Scheme for her village. The men raised all kinds of objections to the scheme but the women were adamant and insisted on the water scheme.

In many training workshops, women discover that they possess the power to actually change conditions they have considered both intolerable and hopeless. They generate their own vision for what they want to achieve, and learn how to inspire others to stand with them to achieve it. After a lifetime of doing only what they have been told, women discover their ability to create their own strategies and action plans. In the months following the training, participants come back together to support each other in achieving their goals.

In this new era of panchayati raj, there are now more than one million women representatives elected to the three-tiers of panchayats who give more meaning for democratic representation, as they become spokespersons of the local community.

Women's political empowerment in the last nine years through the Constitution amendments has exploded several myths, like the belief that they are passive and disinterested in political institutions; only to the well-to-do, upper strata women will come through reservation; only the kin of powerful politicians will enter panchayats through political connectivity to keep the seats for them; and lastly and most importantly, women are only proxy - 'name-sake' – members and they do not participate in the panchayats. Without discounting the existence in panchayats of some women who do fit into this patriarchally oriented framework, one can say that these myths have now been buried. Today the buzzword is that 'women can do it'.

The advantages of Panchayati Raj Institutions are manifold; particularly for women and other hitherto marginalized and oppressed groups. It gives the population in small villages and areas a sense of self-hood, self-esteem, dignity, power and importance. It enables them to find their key role in the machinery of the government, thereby finding their role in shaping the future of their own families, communities and country. It also provides a boost to their self-confidence, especially the women, that if they set their minds to something—there is no end to what can be achieved. The marginalized groups' isolation is reduced greatly, because they feel a sense of connectedness with others and togetherness as they deliberate and discuss on the issues of importance to them.

An enthusiasm to grasp the opportunities available and to translate them into best possible practices is infused into the citizens, especially the women, for whom this presents as a breath of fresh air. The women see that see have been chosen by their fellow villagers and entrusted by the Constitution of India to lead their villages to achieve a healthy and productive way of life. They have the opportunity, power and responsibility to ensure the well being of everyone in their villages. It is also very helpful for capacity building in every individual, man or woman, because it allows them to develop skills to take them forward—such as leadership skills in speaking their vision, listening, communication, negotiation, advocacy, organization and consensus building.

The Panchayati Raj Institution brings every citizen the pleasure of feeling like he or she is a child of the country, with basic rights and responsibilities. A vision for the future is created collectively, for the village. And when the drops combine, the ocean is made from which emerges a vision for the nation as a whole.

6

Devolution of 3 F's to Panchayati Raj Institutions: A Development Paradigm in India

K. KARUNAKAR PATNAIK, *IAS (Retd.)*

India with approximately 5,50,000 villages comprising more than 70 per cent of India's total population, cannot adequately address the local needs. Hence democratic devolution and decentralization is an imperative need. This issue was widely debated even before India achieved independence. Although a lot of structuring and restructuring has been effected to Panchayati Raj Institutions after independence, decentralization or devolution is said to have taken some shape only after the 73rd Constitutional Amendment Act, 1992. The Balwantarai Mehta Committee recommended for creation of democratic institutions as a condition for securing participation in the governance structure and to create a proper climate of genuine decentralization at all tiers. Although PRIs were introduced in most of the states in India following the aforesaid committee's recommendations, Panchayats were generally and mostly considered as development agencies to implement the community development programmes.

Indian constituency is large and diverse. With 28 states and seven union territories and more than a billion people, several states are larger in size and population than many countries with UP alone a population of 131 million almost the size of Brazil. India is a country of diversity, more than 400 ethnic groups speaking a variety of languages and dialects. Therefore, effective representation in a fair and equitable way in such contingency is apt to be sometimes an impossible reality. In a survey of 400 villages it was noticed that 40 per cent villagers reported that they never heard of a single government scheme which number at about 2000 both under state and central schemes for rural development.

In spite of several studies under-taken in the past and recommendations of committees and commissions, Panchayats prior to the enactment of 73rd Constitutional Amendment Act, had neither any definite form nor substance to serve the requirements of the people. Panchayats, in fact, were generally considered as development agencies to implement different development programmes. Even after the 73rd Constitutional Amendment the same situation prevails to some degree in some of the states' governance structure. Inadequate finance and functional responsibilities continue to be the main hurdles in the functioning of PRIs. PRIs in most of the states suffered from several inadequacies. Even in states like Karnataka and West Bengal where powers to levy local taxes had been conferred on Mandal Panchayats (village level) and Panchayat Samiti (block level) respectively, raising of revenue of these bodies became increasingly dependent on revenue transfers from the state or the center. In these circumstances, the often cited apprehension was whether Panchayati Raj Institutions can become viable institutions and to achieve this what pre-requisites are required? It is true that the move to make local bodies truly the third level of governance has rather been incremental. Powers and responsibilities given to local bodies at the district level planning stage is definitely a major step. Some states like Kerala have formulated plans and schemes at the grassroot level earmarking 30 to 40 per cent of state's plan allocations. This is a positive signal. Therefore, in the midst of mixture of successes and failures partly or in some cases almost negligibly, the process of decentralization appears to be tardy. Formation of a remedial mindset queevers around as to whether decentralization should be made efficient, effective and accountable towards achieving an effective institution of self-governance.

"Decentralisation in the context of Panchayats means that when authority.........is transferred from the state to the local governments, the later should have the prerogative of taking decisions "on the planning and implementation of such activity" (Government of India Task Force on decentralisation, 2001). Decentralisation as a government objective is pronounced in the 73rd and 74th Constitutional Amendments focusing on the process of devolution of responsibilities and powers to Panchayats. But it is difficult to address the fiscal framework of Panchayats in isolation from other players in the inter-governmental fiscal system i.e. the center, state and municipal bodies. Fiscal stress at one level is likely to affect all other levels.

Like many other democracies in the world, decentralisation in India has gone through a process of advances and retreats, ups and downs. While advocates of conflicting perspectives on governance and development strategy argue in favour of decentralisation as essential for appropriate participation in governance, technical experts have supported decentralisation as critical to the effective implementation of development programmes. Those who are opposed to decentralisation mostly politicians see decentralisation as diluting political control by putting power into ill-equipped hands and administrators who perceive parallel threats to public management. Decentralisation for sake has made very little progress slowly but incompletely since after 1957. The delay is attributed mainly to the slow pace of legalisation and adoption of ineffective measures. Although there is much to rejoice with the constitutional amendments (73rd and 74th) and affirmative legislations undertaken by states now, the overall picture remains not as a very encouraging one and the overall scenario seems to be rather an unfinished agenda yet. The inadequate legislations and initiatives have not put local governments in right place and rather have failed to endow them with required means to achieve the end results.

With the passing of the 73rd and 74th Constitutional Amendments India embarked upon perhaps the largest decentralization process in modern history through the Panchayati Raj reforms. This is going to be a long and continuing process and any attempt to evaluate its working in its totality is going to be a stupendous task. Experienced hitherto gained after the 73rd Constitutional Amendment has brought home peculiar experimentation process across states in India. Kerala has tried to prove its people-oriented policies whereas Madhya Pradesh under the leadership of its former Chief Minister Digvijay Singh had experimented well-intentioned decentralization projects in the health and education sectors with a model for a district government.

Political history of India richly demonstrates that Panchayati Raj Institutions in India after independence in 1947, were construed to be ideal units to uphold India's democracy. Unfortunately, these institutions were palpably undermined from mid-1960s to 1980s and political power at the center became more centralized specifically in post-1960s after the spilt of the congress party. With widening of power sphere at the state level, the PRIs were left virtually powerless. It is only after the recommendations of Ashok Mehta Committee proposing the PRIs to become organics and integral part of our democratic process that states like West Bengal, Karnataka, Andhra Pradesh and Jammu and Kashmir ushered in a new phase of increased democratic process. Although 73rd Constitutional Amendment provides for a uniform structure and system of representative government, it is still left to the states to decide how much power they will give away through the legislation to the PRIs. As a result of this, variations in implementation of decentralisation and devolution process are noticed across various states in the country. Several research studies have shown that where state leaders have taken bold and sincere steps to support the PRIs and transfer powers, new conflicts have been encountered. In some states PRIs have to compete with parallel structures of governance.

Following the two landmark amendments to the Indian Constitution in 1993 (the 73rd and 74th Constitutional Amendment Acts) a legislative framework was created for introducing the three-tier system of governance for the rural and urban areas in the country. Creation of a three-tier system was made mandatory and states started passing special confirmatory legislations to incorporate in their states laws. Establishment of a State Finance Commission to determine the share of resources to be allocated to Panchayat bodies was a mandatory obligation for the states. Twenty-nine subjects listed in the Eleventh Schedule of the 73rd Amendment covering a broad range of rural development functions were intended to be transferred to the control of elected representatives. The amendments contained potentially far-reaching affirmative-action provisions. These were in form of reservation of seats for women, scheduled castes and scheduled tribes one-third of which are exclusively reserved for women both in seats and offices. Scheduled castes and scheduled tribes are allocated reserved seats in proportion to their population in the constituency with 1/3rd reserved for women of these reserved categories.

The decision to determine the extent of devolution of resources and powers to the three-tiers are left to the wisdom of states. Before the Constitutional Amendment (73rd Amendment) a few states like Kerala, Andhra Pradesh, Gujarat, Maharashtra, Karnataka and West-Bengal had a well-functioning system of local governance. But in most of the states Panchayats were practically moribund institutions with elections held irregularly and infrequently, limited autonomy, resistant bureaucracy, irregular gram sabha and domination in decision-making by power elites. With the new reform measures in granting constitutionals status, seat reservation for disadvantaged groups, ensuring free and fair elections, fixed tenures, designated powers and responsibilities and establishing a mechanism for distribution of finance to Panchayats, the developmental and democratic potential of Panchayati Raj in India was greatly strengthened.

The 73rd Amendment Act addressed some of the problems encountered by the PRIs in the country in the past years and keeping those in view provided the following broad features in the new Act. These are:

(i) Centrality of Gram Sabha to decentralised governance.

(ii) Provision of uniform three-tier PRI structure at village, Block and district levels.

(iii) Proportion reservation of seats and offices of chairpersons at all levels for SC, ST with 1/3rd reserved for SC/ST women.

(iv) One-third of total seats and chairperson offices reserved for women.

(v) Empowering state legislatures to provide reservation in seats and offices for backward classes.

(vi) Uniform five-year term for Panchayats with elections before the expiry of the term and elections within six months if Panchayats dissolved before the term.

(vii) Protection against dissolution by amendment before the expiry of Panchayat term.

(viii) Disqualification from Panchayat membership for those disqualified from election to state legislature.

(ix) Independent State Election Commission to supervise preparation of electoral rolls and control over electoral process.

(x) Twenty-nine subjects eligible for devolution to Panchayats, powers given to states regarding which subjects to devolve.

(xi) Setting up of State Finance Commission (SFC) once in five years to review PRI's financial position and make suitable recommendations for fund distribution to Panchayat bodies.

From the above features of the 73rd Constitutional Amendment, it becomes clear that the PRIs for the first time were granted constitutional status and empowered the socially and economically backward and disadvantaged groups such as dalits, adivasis and women to get into the political process at the grassroot level. Marking a distinct departure from the past experience, the new amendment provided for free, fair and regular elections with fixed tenure of five years for the PR bodies. For the first time independent and constitutionally mandated bodies like the State Election Commission and the State Finance Commission were provided as a regular and uniform pattern of institutions. The amendment definitely tried to bring out political uniformity on the very structure and workings of the three-tier system. It at least perceived popular participation in decision-making and service delivery. This was necessary in the backdrop of a clear absence of delivery mechanism which was even reported in the ninth five-year plan document (1997-2000) which reads as "past experience has shown that many development projects and programmes, having laudable objectives, have failed to deliver the result because of the inadequacies of design and implementation. Time and cost over-runs have become widespread and substantial in public sector infrastructure and development projects. It is common knowledge that the benefits intended to be delivered to the people through development programme in the social sectors have not fully reached the beneficiaries because of the weakness in administrative planning and delivery mechanism."

That the 73rd Constitutional Amendment excluded the Adivasis and other indigenous people from its realm, purposefully or deliberately, is a matter of conjecture only. The

Bhuria Committee (1994) recommended extension of the 73rd Constitutional Amendment provisions to scheduled areas to strengthen institutions of local government on the basis of which the Panchayats (Extension to Scheduled Areas) Act (PESA), 1996 came into force. The outstanding spirit of this Act was that it recognized the vulnerability of the Adivasis to any action against their interests by state functionaries at lower levels of police, excise, forest and revenue department and that the Act endorsed the community oriented Adivasi life in regard to resource base, their community rights with due respect to individual rights, over property. On these fundamental principles, the Grama Sabha is rather placed in the center-stage of Panchayat system of self-rule in the scheduled areas as compared to the non-scheduled areas.

Political decentralisation of rural and urban governments in India is not a new phenomenon although attempt in this direction did not succeed to secure the concept of Gram Swaraj of Mahatma Gandhi in the Draft Constitution of India till they were agitated to be placed in Article 40 in the non-justifiable part to read as "the state should take steps to organize village Panchayats and endow them with such power and authority as may be necessary to enable them to function as units of self-government." Democratic decentralization following the recommendations of Balwantrai Mehta Committee recommendations would have meant devolution of power in terms of resources, powers and authority to the Panchayati Raj Institutions but sadly the committee did not make provisions for fiscal decentralization till the K. Santhanam Committee set up in 1963 which recommended devolution of power to Panchayat institutions to levy special tax on land revenues and homes, consolidation of all grants at state level for eventual devolution to PRIs and establishment of Panchayati Raj finance corporation to look into the financial resources of PRIs and provide loans and financial assistance to grassroot level governments. Failure to implement the above recommendations completely led to the setting up of Ashok Mehta Committee (1978) which recommended for the first time inclusion of Panchayats in the constitution as a political institution instead of the hitherto development organization. In fact, on the basis of Ashok Mehta Committee's recommendations, the states of Karnataka, Andhra Pradesh, West Bengal and Jammu and Kashmir went for amendment/revision of their existing Acts or passed new legislations. The Ashok Mehta Committee broadly recommended:

(i) The district to be the key administrative unit for planning coordination and resource allocation and the management of the rural and urban continuum.

(ii) The PRIs to be a two-tier system with the middle-tier (block) as the base and the Zilla Parishad (district) at the top.

(iii) Representation of Scheduled Castes (SCs) and Scheduled Tribes (STs) in the elections to PRIs on the basis of their population.

(iv) Participation of political parties in elections.

(v) Financial devolution consistent with devolution of development functions to the district level.

On the basis of the recommendations of the committee, for the first time in India, rural local body elections were held in West Bengal in 1978 on political party basis. This was the first experiment in the country. In spite of the recommendations of these committees, the Panchayat institutions continued to be slow in terms of empowerment and in some states they continued to be weak and weaker. Some states like Orissa even managed with two-tiers, the Zilla Parishads being dissolved in 1968 till they were, later-on, reviewed by the state government under the leadership of late Biju Patnaik.

In 1986, the Central Government appointed the L.M. Singhvi Committee which recommended for the constitutional recognition of local self-government and non-inclusion of political parties in Panchayat elections. The L.M. Singhvi Committee observed that local government institutions were relevant to raise revenue resources through exercising taxation powers and for this control mechanism had to be devised. It, therefore, suggested appointment of a Finance Commission to allocate adequate resources for implementing various rural development and poverty alleviation programmes through the Panchayati Raj Institutions. Following the recommendations of the aforesaid committees, the Constitution (64th Amendment) Bill was drafted and introduced in parliament which, unfortunately, failed to get a majority in the Rajya Sabha because it overlooked the states and was perceived as an instrument of the center to deal with the PRIs directly.

However, subsequently, the 74th Amendment Bill (1990) on Panchayats and municipalities was introduced by the National Front government but the bill was never taken up for discussion during its short tenure in office. In September 1991, the Congress Government introduced the 72nd (Panchayats) and 73rd (Nagar Palika) constitutional amendment bills, and finally, on April 24, 1993, the constitutional amendment formally came into force after ratification by more than half of the state assemblies. When both houses of parliament passed the bills, the sequence of bill changed to the 73rd and 74th Amendments respectively. These were historical legislations in the post-independent history of local self-government in India.

It was incumbent upon the State Government to amend their respective state laws to bring in uniformity in the pattern of PRIs in states (three-tier structure) leaving the discretion to smaller states having less than 20 lakh population not to have the middle level Panchayat. As a result, most of the states have adopted the three-tier system as an uniform system of political decentralization. Since implementation of the provisions of the constitutional amendments was left to the wisdom of the states, the states were required to approve the conformity legislation containing powers, functions and procedural details for local government institutions. The state government even were allowed to prescribe new rules instead of going for principal legislation. States like Andhra Pradesh and Karnataka preferred delegated legislation instead of principal legislation even though a lot of speculation and doubts were raised with regard to such matters in implementation, service delivery, capacity building, transfer of responsibilities and powers to rural local bodies. But because of the flexibility given to the states, the 73rd Constitutional Amendment made India one of the most politically decentralized countries in the developing countries of the world and brought in the most distinguishing features of grassroot democracy in the country. Because of the flexibility given to states, a wide variation in the political structure of panchayat bodies across the country is noticed with regard to the size, method for electing chairpersons (direct or indirect), reservation for backward classes, presence of MPs/MLAs in panchayat affairs, election norms, district level composition and methods of dissolution of these bodies and suspension and removal of chairpersons. Even though there is little variation in the average population size of rural local bodies, the fact remains that the intention of the law was to bring the government close to the people. In practical applicability, for example, while Kerala established fewer but larger gram panchayats, Karnataka adopted the opposite approach.

Certain subjects involving core or civic functions of local governments such as drinking water, street lighting, garbage collection, road maintenance and specialized and technical subjects covering primary health, education and social protection are eligible for devolving to rural local bodies. While some governments have transferred some subjects out of 29 subjects indicated in schedule XI, mere nominal transfer of subjects is not enough to enable Panchayats perform those functions. These subjects, in fact, continue to be implemented as activities and sub-activities by line agencies. Most of the state acts have specified functions to be devolved to PRIs but have not been able to transfer administrative or technical control over locally administered programmes. Few states like Gujarat, Karnataka, Kerala, Madhya Pradesh, Rajasthan and Uttar Pradesh have taken measures to transfer functionaries but have faced with strong resistance from different unions/associations. Even where transfers have taken places, these have become minimal/nominal with powers to fire, hire, promote and transfer those staff vested in line agencies. Consequently, Panchayat bodies are reduced to mere salary-paying institutions resulting in government administration still centralised even though it is highly decentralisation politically.

The 73rd and 74th Constitutional Amendment have provided for constitution of State Finance Commissions (SFCs) for the rural and urban local bodies respectively to review and make recommendations on their finances. The Governor of each state was required to set up an SFC within a year from the commencement of the Constitutional Amendment Act and subsequently at the culmination of every five-year period. The amendments also broadened the terms of reference of the Central Finance Commission (CFC) so that it would augment the consolidated fund of states and supplement the resources of local bodies. When faced with incomplete SFC recommendations of hesitation on the part of states, the CFC, the department of

Panchayats and rural development departments have taken additional steps to devolve funds to Panchayats but these have been by and large ad hoc and incomplete. In consequence, a lot of inter-state variation in fiscal decentralization is noticed. While states like Kerala have developed substantial resources to Panchayat bodies, others such as Utter Pradesh have managed only minimal devolution.

In the meantime, although almost all states have constituted SFCs with more or less common terms of reference, there seems to be no common or uniform approach being followed by all the SFCs except that most of them have chosen to stick to the existing tax powers of local governments and suggested the transfer of funds to complement these. The SFCs are required to recommend financial support from the state and the principles for the determination of taxes, tolls and fees that can be assigned to or appropriated by the local bodies. Once the revenue sharing arrangement is designed, the SFC has to recommend the allocation of the revenue that can be shared among different local bodies, both urban and rural.

SFCs in different states followed different ways of determining the resource requirement of local bodies. In absence of clear expenditure assignments, the SFCs were reportedly encountered with problems in such assessment. Many Panchayats, especially GPs in states such as Andhra Pradesh, Madhya Pradesh and Rajasthan neither impose nor collect taxes that they are authorized to because they are perceived to be unpopular with constituents. Among other problems confronted by SFCs are lack of administrative machinery and trained staff for tax collection and availability base of taxes being too low to generate sufficient revenue. Doubting the Panchayat's ability to assess and collect taxes, SFCs in some states did not assign any tax from the state level to the local bodies. Instead, they were in favour of PRIs being given a higher percentage of the state's shared taxes. Based on certain criteria, the SFCs decided on how the total share of the state budget was to be divided between PRIs and municipalities and within each sector. In developing their formulae for transfers to lower-level governments, SFCs were guided by various methods.

The general problem faced by SFCs in recommending a formula is the lack of relevant data. Reliable data is a problem for instance, with per capita incomes for regions smaller than districts, per capita production of agriculture workers and the number of poor families and the quality of infrastructure for all rural local governments. Faced with this data problem, different SFCs devised different methods for devolution of plan funds to local bodies. The following table will indicate the formula of weight age adopted by the SFCs in some states like Karnataka, Kerala, MP, Rajasthan, UP, WB and Orissa.

Indicators	*States*						
Population	33.33	75	75	40	80	25	-
Area	33.33	-	25	-	-	50	-
Poverty	-	-	-	50	20	-	-
Population SC/ST	-	5	-	-	-	-	-
Population of non-desert develop. Programme/Non-drought prone areas Programme/Non-tribal area development (TAD) blocks	-	-	-	10	-	-	-
Persons per bed in govt. hospital	11.11	-	-	-	-	-	-
Road length (in sq. kms.)	11.12	-	-	-	-	-	-
Fincial need	-	15	-	-	-	-	-
Total effect	-	5	-	-	-	-	-
Lack of rural Connectivity	-	-	-	-	-	25	-
Total	**100**	**100**	**100**	**100**	**100**	**100**	-

In matters of adopting formula by SFCs in recommending allocation of funds to local bodies, one popular approach could be the Gadgil formula used for transferring central plan assistance to states. This formula gives a weight of 60 per cent to population, 25 per cent to per capita income, 7.5 per cent to fiscal management and achievement of national objectives and the remaining 7.5 per cent to special problems of states. Another model through which central funds are allocated for employment generation schemes like Jawahar Rozgar Yojana (JRY) is based on the rural population relative to that of the country. Within a state, the allocation is based on an index of backwardness of the districts. This index gives equal weight to the relative SC/ST population in the district (compared to the state) on the one hand, and the inverse of per capita production of agricultural workers on the other.

As the reports of the State Finance Commissions were delayed, the Central Finance Commission (CFC) made an ad hoc provision of 4381 crores rupees (US$920 million) for Panchayats, in equal annual installments from 1996-97 to 1999-00. This was based on the 1971 rural population of 438.1 million and a per capita provision of 100 rupees (US $2.25). These are intended to be matching grants and not meant for salaries and wages. For the five year period beginning the year 2000, the Eleventh Finance Commission (EFC) recommended measures to augment the consolidated funds of the states governments to supplement the resources of the Panchayats as shown in the table below. The EFC grant was also intended for development expenditure and excluded wages and salaries. For the first time, grants to states were conditional on specific monitorable measures of state's level of decentralization to Panchayats.

Third-tier Provisions by Eleventh Finance Commission, 2000

	Annual Grant 2000-2005 (in Cores)		
Category	*Panchayats*	*Municipalities*	*Total*
Total	1600.00	400.00	2000.00
Account-keeping	98.61	-	98.61
Database	197.06	2.94	200.00
Maintenance of Civic Services	1309.33	397.06	1605.15

The civic services included education, primary health, drinking water, street lighting and sanitation.

The Twelfth Finance Commission recommended a total grant of Rs. 20,000 crore to Panchayat bodies and Rs. 5000 crore to Municipalities for the period 2005-10. Out of the funds allocated to the PRIs, the commission suggested the PRIs to be encouraged to take over the assets relating to water supply and sanitation and utilize the grants for repairs/rejuvenation and the O&M costs. Priority should be given to expenditure on O&M costs of water supply and sanitation. It also recommended to earmark 50 per cent of the grants-in-aid given to each state for schemes of solid waste management through public-private partnership. The recommendation of EFC for creation of database and account-keeping was to continue. The inter-se distribution of allocation for the states during the period (2005-10) recommended by the commission is placed in the scheduled below.

In spite of resource allocation suggested by the State and Central Finance Commissions, local bodies continue to reel under fund constraints due to mismatch between demand and supply. In consequence, these institutions continue to depend more on governmental intervention rather than developing and strengthening an inner mechanism for resource raising.

There is a general perception that the Central Government is using its superior financial powers over the states for political ends. This is the case not only with the present UPA government but was also the position with the post-governments in the center. This perception has come-up not because several states are ruled by different political parties but due to many other problems which have cropped up during the last decade. It is a fact that there is a financial asymmetry between the center and states. Invariably there is a mismatch between the needs and assignment of financial powers to the states. More of buoyant revenue sources are assigned to the center and most of the civic and development expenditures are incurred by the states. Aware of this asymmetry, the Founding Fathers of the constitution had provided the mechanism of Finance Commission for correcting this imbalance in a fair manner. Therefore, every five years, a new Finance Commission recommends the criteria and formulae for the quantum of revenue transfer from the center to the states and their allocation among the states. The recommendations of Finance Commission are generally accepted and implemented. The Planning Commission, a non-constitutional entity was set up in 1950 to oversee the socio-economic development of the country in the broad framework of the constitution as provided in the Directive Principles of State Policy. Initially the center started providing financial assistance to states on the basis of specific projects and since 1969 on a formula approved by the National Development Council. This formula is popularly called the Gadgil formula. Even though the planning commission was not a constitutional entity, it has continued to play a crucial role in center-state fiscal relations.

The following important factors have contributed to this predominant role of the Planning Commission namely *(i)* the amount of resource transfer increased overtime even to exceed the devolution suggested by CFC; *(ii)* the Planning Commission has become a permanent body with a sizeable pool of professional staff and expertise and *(iii)* it is headed by the Prime Minister himself as chairman. In fact, major shares of transfer on the basis of CFC and Planning Commission recommendations are based on objective criteria and anchored on pre-determined and transparent formulae; but it is not always the case of other central transfers like the Centrally Sponsored Schemes (CSS) to states. States often complain of too much rigidity adopted in these schemes without allowing flexibility to states to fit into their local needs and conditions. Some states also resent the element of non-transparency involved in the allocation of funds among states. Poor states often complain of absence of counterpart funds for which they are unable to utilize allotted funds. In the present system of things, more enterprising and resourceful states continue to get more benefits and the poorer and less enterprising states are placed at an obvious disadvantage.

Though the implementation of CSS is expected to be closely monitored by the nodal Central Government departments concerned, practically the states do the major work and the Central Government's major task is confined mostly to collection of utilization certificates only. There is hardly any in-built mechanism to ensure that funds allotted are well spent and expected outputs are generated producing intended results. Calamities and disasters are frequent occurrences in one part or the other of the country. Since the formation of the Tenth Finance Commission (TFC) there is a National Calamity Fund (NCF) from which funds are allocated state-wise according to need. State governments normally knock at the door of the center in the event of large-scale calamities such as widespread droughts and floods. The need of states is normally assessed by a central team of officers but there are complaints of lack of co-relation between the intensity of the calamity and the amount of central relief provided which is sometimes influenced by extraneous conditions,

State	Panchayat		Muncipalities	
	Per cent	(Rs. crore)	Per cent	(Rs. crore)
Andhra Pradesh	7.935	1587	7.840	374
Arunahcal Pradesh	0.340	68	0.60	3
Assam	2.630	526	1.100	55
Bihar	8.120	1624	2.840	142
Chattisgarh	3.075	615	1.760	88
Goa	0.900	18	0.240	12
Gujarat	4.655	931	8.280	414
Haryana	1.940	388	1.820	91
Himachal Pradesh	0.735	147	0.160	8
Jammu & Kashmir	1.405	281	0.760	38
Jharkhand	2.410	482	1.960	98
Karnataka	4.440	888	1.960	8
Kerala	4.924	985	6.460	38
Madhya Pradesh	8.315	1663	2.980	98
Maharashtra	9.915	1983	7.220	323
Manipur	0.230	46	15.820	149
Meghalaya	0.250	50	0.180	361
Mizoram	0.100	20	0.160	791
Nagaland	0.200	40	0.120	6
Orissa	4.015	803	2.080	104
Punjab	1.620	324	3.420	171
Rajasthan	6.150	1230	4.400	220
Sikkim	0.065	13	0.020	1
Tamil Nadu	4.350	870	11.440	572
Tripura	0.285	57	0.160	8
Uttar Pradesh	14.640	2928	10.340	517
Uttaranchal	0.810	162	0.680	34
West Bengal	6.355	1271	7.860	393
TOTAL	**100.00**	**20000**	**100.00**	**5000**

political or otherwise. There exists a qualitative difference in the relationship between the Planning Commission and the state governments on the one hand and the union finance ministry and the state governments on the other.

While the Planning Commission is more like a friend and philosopher to the states with its technical expertise without statutory backing over central funding, the Ministry of Finance (MoF) exercises commanding authority and control over central funds. But the Planning Commission, over the years, has tried to maintain its neutrality in contrast to the MoF. In recent years, some state governments ruled by parties not in power in the center have complained of discrimination and step-motherly attitude of the center in the matter of allocation of and control over central funds. The reasons are mainly due to *(a)* A veil of secrecy in the dealings of MoF with the state governments; *(b)* State finance secretaries and their officials have a tendency to rush to New Delhi to solve their liquidity crisis and sort-out payment problems in the face of extended overdraft position and *(c)* The unplanned and often mindless announcements of fiscal packages for particular regions, states or even cities made by politicians and political parties which are not honoured subsequently and these affect directly or indirectly the center-state fiscal relations.

In view of the above, there is an urgent need to review the operation of the system governing center-state fiscal relations. The fiscal position of almost all states is under stress mainly on account of the competitive populism practiced by the State Governments. But at the same time the Central Government can not absolve of its responsibility in contributing to the fiscal mess in the states due to several actions including hefty salary revision in the wake of the fifth pay commission putting pressure on state governments to carryout similar pay revisions for state government employees. It is necessary, therefore, to have transparent fiscal practices and rule-based transfer of funds to states. In this connection, the terms of reference of the Thirteenth Finance Commission may be sufficiently comprehensive to address some of the issued raised above.

How could the impact of Panchayati Raj in India be assessed? Has any such assessment been really made? One of the main difficulties in bringing out such studies is the sheer magnitude, diversity and complexity of the PRI governance pattern obtaining differently in various states of the country. As Mark Robinson puts in one of this writings, much of the available literatures suffer from the limitations of heavy reliance on anecdotal insights, the partiality of authors and empirical data constraints. There appears to be no single authentic source of data that facilitates rigorous comparison or assessment of progress on the basis of a set of measurable indicators. Obviously the task is gigantic and beyond the scope of most organisations.

Another problem was that until recently, majority of social scientists in India were not seriously concerned with Panchayati Raj in particular which resulted in dearth of serious and in-depth research and publications on this subject. The bulk of this research done so far is conducted outside the mainstream of university social science departments by independent research centers or NGOs. As a result, the quality of work is often uneven or is very micro-level in focus. The broad conclusions are typically derived on the basis of very small number of studies conducted in a handful of Panchayats in one region of a single state. Based on research findings and personal insights of years of intensive engagement with policy-makers, officials, academics and discussions with elected representatives it now transpires that the concept of performance of decentralized institutions depends on three major dimensions: effectiveness, responsiveness and process. If these indicators are addressed positively, PRIs can continue to play a major role in the development paradigm of the country.

7

Gram Panchayat Libraries in Karnataka: An Innovative Initiative

B.S. BHARGAVA, K. SUBHA AND D.S. HANUMANTHA RAO

Karnataka state is one of few states in the forefront in regard to the growth and development of the public library system in the country as a whole. The department of public libraries in Karnataka has rendered salutary service by installing a network of libraries through-out the state and is, by way of offering library facilities, striding fast from the capital towards the villages in the direction of evoking an intellectual revolution among the people by instilling in the common man an active interest for reading.

With a view to universalise the right of reading, the Government of Karnataka formulated the Karnataka Public Libraries Act in 1965 and enacted the same thereby laying a sound foundation for the growth of public libraries in this state. To propagate the popular feeling that the Public Libraries are the Universities of common people and to translate that into action, a programme has been chalked out to show an increased interest towards the grassroots by opening Rural libraries in all the Gram Panchayats of Karnataka with a profuse dynamism. It is a milestone, a model and indeed a meritorious point in the very history of libraries in India.

Karnataka state is one of the pioneers in the country in decentralising powers to the grassroots institutions, comprises of 27 districts, 176 taluks, 745 hobilies, 29,193 villages, 6 city, Corporations, 40 CMCs, 81 TMCs and 5,652 Gram Panchayats. It is worth mentioning that, Karnataka is also the pioneering state in the country to establish libraries at gram panchayat level. This was to inculcate among the rural folk an interest to read, to improve the educational standard, a forum for cultural activity and also to cultivate the reading habit during leisure hour.

Karnataka is the 3rd state in the country to establish libraries. The Act facilitates establishment and maintenance of libraries in rural areas. Another important fact is that, the act also provides for collection of library cess through property tax. There are 3,251 gram panchayat libraries functioning in the state (out of 5,652 GPs). Besides the manpower to manage the gram panchayat library, it is the responsibility of the department to provide infrastructure facilities like buildings, furniture, water, light and such others.

Procedure for Establishing Gram Panchayat Libraries (GPLs)

1. Depending on the demand of the local people and if the gram panchayat provides a free building, a gram panchayat library will be opened in such places.
2. The libraries such opened will be managed by a local person studied upto SSLC (pass). The persons thus appointed, will be paid an honorarium of Rs. 750 per month.
3. Following are the provisions for establishment of library at gram panchayat level.

Table-1

Particulars	*For Establishment of New Libraries*	*Ongoing*
Honorary Remuneration @ Rs. 750 per month × 12	9,000.00	9,000.00
Furniture	10,000.00	–
Books	8,000.00	3,000.00
Periodicals	2,3000.00	–
Miscellaneous	200.00	–
Total	**29,500.00**	**12,000.00**

The gram panchayat libraries aim to provide library services to one and all in the rural areas. There is no fee for referring the reading materials in the premises of the library. If one wants to borrow books, he/she should become a member on paying a prescribed membership fee. The membership fee to borrow one book is Rs. 10 and for two books it is Rs. 20.

Objective and Scope of the Study*

(1) To assess the profile of the users of public libraries at gram panchayat level; (2) To assess the effectiveness of public library inculcating to reading effect among the rural masses and thereby enabling them to enhance their knowledge level; (3) To evaluate whether the public library is catering to preference of the uses in terms of books/magazines/newspaper/novels and other relevant reading materials; (4) To elicit the opinion of the users as well as persons managing the public library to enhance the effectiveness and usage of the library at gram panchayat level.

Methodology

The following methodology was adopted for conducting the study:

1. Collection of secondary data,
2. Schedules,
3. Field Survey, and
4. Discussion with experts and focus group discussion.

The districts were divided into four divisions and from each district, two gram panchayat libraries of each taluk was covered in the study (see figure on page 80).

(a) Gram Panchayat Libraries numbering 3251 are spread over in the 176 taluks of the state. Two gram panchayat libraries were selected at random to cover all the 176 taluks. To get a representative sample, the Chief Librarians at districts were consulted. Accordingly, one good/developed library and another average library was selected.

(b) For the purpose of study and to collect primary data on each of the gram panchayat library, it was necessitated to interact with field level departmental functionaries and the users of such libraries. For this purpose 4 schedules were designed, viz., *(i)* District Librarians, *(ii)* Panchayat President/Member/Secretary, *(iii)* Supervisor and *(iv)* Users. As far as users, minimum 10 persons were interviewed.

---

* The paper is generated out of a comprehensive research project report (January 2006), entitled *Evaluation of Gram Panchayat Libraries*; the study entrusted to Institute of Social Sciences, Bangalore by Department of Public Libraries, Government of Karnataka. The authors express profuse thanks to the Director, other staff of the Department and the project for their support and co-operation in conducting the study.

The schedules have been designed in such a way that exhaustive information is collected which will be a bench mark to arrive at findings and to make suitable recommendations.

(c) In total 352 gram panchayat libraries have been covered for the purpose of study which works to about 11 per cent of the total gram panchayat libraries in the state.

Figure
Sampling Procedure

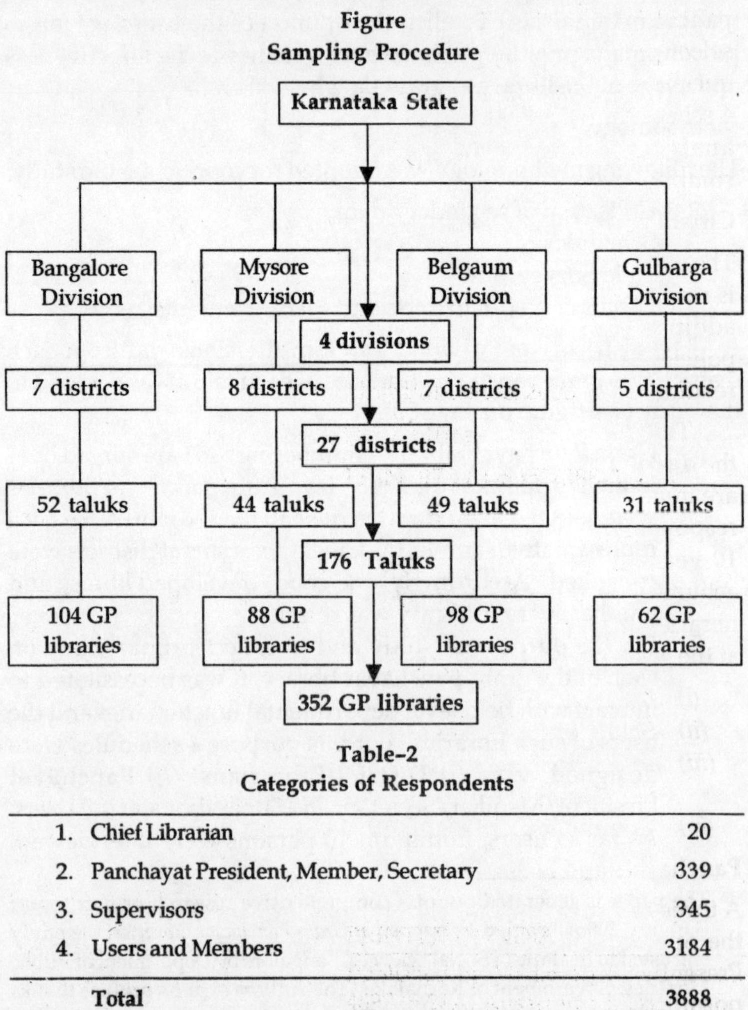

Table–2
Categories of Respondents

1.	Chief Librarian	20
2.	Panchayat President, Member, Secretary	339
3.	Supervisors	345
4.	Users and Members	3184
	Total	**3888**

The study was conducted during 2005-06.

Analysis of Data (Based on Categories of Respondents)

The working of the Scheme (of gram panchayat libraries) has been analyzed based on the data collected from secondary sources, interviews and group discussions. There are common questions in all the 4 schedules used for collection of primary data. Therefore, it was necessary to categorize physical infrastructures availability and opinion oriented common questions. Of the 3251 gram panchayat libraries covering 176 taluks 352 libraries have been selected at random. A few questions are inter-related, and such questions have been analyzed to draw logical conclusions. All the 4 schedules (administered to four categories of respondents) are analyzed category-wise and considered for arriving at comprehensive findings.

Chief Librarians at District Level

The most important person at the district is the chief librarian, who is responsible to carry out the policies set by the department. In addition to spending the money wisely in accordance with the policies of the department, he/she is also responsible for public relations of the library.

The study shows that there are 27 Chief Librarians covering all the districts. It was heartening to note that all the Chief Librarians are qualified in library sciences and maximum number (74%) of respondents have service in a particular district ranging from 5 to 10 years. They also had a good understanding of the district activities. All the Chief Librarians have visited the gram panchayat libraries. They expressed their concern in strengthening the library at the gram panchayat. Their opinions, in brief, are given below:

(i) Own buildings are necessary.

(ii) Salary of supervisors to be increased.

(iii) In some cases, supply of newspapers and magazines are less than the requirement of the readers.

(iv) Computers, Radio and TV to be provided.

Panchayats and Libraries

A three-tier structure of PRIs has been adopted in Karnataka with the operationalisation of the 73rd Constitutional Amendment. Presently, Karnataka has 5,652 gram panchayats having an average population of 5,300 (according to 1991 census). Each gram panchayat is headed by a President. Being the executive head, he is supposed to be knowledgeable about the library, its purpose and activities in the panchayat area. So also the Secretary and other elected members of the panchayat. Promoting economic and social welfare, education and health are the main functions of the panchayat, which will consist of a village or group of villages. As members of the panchayat, their role is very important in the overall development of the community. Their perception of the given issue is, therefore, important.

Most of the elected gram panchayat members interviewed are literate/educated and they also visit libraries. They know the role of library at village level. But there appears to be lack of initiative in providing/facilitating the functioning of library. To begin with, it is just necessary that the elected gram panchayat members take interest in mobilizing voluntary contributions either in kind or cash and maintain proper account.

Panchayat Presidents / Members / Secretaries

In total 339 persons have been interviewed of which 39.2 per cent Presidents, 27.1 per cent Gram Panchayat Members, 25.1 per cent Secretaries, 4.7 per cent Vice-Presidents. Of the 339 respondents, most of them are educated in the order of High School 27.4 per cent, Graduates 23.3 per cent, PUC 15.9 per cent, Middle School 14.7 per cent.

These gram panchayat members will have to know the budgetary allocations to their panchayats and the various programmes that are being implemented. The study reveals that, about 49 per cent of the members know the budgetary allocations. This perhaps may reflect on their involvement in various programmes at gram panchayat level. This also reflects awareness building activities for the facilities under the panchayat.

Being informed about the existence of gram panchayat library the members expressed their desire to improve the activities of the library in order to develop an informed society or community. According to them, the following points need to be considered for effective functioning of the library.

(1) Providing a good building with electricity, water, good sanitary conditions; (2) Proper release and utilization of the allocated funds; (3) To mobilize the public to contribute for library activity; (4) To build awareness among the people about

participation in library activities; (5) To fully support as and when necessary this initiative of the department; and (6) The need for training programmes to the officials and non-officials of gram panchayat about the various schemes of the Government.

Supervisors

To provide materials for library users a librarian must be aware of new publications and must periodically evaluate the materials available. Since budget is limited, the librarian must develop the skill in money management, good judgement about users needs and be informed about latest developments in publication. The librarian should have good knowledge of cataloguing, classifying and arranging books in such a way that the user can locate them easily. At the gram panchayat library the supervisor is the Librarian.

To enhance the effectiveness and use of the GPLs, the Supervisors were interviewed to elicit their understanding, views and perception of the developmental activity. Of the 352 selected gram panchayat libraries, 345 Supervisors could be contacted at the time of survey.

The data showed that while only 29.3 per cent libraries have own buildings, 47.2 per cent library are working in buildings/space provided by the panchayat. The support of the panchayat in promoting library activity is worth appreciating but it also had a negative effect on the smooth functioning of the library. Often these libraries were opened when the gram panchayat office opens. Their stocks were sometimes kept in the library and locked. These items occupied most of the space available for users of the libraries. Some libraries are situated in school buildings, Yuvaka Mandala building and temples. Own buildings are necessary to create a congenial atmosphere. Therefore, there is an urgent need to have the library in separate, own buildings.

It is noticed that, all the Supervisors are not attending the meetings of Gram Panchayats. In such meetings the problems/ bottle necks in running the library could be discussed and resolved locally. As Gram Panchayat meetings are an important forum for finding ways and means of strengthening any activity at the village level and libraries being under the control of gram panchayats, it is necessary for the supervisors to attend the gram panchayat meetings regularly to keep himself/herself aware of the various developments in their gram panchayats. The responses show that 24.6 per cent are not attending the panchayat meetings. The fact cannot be ignored that involvement in these meetings can build a good rapport between the panchayat and the library, thereby helping in effective functioning of the libraries.

With regard to maintenance of income and expenditure in the library it is observed that only 52.2 per cent are maintaining this record.

Level of Awareness

The job of providing materials for library users is a very challenging one. The supervisor should therefore be aware of the materials available and evaluate the need for new ones. The following tables reveal the level of awareness of the supervisors. As regards to the number of users of the library per day, the Supervisors felt that it ranges between 30 to more than 45 persons. If the interests of the regular users are considered, all kinds of reading materials like books, periodicals, magazines, newspapers are required in the libraries. The responses of the Supervisors reveal that, the users show interest in books, magazines and newspapers.

Table-3
Type of Books Preferred More by Users

	Yes	*No*	*No Response*	*Total*
Books	302	36	7	345
	(87.5)	(10.4)	(2.0)	(100.0)
Periodicals	143	195	7	345
	(41.4)	(56.5)	(2.0)	(100.0)
Magazines	295	43	7	345
	(85.5)	(12.5)	(2.0)	(100.0)
Newspapers	203	135	7	345
	(58.8)	(39.1)	(2.0)	(100.0)
Others	163	175	7	345
	(47.2)	(50.7)	(2.0)	(100.0)

It is encouraging to see that the existing nearby schools, colleges make use of the library. 87.5 per cent of respondents said that students were regular visitors. Hence the libraries have to be well-equipped to meet the demands.

The analysis of the level of awareness of the supervisors regarding the terms and conditions of the library, showed a certain degree of lack of awareness. For e.g., about the system as such because the decision on replacement of books lies with the Director and Chief Librarian and that the members can take only two books at a time. The need for orientation is clearly reflected here. The respondents expressed that the old books should be replaced at the earliest as the number of users are increasing and the nearby schools also make use of this facility.

With reference to stock verification 86.1 per cent said that it was conducted periodically. But it is necessary that annual stock verification is done in all the gram panchayat libraries. The Supervisors said that, this exercise helps in identifying loss of books/old damaged books and books lost and cost recovered. However, there is no serious loss as the number of books are relatively less in most of the libraries. Moreover, the available books are under lock and key. In case of loss or books borrowed and not returned the Supervisor being a localite, these books are recovered through personal contact.

Table–4
What Category of People Visit Library Regularly?

	Yes	*No*	*No Information*	*Total*
Common people/ children	271 (78.3)	71 (20.6)	4 (1.2)	345 (100.0)
Agriculturists	242 (70.1)	99 (28.7)	4 (1.2)	345 (100.0)
Students	271 (78.6)	69 (20.0)	5 (1.4)	345 (100.0)
Government employees	251 (72.8)	90 (26.1)	4 (1.2)	345 (100.0)
Businessmen/petty	184 (53.3)	157 (45.5)	4 (1.2)	345 (100.0)
Private employees	148 (42.9)	193 (55.9)	4 (1.2)	345 (100.0)

The table reveals that, the rural mass not only include the farming community but also represent Government/Private employees, petty businessmen, students and common public in the village. In the opinion of the Supervisors, in the order of identified categories, students and common public, government employees and agriculturists, businessmen/industrialists and private employees are the regular users. However, though enrolment of members is open, the frequency of enrolment ranges between 50 to more than 300 in some libraries. Average highest number of enrolment is between below 150. Therefore, it can be said that the enrolment is around the range of 50-150 till date. However, the number of enrolment was quite high in the libraries which have been existing for a longer period or are better equipped.

The use of the library by the villagers in general was on an average a minimum of 50 to maximum of 150 non-members. The significant fact is that library is used by a very negligible percentage of the total population of the gram panchayat. For illustrative purpose, in Mallur GP in Chennapatna Taluk, total population being 6,175, the total literates are 4,452 i.e., 72 per cent. The study shows that, 30 persons use this library everyday. This implies that less than 10 per cent i.e., 0.67 per cent of the literate people visit the library per day. The number of users thus being very less, there is a need to motivate people to use this facility.

The respondents opined that a good building, latest books on various subjects and for competitive exams, magazines, proper water and toilet facilities will attract more people to the libraries, which are the only essential source in remote areas for improving knowledge levels of individuals.

Users / Members

The Schedule IV has a key place in this survey since it reflects the opinion of the regular users of the gram panchayat libraries. An effort has been made to contact minimum of 10 users of library in each of the gram panchayat. The Schedule had as many as 31 questions, because the users opinions are the main indicators for improving the system and for the purpose of drawing the inferences. Among library users, the gender, level of education, occupation and age factor has also been considered.

The study revealed that on an average 74 per cent of users are male and 26 per cent users are female (total of 3184). As far as level of education, it is from literate to Degree including technocrats, but large number of respondents have studied upto high school which reflects the fact that a large number of students use the library.

Several types of occupation was noticed, the major categories being agriculture, business, housework/housewife and teachers. The term *Agriculturists* used here, includes land owner, agriculture labourers, poultry, dairying, animal husbandry and fisheries.

Number of Visits to Library

Of the 3184, nearly 80 per cent of users have the habit of going to library regularly and use the facility. The existence of the gram panchayat library in the vicinity was recognized. 76.2 per cent of the users visited the library frequently to read newspapers and magazines. Highest number of users belong to the age group of 14-25 and 25-50 years.

Facilities Available

Of the respondents (3,184) covering 352 gram panchayat libraries hardly 6.6-12.3 per cent have expressed their dissatisfaction. Though a small percentage, the opinion cannot be neglected. The dissatisfaction related to delay in improving or providing facilities like drinking water, furniture, racks, timely payment of honorariums, supply of periodicals of interests and newspapers.

The data revealed that 64.3 per cent of the respondents have said *good*. But when probed further, 'good' was in the context of the given situation of the local rural area. However, the users were not fully satisfied with the facilities. They expressed the need to improve the given facilities mainly in regard to building, space, furniture, drinking water, toilet and books. Women in the group expressed their need to earmark a specific place for them within the given space of the library.

Quality of Books

The data indicate that 64.9 per cent of the users of all category have expressed the quality of books available are good and 28 per cent of users have the satisfactory opinion. However, there was no improvement in the quality of books. The available books had become old though useful. Procuring new books should be the priority of gram panchayat library

Nearly 2500 respondents (78%) borrow the books as members and the age ranges from 14-50 years. Even as regular users of the library, of the respondents of 3184, nearly 55.6 per cent users borrow books. Majority, that is nearly 80 per cent have said that many people in the locality use the gram panchayat library. This indicates that the people in rural areas are spending some of their time in a fruitful manner.

Gram Panchayat Libraries Help in Improving Knowledge

This indicator has direct relation in totality to quality of books and borrowing of books. 98 per cent of the total users have given positive response. The availability of multifarious reading materials have improved their knowledge. They are able to keep themselves abreast with latest social-economic-political developments mainly through newspapers and magazines. More reading materials would therefore strengthen them.

Opening of the Library

The library has to be kept open for the users on all the 6 working days in a week. 92 per cent of the respondents out of 3,184 states that the gram panchayat libraries are opened regularly. It is noticed from the survey, the opening of library on time has direct relation to the number of people using the library in the locality. In the interest of the users, the Supervisors should be very punctual and keep the library open.

With regard to facilities available in the library, it is linked to the number of users in a day. As mentioned above, when there is good response from the users, (*see* Table 5) minimum infrastructure facilities like chair/table/fan/water/toilets and sufficient light should be provided. But the survey reveal that, in almost all the libraries, chairs/table are provided (98%) but other facilities are not available (viz., fan 80%, drinking water 76%, sufficient light 43% and toilet facilities 92%).

Table–5
Number of Visits to Library

Number of Visits	*Number*	*Per Cent*
Once in a week	337	10.6
Frequently	2426	76.2
Sometimes	404	12.7
No response	17	0.5
Total	3184	100.0

Availability of Space

This is the critical indicator. While the quality of books, facilities available, borrowing of books, knowledge improvement, number of users of gram panchayat library and working hour/opening of libraries are quite encouraging, more than 58.1 per cent of the regular users have found limited space. This may be one of the reasons that some of the users have expressed dissatisfaction about the facilities available. In almost all the panchayats, the rural folk are in the habit of using the library every day. High percentage accounts for visiting library very frequently. While more number of people of all age group like to use the library, limited space and lack of furniture, reading materials and other facilities curtail their enthusiasm.

Infrastructure Facilities

Irrespective of the area or region for the purpose of reading certain basic facilities are an absolute necessity. They are chair/table, ventilation, proper light, drinking water and sanitation. All these are interlinked with that of number of users of the library. However, the data analysis shows that one or more basic features are not available or are not sufficient. For example, chair/table facilities are available according to 98 per cent, while fans are not available according to 80 per cent. Similarly the drinking water facility and availability of sufficient light.

Working Hours

The working hours of the Gram Panchayat libraries is quite satisfactory. People were aware of the membership facilities.

Types of Books Available

In most of the gram panchayat libraries all kinds of reading materials are necessarily kept viz., magazines, newspapers, literature, children books, textbooks, novels, classics, competitive books. But the users opined that most of them are old and rarely updated. The need for adding the latest publications is essential.

Having seen the types of books available in the library, it is interesting and necessary to know the choice of the readers. The respondents (users) were asked a specific question on their preference of books. The given table reveals, the choice of the reader.

Table–6
Which do you Prefer Most

	Yes	*No*	*No Response*	*Total*
Newspapers	2270	905	9	3184
	(71.3)	(28.4)	(0.3)	(100.0)
Other Books	1774	1401	9	3184
	(55.7)	(44.0)	(0.3)	(100.0)
Magazines	2267	908	9	3184
	(71.2)	(28.5)	(0.3)	(100.0)

It is evident from the above, table that though the library possesses certain types of books, the users prefer more latest books to improve their own knowledge and also to take up competitive exams, plan their future, improve their living conditions and the occupation that they are already in. Highest number of users expressed that newspapers and magazines have to be supplied on a regular basis as this was their main source to get updated information on developmental activities, education and career. It is also necessary to have more *books/bulletins/hand books* in agricultural and related activities, encyclopedias, dictionaries and books for competitive exams.

Supply and Donation Books

It is observed that the supply of reading materials is mainly from the department itself. Hardly about 9.6 per cent of the respondents said that the reading materials are supplied/donated. It is thus evident that books are mainly supplied by the department. Efforts to mobilise contributions both financial and in other forms should be initiated.

Extension and Cultural Activity

The library or the vicinity of the library is the place where, most of the rural folk assemble and discuss many issues. The premises being an educative centre, this place could be utilized for the creative, extension and cultural activities. Activities like reading sessions, folk arts, drama, dance, puppet shows, discussions will lure the families to visit the libraries and spread information on its activities to others in the village. But unfortunately this is not happening. Also public contribution for improvement of gram panchayat libraries is dismal. This calls for concrete efforts to mobilize contribution.

Non-users of Gram Panchayat Libraries

It was evident that the percentage of non-users of the library is very high. Hence non-users could not be an integral component of this study for individual interviews. However, we could draw certain facts and inferences. They are:

- In every village panchayat non-users of the library are in plenty.
- Level of literacy is a significant factor for the library use.
- Many factors are common with the users of the libraries such as environment of the location of the library, lack of books of their interest (for instance in one of the village panchayats it was reported that non-users were more interested in books for competitive examinations) absence of other infrastructural facilities.
- Women expressed that they prefer a separate seating arrangements/corner or place for themselves.
- Persons working in the agricultural field since morning till late evening, as reported, have no or little time for visiting panchayat library.

Apparently, given the socio-economic profile of the villagers including high level of illiteracy, the libraries can become the main factor in improving the development indices of a village. It is therefore, evident that to increase the number of users, or in other words to decrease the number of non-users, providing good library building with necessary infrastructure including books of their interest in all the gram panchayats have to be looked into.

Some Unique Cases

Gram Panchayat Library, Galagi Hulakoppa, Kalghatagi Taluk, Dharwad District

The role of the supervisor is very crucial for the effective functioning of the gram panchayat library. The gram panchayat library at Galagi Hulakoppa in Kalghati Taluk of Dharwad district was popular among the people. The library is located in the gram panchayat office building. Though the facilities are poor, outdated and less number of books are available yet the library is functioning well. This is mainly because of the supervisor, who is very enterprising and knowledgeable. He organizes cultural programmes for students in which he also involves the community members. These cultural programmes and other competitive programmes attracts the people along with their families to the library. The youth appears to be very supportive in developing the library. Some more efforts by the department to improve the facilities will make the library activity more visible and useful to the public.

Libraries at Sulla in Hubli Taluk, Samshi and Yare Budihala in Kundgol taluk and Alagawadi in Navalgund taluk are also functioning well.

Gram Panchayat Library, Santhapur, Aurad Taluk, Bidar District

This Library was established in 1988 and is functioning well. There are 2,794 books, local and other newspapers. About 150 people visit everyday and 377 have registered. The gram panchayat members also visit the library. Stock verification is conducted regularly by the gram panchayat secretary. Some departmental information is also available here. The supervisor is very punctual and has taken interest in arranging literacy oriented cultural programmes. He was awarded during 1999-2000, 2004 and 2005.

These supervisors have made special efforts to serve the people and engage in a variety of local based activities that make these libraries an active centre. Short-term training programme to equip the supervisors to assist the public in finding information, getting and arranging library materials, teaching people how to use library resources and to device ways for serving the community.

Gram Panchayat Library, UNCHALLI, Sirsi Taluk, Uttara Kannada District

It is one of the model library in the state. This has been possible due to people's participation. After the establishment of gram panchayat library, the regular users of the library formed a "Readers Forum" and this forum is working to achieve the main objectives of the forum viz. Development of Library, make available large number of books to the readers, inculcate reading habit among children, give priority towards complete literacy, conserve valuable books for future generation, facilitate good guidance from famous writers to young and budding writers, develop interest towards local library, encourage rural art and culture etc. In this direction, the forum could mobilize books and newspapers free of cost to the gram panchayat library. Considering the activities of the readers forum, the local gram panchayats. Unchalli has allotted a land to an extent of 2 Guntas for construction of library building. The forum is also organizing personality development activity, besides bringing out a souvenir called "SUJANA" annually.

A good building with pleasant and comfortable surroundings attracts more people to the libraries. Ventilation and plenty of light, proper arrangement of furniture in hygienic environment will appeal to the public.

Major Findings

The following are the major findings of the study:

- The study reveals that gram panchayat libraries are very useful and essential at the gram panchayat level.
- At the district level, the Chief Librarian is an experienced, knowledgeable and technical person. The Chief Librarians support the establishment of gram panchayat libraries, the need for fund and functionaries to support this activity.
- The panchayat members and officials are aware of the gram panchayat library and expressed keen desire to involve in its activity. But they are not aware of the budgetary allocation for this scheme.
- The supervisors are mainly localities. The percentage of male supervisors are more than that of female supervisors.
- They have good understanding of the library and its needs. But they lack technical knowledge.
- Most of supervisors do not attend gram panchayat meetings.
- The income and expenditure book is not maintained in large number of libraries.
- There is an acute shortage of financial support. It was mentioned that even newspaper bills have not been paid. Also, supervisors are not receiving the honorarium on time.
- On an average 30 to 45 people use the libraries everyday. They represent all sections of the society. Most of the users are students, people having agriculture or related activities and self-employed persons.
- The libraries have inculcated reading habit among the people and the users admit that their knowledge has been enhanced.
- Most of the users visit the library regularly. The age group ranges from 14 to 50 years. The users are not very satisfied with the facilities available.

- The libraries are mostly opened on time and regularly.
- Limited space in the library was specifically mentioned by the users.
- Books are mainly supplied by the Department and rarely donated by volunteers. Public contribution for improving the library activity was less or generally nil.
- It was found that though the libraries possess certain types of books, they are mostly old and not updated. The users preference is thus not catered to.
- Most of the libraries do not have own building. They sometimes function in the gram panchayat office; some gram panchayat libraries need immediate attention.
- It is evident that there is a high percentage of non-users of the library in the rural areas.
- Discouraging factors are common with the users of the libraries such as environment and location of the library, lack of books of their interest and absence of other infrastructural facilities. Women expressed that they prefer a separate seating arrangements/corner or place for themselves, as available space in the library is less.
- Though some people are aware of the existence of these libraries, a large number of the villagers were ignorant about these libraries.
- Publicity about gram panchayat libraries was very low, which has led to lack of awareness among the people.
- Own building, adequate finance, updated reading materials, good number of chairs/tables/racks in addition to drinking water and toilet facilities are crucial for promoting the library activity.

Suggestions and Issues having Policy Implications

The *information revolution* ushered in by communication and computer technology is bound to effect the social and economic order. The science and technology revolution has transformed the capacity to retrieve, store, process and transmit massive flows of information. Today, all this is possible with unbelievable speed. Alvin Toffler, in his book, *The Third Wave*, considers information through technology as holding the potential for great social change. It will stimulate learning and will in turn kindle creativity. If intellectual advancement is the aim, then informationalisation of the society is the means.

Perhaps the Department of Public Libraries has understood this very well and started its extension activity by establishing libraries across the state. Karnataka is the first state in the country to establish libraries at gram panchayat level. Out of the total number 5,652 gram panchayats, libraries have been established in 3251. The study reveals that, these libraries by and large are working satisfactorily. However, shortcomings have been noticed which directly relate to maintenance of libraries. Based on the observations the following suggestions are recommended for the consideration of the government.

Suggestions

1. The officers of the Department of Libraries at District level shall be made responsible to co-ordinate with the respective zilla panchayats for implementation/utilization of the budget earmarked to the gram panchayats without any lapses.
2. It is necessary that gram panchayat Presidents/Vice-Presidents and other members be motivated for mobilizing funds through voluntary contribution from various means for improving the libraries. For this purpose, the Department of Public Libraries may consider the possibilities of organizing a sort of workshop or awareness building camps to the elected gram panchayat members regarding the role of gram panchayat in growth and development of the gram panchayat libraries.
3. It is necessary for the department to have own buildings for running the library at gram panchayat level. The gram panchayats can also identify available vacant community land in the village, raise funds from voluntary organizations/voluntary contributions to facilitate to have own building for library and keep separate account.
4. Nearly fifty per cent of the libraries have not maintained the income and expenditure statements pertaining to the libraries. The Supervisors and the gram panchayat Secretaries require a short-term training on maintenance of income and expenditure. The department may correspond with CEOs of the respective districts on this issue to take appropriate decision in the matter.
5. In the state, some of the users have expressed their dissatisfaction about the available facilities. The department should make provision for basic facilities like drinking

water, furniture, supply of magazines, newspapers and books, so that, people from all sections can use the institution. Similarly, the quality of books will reflect the quality of library.

6. The department shall identify the nature of periodicals required by the users, keeping the farmers in view. Journals in Kannada on farming, and co-operatives and related issues shall have to be subscribed by all the gram panchayat libraries. For this purpose, the library department can correspond with Agriculture University, KVK, Department of Agriculture, Department of Horticulture, Animal Husbandry and Veterinary Services, fisheries, sericulture, KVIC etc. It should also mandatory for all departments to send their literature to gram panchayat libraries.
7. A register/suggestion box has to be maintained in the gram panchayat libraries to seek the opinion of regular users as to the kind of books/periodicals that they look for. The Supervisor shall review these opinions once in three months and bring the facts to the notice of the district librarian for arranging such periodicals.
8. The gram panchayat members and the supervisors shall induce the regular users to become the members. So that, atleast for having availed the membership facility, they will bc using the books/periodicals. Similarly, the Supervisor/gram panchayat Members/gram panchayat Secretary including taluk panchayat Members of the village shall explore possibilities for donating books.
9. Success of any activity depends on people's participation. The library premises should become a place for creative and cultural activities. For this purpose, the library supervisors and the gram panchayat secretary and elected members should be motivated. Available local NGOs/VOs may be requested for sparing their valuable time and give constructive suggestions.
10. The department and district administration may jointly organize a sort of *movement*, once a year just like Vanamohothsava and Traffic Week.
11. Timely payment of honorarium to the supervisors is a crucial issue in addition to periodic enhancement for proper maintenance and smooth running of the library.
12. As could be seen from the budget allocation to the

department the funds available is too less. The collection of cess should be done regular and the grant to gram panchayat of Rs. 3,000 per year should be released regularly.

13. The need for a trained hand to head the gram panchayat library was evident. Therefore, short-term capacity building programme for the Supervisors has to be introduced.
14. Computerisation of Gram Panchayat Libraries will attract more users.
15. More publicity about the gram panchayat libraries is essential. Book exhibitions, Leaflets/Handouts, Notice Boards/Walls of gram panchayat, Raita Samparka Kendra, Schools, Hospitals and Post Office could be used to popularize the library activities.
16. To establish library development committees under the Chairmanship of Gram Panchayat President, in villages comprising of people from different walks of life to take care of the overall development of libraries.
17. A proportional increase in the budget allocation every year for gram panchayat libraries has to be initiated. At least 10 per cent increase over and above the previous financial year, so that every year there is a proportionate rise in the allotment.
    1. As far as possible preference should be given to women as Supervisors. It may be suggested that not less than 33 per cent quota be considered.
    2. In phases, computerisation can be considered. This assumes importance in view of the fact that the Government of India is seriously thinking to link up gram panchayats through e-governance system in phased manner and Karnataka has already taken initiatives in some departments in this direction.
    3. *Village knowledge centre*: The libraries should be developed as village knowledge centre serving the interests of the local people and meeting their information requirement.
    4. Immediate steps should be taken to establish gram panchayat libraries in all the gram panchayats of Karnataka.

Libraries form a vital part of the education system making available knowledge accumulated through the ages. It is considered as one of society's most useful service institutions. They should therefore house a wide variety of materials that inform, educate and entertain especially in today's context of globalization and liberalization. As more and more information becomes available, computers can help libraries to cope with this growth. Adequate funds will help in serving the community in a better way. In Karnataka, the study shows that though the local libraries developed very slowly, today there are several thousands of local libraries. They are catering to the educational needs and stimulate the learning process of the community. This is a very encouraging trend. Since libraries serve as a centre for a wide variety of educational media, immediate steps should be taken to establish gram panchayat libraries in all the gram panchayats.

Subsequent Development

The Department of Public Libraries, Government of Karnataka, has been taking many steps for strengthening the number and quality of services at gram panchayat library level after making an evaluation study as referred to earlier.

The following are worth mentioning:

1. A Rs. 300 crore plan to be implemented in five years has been chalked out for construction of buildings for libraries in all gram panchayats.
2. According to the plan 1,000 library buildings will be built every year at a cost of Rs. 4 lakh (*The Hindu*, 28.01.2007).
3. The Government has decided to set up Library Development and Monitoring Committees (LDMCs) at every gram panchayat to revive public library system in rural areas. It is because in the absence of a monitoring authority, the system had weakened library network in villages.
4. If the new system (LDMC) comes into effect, things can be set right and libraries in every gram panchayat will become truly hub of knowledge.
5. The LDMC will be headed by president of the respective gram panchayat and headmaster of local primary or high school, a woman representative and four readers will be its members. The primary duty of LDMCs is to ensure that libraries function properly and recommend measures to improve them.
6. A state level panel will be formed to suggest measures for developing public library network in rural areas (*Deccan Hearld*, June 20, 2007).

8

Constitutional Laws Vs Community Laws: Conflict and Synergy

G. PALANITHURAI

Introduction

The 73rd and 74th Amendments to the Constitution of India have enabled the marginalized and the oppressed to move into the power structure in grassroots governance. The two amendments have a rich potential to transform and alter the nature of governance and social dynamics.[1] To realise the potential, the state has to play an effective role. Dalits got elected to local bodies but they are not allowed to function independently as leaders and discharge their responsibilities. Women got elected to local bodies and they are not allowed to sit in the office and discharge their responsibilities. In such a way barriers and obstacles are created by the leaders of traditional institutions.[2] They are drawn towards governance because seats have been reserved for dalits and women. The constitution grants such opportunities but the community rejects them. Why this syndrome is a major question to be probed. The whole exercise is around the interface between the state created institutions and the community evolved institutions.

Context

After the departure of the colonial power, the modern state system provided an institutional mechanism to govern and administer the society and achieve development based on the western model of parliamentary democracy. The Afro-Asian countries borrowed this model and adopted the same without much adaptation to suit the local conditions. The Afro-African countries are known for their strong traditional structures for community governance. One would find strong resistance to reform in certain aspects of the society and more particularly on governance. That is why we find a new syndrome of modernity in tradition and tradition in modernity in many of the socio-political processes of the society. In one aspect the modern state had and has to be very strong on dismantling certain structures and practices to enable the marginalised to emerge as respectable citizens and claim their entitlements. It is unfortunate that beyond enacting legislation and evolving policies, the state has not shown vigour in translating the legislations and the decisions into reality. Further in the Afro-Asian countries people do not understand the importance of representative democracy.

Despite its being in practice for several decades, people do not understand the process of governance under representative democracy excepting 'voting'. As a result the governing mechanism superimposed on the society from above on the premise that if the state apparatus is expanded all developmental responsibilities will be handled effectively and that thereby society will be modernised and equity and equality will be achieved; by efficiently handling the state institutional mechanism economic development will be achieved through the western mode of production and the consequent development will be distributed equitably through the government institutions. The above premise has another underlying principle and assumption. That is the political institutions and state institutions will have the efficacy and efficiency to transform the society from backwardness to modernity. While evaluating the whole process of governance and development over a period of time it has been noticed that the avowed objectives have not been achieved through the structures created through the state apparatus. The state system has failed miserably.[3] The problems confronted in the formative years of establishment of governance after the departure of the colonial administration have continued to remain and new kinds of problems and issues have emerged due to the impact of modernisation, industrialisation and democratic governance through representative democracy. The countries which are facing severe crises in governance and development are in search of alternatives. The organisations and institutions which are working at the global level in development and governance have also analysed the problems with the objective of finding out an institutional mechanism suitable to the ethos of the society and a suitable methodology for development. It is now widely accepted that pluralistic and widespread governance will be effective in managing the affairs of the society and hence authority and power should be spread at different levels and multiple centres of power have to be established.[4] Further the democratically elected governments have to be further deepened through decentralisation of powers.[5]

Thus, people have to be empowered to tide over the problems in governance. In this strenuous journey it is found that each and every society has its own institutional mechanism evolved over a period of time to manage its own affairs and they are dormant since the state apparatus has extended its tentacles to the grassroots as development bureaucracy and street bureaucracy work for development as per the direction of the government from above. Though they are dormant, they are having control over the community in performing certain minimal functions and hence they try to influence the state institutional mechanism to act according to their wishes.

As a result, the government, through its policies, programmes and schemes could not achieve the planned target. So micro institutional structures working at grassroots were identified as effective and feasible. To achieve local development and to achieve social reconstruction to address the issues of social justice, local institutions are considered appropriate. This was the new premise found out throughout the world.[6] But the local institutions have to be reformed as they are traditional in character and not inclusive and gender sensitive. Hence it was planned to create local institutions to achieve development legitimately and to perform the functions of the local institutions evolved by the communities.[7] Such local self-governance created by the modern governments has gained attention throughout the world.[8] Around eighty countries are seriously involved in creating an alternative paradigm of governance and development. This new initiative is the result of the failure of the big governments in delivering services and goods, because, in many of the developing countries, state systems became weak and hence could not manage the society for reform.

All over the world, local bodies are being given due recognition through various means to establish them as institutions of governance legitimately and well within the framework of constitutional governments. Brazil, Denmark, France, India, Italy, Japan and Sweden have given constitutional status to local governments. Australia and the Untied States of America have given due status in state or provincial constitutions. New Zealand, the United Kingdom and a large number of countries have enacted legislation to accord recognition to the grassroots institutions. China is an exception as it has accorded status only through an executive order. By doing so, the governance mechanism at the grassroots has been formalized and legitimized. Institutional structures are created everywhere.[9]

In India, the 73rd Amendment has been introduced and consequently the provincial governments have enacted conformity legislations. Elections have been conducted and representatives have been positioned. Since reservation was given, in the Amendment and in the State Act, women and dalits were elected to different positions of rural local bodies. The whole process of activating grassroots democracy meets with stiff resistance from the communities in many places in India. The constitutionally created structures are allowed to function at the grassroots but not with the full participation of people. Community organisations are vibrant in involving the people in local activities. The problem starts from the election itself. In many places women and dalits are allowed to contest in the election on conditions. But, after the election, they are not allowed to function as representatives of the people. If they are women, the males of their family handle power.[10] If they are dalits, dominant community leaders handle power.[11] In some places the positions are auctioned openly by the leaders of the traditional Panchayats. In a few places a small group in the traditional panchayat decides the individual to be the leader. In some places where the seats are reserved for dalits, community leaders resist the election commission's attempt to conduct the election.[12] Indian society is not an equal society. It has got social inequality, economic inequality and discrimination in terms of gender and marginalization. Despite the fact that provisions are made for the marginalized groups to participate in governance through the Constitution, the leaders from among dalits and women are not allowed to function.

For the first time in India, after Independence, the western model of democracy penetrates into the rural areas through the

73rd Amendment to the Constitution. Wherever, the society is modernised and oriented in representatives democracy, women and dalits are allowed contest in the election and they are being supported by the communities to carry out their duties and responsibilities. Wherever, the society is modernized and not properly oriented in representative democracy, women and dalits are allowed to contest in the election but not allowed to carry out their work. Wherever women and dalit leaders are having leadership skill and understanding, they interface with the traditional structures and manage the institutions so as to deliver services and goods effectively to the satisfaction of the people. Wherever, the women groups and dalit groups are active and cohesive and have got orientation, however weak the women and dalit elected leaders, they are being supported by the groups and they are made to function effectively. Wherever the women and dalit leaders are weak and communities are also not supportive to the legitimate constitutional governing institutions, the traditional leaders assert themselves and control the constitutional institutions. Wherever, the societies are not modernized and people are not oriented in representative democracy with a weak bureaucracy, traditional institutions never allow the constitutional institutions to take shape through election. These are some of the premises emerging from our experience with local governance in India.

After the conduct of the elections, women and dalits are in position in the governance institution. To carry out the activities of the local institutions the leaders have to equip themselves by building their skill, capacity and capabilities. When they build the capacity and capability they can manage the institutions, mobilize the people for effective participation in governance and development, and interface with traditional institutions and government institutions at a higher level.[13] Managing the local bodies is not a single man's or woman's show. It requires the support of the family, peers, political party, civil society, and community leaders. It is a skilful job by which synergy among different stakeholders can be achieved.

In many places even in a modernised society, traditional institutions still do look after the affairs of the community such as temples, community properties especially commons and more particularly water and local disputes. The traditional institutions have a valid framework of governance to manage the commons, conduct temple festivals and resolve minor disputes. They also operate a huge corpus fund.[14] Since there is an accepted and standard mechanism to operate a funds from the corpus fund in a transparent way the community reposes confidence in the leadership. While looking at the basic principles of these traditional structures one finds modern indicators of good governance, namely, accountability, responsiveness and transparency but not inclusion of gender and marginalized groups. In many places even the leadership is also on a rotation basis or on the basis of election. After the Tsunami in Nagapattinam District, many of the fisher-folk Panchayats have been democratized by which election was introduced and women were also included in the committee for governance.

Whenever, the bureaucracy is effective, it interferes in the functioning of the traditional structures when the traditional structures disturb the normal functioning of the constitutional structures at the grassroots. Wherever, there is synergy between the two, it plays a supportive role.[15] The traditional institutions which are vibrant in some places by their performance and credibility are able to bring the constitutional bodies under their fold for which the community is also supportive. By doing so, the corpus of the traditional structure is enhanced by using the commons of the constitutional institutions.

The people who are the major source of support to both institutions make a balanced act by extending support to both in many places, extending active support to traditional institutions and passive support to constitutional institutions. In some places where there is active social conflict and the affected people are the marginalized, they extend support to the constitutional panchayat and discourage the traditional Panchayat. In a few places both are in action and intense conflict prevails between the two with the support of two groups supporting them. People know the roles of both institutions. If they feel both institutions are active and deliver services reasonably they extend support to both, because people are economically and politically rational. In the event of failure of the state structure in delivery of services, people have no option and hence whatever mechanism is available at grassroots has to be supported. Whenever, the conflict is intense between the collectivities within a geographical area where the constitutional panchayat is co-terminus with the traditional panchayat, the civil society and media have to play an active role to expose the malady and seek the intervention of government institutions. It has been demonstrated that local institutions are vibrant and capable of achieving local development[16] but, at the same time, local development should be on a equitable basis. To achieve this the constitutional institutions have to be strengthened. The search is on throughout the world to find ways and means of strengthening the constitutional institutions.

Experiences in India

It is unequivocally clear from reports that women and dalits have come to power at the grassroots. Really they have formed the critical mass. But the critical mass has to perform the critical function. To perform the critical function an array of steps are to be taken at different levels starting from the federal government to the local society in a variety of ways. The women and dalit leaders have started their struggle and many of them are emerging as models in achieving development and social justice after surmounting all the barriers and obstacles.[17] Still many of them are in struggle and have not achieved any result. Capacity Building is being done by various training institutions, support structure is being created at different levels to extend handhold support to leaders who are in struggle. The media has been oriented to capture the success stories and the struggles of the marginalized leaders for effective intervention of the state authorities.[18] Political parties which are pro-grassroots-democracy periodically represent the problems of the leaders of the marginalized groups in the Provincial Legislative Assembly through their representatives. The women leaders and dalit leaders who have deep commitment to social transformation and rural development have formed their own organisation to raise their voice. While looking at the process of strengthening the grassroots democracy, one cannot under estimate the positive elements of the traditional structures which cannot be achieved through the modern state structure. The negative aspects of the traditional structures can be eliminated through an effective synergisation between the two. It has taken place in many areas in India.[19]

Case Studies from Tamil Nadu

When four Gram Panchayats Keeripatti, Pappapatti and Nattarmangalam of Madurai District and Kottakatchienthal in Virudhunagar districts were not allowed to have dalit leadership it was effectively tackled by the District Administration. The whole state machinery helped to conduct the election by undermining the traditional structures. It is the best example to demonstrate how the state structures effectively intervened and restored democracy for inclusion. When *sati* was practiced in Madhya Pradesh, the government fixed the responsibility on the constitutional Panchayats and stopped the development grants to the Panchayats by which *sati* was eradicated effectively through the constitutional Panchayats. While protecting the commons from the encroachment of the influential leader of caste and party, Urapakkam Gram Panchayat leader Ms. Menaka gave her life by which she created awareness among the people about the importance of natural resources.[20]

The President of K. Rayawaram Gram Panchayat in Pudukkottai District, Mrs.Rani Sathappan, accommodated the traditional panchayat in the fold of the constitutional Panchayat and delivered services effectively for about ten years and won several awards for her outstanding performance. She ably demonstrated her leadership in managing the traditional Panchayat. Even the traditional Panchayat leaders appreciated the effective performance of the woman leader.[21] She shared with the traditional panchayat many of the responsibilities in the best interests of the community and the traditional Panchayat ably fulfilled all its responsibilities. Thus one can find synergy between the two structures.

Nattukottai Gram Panchayat in Sivaganga District was headed by a traditional Panchayat leader Mr.Ramanathan who has emerged as an outstanding leader in achieving infrastructure, development and social justice. He was the President of both the structures and worked for social justice and got several awards.[22] He held the position for several decades. In the absence of the constitutional Panchayat he carried out all the welfare activities in the village through the government departments. He continued to be the traditional Panchayat leader. It is very vibrant in this Panchayat. A cultured and well-oriented leader, he is sensitive to social justice and so worked for social equity and equality. It is to be noted that this district is known for conflict between traditional Panchayats and constitutional Panchayats as traditional Panchayats practice untouchability. But this Panchayat emerged as a model for social justice due to his leadership.

The Maravamangalam Gram Panchayat leader Mr. Annadurai was very popular among all segments of the society and got the support of all for all his transparent development activities. He used to keep the traditional Panchayat within the fold of the constitutional Panchayat. By doing so he succeeded in all his attempts.[23] It is to be noted that he belongs to the Communist Party of India. Normally the left parties are against the functioning of the traditional structures. Despite the poor presence of left party supporters in this village he was elected President because of the support extended by the community through the traditional structure. He worked hard to achieve social justice for which there was no resistance from the traditional structure. Hence he worked comfortably with the traditional Panchayat.

Noothulapuram Gram Panchayat President Ms. Kala, a dalit woman, carefully developed a design to work effectively for the betterment of the dalits by aligning with the traditional Panchayat leaders. The dalits called it a compromise but she called it a strategy. According to her, one can be in struggle if suppression of the dalits happens. But, to achieve development for a marginalized section, aligning with the traditional Panchayat is not a bad formula.[24] She argued that for her victory in the election, the traditional leaders also worked. When they were not against any development work for the dalits why should one develop an antagonistic attitude towards the traditional leaders?

Kuthampakkam Gram Panchayat President Mr. Elango, by his extraordinary leadership qualities, fought with the bureaucracy and made the Panchayat a self-governing institution. By his performance he transformed the entire village and more specifically the dalits. He is a model for other Dalit Gram Panchayat leaders.[25] His leadership is accepted by the Community as he has demonstrated his leadership.

Ms. Pappa, President of Atthankaraipatti Gram Panchayat, formed a Dalit Women Federation to help the other dalit women leaders. She relentlessly waged a struggle against the political party leaders of that area. She succeeded in all her attempts. Thus the leaders of constitutional Panchayats have successfully transformed the development politics at the micro-level with different strategies.[26] Madurai, Sivaganga and Virudhunagar and some of the southern districts are known for the practice of untouchability and the strong presence of traditional community structures. Many reports both from research institutions and civil society organisations reveal that the constitutional Panchayats headed by Dalits are not allowed to function independently. But the cases explained above are mostly from the above districts. How were they able to succeed? It was because of the extraordinary leadership of the individuals. The leadership plays an important role in transforming institutions and society.

It has been demonstrated that the state structure as well as the traditional structure have strengths and weaknesses in terms of delivering services and achieving equity. In the absence of a vibrant local democratic mechanism, the traditional structures keep the people intact with them.

The traditional structures can be weakened by the effective performance of the state structures even at the local level. In the absence of such strong and vibrant state structures the traditional structure will maintain its primacy. In terms of leadership, the traditional leaders are known for their integrity, honesty and rectitude in handling finance and delivering services. Acceptable norms have been evolved over a period of time with the participation of the members of the community. Hence it is all known to the people whereas the western model of governance is not known to the people. The local governance institutions created through the central and provincial governments have to imbibe the nature and character of the traditional institutions after eliminating the negative features of the traditional institutions.

Conclusion

Constitutional institutions created at the grassroots should be made vibrant and they have to shed their present character of unresponsiveness to the demands of the people. A constant drive should be maintained from the upper level governments to strengthen the constitutional structures for which mobilisation of the people is imperative. The elected leaders have to be equipped to carry out the roles and responsibilities of the grassroots institutions. Equally the traditional institutions have to be democratised and they are to be integrated with constitutional Panchayats. A meaningful synergy between the constitutional structures and the traditional structures will produce needed results from the grassroots institutions.

NOTES AND REFERENCES

1. The following works reveal the potentials of the Grassroots institutions created through the historic amendments: Nirjoa Gopal Jayal, Amit Prakash and Pradeep K. Sharma (eds.) *Local Governance in India: Decentralisation and Beyond,* New Delhi: Oxford University Press, 2006; L.C. Jain (ed.) *Decentralisation and Local Governance,* New Delhi: Orient Tong Man, 2005; Girish Kumar, Local Democracy in India: Interpreting Decentralization, New Delhi: Sage Publications, 2006; and G.Palanithurai (ed.), Dynamics of New Panchayati Raj Systems in India, New Delhi: Concept Publishing Company, 2004, Vols. I, II & III.
2. G. Palanithurai, *Process and Performance of Women and Dalit Leaders,* New Delhi: Concept Publishing Company, 2004.
3. Bidyut Chakraparthy and Mohit Bhattacharya (eds.), *Administrative Change and Innovation : A Reader,* New Delhi: Oxford University Press, 2005.
4. L.Hooghe and G. Marks, Unraveling the Central State, but How? Types of Multi-level Governance, *American Political Science Review* 97:2 (2003) pp. 233-43.
5. Samuel P. Huntington, *The Third Wave: Democratization in the Late Twentieth Century,* Norma: University of Oklahoma Press, 1991.
6. James Manor, *The Political Economy of Democratic Decentralisation,* Washington DC: World Bank, 1999.
7. George Lutz and Wolf Linder, *Traditional Structures in Local Governance for Local Government,* (Report of a Project commissioned by the World Bank), Bern: Institute of Political Science, 2004.
8. Warren Magnusson, *Protecting the Rights of Local Self Government, Canadian Journal of Political Science,* Vol. 38 : No. 4 (Dec., 2005) pp. 897-922.
9. Warren Mangnusson, *Op cit.*
10. G.Palanithurai, *Empowerment of Women: Problems Faced by the Elected Women Representatives* (Monograph), Gandhigram: Rajiv Gandhi Chair for Panchayati Raj Studies, 2001.
11. G.Palanithurai, *Dalit Leadership in Panchayats* (Monograph), Gandhigram: Rajiv Gandhi Chair for Panchayati Raj Studies, 2003.
12. G.Palanithurai, *Third General Election to Local Governments in Tamil Nadu: Expectations and Shocking Realities,* New Delhi: Concept Publishing Company, 2007.

13. G.Palanithurai, *Experience of Training and Capacity Building of Local Body Leaders,* New Delhi: Concept Publishing Company, 2007.
14. V. Ragupathy, *Participatory Management of Natural Resources,* New Delhi: Concept Publishing Company, 2003.
15. G.Palanithurai, *Synergisation of Traditional Panchayats with Formal Panchayati Raj System in Managing Community Affairs,* Gandhigram: Rajiv Gandhi Chair for Panchayati Raj Studies, 2003.
16. Hari Mohan Mathur, *Administering Development in the Third World: Constraints and Choices in the Third World,* New Delhi: Sage Publication, 1986.
17. G.Palanithurai, *Change Makers at Grassroots Democracy,* New Delhi: Concept Publishing Company, 2007.
18. G.Palanithurai, *Media and Grassroots Governance* (Monograph), Gandhigram: Rajiv Gandhi Chair for Panchayati Raj Studies, 2004.
19. Kripa Ananthpur, *Interfaces in Local Governance: A Study in Karnataka,* Chennai: MIDS, 2004 (Working Paper, 187); Kripa Ananthpur, *Rivalry or Synergy? Formal and Informal Local Governance in Rural India* (Working Paper, 226), Sussex: IDS, 2004.
20. The Tamil Nadu Federation of Women Presidents, *Voices of Women Presidents of Panchayat Governments in Tamil Nadu,* Chennai: Human Rights Advocacy and Research Foundation, 2004.
21. G.Palanithurai, *Leadership Matters at Grassroots Governance: Path Finders Series IV, K.Rayavaram* (Monograph), Gandhigram: Rajiv Gandhi Chair for Panchayati Raj Studies, 2004.
22. G.Palanithurai, *Leadership Matters at Grassroots Governance: Path Finders Series VI, Nallukottai* (Monograph), Gandhigram: Rajiv Gandhi Chair for Panchayati Raj Studies, 2004.
23. G.Palanithurai, *Leadership Matters at Grassroots Governance: Path Finders Series XIII Maravamangalam* (Monograph), Gandhigram: Rajiv Gandhi Chair for Panchayati Raj Studies, 2005.
24. G.Palanithurai, *Leadership Matters at Grassroots Governance: Path Finders Series XXII, Noothulapuram* (Monograph), Gandhigram: Rajiv Gandhi Chair for Panchayati Raj Studies, 2006.
25. G.Palanithurai, *Leadership Matters at Grassroots Governance: Path Finders Series V, Koothampakkam* (Monograph), Gandhigram: Rajiv Gandhi Chair for Panchayati Raj Studies, 2004.
26. G.Palanithurai, *Leadership Matters at Grassroots Governance: Path Finders Series XXIII, Aathankaraipatti* (Monograph), Gandhigram: Rajiv Gandhi Chair for Panchayati Raj Studies, 2004.

9

Educating Children in India: Policy and Perspectives

SNEHALATA PANDA

Since 1950 targets were set and revised in our country to fulfill the objective of universal elementary education for children. In 1950, it was envisaged to achieve the goal within ten years. But due to paucity of infrastructure facilities, personnel and availability of funds this goal could not be realised. In 1965-66 the period was revised to 1975-76. Again the working group set up by the Planning Commission modified it to the end of the Sixth Plan, that was 1984. Kothari Commission suggested attaining this goal by 1986. National Policy on Education (NPE), 1986 envisaged that all children reaching the age of eleven years in 1990 would have at least five years of schooling in regular schools or in non-formal mode. It also stipulated that by 1995 all children up to fourteen years of age would have access to free and compulsory education. NPE and the revised Programme of Action (PoA) 1992 by the Ministry of Human Resource Development (MHRD) made specific achievement of this target before entering the twenty-first century. The National Development Council, in its forty-third meeting, specified universal elementary education for children and complete eradication of illiteracy among the adults. In the 1993 summit of nine high population countries held in New Delhi, it was suggested to achieve this goal by the year 2000.

The Education Ministry resolved in 1998, to pursue elementary education in the mission mode. But the 83rd Amendment to the constitution is a milestone in the road that independent India had tramped through to keep up its constitutional obligation to redeem children from the scourge of illiteracy. It guarantees free and compulsory education for children in the age group of 6-14. Apart from being a fundamental right it makes a fundamental duty for the parents to provide education to their children in this age group. The amendment supersedes Art. 45, which provided for free and compulsory education up to 14 years as Directive Principle of State Policy specifying that *the state shall endeavour to provide free and compulsory education to all children within the age group of 14 years.*

This was in consonance with the Supreme Court Judgement[1] that free education for children up to the age of fourteen is a fundamental right. A number of programmes in and outside the five year plan agenda like Operation Blackboard, Non-formal education, Teacher Education, Mahila Samakhya, and several state specific Basic Education Projects got underway to ensure universal elementary education. Over a period of time along with expansion of education facilities, enrolment and retention of students has been focused with improvement of quality. Sarva Sikhsha Abhiyan (SSA) is currently in operation to fulfill these objectives.

SSA follows other programmes like District Primary Education Programme (DPEP) which started in 42 districts in the year 1994 in seven states and expanded to 272 districts covering 18 states by the year 2002.The programme aimed at providing quality primary education to all children, access to all children to primary education or equivalent non-formal education as the case may be, reduce gender and social groups gaps in enrolment, drop out rate and learning achievement score to less than five per cent and over all dropout rate by 10 per cent. It also aims at raising average achievement results by 25 per cent over measured baseline levels. During the period various activities like community mobilisation, construction of new school buildings and classrooms, teacher training, improvement of teaching and learning materials, bridging gender and social disparities in schooling, support services for the mentally and physically challenged, alternative educational facilities for children not having facilities for entering regular schools, monitoring of the programme through Educational Management Information System (EMIS) were taken up to reduce drop out , provide access to school for out of school children, improve the quality of education with an impact on achievement levels of the pupil.[2]

SSA integrates several other programmes introduced after the National Policy of Education 1986. These schemes were Operation

Blackboard, (OBB), Teacher Education, National Programme of Nutritional Support for Primary Education, (NPNSP) Mahila, Samakhya, Education Guarantee and Alternative Innovative Education, District Primary Education Programme (DPEP), Lok Jumbush Project etc. The OBB aimed at improvement of infrastructure but after implementation of SSA no fresh recruitment to teaching posts have been taken under the scheme and improvement of infrastructure is enlisted in SSA programme. It was launched in 1987 to provide minimum essentials to primary education in the country. But lack of accommodation, teacher ignorance in the use of teaching materials and non-replacement of breakage were the major hurdles for its success. The revised programme included expansion of OBB to upper primary level, teacher training, provision for replacement of breakage by the State Government, women to constitute fifty per cent of the teaching personnel, make it an integral part of micro planning, use of low cost and locally available material for construction of schools/ classrooms, replacement of breakage and teacher education emphasized rigorous criteria for teacher recruitment for which MOUs were signed with the concerned states. But after the IX Plan it has been merged in SSA.

Sarva Sikhsha Abhiyan (SSA)

SSA is a time bound programme to Universalisation of Elementary Education (UEE) through community owned quality mission mode, which provides opportunities to children to develop their human capabilities. It focusses on promoting social justice and involvement of panchayat raj institutions, school management committee, slum level education committees, parent teacher association, mother teacher associations, tribal councils and other grassroots level structures in management of the elementary schools. Partnership between centre and states as well as local government institutions with freedom to the state governments to develop state specific and area specific programme for development is the hallmark of SSA. For this a separate department of Elementary Education and Literacy has been created. The Central and State Governments in partnership with local governments and community have implemented the scheme. A National Sarva Sikhsha Abhiyan Mission under the chairmanship of the prime minister and State Sarva Sikhsha Abhiyan Mission under the chairmanship of the chief minister of respective states have been established. The National Sarva Sikhsha Mission in consultation with the state mission has to play an important role in capacity development needs of a district and regularly interact with state implementation societies. The State Mission Authority for Universal Elementary Education looks after planning and implementation in coordination with other departments relevant for success of the programme. The states have state level implementation society. The existing structures in District Primary Education Programme (DPEP) are suitably modified to meet the requirements of UEE. There are also district and sub-district units. Active involvement of NGOs for expansion, implementation, advocacy of the programme with accountability fine-tunes the programme to civil society participation.

Specific characteristic of the scheme are community involvement, bridge schools, quality education, better infrastructure with emphasis on comprehensive early childhood care, learning about their environment, do away with regional and gender gap in providing opportunity for elementary education and quality education with thrust on education for life, rationalization of inter and intra district variations in pupil teacher ratio, teacher training for capacity building etc., which give it an edge over earlier programmes in terms of quality, quantity and time bound achievement.

The principal objective of SSA is to provide universal elementary education of satisfactory quality for all children by the year 2010. Its time bound programme envisages enrolment of all children in school by 2003, completion of five years of schooling by 2007, eight years of schooling by 2010, adjoinment of gender and social category gaps by 2007 and universal retention of enrolled students by 2010. An important aim is educating out of school children.

To achieve these goals the strategy adopted are, institutional reform, which includes allocation of finance, assessment of educational administration, review of State Education Act, status of education of girls and other disadvantaged groups with timely monitoring and appropriate evaluation. It lays stress on functional decentralisation through community participation and many other existing structures of administration in the locality to enlarge the sphere of accountability. Its duration in a state will depend on the

District Elementary Education Plan prepared by the DPEP to cater to its specific needs.

Continuous financial allocation is imperative for the success of this programme. Accordingly the budgetary allocation has been sustained by the Central Government despite reduced obligation to the social sector services after adopting the market model for economic development. The General Budget of 2006-07 has allocated Rs. 10.041 crore for this programme in 2006-07. This is an increase by Rs. 2885 crore from the budget provision of the previous year. Among others the amount has to be utilized for construction of 500,000 additional classrooms and appointment of 150,000 teachers.

Earlier the financial share of the center and states were fixed in the ratio of 50: 50 after the Tenth Plan. But due to resistance from states it was revised in the Union Cabinet meeting held on 13 September, 2007. The central share will be 65 per cent for the first two years of the XI Five Year Plan, 60 per cent in 2009-10, 55 per cent in 2010-11 and 50 per cent in the last year of the plan that is 2011-12. Which will continue during the XII Plan period. Expenses for up gradation, maintenance, repair, teacher training are the lookout of the Village Education Committee, School Management Committee, Gram Panchayat or any other organizations stipulated by a particular state. It specifies availability of a school with in one kilo meter, one teacher for every 40 children, at least two teachers in every primary school, classroom for every teacher, a room for the headmaster in every upper primary school, free textbooks to girls, SC and ST students, upgradation of EGS to regular school or setting up a new primary school. It has also provision to integrate physically and mentally challenged children in disabled specific schemes with a financial allocation of Rs. 1200 per annum. Innovative schemes for girls' education and interventions for children of SC and ST category and computer education are provided for which Rs. 15 lakh for each project is earmarked. Interventions for out of school children and mainstreaming the dropouts through remedial and bridge courses with community mobilization makes the SSA a reasonably good scheme for eradication of illiteracy among the children in the country. The State Institutes of Educational Management and Training are given Rs. 3 crore, Rs. 200 has been allocated for replacement of non-functional school equipment, teachers are allocated Rs. 500 per year with the condition of transparency in fund utilisation.

Sustainable finance apart, it specifically stresses on institutional reform wherever necessary as the key factor to achieve its stated objectives and improve the delivery system. The institutions like NIEPA, NCERT, NCTE, SCERT, SIEMAT are targeted for capacity building, improvement of quality and unremitting support to resource persons.

Other strategies are involvement of the community, its administrative structures, women's groups to make them responsible stakeholders in the success of the programme. It is the community culture overstrained by economic construction which hold back children to get enrolled in schools and continue education. Transforming the community culture through sensitization about the importance of education for children will ensure there all round development. Community leaders preferably women are provided with a daily allowance of Rs. 30 per day for attending training. Community has to be involved in planning, monitoring programmes with full transparency relating to finance and education, which has to be correlated by Education Management Information System (EMIS). The community based monitoring system through micro-planning, survey and transparency in financial transaction and coordination between teachers, parents and the Panchayat Raj Institutions are significant features of SSA to improve mainstream educational administration.

SSA stipulates that habitation, as unit of planning shall be the basis of district plans. The district shall prepare elementary education plans. Mere enrolment and provision for free food, clothing and reading material will not enhance their capabilities. Therefore, it has stressed on quality of education by "sustainable support system of resource persons, creation of block or cluster resource centers, consistent training for the teachers to enhance their skill, effective teaching and learning methods and keep them abreast of relevant and effective teaching methods. For quality improvement 20 days of in service course has been stipulated for all teachers and 30 days orientation course for the newly recruited.

The quality of education in private schools being superior, parents prefers these schools even though education in these institutions is expensive. As a result number of students in government primary schools has come down to an alarmingly low level. SSA has taken note of this factor and envisages cost effective primary education through public private partnership. Thus the over all strategy envisages, involvement, autonomy, decentralisation, quality, universalisation and a comprehensive approach to elementary education with accountability of the community. The programme for implementation and budgetary provision to sustain the programme makes it a better programme in comparison to earlier schemes to universalize elementary education though existing schemes of the department of education merged with SSA after the IX Plan except the National Programme for Nutritional support to primary education.

The statistics[3] reveal that this national flagship programme has achieved considerable success so far primary education is concerned. Till December 2006, more than 2.40 lakh schools were opened, 1.57 lakh school buildings, 6,50 lakh additional class-rooms, 2.03 lakh toilets were constructed and 1.57 lakh drinking water facilities have been provided. The access to primary education has been almost universalized. Quite a few children studying in education guarantee scheme and alternative and innovative education have been mainstreamed. Selected Educational Statistics (SES) 2004-5 reveal that 94 per cent children in the age group of 6-14 years were enrolled. The Gross Enrolment Ratio in primary school was 108.56 per cent (boys 111.41% and girls 105.48%), the dropout rate has declined by 10.54 percentage points at primary with 15.08 percentage decline for girls during 2001-05. The Gender Parity Index (GPI) in lower primary reveals above 90 in several states and in upper primary it has increased to 0.88 District Information System for schools (DISE) 2005-06 reveals that the share of ST students was 9.02 per cent, SC students 18.64 and their transition rate from lower to upper primary was 83.36 per cent during 2005-06. The number of out of school children which was 3.20 crore in 2001-02, was reduced to 70 lakhs in April 2006. By December 2006, 8.22 lakh teachers were appointed and trained, remedial teaching was imparted to over 43 lakh children, 6.12 lakh eligible students were given free textbooks. Computer aided learning to upper primary level and independent testing of children were introduced. The SSA covers all states and Union Territories and reaches out to 19.4 crore children in 12.3 lakh habitations. Its goal of all children in school by 2005 has been satisfactory as the above statistics reveal. Alternate school; back to school too, have been satisfactory. Progress at this rate might result in bridging the gender gap at the primary level by 2007 and at the elementary level by 2010.

Appraisal

An assessment by the Education for all, Government of India, MHRD in November, 2005 shows that the number of out of school children dropped to 10.4 million in 2005. Enrolment has increased because of setting up of large number of small schools and bridge courses who were to be mainstreamed in to regular schools. The goal of all children to complete five years of schooling by 2007 and eight years of schooling by 2010 depends on the continuation of education beyond the third grade. High retention and completion rate will ensure attainment of the goal of the programme. Girl's enrolment has increased but it has not reached 100 per cent. It also states that the difference in boys and girls enrolment is still disappointing in upper primary schools. Though the enrolment has increased, adequate number of teachers has not been recruited and many of those recruited are not trained to enhance their capabilities. Now that enrolment is almost satisfactory the next area, which demands attention, is effective functioning of schools and enhancing the quality of their outcomes. Therefore, a proper monitoring of school and teacher grants is necessary for its cumulative effect in satisfactory functioning of schools. For quality improvement establishment of independent organisations is needed which should not be subordinate to SCERT and SIEMAT. Recruitment of women teachers has increased but still needs attention particularly in areas where social stigma keep women out of education and employment as teachers. There are a number of schools in habitations inhabited by marginalised groups and lack in infrastructure affecting quality education. It suggests for special measures to be taken to check teacher absenteeism and implementation of teacher grievance redress mechanisms. Non-availability of data in enrolment of private unrecognized schools is an important factor. Mere expansion of schooling facilities and coverage of children will not be a better approach to elementary education. It is their functioning, performance of students, quality of teachers and management of funds, which need attention.

The Comptroller and Auditor General (CAG) Report for the years 2002-03 and 2004-05 relating to SSA Delhi shows that planning of the scheme was centralized. It has noted decrease in number of students, shortage of teachers and lack of study to evaluate the impact of SSA. Large number of students remained out of the purview of schools and earned their livelihood. Only fifty per cent of the enrolled students attend classes. Despite availability of funds there was staff shortage to monitor the programme. Parents are reluctant to send children to school because of distance of the school, economic constraint and age of the student. If this is the scenario of primary education in Delhi it may be worse for rural areas due to conservative attitude of the parents and economic constraints.

The CAG report for West Bengal states that universal enrolment target has not been achieved and dropout rate in class 1 to IV was as much as 76 per cent. The state spent only 47 per cent of the allocated funds. As regards physical infrastructure it stated that only 20 per cent of the schools had one classroom, 19 per cent had no drinking water, and 41 per cent had no toilet facility. There was no separate toilet for girls in 81 per cent of the schools. Expenditure was more in buying computers, air conditioning machine, fax and type writer machines.[4] The Third Joint Review Mission State Report, West Bengal January 12-20, 2006 revealed that in the state the number of out of school children was reduced from 3.35 lakhs in 2003 to 1.88 lakhs in 2004-05, girls enrolment was 49.58 per cent, disadvantaged groups have been provided access to education, Sishu Bikash Kendras have been upgraded providing alternative education, community involvement is helpful in the progress of enrolment of children, satisfactory progress has been achieved in bridging, gender and social category gaps, locally recruited teachers are performing better, and playing an important role in enrolment of children, Village education committees are completely involved in managing school funds. The state has introduced Integrated Learning Improvement Programme as an innovative programme.

But the other part of the story is not very encouraging. There is paucity of regular school, alternative schooling is under resourced, only 25 per cent of teacher vacancies have been filled up, non-receipt of total DPEP approved funds has affected payment to teachers, cheques are delayed for encashment, registers are not updated, construction of school building and additional classroom is unsatisfactory, teaching learning materials have not reached schools, training for in service teachers is not satisfactory, no annual plan programme has been prepared for teacher training. Although funds are transferred procurements by the transferee is not monitored. Paucity of institutional structure affects quality education. There are multiple organizations for the SSA but lack of coordination between them has affected education. The SPO and DPO are not integrated with existing institutional set up. Of course the Managing Committee has control over staff but the Village Education Committee has no control. In Orissa too, a number of children in the age group of 6-14 are out of school.[5] Even though alternative schools and new primary schools have been opened. The EGS ad AIE that has replaced the Non-Formal education scheme is operating in all 30 districts of the state involving government as well as NGOs have not been successful either. But enrolment of students in both the sectors is encouraging and para teachers have been appointed. Their activity has extended to out state, that is Hyderabad in Andhra Pradesh and camp schools have been set up for migrant families, orientation courses have been organized for almost all stakeholders like the community. Though schools are opened widely primary aim of access to universal elementary education and retention till they attain the age of 14 still remains elusive for a number of children.

Perceptions and Suggestion

Education is fundamental to children for their optimum growth and development in all areas like health and hygiene, language and communication, physical, emotional and intellectual development, personality building and adjustment with their immediate environment as well as the larger community. Early childhood educational experiences determine the quality of human resource, which in turn indicate the socio-economic progress of a country. Therefore since independence India has made remarkable effort in universalising primary education by increasing the number of schools, teachers and enrolment of students. As a result the Gross Enrolment Ratio (GER) has exceeded 100 per cent at the primary stage, 94 per cent of the rural population has schooling facilities for elementary education but non-attendance, gender and social gaps, dropout, inadequate staff, centralised planning, lack of infrastructure continue to be the problems.

The main obstacles to education for children are, rural poverty, increased population, lack of financial resources, attitude of parents and low official priority. Education for children in our country suffers from lack of quality, high dropout rate, and perception of its irrelevance for economic benefits. Statistics reveal that one in five children is over or under age, one in three drops-out before completing the primary stage and one in two children do not have clean drinking water or toilet facility. Literacy percentage varies from 90 per cent among the rich children to a meager 17 per cent for the poor. Differences in enrolment among peasant households and medium to large landowners are almost twenty percentage points. The educational profile in India varies from state to state with no linkage to economic resources of the state as Kerala has 90 per cent literacy but low income compared to a high income state like Punjab which has only sixty per cent literacy. Government statistics reveal that more than half of rural India school dropouts often relapse to illiteracy. Despite efforts made so far, schools are located at a great distance, there are no infrastructure even black boards and a single room houses all the students of the school. In some regions schools cannot open during inclement weather and classes are conducted in open air. It is rather disappointing to note that the vision for a knowledge society stumbles when statistics reveal that every third illiterate in the world is an Indian, more than six crore children of 6-14 years do not attend school, many work as child labourer and out of every ten illiterate seven are women. Among the tribals 91 women out of 100 are illiterate. The dropout rate in this category is very high. Nearly one-lakh schools have no buildings though unspent funds high and teaching materials are under or unutilised. As per the Human Development Report by international standards India fares low in comparison to Sri Lanka so far education is concerned and in female literacy Sub-Saharan Africa fares well than India.

The National Policy of Education 1968 marked a new strategy for radical reconstruction of education system in the country but due to lack of proper implementation, funds crunch and organisational support the problems of access to education, quality, quantity financial outlay etc., most of its stated objectives remained unachieved. Infusing Indian way of thinking and making the human resource meet the challenges of the present situation, the goals of secularism, socialism, democracy and professional ethics are facing challenges. In rural areas education suffers from inadequacy of infrastructure and trained staff. SSA is a right approach in this regard but some of the earlier problems continue to hamper the success of this programme. My personal observations and interaction with people in some villages of Orissa revealed that an overwhelming number of parents view that primary education is essential for children indicating their willingness to send their children to school though about girls' education the conservative attitude persists. Also economic reasons do not restrain children to get enrolled in the school as many of them do not work. Some students have withdrawn from school because the environment is boring, due to quarrel and exchange of blows with their classmates, strict discipline and control of their movement. Even if primary education is free, parents incur some expenditure for sending their children to school which even though low many are unable to afford. For girls the common view is that they have to marry and will not do remunerative job for which education is not necessary. They are yet to realise that education has many facets and essential for healthy existence. Though SSA has laid emphasis on infrastructure, many schools do not have proper facilities to accommodate children. Where the building is good it is utilized for some other purpose than accommodating pupils. Even teacher student ratio is not satisfactory though official statistics indicate bridging of this gap. Surprisingly many students are not able to read and write after being enrolled in school for pretty long time. This might be due to absence of teachers in school, lack of time to teach and personal attention to students. Many of them are not paid on time and are engaged in teaching all the classes in single teacher schools. The distribution of midday meal has diverted their activity to cooking and food distribution and controlling children particularly at the time of food distribution. Now the scheme has been expanded by including children in upper primary stage in government and government aided schools, besides education guarantee scheme and alternative and innovative education centers in two phases. In the current financial year it will include 3479 educationally backward blocks and next year it will include all areas of the country.[6]

But a better approach would be payment against each day of attendance in the school for a student in cash, which should be deposited, in the local post office or bank in a joint account to be operated by the student, parents and the headmaster of the school. This amount cannot be withdrawn till the student finishes schooling up to the age of 14 years. This will be a better substitute for food and dress now provided in schools. The midday meals programme has kept the teachers engaged in looking after cooking and distribution of food rather than teaching the pupil. Similarly students attend classes when food is provided. It is reported that attendance is almost full when eggs are given with rice and dal. The students are interested more in food than learning. Such attitude is adversarial for quality learning. Monetary payment will create positive attitude to attend school, learn and sustain attendance. Initially this can be started at 50:50 ratios that are food distribution for three days and saving the expenditure for other three days in a week. Gradually the scheme can be withdrawn and payment against expenses for food and dress shall be substituted.

It is welcome that the Controller General of Accounts (CGA) will implement monitoring system for assessing the expenditure on 27 central government schemes entailing a cost of one lakh crore which will be available for public viewing in its website. This will ensure transparency check wastage and improve performance. The course component of elementary education should be made more interesting for retention and continuation of students. For this the teachers have to play important role. The syllabus should be revised keeping in view the changes. Communicating in a language that will be understandable for the student .Affection, care and friendly environment will have better effect.[7] The method of story telling and play mode is effective which should be universalised.

At the moment SSA is a good programme but its success depends on implementation, monitoring, dedication and commitment of all the stakeholders. One of the thrust areas of 'National Policy of Education' was responsibility to Panchayati Raj Institutions in the management of education. They have to recruit personnel, generate resources, allocate funds, prepare budget, approve expenditure and supervise academic performance. The Committee on Decentralised Management of Education stipulated establishment of Village Education Committees (VLC) consisting of the panchayat chairman, the head teacher or head master, and persons having concern for education. It includes representatives of parents and other marginalised groups. One third of the total members of VLC should be women. These representatives have to take care of enrolment of children, check dropouts and supervise repair and construction of school buildings. Community involvement is the basic requirement for enhancement of student enrolment, sustained attendance and effective teaching. In Kerala community involvement in quality education has yielded positive result .The VLC should realise the enormity of its responsibilities in educating children which can automatically improve the current state of affairs over-involved in low quality education, leakage, absenteeism, diversion of funds and many other deficiencies.

REFERENCES

1. JP Unnikrishnan Vs. Andhra Pradesh, 1993.
2. http://www.jmi.nic.in/Events/Events 03/DPEP.
3. http://www.indlaw.com
4. http//jharkhand.org.in
5. http://opepa.in.
6. *The Hindu*, 14 September, 2007, p. 15.
7. 'Teacher Canes, Pupil Faints', *The Times of India*, Bhubaneswar, 3 September, 07, p. 1.

10

Rural Development Through Panchayati Raj Institutions: Strengthening a Participatory Democracy in India

N.S. GEHLOT

Decentralisation is "a new mantra of governance", but in Indian context, it is narrow in the administration of poorly governed northern states, as decentralisation would lead to more powers in the hands of a feudal elites at the grassroots levels. That is why centralised planning still prevails in our federal set-up against the very spirit of 73rd and 74th Amendments. The 'Centre' with funds and bureaucrats has not disappeared or its character has not changed in the administrative devolution of power. What is needed is replacement of it with decentralisation and with intellectual pluralism as a guiding principle of planning for development.

This contradiction calls for a rethink of the planning process. The solution lies in decentralising the process. States have their planning boards, which can coordinate work at the grassroots. Panchayati Raj Institutions should be asked to work on localised plans. Problems and concerns specific to a particular area will then get enough attention. This will also make the process more democratic and inclusive. The People's Planning exercise initiated in Kerala in the 1990s offers lessons for a decentralised and participatory approach to policy-making. If backed by sufficient funds and judicious redeployment of bureaucrats, grassroots planning could help states to cut down project costs and maximize benefits to the people. At present, planning is an exercise undertaken by a small group of babus who follow state economic models handed down by 'experts' and 'consultants'. This boxed approach only alienated people (*aam admi* of India), the intended beneficiaries. Development is after all a political problem and it needs the involvement of the people at large.

How to have a Responsive Administration?

The conference, convened by Cabinet Secretary B.K. Chaturvedi on 19th July, 2006 discussed the changes for making the administration more responsive to the requirements of 21st century. It was particularly concerned about the procedural bottle necks that keep the poor and dalits from accessing a ration card or copies of land record and other kinds of documents. The focus was rightly concerned on the implementation of schemes like Rural Employment Guarantee Programme; National Rural Health Mission, Right to information Act, the Bharat Nirman, poverty eradication, the mid-day meal scheme etc. which shall definitely have a vital bearing on country's aspirations for double-digit growth rate. Herein, the Panchayats shall have to be recognised as 'agency' to increase the reach of the schemes to the downtrodden, keeping in mind to arrest the ongoing trends of corruption, caste politics and violence.

Strengthening a Participative Democracy

There was much discussion on increasing the strength of Lok Sabha seat on the basis of population. In order to avoid North-South divide, a better solution was proposed to have favoured to keep the inter-state allocation of Lok Sabha seats intact while read just constituency boundaries to reflect population changes. The same arrangement applies for Legislative Assemblies as well. In order to a balance between rural and urban areas and to maintain arithmetical parity in terms of population, the Panchayats and Municipalities, 1992—a third ties of governance under the 73rd and 74th Constitutional Amendments-should be given due representation in the State Assemblies/Parliament or by creating Legislative Councils for states (at present the council exists only in five states in our federal structure). Today, we need our Panchayats and Municipalities as much as we need our Assemblies and Parliament and it is suggested that the voice of the people should be heard to strengthen a participative democracy, instead of adding a few hundred more MPs in Parliament to represent increased population which shall increase expenses to the tax payers.

On the other hand, our democracy needs functional reforms to make it more accessible to ordinary people to be more say in them. According to Harsh Mander[1], more numbers of powers are needed not in Parliament but in panchayats and municipalities. Many critical decisions have far-reaching effect on the lives of ordinary people and they have no say in them. For example, the economic policies of globalisation, for which we need deliberative forms of democracy such as referendums and citizens' juries. We need to strengthen the rights of citizens to hold governments and their representatives more accountable. The Right to Information Act has done more for Indian democracy than the creation of a thousand new MPs. It should not be possible for governments to suppress democratic freedom and popular discontent with armed forces or anti-terror laws. Democracies are as much about the rights of minorities as it's of majorities, and therefore religious minorities, Dalits, and women, need to be defended and strengthened.

The elegant circular structure that house Parliament in Delhi does not need to be populated further. The defence of democracy requires greater powers for the real rulers of this land, the people themselves. Until this is done, farmers will continue to extinguish their lives unheeded, and Sharmila from Manipur may refuse food and water for another six years but still never be heard by those she and her people elect.

Reviving Rural India

We have confirmed statistics of suicide by 25,000 farmers since 1997. About 80 per cent of India's population still lives in rural areas where consumption has actually declined in the last fifteen years. In fact, we have a sub-Saharan African in our mindset. How can we talk of marching forward or of a software park in the conditions of shortage of onions; rising price commodities like gas, milk, petrol, wheat etc. This kind of depressed situation must be stopped and farmers' class should be made to live in a decent condition, for which the govt. must change their mindset by restoring a bold and-revolutionary approach. The govt. should depute a team of 10 to 12 young officers of rural background to every block of villages as 'developers' with a mandate to act as change agents. The team should be led by a project leader who must be empowered to achieve desired results in the given time frame and budget.

The responsibilities of the team should be the following: Undertake watershed development, construct check dams and tanks, dig wells, popularise drip irrigation, ensure safe drinking water supply and prevent soil erosion; motivate farmers to sell their produce directly to urban consumers and construct cold storage facilities; obtain help from agricultural universities to improve farm productivity, train farmers.

There is also an urgent need to abolish outdated laws like APMC Act which force farmers to sell their pr6duce only to market committees controlled by influential politicians. Farm produce should be allowed to be sold freely across state boundaries. Government should protect our farmers' interests in WTO negotiations or in building SEZs. We must prevent developed countries, which give huge subsidy to their farmers, from dumping their farm produce on us at cheap prices.

Finance Minister P. Chidambaram budgeted Rs. 50,000 crore for the Bharat Nirman programme in 2006. But Rajiv Gandhi had famously observed that only 15 per cent of development funds actually reaches intended beneficiaries. The Centre also depends on a matching effort by the State Governments. State Governments need to strengthen the delivery mechanism.[2]

We need an economic revolution that starts in villages, not one that bypasses them. And we need a creative solution for such a revolution.

Bharat Nirman Programme

The Central Government led by U.P.A. has announced massive programmes for the renewal of Urban Centre for Bharat Nirman, for which guidelines and monitoring system have been laid down to implement programmes. The major objectives of the programme are as follows:

(a) One crore hectors of un-irrigated land will be irrigated; *(b)* all villages whose population is 1000 or more and 500 or more in hilly areas will be connected with roads; *(c)* over 60 lakh houses will be built in villages; *(d)* 74,000 habitants which do not have access to safe drinking water will be provided these facilities, and *(e)* each and every village will have at least one telephone connection. This programme if enforced honestly, has tremendous potential to solve the problem on unemployment, abolish poverty and create new wheat for the country, provided proper planning is made and care is taken of investment and people's involvement is ensured. It needs huge money to spend.

It may be recalled that the Indira Awas Yojana has been introduced by Central Government since several years. Any survey of the houses constructed under Indira Awas Yojana would virtually reveal that most of the houses have been dilapidated, as they were constructed without any norms or standards. Besides, the Government should reconsider the existing policy of construction houses for the people from Scheduled Castes, Scheduled Tribes or minorities at a distance from the habitats. This may perhaps keep them away from the national stream and perpetuate the existing caste system.

Before constructing 60 lakh houses in a random manner, according to Dr. Mohan Dharia,[3] a long-term plan should be undertaken to reconstruct our villages. It is well-known that various tribes created their own habitations and housed were built from the point of view of security. Naturally no care was taken of health or sanitation. On this background restructuring the whole village habitation providing all possible amenities should be considered by the Government.

Programme of restructuring 6 lakh villages is indeed, a Herculean task and enormous investment may be required for the same. However, if we plant species like Bamboo, Casuarinas, Poplars, Teak etc., on a massive scale in the earnmarked area, within next 10 to 15 years such plantations would share maximum part of the expenditure required for reconstruction. With a visionary approach the farmers staying in the villages may be asked to reserve about 4000 to 5000 sq. ft. area from their field only for plantation of tree species, to erect a house in future. It may be possible to have small house with all amenities, cattle shed and storage for food grains along with kitchen, garden. This will also require perfect planning for every village. The Government should reconsider the whole programme of constructing houses without such planning. Similarly, National Agencies or Missions as suggested above should be constituted to effectively implement objective of the programme. It would be advisable to get these objectives scrutinised from the Planning Commission before introducing the programme with proper planning and adequate mechanism to monitor the same and to keep them away from competition.

Posting Doctors in Rural Areas

In 2006, the Health and Family Welfare Ministry proposed compulsory rural postings for all MBBS students but due to stiff resistance the plan was shelved. But the ministry once again, after discussion of the matter with Medical Council of India and other professional bodies, has made up the mind to have a legislation making it mandatory for all doctors to undergo one-year rural posting before they get a permanent registration. And the steering group *National Rural Health Mission* has approved it. It is like that of the Chinese model where it is mandatory for all doctors to undertake the fresh job at rural areas. This policy should be the basic part of infrastructural facilities to look after the health of rural masses. Around 26,000 doctors are posted at the health and community centres, but about 30 to 40 per cent of doctors do not report for work. The compulsory postings would ensure better health facilities for people living in the rural areas. The manner in which cases of dengue fever have been reported in Sept.-Oct. 2006 in the country, underlines the need of such a law. Though it was epidemic yet it is matter of concern. We need to create masses awareness through young doctors while roping schools in this mission to contain such diseases.

Government health services are pathetic, with either employees or drugs missing from primary health centres on most days. Only one-fifth of all medical services are supplied by the Government, the lowest proportion in the world. What is the way out? First, some states should experiment with education and health vouchers given directly to households, who will have the option to use these in government or private schools and clinics. The ensuing competition will raise standards. Second, we must end the license—permit raj that strangles private school growth. Third, we should devolve budgetary powers to panchayats so that they can directly hire doctors and teachers, and not have to depend on unshakable staff from state capitals. Fourth, local governments should have the power to withhold the wages of staff that are absent on any day. Fifth, private universities must be encouraged rather than banned, and foreign universities should be allowed to open campuses in rural sector. Such reforms will be just a starting point. We have a long way to go.

A Lesson from Singur Land Acquisition

The UPA Government has enacted the SEZ Act, which needs changes in its rules (Special Economic Zones), specially on land acquisition, tax concessions and labour laws. The way the Trinamul Congress supremo launched movement against Tata Motors plant in Singur (West Bengal) underlines the flaws in the land acquisition procedure for industrialisation. Even Land Acquisition Act, entacted by British India in 1894, no industralisation should be allowed at the cost of cultivators' land which is fertile. The matter needs to lay down new national guidelines.

In the light of liberation and globalisation viz-a-viz the spate of farmer's suicide in the recent years, our agri-trade policy needs to be reshaped in a way that the SEZ initiative adds new dynamics in the food security because, agriculture sector in India has long become economically unviable. Probably against this backgrounds, the UPA Government endorsed Congress President Sonia Gandhi's concern on acquisition of farmer's land for industrial purposes including creating SEZs. The Centre has directed state governments to ensure that SEZs are built only on wasteland or in fertile fields and farmers should be rightfully and adequately compensated for acquiring such land. The concept of economic development should not be carried out at the cost of farmers and peasants. At present, India has approved 164 such zones to boost exports and economic growth, aiming to attract petro chemicals, auto parts, IT, bio-technology, jewellery and electronics firms with investment of at least 22 billion over three years.

That the above cited crisis does not get aggravated further, the prevailing practice of controlling food trade by middle men to procure crops should be broken down to ensure the role of FDI in food retail. The structure has to be reshaped. The government should incentivise retail companies to procure directly from the fields, particularly from farmer cooperatives. Policies, especially related to credit, should be put in place to encourage the latter's formation on the lines of self- help groups. Women self-help groups should be encouraged to take up local procurement of farm produce, if need be. Cooperatives have been successful, most famously in the dairy sector, and to some extent in sugar and plantation crops. It is time we explored this option in the case of food grains and with food majors, including multi-nationals. The retailers, in turn, could help farmers access not just the market but also technology and credit to boost productivity. Such a relationship could work not because of any altruistic reasons but for sound business reasons. Geography and climatic variations offer India the possibility to be the world's food basket. On the other hand, declining productivity and low prices have been the bane for agriculture in India. The entry of food majors could open up new markets for farmers, drive out middlemen and fetch producers better prices. Assured business would also empower farmers to risk diversification of crops. Besides formulating policies that would encourage a healthy retailer farmer arrangement, the state should step up public investment in irrigation and electricity. Now Jai Kisan slogan should not continue to be an empty slogan.

While keeping in view the events of West Bengal viz-a-viz SEZs, the Apex Chambers like C.I.I., FICCI and ASSOCHAM have agreed to compensate to farmers for their land cost as per market rates and the members of the displaced families be given alternative employment. According to our President APJ Abdul Kalam, India can be move into 10th position (now holding 43th position in global competitiveness), if following important factors, namely knowledge, technology, innovation, resource investment, customer loyalty, quality and value of products, employee productivity, working environment and a creative leadership—are taken into consideration. Rehabilitation, not displacement should be the focus of new SEZ's policy. It needs a carefully study and its implications on social sector.[4]

Accountability of NGOs

In a globalised world, it's not just the government that affects the lives of people, but NGOs too. So if the government can be held accountable to internal and external stakeholders, why not NGOs? This is a debate that's now seeing some fruition. Over the last decade, NGOs have proliferated in India, while remaining relatively unregulated. There are an estimated 12 lakh NGOs, over half based in six lakh villages. But many do good work, but lack of accountability has allowed less-credible NGOs to undermine the work of the credible ones. This has led to a dilution of trust between donors and beneficiaries. In order to celebrate good work and raise confidence, Credibility Alliance of London (CA), an initiative by voluntary organisations to enhance good governance within the sector, was started in 2004.

For this accountability and transparency, the public mobilisation shall have to be streamlined at the village level. They should have to standarise their accounts, reports and other things. We cannot effort to a sliding of public morality.[5]

Accountability of Civic Bodies

Urban Development Ministry's Model Municipality Disclosure Bill, to be adopted by states pitching for funds under the Jawaharlal Nehru Urban Renewal Mission (JNNURM) to revamp the crumbling infrastructure, calls for municipalities to put in public domain details of services being offered and their quality. The civic bodies also have to provide details about their financial health on a quarterly basis. "The move will empower people to demand better quality of services as promised by civic bodies in their disclosure details." The model Bill, aimed at injecting transparency and accountability into varicose municipal administration, will require civic agencies to disclose their financial statements within two months of the end of each quarter and for the full year within three months of the end of the financial year. In fact, the purpose of it is to put a check on growing tendencies of competition in these bodies, to evaluate the civic agencies' performance and enforce accountability on officials and staff. The bodies will have to maintain and publicise official records of subsidy (programmes) while revealing decisions. made by their bodies" councils/ committees. This should be applicable to Panchayat Raj Institutions which need to undertake systematic rural reforms. As such no system of governance is effective without accountability. Gram Sabha should be permitted to hold Panchayats accountable and responsive.

In UP, the elections to the local bodies were held in October, 2006, in which Minister Sanjay Garg resigned due to the excesses committed by the police on minorities in his own constituency. Such events/developments can be prevented if the range and scope of the Election Commission of India is further enlarged and brought in its preview to ensure that the entire state level electoral machinery does function under its command and supervision. The grassroots level democratic institutions shall have to be strengthened while keeping control over mal-practices involving caste politics etc. Without this, the fruits of good governance can not be procured at grassroots level.[6]

Rural Development through NCAER[7]

In a first of its kind estimation of infrastructure deficit in rural areas, the National Council of Applied Economic Research (NCAER) has estimated an investment of Rs. 1,58,310 crore in telecommunications, power, roads and transport, water and sanitation. Pointing to the fact that rural India faces more acute shortage of infrastructure, the *India Rural Infrastructure Report,* released in December, 2006, made a strong pitch for decentralising and localising the provision of these services in addition to seeking newer financial instruments. Today, rural areas 23.98 per cent minorities in and 30.41 per cent urban areas are living below poverty line.

According to the Report, The capital needed to build infrastructure is a small percentage of the total expenditure that would be needed to be incurred by states (for operation and maintenance). Nor do the capital costs include central funds that would be needed to be spent on administrative expenses and subsidies. Probably, this is the first time that the focus has been stressed on Rural India, and that too on strengthening infrastructural facilities through the 11th Plan. Much shall depend on the concept of 'good governance' and the priority of local administration.

India Needs Another Green Revolution

Our President, Dr. A.P.J. Abdul Kalam has stressed the need for a 'second Green Revolution' based on practical applications of latest technological innovations in the age of globalisation to meet the future food needs of common man necessitated by increasing population growth. It needs to focus on agriculture sector, which is still backward. The President said so while inaugurating the Global Forum on Agricultural Research—GFAR.

Of course, 'water' could not lead wars in the near future, as per UNDP's report, but hydrologists have pointed out to exploit earth water plant net (Oceans) that has 97 per cent of its water, as water needed to grow food, support industries—and maintain the environment. As per the UNDP's Human Development Report 2006, by 2025, over billion people across the world over would be facing water crisis.

To Conclude

Democracy in India has to move from elections to development and the same has to be extended to all organisations and institutions. Our family, religious institutions, political parties, educational institutions and development organisations have to be democratised. As there is no democratic spirit in our institutions, the organisations have to be democratic accountable and responsive in its functioning. Many of our constitutional provisions are not operationalised because they are countered by the practices of the communities. As our activities are in a feudal mode, community practices are taking upper hand to sabotage the provisions of the Constitution. There are numerous examples to mention where the caste Hindus has not allowed the Dalits to contest in the Gram Panchayat elections. Thus, communities have totally pushed the constitutional provisions away from the grassroots. It is a paradox that the caste based communities have reservoir of energies, talents, skills, knowledge, capacity and capability but they are not being harnessed, and instead in the name of expansion of government they are annihilated and allowed to die. But there are certain practices which are antithetical to democracy which are being allowed to survive. As a result, the anti-democratic feudal elements have perfectly buckled with our electoral politics and bureaucratic development activities.

To overcome these problems, late Rajiv Gandhi when he was the Prime Minister, took the initiative to introduce series of reforms and of which economic reforms and political reforms were phenomenal. In political reform he intended to deepen democracy, change the character of our democracy, bring the development initiative from below by changing the total paradigm of development and made it an inclusive and gender-sensitive democracy. This would create a change in our society and show the way to other societies in the world by involving the people as stakeholders. The reform which he initiated in economy has paid rich dividends to those who have enhanced their capability and skill. But the poor and the unskilled are still marginalised.

The reform which he initiated on decentralisation has brought the marginalised to the central stage for governance. But handling power by them has yet not taken a shape. The Dalits have come forward but caste politics and discrimination have presented them.

The people who are marginalised now have to build their capacity and negotiate for power and resource to develop themselves on their own. New forces are emerging. The Panchayati Raj system, therefore, has to be freed from the clutches of political parties by declaring the grassroots institutions non-party based context. The new forces of youth groups have to actively involve themselves in the grassroots institutions. The civil society organisations have to build the capacity of the local body leaders. Along with the capacity building, people have to be mobilised to participate in Gram Sabha meetings. Constantly providing support to the dalit and women Panchayat leaders to manage the Panchayats is the need of the hour. By supporting and strengthening the constitutional Panchayats, the customary and traditional Panchayats have to be democratised and a synergy has to be established between the traditional Panchayats and constitutional Panchayats. All activities, especially, development initiatives have to be undertaken.

With the active participation of stakeholders delivery of services will be done effectively. Grassroots empowerment is more important than grassroots development. A new citizenship culture has to be created at the grassroots. By doing so the self-dignity of the poor, marginalised, women and Dalit will be restored. They should have a feeling that they can decide their destiny on their own. All major changes in the electoral politics came after Rajiv Gandhi through the Panchayati Raj Institutions have created revolutionary changes, but this new arrangement is yet not properly shaped to function with autonomy. Today, forces are working against the devolution of powers, inclusion of women and Dalit in governance. To overcome this kind of barriers and obstacles, a movement from below has to be initiated which will strengthen grassroots democracy.[8]

Taking E-Governance to Rural Areas

In a bold step, the BJP Governments of M.P. and Rajasthan have shown assertion to take e-governance to rural areas and ensure villages 24 hr. service of electricity. The plan is good but would face a cropper if power supply in rural areas is not improved. It is yet not clear how will computes work without power supply? These states have been facing a power shortfall since last two years. Even farmers in villages are troubled over the non-availability of electricity, apart from the crisis the student community faces the power crisis during examinations. The idea of e-governance is good for bringing transparency and good governance as it would connect the Government Secretariat to the key villages. The reality is that more than 50 per cent of the states' websites are either defunt or not up-dated in the wake of power-crisis. The states shall have to prioritise the supply of power before the e-governance is to be introduced in the rural sector for development. Without ensuring power supply no development is possible. The farmers have already protested and blocked the offices/highways against power crisis and faced bullets also.[9]

Unfortunately, our Budget 2007-08 claims to be dedicated to the Kisan cause but it has little to say about the crisis of rural infrastructure, particularly power. Instead, it talks of fertilizer outlay/subsidy which helps the industry rather than the farmers. Besides, fertilizer than the farmers. Besides, fertilizer cannot be more important than bizli, sadak, paani, housing, telecommunications. If rural infrastructure is overlooked in any budget, all poverty alleviation programmes shall withhold the overall growth plan, namely the Bharat Nirman or other schemes. Both the power and agricultural sectors are equally important.

REFERENCES

1. 'RTI can do more for Democracy than a thousand MPs', *The Times of India,* New Delhi, Oct. 15, 2006.
2. Arun Firodia, 'Reviving Rural Indian', *The Times of India,* July 6, 2006.
3. Dr. Mohan Dharia is President of Vanarai, Pune and former Deputy Chairman of the Planning Commission and has given his reflection on the programme, *South Asia Politics,* February 2006, pp. 6-7.
4. In West Bengal, forcefully acquisition of farm land at Singur for TATA Motor's proposed project of small car unit, triggered mass movement because of not paying adequate compensation to farmers. This was led by Trinamul Congress Supremo Mamta Banerjee & attacked by the police. Now the Left Government had to suspend the scheme.
5. Surendra Mushi and GG Biju Paul Abraham, *Democratic Societies of Globalisation,* New Delhi, Sage Publications, 2004.
6. In a classic but first-ever judgement, the court of India ruled that the State Election Commissions can under no circumstances postpone elections to Panchayati and Municipalities after the completion of their 5 years term. The only exception to timely holding

of elections could be man-made calamities, such as riots and breakdown of law and order or natural calamities. This ruling will strengthen grassroots democracy. The petition was related to holding the elections of the Ahmedabad municipality and the pressure was put on the Government to hold the timely elections. *The Times of India.* New Delhi, 21 October, 2006.

7. *NCAER's India Rural Infrastructure Report,* released on 31-12-2006.
8. Sec. 'Indian Democracy: A Re-thinking' *South Asia Politics,* New Delhi, December 2006, pp. 30-31.
9. The issues relating to institutional structures and dynamics of global governance, the fallout of gender, caste class, ethnicity and religious political processes have been thoroughly discussed in the book, Manorajan Mohanty, Richard Baum and Rong Ma (Eds.), *Grassroots Democracy in India and China: The Right to Participate,* New Delhi, Sage Publications, 2007.

11

Public Accountability, Community Empowerment and E-Governance

DAMODAR ROUT

Let us believe that *e* in empowerment and *e* in e-governance are one and the same. For me *e* is always equal to empowerment be it constitutional or informational, be it resources database or information management.

We all know that distance from power is poverty. The majorities of the world's poor are rural, live far away from centers of power, and will remain so for several decades. Rural poverty is reflected in poor-nutrition, inadequate shelter and low-health standards and creates a vicious cycle of poverty that flourishes on its own.

The role of local-self-government, as an instrument of poverty reduction must be given a re-look. Many Government, institutions, and project managers are reluctant to carry out impact evaluations because they are deemed to be expensive, time consuming, technically complex, and because the findings can be politically sensitive, particularly if they are negative. In poverty-reduction, as in growth, India is typical of other developing-country democracies, having achieved steady but not spectacular success. Very few democracies have eradicated poverty. Other countries have democratised after becoming quite rich. We believe that inequality in different dimensions and institutional arrangements play as key a role in this as markets do, and this links to our empowerment discussion.

Participatory and decentralised management, apart from securing democratic control and developing human potential, often improves the cost-effectiveness of a range of actions, from developing new seed varieties through micro finance to rural schools and public works programmes. Special measures are needed to enable the poor to participate.

The Constitution of India was adopted in 1950. It has envisaged (Article 40) that "the state shall take steps to organize village Panchayats and endow them with such powers and authority as may be necessary to enable them to function as units of self-government." This provision of the Constitution was primarily advisory. In the following FIVE decades, some sporadic and indifferent steps were taken by some of the state governments to organise Panchayats; but they were invariably denied any meaningful powers and authority and, worst of all, the elections were seldom held at 5-year intervals as required.

The 73rd Amendment to the Constitution of India dated 24 April, 1993, directed all state legislature to amend their respective Panchayat legislation to conform to the Constitution Amendment, within one year. All the states complied and adopted new Panchayat legislation by 23 April, 1994. By April 1995 all the states were expected to complete decision on new Panchayats—and those who delayed ran the risk of losing central government assistance.

Local Government : An Instrument of Poverty Alleviation

Having discussed broad features of local self-government structure poverty issue on which there is some measure of consensus, I may now turn to approaches and policies that are more often contested or where unresolved institutional and political economy issues leave considerable scope for further analytical discussion and more empirical work.

One approach, popular in some international lending agencies and donor countries, is to rely primarily on market-based growth and then to take care of those who fall through the cracks of the market process with targeted public welfare programmes and the provision of infrastructure.

Another approach is to give much more emphasis to various forms of massive public intervention in directly improving the health, education, and nutrition of the poor.

A third approach, which has received less attention, is to move some distance away from both state patternalism and the harshness of market processes and instead to rely more on local self-governing institutions and community involvement to improve the material conditions and autonomy of the poor. The issue is not just the administrative decentralization or better co-ordination of delivery mechanisms that is sometimes urged.

An anti-poverty programme cannot be effective or sustained, particularly under the usual politics of scarcity, without active and vigilant participation by the poor, demanding the benefits as part of their minimum social and economic rights. But in most parts of the world the poor are much too weak and fragmented to get organized – and even getting organized may not be enough.

India

A Rural-Urban Relationship Committee, set up by the Government of India in 1963, pointed out that local government can no longer remain merely instruments of political education and civic conscience, but have to become institutions for the promotion of social and economic development of local community as well as an integral part of the National Government. Thirty years later the Seventy-third and Fourth Constitutional Amendment Act, 1992 has given effect to these by providing more power at the local level.

Pakistan

Ironically, local government has been strong under military regimes, not under democratic elected ones.

Rural poverty alleviation through economic and social development was high on the state agenda in almost all countries of the Asian and Pacific region during the second half of the twentieth century. To achieve that goal, several development models were experimented with. These ranged from state-driven import substitution to market-driven export promotion models, from agriculture focused to infrastructure-focused models and from the trickle-down approach to directly focused programmes.

Legislation alone cannot empower people. Empowerment of the rural poor through decentralization in poverty alleviation actions needs a detailed examination with reference to Asian and European Experience. Most Decentralization Theories identify two essential ingredients: Local Accountability of leaders to their people, enabling greater efficiency and greater equity; Discretionary powers in the hands of local leaders so that their powers have meaning to local people who then have an interest in accountability. Accountability is more than elections; it is also based on procedures, culture, knowledge and identities.

E-Governance and Good Governance

Good Governance is increasingly cited as a key component in any successful strategy to reduce poverty. Decentralization of authority and responsibility is a key factor in good governance. Good governance is concerned with institutionalizing democracy in such a way that the structure produces the expected functions. A recent study has argued that the persistence of poverty in most countries has its origins in problems of governance rather that in an inadequacy of resources. Information technology can bridge this digital divide.

Participation of the Rural Poor : Mixed Experience

There has been a constant debate on the methods and sequence of enabling people to participate in the development process. Earlier development strategies treated people as "object" or "target groups" to whom development was to be delivered by outsiders. Those concepts perceived the rural poor as passive recipients who wait for outsiders to come to their assistance. Such an approach might work in a relief operation but certainly not in the empowerment of the rural poor.

Raj of Panchayat or a Case of Panchayats

Democratically elected representative panchayats are far more effective means for containing (though not eliminating) corruption and ensuring accountability than is generally recognised. If decentralised planning and implementation leads to even a modest reduction in waste and leakage—there will be a dramatic improvement in effectiveness in all aspects of the programme.

Revitalized local government is essential if many of the government's aims are to succeed. Public faith in politicians and their institutions in fragile. The need to restore the link in people's minds between their vote and the services that their lives is urgent. Local democracy is the place to start. The open question still remains why Panchayati Taj as an instrument and mechanism of poverty reduction. It is the panchayat that can reduce the distance of poor from power.

Tradition

Panchayats are an ancient form of local government based on the idea that when five (panch) elders come together, God will be present.

To conclude I would like to say that decentralisation is a process of participatory development—a case of rule clarity and role clarity. Thus open question is a policy for pro-poor-growth with emphasis on poor. Potential for poverty reduction is better than there is strong coalition of the poor that can pressure the government to act in their favour.

12

Democratic Decentralisation and Participatory Planning in Kerala: The Locomotive of a New Development Culture

MOHANAN B. PILLAI

Introduction

Ever since the launching of the campaign for democratic decentralisation and participatory planning by the CPI(M) controlled Left Democratic Front (LDF) Government in 1996, Kerala has, once again, become the locus of international attention thanks to the sudden transformation of the state as the location of innovations in local democracy and participatory development, in the age of globalisation. Development thinkers, social scientists, policy makers and activists from other states in India and abroad have detoured the charming villages of Kerala to get a feel of the nature and dynamics of decentralised democracy at the grassroots level. All of a sudden Kerala has become the most favoured destination of academic tourism as everyone wanted to know what is happening in the red-bastion in the South -west strip of India.

Many western writers who have been studying Kerala for several years have show-cased the decentralized planning campaign as an alternative to the economics and politics of corporate dominated globalization. For writers and activists from other states in India, Kerala has emerged as a replicable model of democratic decentralisation within in the framework of 73rd and 74th Amendments to the Constitution of India that came into effect in 1992.

Back home the people's Plan Campaign for Decentralised Planning (PCDP) generated heated arguments, debates, discussion as also controversies of unprecedented nature. The Left intellectuals in Kerala who took positions in the 'right' of the 'left-centre' and 'left' of the 'left- centre' and 'far- left' of the 'left -centre' enriched the intellectual horizon of Kerala with illuminating ideas and arguments. Interestingly, there was virtually no participation in the debates from the side of the leaders and supporters of the non-left formations in Kerala represented by the Congress (I) party led United Democratic Front (UDF).

The media in Kerala, both print and electronic, sensationalized the whole debate by crossing even the fault-lines of decency and civility. Two of Kerala's most circulated newspapers have substituted meaningful discussions with personal attacks and mudslinging. They found in the debate a handy stick to beat the CPI (M).

The media in Kerala, both print and electronic, sensationalized the whole debate by crossing even the fault-lines of decency and civility. Two of Kerala's most circulated newspapers have substituted meaningful discussions with personal attacks and mudslinging. They found in the debate a handy stick to beat the CPI (M).

It is evident that some comrades, friends and fellow travellers of the CPI (M) seemingly failed to comprehend the development implications of the politics of democratic decentralisation in its proper spirit. For instance, the far- left deviation of M.N.Vijayan, a Professor of Malayalam language and literature, who served as Editor of CPI (M)'s weekly Magazine, is noteworthy. In fact, Vijayan was resigning as Editor of *Desabhimani weekly* in protest against what he perceived as the party's deviation from conventional party programme and strategy. At the same time, CPI (M) had expelled one of its committed comrades, the people's science movement activist and scientist M.P. Parameswaran for his over enthusiasm for decentralized planning programme which the party thought a kind of right deviation. The CPI (M) leadership in unequivocal terms made it clear that right deviation is not the answer to far-left adventurism. What was perceived as 'far-left' adventurism and right deviation of two of CPI (M)'s prominent intellectuals in Kerala combined with the unethical journalism of certain newspapers and news channels have given enormous amount of embarrassment for the state unit of CPI (M) at a time when the party was engaged in a process of repositioning itself in the society and polity of Kerala with a new political strategy. Why CPI (M) thought of initiating a new political strategy in 1996? What exactly is the 'new' in the strategy initiated? What is the meaning and content of the new development culture that the CPM was talking about during the late eighties?

Overview of Literature

The debate on decentralization in Kerala is very active and vibrant from the 1990s. EMS (1992) has suggested that Panchayati Raj Institutions (PRIs) should be made important instruments for the extension of democracy at all levels of administration and for the solution of serious problems in socio-economic development. He pointed out that PRIs could be micro-level institutions for development of agriculture and petty production sector. V.K. Sukumaran Nayar (1992) argued that decentralisation should start with political parties. V. Ramachandran (1992) drew the attention to the need for enough preparation before implementation of any programme on decentralisation.

Jose Chattukulam and P.G. Padmanabhan (1998) brought out a critical analysis of Kerala Panchayati Raj Act, 1994. Jose Chattukulam and M.S. John (1998) examined the Sen Committee Recommendations on devolution of powers and identified certain problems with it. They have expressed the view that we cannot set up local self-government by extending sectors of activities or by providing more funds to local bodies. Self-governance could be realized only through creating institutions in which there should be complete freedom for decision-making and for utilizing financial resources without external control and interference.

People's campaign for development planning added a new chapter in the annals of democratic decentralisation efforts in Kerala. This has also been extensively reviewed by academics and activists in the fields of Development Studies. Those include Thomas Issac (2000) Isaac and Franke (2000), Mohanakumar S. (2000), V. Rajendran Nair (2000), Sajith Sukumaran (2001), Rashmi Sharma (2003), B. Mohanan (1998, 2003, 2005), Richard Franke and Barbara Chasin (1995). All these writers have praised PCDP, identified certain weaknesses of the programme and suggested measures for further improvement. However John and Chattukulam observed that institutions created with state patronage would not serve the interest of democracy at the grassroots level. B. Mohanan (2002) studied the reasons for low participation in the *grama sabha* meetings in Kerala and arrived at the conclusion that people's participation in *grama sabha* in Kerala was drastically low because of the effect of civil society.

The extensive literature on Kerala's decentralisation movement can be grouped into two distinct categories. The academic writings on Panchayati Raj Institutions and democratic decentralisation up to 1996 constitute the first category. The second category of literature started burgeoning ever since the launching of people's campaign for decentralized planning and development. The post-1996 literature could be classified into four groups. Firstly, the insider's view as presented by Thomas Isaac and his associate-activists in the campaign for decentralisation. The extensive writings which have assessed and reassessed the merits and demerits of PCDP from a purely academic point of view from the second category of literature. The debates on the ideology of people's plan campaign represent the third category. Analysis by the intellectuals of the far-left school viewed it as the implementation of the neo-liberal agenda of governance. Finally, the writings of the foreign scholars who projected Kerala's decentralized democracy as a viable alternative to corporate dominated globalization. However, the contextual and domestic compulsions that necessitated the launching of the programme have not received adequate attention.

Efforts at Democratic Decentralisation in Kerala

The history of efforts at democratic decentralisation in Kerala goes back to the early days of formation of the State. The Administrative Reforms Committee (1958) under the Chairmanship of the then Chief Minister, EMS Namboodiripad, suggested a two-tier local government set up with Panchayats and Municipalities at the grassroots level and District Councils at the district level. The District Council Bill was introduced in the Kerala State Assembly in 1958. But the bill could not get passed because the EMS Government was dismissed by the Central Government and the Assembly was dissolved in 1959. In 1967 the second EMS Government wanted to enact the two-tier local government set up. The Kerala Panchayati Raj Bill was introduced in 1967. The Government resigned in 1969 and the bill lapsed. A Kerala District Administration Bill was passed by the Congress Government headed by A. K. Antony in 1979 which was originally introduced in 1971 and re-introduced in 1978 but no attempt was made to implement it till 1987. The LDF Government of E. K. Nayanar (1987-91) took measures to implement the Act. Elections to District Councils were held in February 1990. In the next Assembly Elections the LDF lost power and UDF Government under the leadership of Congress leader Karunakaran came to power. The UDF Government of Karunakaran took back all functions and powers transferred to the District Council in the very first decision of the new government.

It is at this juncture that the Government of India came out with the 73rd and 74th Amendments to the Constitution of India to have uniform pattern of local bodies all over India and to provide constitutional status to them.

Kerala's experiment with decentralisation has always been affected by the sharp political division in the state on rightist and leftist lines ever since the dislodging of the first Communist Government through the so-called liberation struggle. The two major coalitions of Political Parties the Left Democratic Front (LDF) and the United Democratic Front (UDF) have approached the question of democratic decentralisation with contrasting interests and ideas. It has been well-documented that the LDF tried to push forward the decentralization programme earnestly whenever they controlled the State Government. However, Kerala could not succeed to present a viable model of decentralized governance till the PCDP was launched in 1996 because of the alternating of governments between LDF and UDF on every five year intervals. The PCDP has provided an opportunity for both protagonists and opponents of decentralization for learning and experiencing grassroots democracy.

The campaign for decentralised planning and local democracy was in fact, a clear departure from the existing strategies and programmes of the left in Kerala. In the context of the serious setback suffered by the Communist movement at the global level in the aftermath of the demise of Soviet Union, the CPI(M) leadership in the state might have felt that if the CPI (M) was not addressing the development crisis of the state the party might be facing the threat of redundancy. In fact, this is not the first time that the CPI (M) is coming out with a new agenda for action for the attainment of its brand of socialism. Krishnaji has identified three such phases in the history of communist movement in Kerala. The first one was before the formation of the State in 1956 when the communists were engaging exclusively in class struggle along "orthodox" lines on behalf of workers and peasants, marked by much violence. In the second period from 1957 to the early 1970s the communists experimented with ways of both ruling the state under the Indian democracy and transforming property relations to the extent possible with out giving up militancy. The third phase is from 1970s which is characterized by the total absorption of the communists in the electoral politics (Krishnaji 2007).The kind of total absorption of the communists in the electoral politics as encapsulated by Krishnaji is the creative response to contextual compulsions and challenges.

The Crisis Narrative and the Left Response

In the late eighties and early nineties several studies questioned sustainability of the celebrated Kerala model of development because of the absence of the support system of required level of economic growth.

This phenomenon of social development sans economic growth has been explained in terms of the redistribution strategy adopted by successive progressive governments of the State in response to public action through mass mobilisation. In the eighties and early nineties, the left intellectuals in the state had also started subscribing the view that Kerala model of development was facing a severe crisis of sustainability. Social sector achievements could not be maintained further without addressing the issue of sluggish economic growth. They had arrived at the conclusion that without increasing production and productivity in agriculture and petty production sectors, the state would fall into the morass of deep crisis.

At this juncture it is pertinent to have a look at the left response as explained by Thomas Isaac, the chief activist of the people's plan campaign. He refers to various studies undertaken by scholars of the Centre for Development Studies (CDS, Trivandrum) and the speeches and writings of EMS Namboodirpad.

In 1991, CDS Economist, Dr. Krishnan came out with empirical evidence that the rate of growth of wages was higher than the rate of growth of productivity in the state.

Even before that in 1989 EMS Namboodiripad published a pamphlet entitled *Politics of Development* in which he proposed the need for a new political culture in the state for development. Since then he had been articulating his views for a new strategy. For instance in 1991 as a response to Dr. Krishnan's findings he said self critically:

> "I don't claim that the approach of the workers and peasant organizations and political parties leading them are above fault. While they struggle for their rights and demands they have to realize the importance of improving production and productivity in agriculture and industry. Mass organizations of workers and peasants and other sections of people and political parties giving leadership to them have to come forward to increase production in the public and private sectors and help to mobilize capital for social investment. I want to publicly state our commitment to rectify mistakes, if any, in this respect from our side" (EMS in 1991 as quoted by Thomas Isaac, 2000:45). EMS was bold enough to admit the fact that the problem of sluggish economic growth, was partly due to the mobilization strategies of the communist party. He candidly admitted that while organizing struggles for rights and demands, the mass organizations did not pay due attention to issues related to production and productivity. He further publicly expressed his commitment to rectify mistakes, if any.

Further, he said that leaders and workers of mass organizations had to come forward to increase production and productivity in both public and private sector. Another most significant point in the statement quoted above is his views on the role of mass organizations in helping to mobilize capital for social investment. In another occasion he said:

> "Kerala faces today an intense economic crisis in production—agricultural and industrial. I am inclined to believe that while we have spent much time and attention on 'social sector' issues of welfare and improvement of the living standards of the people we have not paid enough attention to or adequate concern for pressing problems of economic growth and material production. I

make a request: let not the praise that scholars shower on Kerala for its achievements divert attention from the intense economic crisis that we face. We are behind other states of India in respect of economic growth and a solution to this crisis brooks no delay. We can ignore our backwardness in respect of employment and production only at our own peril" (EMS 1994 as cited in Isaac 2000:44).

He admitted that Kerala is behind other states in India in respect of economic growth and generation of employments. He had reasserted his views that the organized strength of the mass organization could be mobilized for increasing production and productivity:

"Our greatest assets are our mass organisation and the democratic consciousness of our people. The combined strength of all mass organisations in the state is about ten million. Besides, there is a vast net work of cooperative organisations of the library and literary movements. I am aware that there are some people who consider all these to be the bane of Kerala society. I have devoted my life to mobilizing the people for radical transformation of our society, and I cannot but disagree with such perceptions. I feel that one big question that we face is whether the organized strength and political consciousness of our people can be used to increase production and productivity. I would like to answer in the affirmative" (EMS 1994 as quoted by Thomas Isaac, 200:26).We have reproduced the excerpts from the writings and speeches of EMS Namboodiripad as quoted by Thomas Isaac to substantiate that the theoretical base of the campaign had been provided by no less a person than EMS, the veteran theoretician and tactician. From the extracts cited above we could see the following. Firstly, EMS in unequivocal terms underlined the importance of production and productivity for sustaining the achievements in social sector. Secondly, we should do all possible to overcome the challenges of economic growth and past mistakes had to be corrected. Thirdly, he articulated the view that the organized strength of mass movements should be used for increasing production and productivity.

Marxist In-house Dialogue

CPI (M) continued the development debate initiated by EMS on its own platform. A Round Table was organized under the auspices of the theoretical of journal of CPM in Kerala. Left political party leaders and academics participated in it. A discussion document was prepared and submitted to the party for further debate and action.

The starting point of the discussion document was reference to the Kerala model of development with its social sector achievements and underlined the following:

Kerala has been successful in providing the basic needs of the people. Kerala's achievements have resulted from redistributive strategies in response to mass pressure from below. The left carries forward the progressive legacy of earlier social reform movements. The struggle of the left has not been only for land reforms and wage increases, but for the right to shelter, education, health care, safe drinking water and other basic needs. The social sector achievements did not have a complementary positive impact on economic growth. Despite land reforms there was no remarkable improvement in agricultural productivity. Despite educational expansion industrial modernization and diversification remained retarded. As a result unemployment was three times the national average. The quality of the social infrastructure was deteriorating. The fiscal crisis of the state was rendering it incapable of intervening in the crisis. In the absence of economic growth it would not be possible to sustain redistribution strategies. The economic stagnation had serious political implications – unemployment, growth of caste based movements etc. Right wing ideologies were attacking the left that the left had no programme for increasing production. They said stagnation resulted from the redistribution strategies of the left. The critics said that (1) the left had fulfilled its historic role in bringing about more equitable distribution and (2) now it should make way for market forces in order to achieve rapid growth.

On the basis of the debate initiated by EMS an International Congress on Kerala Studies was organized in August 1994 under the auspices of AKG Centre for Research and Studies. According to Thomas Isaac and other organizers of the conference the International Congress on Kerala studies was "an important landmark in the move towards a broad social consensus on the development of the state". As a result of continuous discussions and debates a coherent strategy with two pillars was evolved by 1996 to address the development crisis of the state. The first pillar is "resolute state intervention" in power sector and inviting private capital in electronics, light engineering and other industries, where the state had comparative advantage. The second pillar which is considered as the "centre piece" of the strategy was decentralization with the involvement of the masses for increasing productivity in small scale sectors and to improve the quality of life in public services.

Thus, the people's plan Campaign is a product of a dialogue among the left intellectuals in Kerala about the crisis that gripped the much publicized Kerala Model of Development. The state has achieved high quality of life without proportionate increase in economic growth. This is an outcome of mobilization of masses by left forces for redistribution of wealth and appropriate government intervention. But by the end of the eighties this development model had fallen into a severe crisis because of stagnation in production sectors and quality erosion in service sectors. As has already been noted following are the problems identified in productive sector: *(i)* the virtual stagnation of the agricultural sector; *(ii)* the deplorably lower level of productivity of important crops; *(iii)* growing apathy among cultivators; *(iv)* structural decay of the industrial sector dominated by ailing traditional industries; *(v)* rapid deterioration of power situation and *(vi)* overburdening of fragile ecosystem etc.

Krishnaji observes, "the efforts culminated in a massive 'people's campaign for decentralized planning', and later to the implementation itself, following an LDF victory in 1996...... EMS repeatedly emphasized his faith in decentralization as a means for helping the poor in their day-to-day struggles against oppression and exploitation. He also talked about and wrote about amicable solutions to be found through collective bargaining and discussions. The ideology formulated new during the 1990s had thus elements of pragmatic compromise, tinged by voluntarism: hopes about whole communities participating in a planned economic betterment of the poor. The implementation of the scheme in 1996, with the devolution of substantial part of plan funds to the local village bodies, was an act of rare political daring"

(Krishnaji, 2007). Krishnaji has, in fact, captured the meaning and content of the decentralized planning movement when he had written that it was a pragmatic compromise tinged with voluntarism.

Contributions of Younger Marxists of Kerala

As has rightly been observed by Krishnaji, the programme formulated in 1990s is a pragmatic compromise and an act of rare political daring due to domestic compulsions that it is partly a creation of setbacks for communist movements the world over in the context of demise of Soviet Union. No doubt EMS laid the foundation for it. However, the whole complex edifice of people's plan campaign has been built brick by brick by the comparatively younger generation of Marxists of Kerala. About this Richard Franke raises two questions."Can we go beyond the earlier Kerala model of public action to generate a high material quality of life through redistribution by adding to that model a mechanism for an egalitarian strategy of growth? And if we wanted to do that what would be the fuel?" Franke himself answers these questions thus. He is of the opinion that the new generation activists of Kerala had come to realize by 1980s certain facts about the new world. While maintaining intense respect for the sacrifice and idealism of the older activists for their fight for land reforms and higher wages and benefits for the poor, they found immense potentialities offered by non-violent action for social change. They have been inspired by Gramsci's thinking rather than by the long march of Mao's army. Also they have realized that time has come to move beyond traditional activism of the left in the spheres of land reforms, wage increase, improving working conditions and overcoming caste discriminations to newer frontiers of gender equity, environmental protection and expanding democracy through building community. They felt that struggles would have to become less mechanical and more democratic and participatory. Here Franke raises another question. Why did they arrive at this historically significant breakthrough? He answers: "I can only tell you at this time that the US movements of the 1960s had a profound effect on their thinking. And the evolution of the Italian communists with their emphasis on cooperatives and local government accountability struck strong chords in Kerala. The collapse of the Soviet Union in turn welcomed the position of the old left forces and created an opening for the younger activists who were reading green and feminist literature. And looming behind all these intellectual developments was Mahatma Gandhi, whose teachings on village self-sufficiency, exemplary simple life style, and economic growth as a means to benefit the most needy have continued to inspire each new generation of activists in Kerala" (Franke, 2001).

According to Franke the new generation Marxists of Kerala has been influenced by green and feminist literature as also by the writing of Gramsci and teachings of Mahatma Gandhi. Richard Franke is the academic collaborator of Thomas Isaac. Therefore his narrative about the orientation of the younger generation of the Marxists bears the authenticity of an insider. The new role of the younger generation Marxists of Kerala has been succinctly summarized by Patrick Heller as an attempt to 'de-Leninise' CPI (M) in Kerala. Heller writes that historically CPI (M) does not have any intense affinity for democratic decentralization and the organizing principle of that party is democratic centralism. Then why the key elements in CPI (M) embraced decentralisation?

To answer this question two developments have to be singled out, according to Heller. "First, the party has come to recognize the limits of its electoral appeal and in a context of competitive party politics has identified decentralization as encompassing a set of interests and issues that can appeal to new post-class struggle constituencies. Second, the embrace of decentralization marks a tacit recognition of that the redistributive capacities of the developmental state have exhausted themselves. If a strong, centralized and interventionist state did secure many of the benefits associated with the Kerala model, the second generation social development challenges Kerala faces call for a fundamentally different mode of governance" (Heller, 2000).

Thus, the launching of the campaign for decentralized democracy and participatory planning is an outcome of the burning desire of the younger activists with in the CPI (M) with the blessings of EMS to create newer institutions, on the solid foundations of achievements of yester years, that could address the challenges of environmental degradation, gender equity and above all economic growth.

PCDP and Economic Growth

Over a period of ten years, by utilizing the funds devolved to the local bodies, several kilometers of new roads in rural areas have been constructed. Houses for homeless have been constructed, drinking water projects implemented with community participation. Krishnaji observes:

> "The results of Kerala's democratic decentralization experience show in fact that a major part of the plan funds had gone in support of the so-called social sector, through the construction and improvement of roads, move tangibly for provisions of public toilets and houses for the poor and so on" (Krishnaji, 2007).

When it comes to production and productivity the record of PCDP is not on par with achievements in infrastructure and allied sectors. It has been reported that the projects under taken particularly in agriculture sectors, are not sustainable. However revival of cultivation of labour intensive crops such as paddy is difficult because of land ownership pattern and because of "non-availability of labour for time bound operations such as harvesting and other types of mass work. Labour in Kerala is withdrawing from manual work" (Krishnaji, 2007). At the same time in several places micro-enterprises have been started by *Kudumbasree* cooperatives and self-help groups. These units are now successful in establishing backward and forward linkages. In certain locations marketing companies have been registered for marketing of the products of micro enterprises on common brand name (Thomas Isaac, 2007). After observing the PCDP for the first three years Franke has written that thousands of new acres of land have been brought into cultivation. It recorded an increase of 5.6 per cent. The long stagnated agriculture sector, recorded a growth in 1988-99 by 3.82 per cent compared with an average of 1.3 per cent in the previous 3 years. Industrial sector rose by 7.2 per cent and more than 100,000 new jobs were created. It represents possible 5 per cent decrease in the employment rate of Kerala (Franke, 2000).

In this context it would be appropriate to have a brief mention about recent trends in economic growth of Kerala. Achin Chakraborty, K.P. Kannan, P.D Jeromi and a number of other economists have, of late, reported that Kerala economy is growing. Chakraborty observes that "growth has not eluded Kerala after all".

He says that Kerala's SDP has been growing at a rate closer between Kerala's achievements in education overseas migration of job seekers and flow of remittance at phenomenal proportions (Achin Chakraborty, 2005).

Similarly, K.P. Kannan (2005) talks about a turn around in economic growth. He is of the opinion that the state which has shown high human development and low economic growth is of late, exhibiting a new phenomenon of accelerated economic growth since the late 1980s. This is a contribution of economic reforms and massive flow of remittances. Now the challenge is addressing the issue of unemployment of its educated youth and ensuring equitable participation to women in all walks of life. P.D. Jeromi (2003) has made an analysis of the performance of Kerala in different sectors and found that, the state has recorded growth in the tertiary sector. According to him there is a revival in the growth of the state income during the 1990s from a phase of low growth during the eighties.

All these economists have noted that the growth recorded is in the tertiary sector only with the significant share of tertiary sector the state's economy has become a service oriented economy. There is persistent decline in food grain production and the state continues to be industrially backward (Jeromi, 2003).

The economic growth that has been reported by leading economists coincides roughly with the period of PCDP. This is not to say that PCDP is responsible for the reported economic growth. However, it has a role in bringing in certain attitudinal changes that in turn might have promoted investment in the tertiary sector. Even though the productive sector did not show impressive growth, the trends of growth recorded in tertiary sector, brings home the point that the hurdles in the way of capital development is being removed. No doubt a new entrepreneurial culture is in the making in Kerala. A new work ethics is being shaped. There are concrete evidences to show that the state is gradually making a departure from the century old agitation mode.

The Arduous Journey Through the New Development Culture

Decentralised planning campaign which has now completed ten years of its implementation is definitely a revolutionary decision and bold step in the history of planned development in India. This internationally noted programme has received both laurels and brickbats; and it is quite natural while considering the complexities and dimensions of the programme.

The most important feature that could be observed about the programme is that it deviated from the mainstream theory of people's participation and local governance as propagated by World Bank. The criticism that Thomas Isaac and other plan activists facilitated the backdoor entry of World Bank's neo-liberal agenda of development has no basis at all. In the World Bank concept of decentralized governance and participatory development NGOs got a prominent place. In the people's plan campaign NGOs did not get accommodated. Instead, the constitutionally established Local Self-Government Institutions themselves prepared their plan proposals with people's participation. To mobilize people at the local level as a support system to LSGIs, the People's Science Movement in Kerala (KSSP) took the lead role assisted by individual volunteers drawn from among school, college, university teachers and sectoral organisations of State Government employees, all affiliated to CPI (M).

Here it is noteworthy that the teachers and government employees who took part in People's Plan activities were not officially representing their sectoral organisations; they participated in PCDP activities as members of KSSP. It is very significant to note that the sectoral organisations of CPI (M) did not cooperate with PCDP as it was desired by EMS.

The mass organizations have been given training to work on the basis of their understanding of the economic, social and cultural issues in the sector they are operating. For instance a union in the industrial sector would be organizing agitations to get their demands accepted. Similarly agricultural workers union, students union, teachers' organizations, women's associations etc., would be organizing and articulating their demands through agitation methods. In other words, the methods of all mass organizations are that of agitation.

All on a sudden putting agitation on backburner and involving in development work was unthinkable for a sizeable section of the organized masses, if not all. The important aspect of Kerala's development experience has been the intervention of the state to bring about distributive justice. The compelling factor in this kind of state intervention is that it is the response of the state to the pressures and demands of common people articulated through mass movements.

The CPI (M) can take the credit for organizing all sections of the people in Kerala. The organizations of government employees, teachers, students and labourers are very vocal in articulating their sectarian demands. These organizations controlled mainly by CPI (M), till the initiation of People's Plan, were not ready to make minor sacrifices for overall growth and welfare of the state as a whole. This has created a situation where the political society in Kerala has become an arena for pressurizing the government for the attainment of sectarian demand; no concern for production and productivity.

EMS in the last few years of his life devoted his intellectual prowess to re-canalize the organized strength and political consciousness of mass organizations to increase production and productivity.

Even though the mass organizations of CPI (M) did not participate in PCDP programmes officially, the involvement of several members of various organizations through the KSSP route did have a "de-schooling" effect on mass organizations in Kerala. This is evident from the slow percolation of changes in the nature of production relations in Kerala. The trade union militancy for which Kerala was known till the eighties is waning rapidly. The state is now encouraging private investment. The *Bandh/Harthal* culture etched in Malayalee psyche over several decades shows a trend of getting erased. It is very clear that the campaign for democratic decentralization and participatory planning succeeded in ushering in an attitudinal change of long-term import in the organized sector of Kerala. A gradual transition from agitation mode to a kind of politics of community integration is in the making.

This is in fact a major departure from the past. From the social history of Kerala roughly from 15th century onwards one could glean the way that the typical Malayalee work culture got shaped and got transmitted through generations. Even though protestant Christianity embarked on Kerala shores around fourteenth century the protestant work ethics failed to percolate into the *Keralam* of that age because caste system controlled the relations of production.

The colonial capitalism did have a chain effect on production relations in Travancore and Cochin. About that Geneveve Lemercinier writes: "our empirical analysis also revealed diversity in the reaction of the social actors to the changes brought about in the traditional economic order by the particular form of colonialism that developed in Travancore. Now this diversity was not unrelated to caste belonging. Without wishing to generalise these observations so as to include all their members, it would appear that certain castes and similar groups entered more easily than others into this process of change. We have already noted, indeed, that some Syrian Christians had readily involved themselves in big agricultural and commercial projects...... A rather similar attitude could be observed among the Ezhavas who very quickly oriented their cultivation towards export crops, and developed small manufacturing industries for the process of coconut fibers and the production of coir" (Lemercinier, 1974:179).

It is significant to note that on the plane of social relations of production massive changes had been introduced by colonial capitalism. It had helped the emergence of local entrepreneurs particularly among Syrian Christians. But this trend did not sustain. The new education system, that was emerging, did not help the development of productive forces in the rural milieu because the objective was oriented towards serving the interests of colonial capitalism. Secondly, "the cultural models involved in the production of kinship relation were not damaged......so that the persistence of rural dominance in the economy created conditions favourable to the reproduction of a culture supporting the stability of practices of traditional type" (*Ibid.*, p. 185).

In short the feudal values had reproduced it whatever be the mode of production. This in turn had shaped very much the nature of social reform movements also. The social psyche of the right (over) conscious Malayalee whose life ambition had been to enter into the government bureaucracy irrespective of the size of pay packet had thus been formed. Employment in the bureaucratic structure of the government had become the criterion of social status. This had had twin effect. Firstly, the entrepreneurial talent started sprouting during the initial period of introduction of colonial capitalism did not flourish. The economic behaviour of the Syrian Christians and Ezhavas stand testimony to it. The Syrian Christians had entered into money lending business rather than taking the risk of investing in production sector. If at all they had invested in production sector it was outside the territorial boundary of Kerala. Secondly, the new education system introduced by the colonial power grew in such a way that it produced only stenographers, typists, clerks and teachers (PM Mathew, 2005). No concerted effort during the colonial period or even after the attainment of freedom towards entrepreneurial talent development.

The left in Kerala used to boast that they are the inheritors of the progressive legacy of the social reform movements of the pre-independent period. They are, in fact, the inheritors of not only the positive legacy of social reform movements but the negative legacy also. We have noticed that Protestant Christianity had failed to induct protestant work culture into Kerala society. Similarly, the Marxists of Kerala mobilized the masses for redistribution of wealth, without touching the dominant values of the caste system; and it is to be reiterated that they have been successful in the re-distribution of wealth. As the way Protestant Christianity failed to bring in protestant ethics, the communist movement has, by and large, failed to utilize the collective strength of their mass organizations for increasing production and productivity side by side with the agitations for maximizing the welfare of the working class.

In the context of far reaching changes at the global level as also the compulsions of the domestic situation, including the political demography of the state, the CPI (M) was forced to come out with a strategy that could ensure a complete break with the historical legacy of negative attitude towards production and productivity.

Concluding Observations

From the foregoing, it is quite clear that the politics of democratic decentralisation and campaign for people's planning initiated in Kerala is the outcome of the quest for a new agenda for action in response to the development challenges of the state political demography and the contextual compulsions. It evolved through the writings of EMS, specifically between 1989 and 1994. In fact, democratic decentralisation was a pet theme of EMS from the early fifties. However, the people's plan phase of communists' engagement with decentralization is radically different from ideas and strategies of the earlier period. Apart from EMS' appeal for utilizing the collective strength of mass organizations for production and productivity, the new generation Marxists of Kerala has contributed substantially to the operationalisation of the new politics of democracy at the grassroots level with the objective of breaking the limits and limitations imposed by the political demography. The attempts of the younger activists of the party has been to rescue the party becoming redundant in the context of new challenges to socialist movements the world over as also further advancement of the left in the state by befriending the social formations that are historically hostile to communism in the state.

It is clear that more than anything else circumstances within the state compelled EMS to formulate a new strategy with the active assistance of the new generation activists to replace partly the orthodox lines of class struggles on behalf of masses marked by agitation and resultant violence. PCDP did not bring massive increases in economic productivity. However, Kerala society's attitude towards economic production and productivity has changed tremendously after the implementation of PCDP. Previously there was organised resistance against private investment. In other words, the focus of the state has all along been on distribution rather than growth of income and therefore the society developed a kind of negative attitude towards private sector investment. The general perception has been that private investment is a means of exploitation of workers. Now attitudinal changes are on the horizon of Kerala society. Private investment is being promoted. The global investors meet during LDF regime and the singing of smart city agreement for investment in information technology between the LDF Government and the Dubai based company vouch for the changing attitude towards private investment. Kerala society, of late, is not patronising trade union militancy. The state is no longer investor unfriendly. On the whole, the Kerala's political culture of inflated consciousness about one's own rights that got shaped through a hundred years social history and that stood in the way of economic growth started showing signs of melting out. Thus a new culture of development rooted very well in the dynamics of parliamentary democracy is in the making, thanks to democratic decentralisation initiative. For the new generation Marxists of Kerala Gramsci as also Mahatma Gandhi are equally important for developing strategies for overcoming the demographic limitations of the left in Kerala.

The mainstream print media of Kerala who sensationalised the campaign, it seems, have failed to grasp the meaning of parliamentary road to socialism and it's far reaching implications, for the society and polity of Kerala, by way of the 'de-leninising' process in the programme CPI (M).

REFERENCES

Achin, Chakraborty, 'Kerala's Changing Development Narratives', *Economic and Politica Weekly,* Vol XL No.6 Feb.5, 2005, pp. 541-47.

Franke, Richard, W. Franke (1996): *Life is a Little Better: Redistribution as a Development Strategy in Nadhur Village, Kerala,* New Delhi, Promilla and Company Publishers, 1996.

Richard, W. Franke and Barbara H. Chasin, *Kerala: Radical Reform as Development in an Indian State,* Oakland, C.A. Food First, Second Edition, Also New Delhi, Promilla and Company Publishers, 1994.

Richard, W. Franke and Barbara H. Chasin, 'Power to the Malayalee People'. *Economic and Political Weekly,* Vol. 32, No. 48, 1997, pp. 3061-68.

Richard, W. Franke and Barbara H. Chasin, 'Fueling Economic Growth Through Democratic Participation' http://chss.montclair.edu/anthro/fuelinggrowth.htm, 2001.

Genevieve Lemercinier, *Religion and Ideology in Kerala,* ISDA, Trivandrum, 1994.

Government of Kerala, State Planning Board (1996): *Janakeeyaasootrana Prasthanan: A Handbook* (Malayalam), 1996.

K.P. Kannan, 'Kerala's Turn around in Economic Growth', *Economic and Political Weekly,* Vol. XL, No. 6, 2005, pp. 548-53.

N. Krishnaji, 'Kerala Milestones: On Parliamentary Road to Socialism', *Economic and Political Weekly,* Vol. XLII No. 23, 2007, pp. 2169-76.

B. Mohanan, 'Controlling Corruption at the Grassroots: Lessons from a Decentralised Participatory Development Administration', *ISDA Journal,* Vol. 8, No. 2, 3 and 4, April-December, 1998, pp. 245-65.

B. Mohanan, 'Pradeshika Jenadhipathyavum Keraleeya Civil Samooham', *Bharanachakram,* (Malayalam) Book 27, Vol. 12, December, 2002, pp. 8-11.

B. Mohanan, 'Decentralised Governance and Development in the Context of Globalisation: Lessons from Kerala', *ISDA Journal,* Vol. 13, No. 2, April-June, 2003, pp. 417-55.

B. Mohanan, 'Decentralised Planning and Development in the Context of Globalisation: Lessons from Kerala', *South Asia Politics,* July 2003, pp. 36-42.

B. Mohanan, *Decentralised Governance and Participatory Development: Issues, Constraints and Prospects*, Concept Publishing Company, New Delhi, 2005.

S. Mohana Kumar, 'From People's Plan to Plan sans People', *Economic and Political Weekly*, Vol. 36, No. 16, 2002, pp. 1492-7.

Nair, Rajendran V. Nair (1999): 'Political Socialisation and Empowerment of Women: Experience from the People's Plan Campaign', *ISDA Journal*, Vol. 9, No. 4, October-December, 1999, pp. 263-94.

V.K. Sukumaran Nair,(1992): 'Decentralisation should Start with Political Parties' *ISDA Journal*, Vol. 2, No. 4, October-December, 1992, pp. 267-72.

EMS Namboodiripad, 'Democratic Decentralisation in Kerala Today', *ISDA Journal*, Vol. 2, No. 4, Oct.-Dec., 1992, pp. 263-65.

Patric Heller,'The Politics of Decentralisation in Kerala', South Africa and Porto Alegre", http://localgovkerala.net/LSGD Links?Research/Books 12.asp, 2001.

T.M. Thomas Issac, *Local Democracy and Local Development: The People's Campaign for Decentralized Planning in Kerala*, New Delhi, Leftword Books, 2000.

T.M. Thomas Issac, Richard, W. Franke and M.P. Parameswaran,. (1997:'From Anti-feudalism to Sustainable Development: The Kerala Peoples Science Movement', *Bulletin of Concerned Asian Scholars* 29 (3), 1997, pp. 34-44.

T.M. Thomas Isaac, The Politics of Democratic Decentralisation (Malayalam), DC Books, Kottayam, 2005.

World Bank, *Entering the 21st Century: World Development Report 1999/2000*, New York, Oxford University Press, 1999a.

World Bank, *Beyond the Center: Decentralising the State*, Washington, D.C., The World Bank, 1999 b.

World Bank, *World Development Report: The Challenge of Development*, New York, Oxford University Press, 1991c.

13

Capacity Building for Rural Development Personnel and Panchayati Raj Functionaries in India

M. L. SANTHANAM

Introduction

The impetus to the development of the country is being given by the Panchayati Raj system also known as Local Self-Government. Thanks to the vision of Sri Rajivi Gandhi, the late Prime Minister of India who believed that development of India is possible by strengthening the grassroots institutions. These institutions are peoples. organisations comprised of groups of individuals from the area who know the cultural, social, environmental and economic conditions of the locale. It is necessary that they "need to be prepared to understand the programme, implement them successfully and evaluate to see the effectiveness of these programmes. This requires that they need to undergo a process of capacity building to make them efficient and effective in taking the programmes to the people of the area. This is usually done by organising a number of training programmes to all the categories of elected representatives and the officials designated to implement the programmes. Training is a tool for capacity building.

In this chapter an attempt is made to understand the concept of Capacity building and present a systems approach to training which would fulfill the needs of the participants.

Concept of Capacity Building

Having realised the importance of making people to be fully competent to face all eventualities, it is time to understand what capacity building mean.

The lead within the UN system for action and thinking in this area was given to UNDP and it has offered guidance to its staff and governments on what since the early 1970's. This involved building up the ability of 'basic national organisations, in areas such as civil aviation, meteorology, agriculture, health, nutrition to do their tasks well. All UN specialised agencies were supposed to be active in support of capacity building in the areas for which they were technically qualified e.g. FAO for the rural sector and agriculture, WHO for health etc., but they achieved mixed results

Specifically, capacity building encompasses the country's human, scientific, technological, organisational, institutional and resource capabilities. A fundamental goal of capacity building is to enhance the ability to evaluate and address the crucial questions related to policy choices and modes of implementation among development options, based on an understanding of environment potentials and limits and of needs perceived by the people of the country concerned.

In 1991, UNDP and the International Institute for' Hydraulic and Environmental Engineering defined 'capacity building' as

- the creation of an enabling environment with appropriate policy and legal frameworks;
- institutional development, including community participation (of women in particular); and
- human resources development and strengthening of managerial systems.

Capacity building may also be defined as "activities which strengthen the knowledge, abilities, skills and behaviour of individuals and improve institutional structures and processes such that the organisation can efficiently meet its mission and goals in a sustainable way."

UNDP recognises that capacity building as a long-term, continuing process. In which all stakeholders participate (ministries, local authorities, non-governmental organisations, professional associations, academics and others).

Capacity building often refers to assistance which is provided to entities, usually developing country societies, which have a need to develop a certain skill or competence, or for general upgrading of performance ability. Most capacity is built by societies themselves, sometimes in the public, sometimes in the non-governmental and sometimes in the private sector.

Why Capacity Building is Needed?

- The issue of capacity is critical and the scale of need is enormous, but appreciation of the problem is low.
- The link between needs and supply is weak.
- There is a lack of realistic funding.
- There is need for support for change.
- Training institutions are isolated—communications are poor.
- Development of teaching materials is inefficient.
- Alternative ways of capacity building are not adequately recognised.

Capacity Building is much more than Training

It includes the following:

- Human resource development, the process of equipping individuals with the understanding, skills and access to information, knowledge and training that enables them to perform effectively.
- Organisational development, the elaboration of management structures, processes and procedures, not only within organisations but also the management of relationships between the different organisations and sectors (public, private and community).
- Institutional and legal framework development, making legal and regulatory changes to enable organisations, institutions and agencies at all levels and in all sectors to enhance their capacities.

Who are the Clients?

The needs for capacity building are always changing. There are no ready solutions, and any programme must be appropriate for the local situation and organisation.

Local Government, Communities and NGOs are the main clients, but central government and the private commercial sector also need support. Community groups, often with strong NGO support, need to improve their capacity to plan, organise and manage their neighbourhoods. Departments of local government play an increasingly important role in enabling community groups to enhance their capacities and effectiveness.

There are very direct implications for development education in the area of human resource capacity building since by definition the term (and the process) has education, both formal and non-formal, at its core.

In its broadest interpretation, *The Food and Agricultural Organisation* observes that capacity building encompasses Human Resource Development (HRD) as an essential part of development. It is based on the concept that education and training lie at the heart of development efforts and that without HRD most development interventions will be ineffective. It focuses on a series of actions directed at helping participants in the development process to increase their knowledge, skills and understandings and to develop the attitudes needed to bring about the desired developmental change.

Another essential mechanism for capacity building is partnership development. Partnerships give a local NGO access to: knowledge and skills; innovative and proven methodologies; networking and funding opportunities; replicable models for addressing community needs and managing resources; options for organisational management and governance; and strategies for advocacy, government relations and public outreach.

Components of Capacity Building

1. *Technology transfer*: The process by which innovations are diffused among service providers to improve how intervention effectiveness and scientific research is translated into programmes and practice.
2. *Technical assistance:* The provision and/or facilitation of culturally relevant and expert programmatic, scientific, and technical advice (mentoring/coaching) and support. CBB members provide assistance to grantees in areas such as organisational implementation, infrastructure development, adaptation and tailoring of programme behavioural interventions, and evaluation.
3. *Training*: Curricula development, delivery of curricula and coordination of training activities to increase the knowledge, skills and abilities of trainers, educators and service providers. Training focuses on the delivery of effective programme interventions and strategies, such as counselling

Training activities also include facilitation skills, recruitment strategies, adaptation and tailoring guidance that increases knowledge, skills, and abilities required to implement HIV prevention interventions, and programmes and services. Trainings are provided directly to service providers for implementation or to educators/trainers in a Train-the-Trainer (TOT) format for further dissemination. Facilitation of trainings is provided in English and Spanish.

4. *Information dissemination*: Distribution and sharing of relevant and current information through print materials, mass media, presentations, websites and the like.

Training as a Tool for Capacity Building

Training has become an integral part of the development of any organisation and capacity building of its personnel. Capacity building means enhancing the effective and efficient performance of the personnel on their job, by providing inputs such as knowledge, skills, communication, interpersonal relationship, motivation etc. Training is used as a tool for capacity building.

Training may be construed as an art and science of helping the employees and the management in acquiring knowledge and skills for achieving the objectives of the organisation. Training is performance oriented. Changes in behaviour can only be brought out if effective learning takes place. To achieve this purpose, the training programme and learning material should be systematically prepared keeping in mind the learners so that the desired change in behaviour can be obtained. Training facilitates improvement in knowledge, strengthening and developing new skills and aims at creating an environment for attitudinal change towards favourable direction.

In essence, training and development within the organisation is the acquisition of knowledge, skills and attitude, which enable the people to achieve current and future objectives. In short it can be said that the training and development can contribute to success of the organisation/programme for enabling the personnel to

- improve the performance of the job.
- improve the quality of the work and reduce the wastages and errors.

- Achieve job satisfaction.

  This can be achieved if the training programmes are well thought out, organised by following the training cycle, which involves –

- Job Analysis;
- Need Identification;
- Defining the Objectives of Programme;
- Specifying the Programme Content;
- Methodology Intended to be Followed;
- Evaluation of the programme; and
- Follow-up.

"Systems Approach" to Capacity Building

Derived from Greek word "SYSTEMA" means *"An organised Relationship among Functioning Units* or *Components."*

- System may also be defined as "an Orderly Grouping of Interdependent plan to achieve a specific Objective."
- Development of training can be viewed as a system and can be analysed into its sub-systems and how they interact with each other.
- A training system may be defined as rational arrangement of inputs, technology, people, material, events and process designed to elicit behavioural outputs increasing organisational effectiveness.

Systems Approach Provides Insights into the Domain of Training in Two Ways

Training can be viewed as a system which interacts with other systems such as infrastructure, Personnel selection, ergonomics, etc.

The development of training programme can itself be viewed as a system and can be analysed into its sub-systems and how they interact with each other.

In this chapter this approach is emphasised for improving the efficiency and effectiveness of the Rural Development training because of the fact that training programme is taken for granted by the participants, the training institutions and deputing agency which nominates/deputes their officers for training.

The Diagram given below Indicates the Process of this Approach

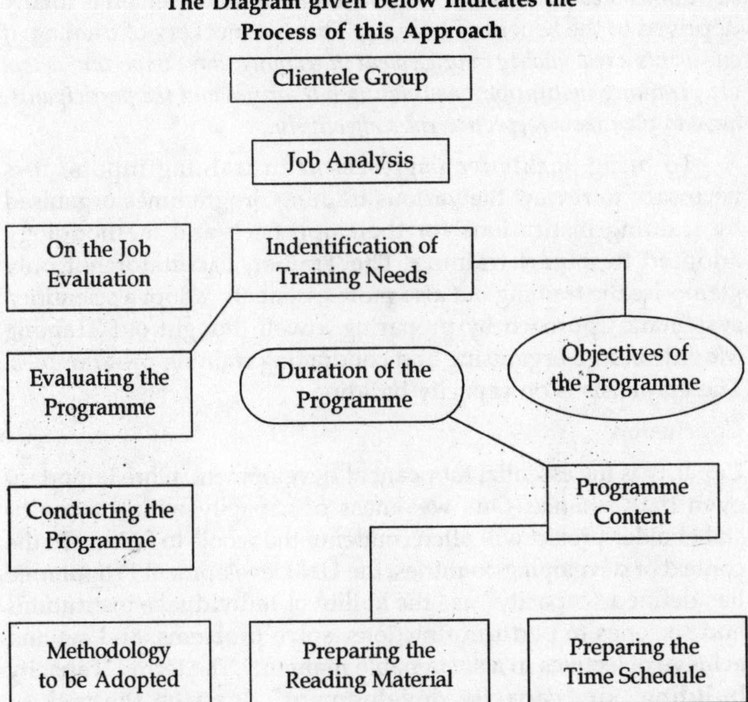

First of all, the participants come to the training programme with their own agenda and attend the training programme to achieve their personal goals.

It disheartens and disappoints to note that still today some of the training programmes are organised by some institutions and trainers by just preparing a time table only with scant respect to identify the need for training, defining the objectives and specifying the programme content. In short it can be said that a preparing a time-table and engaging few guest speakers according to their convenience to talk on the topics of their interest to the participants, arranging a sight seeing trip under the banner of Field Visit, is training. Further, it is observed that the nominating authorities depute some officers of their choice whose participation in the training programme would not improve the performance. To make it explicit, functionaries who are not wanted by the department or about to retire are deputed for training. Sometimes a particular official repeatedly attend the programmes at S.I.R.D., say about 6 to 7 times in a year whereas another person is totally deprived of the benefit of training. This is a mockery of training. *If one wants a real quality improvement in training, three important actors viz., training institution, nominating authorities and the participants, have to play their respective roles effectively.*

To bring *qualitative improvement* in training inputs, it is necessary to review the various training programmes organised by training institutions for their approach and methodology adopted to impart training. The Trainer/Facilitator not only glamorise the training but also more essentially adopt a scientific/ systematic approach by preparing a well thought out Training Module before organising and conducting training programmes. The emphasis is on capacity building

Conclusion

Capacity is the essential lubricant of development, more important even than finance. One weakness of capacity within a multi-stakeholder project will often condemn the whole to failure. In the context of developing countries, the UN Development Programme has defined "capacity" as "the ability of individuals, institutions and societies to perform functions, solve problems, and set and achieve objectives in a sustainable manner." The terms "capacity building" or "capacity development" describe the task of developing levels of human and institutional capacity. Whatever be the terminology, capacity building remains one of the most chaellenging functions of development.

REFERENCES

Internet clippings.
Lecture notes of self.

APPENDIX

Seventh Round Table of Ministers In-charge of Panchayati Raj—Jaipur, 17-19 December, 2004

Capacity Building and Training

1. Training and communication ought to reach all PRI functionaries and elected representatives, viz,
   - *(i)* Gram Panchayat Members, Chairpersons and Office bearers,
   - *(ii)* Intermediate Panchayat Members, Chairpersons and Office bearers,
   - *(iii)* District Panchayat Members, Chairpersons and Office bearers,
   - *(iv)* All officials concerned at National, State, District, Intermediate and Village level; and
   - *(v)* Standing Committee members at all levels.
2. There should be special effort made towards sensitising the media, political parties, representatives in the legislatures, civil society organisations and citizens,
3. There must be special campaigns for mobilisation of Gram Sabha members.
4. There must be special training for Women, SC/ST representatives as well as first time entrants into the Panchayat system within 3 months of their entry.
5. Training for PESA areas should be designed so as to have regard to the cultural traditions and special needs of tribal people.
6. Training and communication should not be viewed as a single one-time intervention but should be a continuous, ongoing process leading to enhanced sense of self-esteem and confidence. Training should cover both the "before" and "after" election periods. Initial training and communication should reach all elected representatives within one year.
7. For those panchayat members who need it, a functional literacy training course should be undertaken immediately after their elections.
8. The panchayats should be encouraged to have a sense of ownership of the training programmes and play a major role in designing content and mechanisms of training. To

this end, there must be representation for panchayat members in the governing boards of training institutions that cater to their needs.

9. Content of training should press on strategic and technical aspects and should be based on a systematic Training Needs Analysis arrived at through multi-stakeholder consultative workshops, which would precede the design of training modules and materials.
10. There should be a minimum core curriculum that is common across the States adapting to suit local contexts. Core curriculum should include:
    - *(i)* Vision on purna swaraj through Gram Swaraj;
    - *(ii)* Principles of secularism, equality and human rights emanating from the Constitution of India;
    - *(iii)* Gender equity and social justice;
    - *(iv)* Status of human development;
    - *(v)* Poverty alleviation;
    - *(vi)* Participatory planning, implementation and monitoring;
    - *(vii)* Right to information and transparency;
    - *(viii)* Social Audit; and
    - *(ix)* Rules and regulations covering Panchayati Raj.
11. Overall perspective of training must reinforce issues of social equity, gender sensitivity and justice among all participants in the process of govemance through panchayati raj, including all levels of the bureaucracy.
12. Thematic curriculum should include:
    - *(i)* Human Resource Management,
    - *(ii)* Natural Resources Management,
    - *(iii)* Disaster Management,
    - *(iv)* Financial management, including own resource management and accounting, and
    - *(v)* Sectoral approaches into providing basic human needs.
13. Training strategy should be inclusive, participative and interactive and a composite mix of various interventions:
    - *(i)* Face-to-face participatory training;
    - *(ii)* Exposure visits;
    - *(iii)* Peer training/learning;

(iv) Satellite training;

(v) Radio/cassettes/films;

(vi) Traditional means of communication;

(vii) Newsletters, updates and digests of replies to *Frequently Asked Questions;* and

(viii) Resource centers and Help Desks for Panchayats.

14. Training content and processes should be relevant to the ground reality of elected representatives. It should continue to develop and evolve based on feedback and impact assessment. Training should become a two-way process so that feedback can help in reforming the content and process of training, as also result in systemic changes in Panchayati and government functioning.
15. States should move towards formation of training networks and collectives to share experiences, learn from each other, and access material from each other. States should also institutionalise collaboration with community based organisations at the State, District, and Block level.
16. Training should inspire elected representatives to form federations or collectives and facilitate them to voice their demands for genuine devolution and development.
17. Trained members should be encouraged to become resource persons for further training of panchayat representatives, peer to peer learning, both within and outside the state through regional or national tie-ups should be encouraged and supported.
18. Training should include exposure to best practices through visits to other panchayats.
19. All open universities may tie-up with IGNOU and build linkages with the SIRDs and other like institutions engaged in training and capacity building.
20. Training programmes shall be designed especially for the secretarial and technical staff working with panchayats through institutions such as IGNOU. Such training programmes should lead to formal certification on achieving prescribed standards of learning.
21. Education in democracy and the constitutional role of panchayats as institutions of local self-government should be made part of school curricula.
22. It shall be the endeavour of the Central Government to

provide in as short a time as possible a panchayat capacity building fund through the Ministry of Panchayati Raj, which could include a certain percentage of central transfers specially earmarked for that purpose. Similarly, state governments should also create a Panchayat Capacity Building Fund for periodic training.

23. There should a national perspective plan on decentralised training and capacity building for all PRI functionaries with specific objectives time-frame and resources.
24. States can benefit by the use of pedagogy and training techniques with information accessible to all. The Ministry of Panchayati Raj could develop a repository of training programmes, including training resources and manuals developed by the Commonwealth. Development of master modules in training in issues of gender, poverty, mass communication etc., could also be developed.
25. Independent training impact assessment studies should be periodically undertaken to assess the outcomes of training and inform emerging needs for follow-up.
26. States shall work towards up gradation of training centers, such as SIRDs, and extension training centers at the district, block level and below.
27. With respect to the training needs of panchayati members from the Union Territories and States with Sixth Schedule areas, the Government of India would identify an SIRD or a group of institutions that could undertake the training.

14

Right to Information Act in India: Rhetoric and Reality

I. SATYA SUNDARAM

People's active participation in the development process has been recognised as an indispensable condition for the success of development schemes, particularly pro-poor programmes. Transparency and accountability are the bedrock of democracy.

The Supreme Court of India has from time-to-time interpreted right to receive and impart information (right to information) as part of the Article 19 of the Constitution. Thus, there should be an effective mechanism to put power of legislature, executive and even judiciary under the scrutiny of general public. A well-informed and enlightened society is vital for the successful working of democracy. It facilitates informed criticism and a better understanding of official policies and makes the public vigilant. Our experience shows that the right to expression is meaningless without the right to information (Kavaljit Singh, 15).

Information is power. Government department have a tendency to conceal information. To that extent, the quality of governance suffers. The Supreme Court, in its landmark decision in S.P. Gupta's case, way back in 1980, aptly observed: "No democratic government can survive without accountability and the basic postulate of accountability is that the people should have information about the functioning of the government. It is only if people knowhow government is functioning that they can fulfill the role which democracy assigns to them, and make democracy a really effective participatory democracy."

Past Effort

It is interesting to the note that some states had already passed Acts towards right to information. These states include : Rajasthan, Goa, Tamil Nadu, Madhya Pradesh, Karnataka, Maharashtra and Delhi. But, these Acts are not effective because of a large number of exemptions. Of course, the experience of Rajasthan was somewhat different as here a very strong grassroots movement for right to information had emerged (Bharat, Dogra, 2006 : 10).

The Representation of the People Act, 1951 has recently been amended. Under the newly added Section 33-A, a candidate is required to furnish in the nomination paper the following information : *(i)* accusation of any offense punishable with two or more years of imprisonment in any case including the framing of charges in pending case; and *(ii)* conviction of an offense and sentence of one or more than one year imprisonment in the form of affidavit.

The Water (Prevention and Control of Pollution) Act, 1974 and the Air (Prevention and Control of Pollution) Act, 1981 contain provisions for disclosure of information about air pollution. However, both of these laws allow for the withholding of information if disclosure is 'against the public interest'.

Under the Consumer Protection Act, 1986 the consumer has been given the right to be informed by the trader about the quality, quantity, potency, purity, standard and price of goods and services, as the case may be, so as to protect the consumer against unfair trade practices. This is intended to save the consumer from unfair trade practices.

Of course, the existing laws try to protect the right to information. For instance, the Factories Act, 1948 provide for compulsory disclosure of information to factory workers regarding dangers including health hazards and the measures to overcome such hazards arising from their exposure to dangerous materials.

The RTI Act

The Right to Information (RTI) Act has special relevance to the present Indian situation which has been besmirched by rampant corruption, nepotism, abuse of authority, misuse of funds, political interference in administration, vindictive harassment, of upright officials and judges, subversion of the due processes of law and justice and the growing nexus between politicians and criminals etc (M.K Heble, 1992:17).

The RTI Act came into effect from October 12, 2005, the important features of the Act are:

- The Act provide for appointment of information officers at various levels—national, state and district etc.
- There is a formidable list of 17 categories of information which a public authority is mandated to disseminate within 30 days. Of course, information relating to life and human rights should be provide within 48 hours only.
- The Act has fixed only nominal fee for providing the information. However, people living below the poverty line need not pay any fee.
- The information can be disseminated through the notice boards, newspapers, pubic announcements, media broadcaste, the internet, or any other means.
- Failure to provide the relevant information within a specified period will incur a penalty of Rs. 25,000. An aggrieved party may file an appeal before the Central Commission. The Courts have no jurisdiction in this matter.
- In the application, the information sought should be clearly mentioned. The reasons for seeking information need not be given.
- All administrative officers of public authorities have to appoint Public Information Officers (PIO). For any delay in providing information, the PIO will be punished with a penalty of Rs. 250 per day.

The Act defines information as any material in any form including records, documents, memos, e-mails, opinions, advice, press release, circulars, orders, logbooks, advices, press releases, circulars, orders, logbooks, contracts, reports, papers, samples, models, data, materials held in any electronic form and information relating to any private body which can be accessed by a public authority under any other law.

The act requires officials to take seriously Section 3 which makes it incumbent on public authorities to "maintain all records duly catalogued and indexed" and to provide "as much information suo motu to the public at regular intervals."

Thus, the RTI Act contains all important provisions which bring administration closer to people. The common man may seek initial help from an institution or agency.

Some Problems

There is no conceptual clarity regarding some provisions of the Act. For instance, do file nothings come under the Act? While the 2002 RTI Act, drafted by the NDA Government, specifically stated that file noting should be excluded, there was no such exemption in the 2005 Act amended and passed by the UPA Government.

The Department of Personnel and Training (the Ministry that drafted the RTI law) feels that file noting can be kept secret as these are crucial pointers to how and why decisions were taken and who were behind them.

The Chief Information Commissioner, Wajahat, Habibullah observed, in January 2006, that file notings are part of the definition of information. He, however, felt that "decisions on whether particular file notings can or cannot be given to applicants under the RTI Act will be made by the Commission when appeals are decided by us from time-to-time." (The New Indian Express, January 12, 2006).

The executive is not exhibiting sincerity in dealing with cases relating to corruption. There are cases against small people like shop owners and food department officials. The entire vigilance and anti-corruption set-up in the sates is underthe control of the executive. Often complaints have to be made to the same set of people against whom one has complained (Arvind Khejriwal, 2005:64).

The states and local administration have not taken RTI Act seriously. Many government offices and departments do not even display the name of the Principal Information Officers (PIOs) and assistant PIOs.

In some cases, information I provided, but it is not satisfactory. The fact is, information in intelligible form should be maintained systematically as per the Act, but is to being done. It is further observed that only voluntary organisations are seeking information but not the lay public (*The New Indian Express*, December 5, 2005).

Also, there is short of staff at all levels. Hence, it becomes difficult to provide relevant information within the stipulated timeframe. The Act can also be misused by unscrupulous politicians.

Some states insisted that the information received is not to be used for other purpose. In Orissa, the proof of residence should be attached to the application. Such conditions certainly undermine the utility of the Act.

Should government officials play a key role in the functioning of the commissions? The answer may be, no. But, the head of the Central Information Commission, Mr. Wajahat Habibullah feels that their services can be used as they will be in a better position to be able to guage if something has been concealed or openly stated which is what is required by the Act (Interview with Wajahat Habibulla, *The Hindu*, November 4, 2005).

The constitution of central information commission, and state information commission is also important. Whereas the Act suggests that non-bureaucrats should serve these commissions, most commissions appear to be from the IAS cadre. Another problem is, even when officials function sincerely, political interference may still be there. This would certainly dilute the efficacy of the Act. It is a shame that there is no effective enforcement of this salutary legislation (Sorabjee, 2006).

There is 'conflict' between RTI Act and the Official Secrets Act (1934). The latter has been strongly criticized by journalists, jurists, and social activists. This Act was enacted by the Britishers, but our government too use it to muzzle the freedom of the press and the struggles of the poor, and the marginalised sections of the society (Singh, Kavalit Singh, 1990:17).

According to former Chief Justice, P.N. Bhagwati, "The disclosure of information in regard to the functioning of government must be the rule, and secrecy an exception, justified only where the strictest requirement of public interest demands."

The citizen has to wait for 30 days to get relevant information. Because of this delay, the information provided may not be of much help.

There are too many exemptions. In the name of national security, and defence, information can be withheld. As if this is not enough, information cannot be sought under Sections 8 and 9. It has been rightly pointed out that in the hands of an opaque bureaucracy, the interpretation of an exception can be expanded in way that could undermine the intent of the RTI law (Pamela Philipose, 2005).

The Act does not apply to the private sector. But, in some important sectors like health, private sector is predominant. There is no check on the malpractices indulged in by the private doctors.

Another lacuna of the Act is that it has ousted the jurisdiction of the regular courts, thus leaving the aggrieved citizen in the lurch.

Measures Needed

In the government circles, so far priority is given to secrecy. The Information Act would be effective only if there are political reforms. There should be a change in the mind-set of top officials.

There should be a nation-wide discussion on right to information act. The interface between officials and common people should be ensured. The ordinary people should be aware of all the provisions of the act.

In order to promote understanding of various provisions of the Act, civil servants at all levels should be trained. As there are many practical problems in the implementation of the Act, training classes need to be conducted periodically. Also, there should be a mechanism to ensure consultation/dialogue between people and officials.

It is not enough if people get information under the act. The people have the right to knowhow the departments are functioning, how the decisions are taken and how the guidelines are prepared.

Seventy per cent of all government decisions and policies are based on file notings by officers throughout the bureaucratic hierarchy as a file moves up. As such, if they are excluded from the Act, it amount to killing the act. In fact, the "note file" discloses the link between the reasoning and the ultimate conclusion. "The person dealing with public matters, should have the humility to accept other points of view arrived at after careful discussions. The note file need not always be used as weapon against administrative officers (Ashok Kumar Sahay and Kshirod Chandra Patra, 2006:30). If file notngs form an integral part of RTI, it can transform the culture of rule in India (Amitab Mukhopadhyaya, 2007:88).

The NGOs should help people acquire the relevant information. They can explain the benefits and importance of the right to information. In fact, the Act emerged because of the efforts made by the NGOs. The NGOs therefore should see that the Act is implemented properly.

The rural people are reluctant to visit government officers for various reasons. The NGOs have to help such people.

In a major directive, the Appellate Authority under the Right to Information Act has ruled that the assets and liabilities statement of an officer is not a document that is private or confidential (*The New Indian Express,* January 10, 2006). This means that the scope of the RTI Act is large.

Civil society and the saner element in the government and legislature would need to be on constant vigil to ensure that the vested interests do not hijack and subvert the agenda of RTI Act (Niranjan, Oulac, 2005:4872).

Two things are very important : *(i)* an awareness campaign is required to highlight the features of the Act, and *(ii)* given the socio-economic background of the poor, the mass media and NGOs have to play a vital role in ensuring justice under the Act (I Satya Sundaram, 2006:32).

Also, the agencies responsible for implementing the act should not be starved of funds and facilities so that they can function to their full efficiency (O.P. Kejriwal, 2006:941).

Some intellectuals are trying to float a public forum to monitor the implementation of the RTI Act (*The New Indian Express,* December 12, 2005).

In spite of its limitations and shortcomings, the RTI Act has come as a boon. It is a powerful tool to hold the state accountable and secure the service to which he/she is entitled. In India, there are endless irregularities–delays in the execution of projects costing crores of rupees, misuse of funds, malpractices in administration etc. The officers, under the act, will have to play a proactive role in guiding the public to access information and in ensuring that the public authorities adopt a positive attitude in dealing with citizens and in disseminating information.

The panchayats have been empowered through the 73rd Constitutional Amendment. In some cases, funds are directly routed to panchayats for the implementation of development programmes and welfare schemes, and the distribution of subsidies. But, the functioning of the panchayats is yet to be streamlined as many irregularities still continue. The RTI Act empowers the tax payer to question the manner in which public authorities spend the money. The act, however, needs to be seen as an opportunity not just to unearth corruption but also prevent its occurrence (Venkatesh Nayak, 2006 : 331).

India is predominantly rural, and the panchayats will contribute a lot to the effective implementation of the Act. The awareness is imperative for common people both to knowhow they are governed, and to participate actively in the process of auditing their representatives (Sita Ram Kumbhar, 2006:337). Of course, the Gram Sabha should be revitalised. An effective implementation of RTI Act would lead to good governance which is a pre-condition for steady and satisfactory growth of the economy.

REFERENCES

Amitab Mukhopadhyay, 'File Noting and Govern mentality', *Seminar,* January, 2007.

Arvind Khejriwal, 'Holding Officialdom Accountable', *Seminar,* July, 2005.

Ashok Kumar Sahay and Kshirod Chandra Patra, "Survival of Democracy Needs RTI Act', *Mainstream,* September 29, 2006.

Bharat Dogra,'Right to Information', *Frontier,* March 26 – April 1, 2006.

I. Satya Sundaram, Review of a National Seminar on Right to Information', *Southern Economist,* March, 2006.

Kavaljit Singh, 'Right to Information : Issues and Suggestions', *Mainstream,* April 21, 1990.

M.K. Heble, 'Right to Information, a sine quanon' for Democracy', *The Hindu,* October 13, 1992.

O.P. Kejriwal,"Right to Information Act' : Loopholes and Road Ahead', *Economic and Political Weekly,* March 18, 2006.

Oulac Niranjan, 'Right to Information and the Road to Heaven', *Economic and Political Weekly,* November 19, 2005.

Pamela Philipose, 'Kingdom of the Officials Secret', *The New Indian Express,* December, 26, 2005.

Sita Ram Kumbhar,'Role of Civil Society in Taming Development through Information', *Social Action,* October-December, 2006.

Soli J. Sorabjee, 'The Right to Information', *The New Indian Express,* May 21, 2006.

Venkatesh Nayak, 'Governance in a Rights Framework and the Right to Information', *Social Action,* October-December, 2006.

15

Emerging Challenges on Reservation Policy of Panchayati Raj Institutions: The Case of Women Representatives in India

PRAMOD K. MISHRA

When the 73rd Constitutional Amendment was introduced in 1992 in order to inject new life to the decadent Panchayati Raj Institutions in India (PRIs), it was expected that most of the states in India will implement them in letter and spirit. With 33 per cent reservation provided to women in the 3-tier system of the PRIs and benefitting reservations to the SCs and STs in due proportion to their population it was expected that the situation will improve in our grassroots organisation.

But in reality when one looks at the grassroot realities in the working of Panchayati Raj Institutions, one notices several gapping holes. The three decades of nineteen fifties to nineteen eighties saw phases of revival and neglect of these vital grassroots institutions of local governance with heavy social and political costs for the rural areas. The patchy progress of development initiatives, lack of people's participation and support led to realisation of the need to depend democracy and develop inclusive and capable institutions of local governance.

The 73rd Constitutional Amendment in 1992 adding Part IX to the Constitution for mandating vibrant Panchayat institutions drew upon the efforts made by different states to organise Panchayats in the four decades since the Constitution became effective. It sought to include essential features for their continuous existence with more inclusive membership and with adequate powers and resources. It also included a complete three-tier Panchayati Raj structure instead of village Panchayats only as initially expected in Article 40 as an essential uniform structure for the whole country.

Even with these features included in the Constitution itself by this Amendment the subject of Panchyats still continues to be within the competence of the states. Hence, a number of steps of implement these provisions had to be finally fashioned by the state legislature while bringing their Panchayat legislations in conformity with this Amendment.

The paper while broadly highlighting on the salient features of the 73rd Amendment relating to the election of PRIs, will evaluate the gross violations of these provisions by the different Indian states. Our broad hypothesis is that most of the state government in course of their implementation of the 73rd Amendment have often modified their implementation mechanism primarily to suit to the petty interests of the ruling parties and their power-hungry politicians.

Crucial Provisions on the Election of PRIs under the 73rd Amendment

It provides for : *(i)* Fixed five years' tenure for all Panchayats and their office bearers with no powers to extend this period as was being done earlier by the State Governments extending the period for one reason or the other and thereby avoiding/delaying regular elections *(ii)* Elections to all Panchayats by independent State Election Commissions to be set up by the states *(iii)* All Panchayat memberships to be by direct election from territorial constituencies of the Panchayat area i.e., no nominations or co-option etc. The only exception given for ex-officio membership of MPs/MLAs and to presidents of lower ties Panchayats in the higher level Panchayat bodies *(iv)* For chairpersons, the state Panchayats legislations can provide for election of Chairpersons of the village Panchayats directly by all voters or indirectly by the members of the Panchayats but Chairpersons of the district level and intermediate level Panchayats are to be elected by their members only *(v)* Reservations for weaker sections of SC/ST and for women in the membership as well as in the Chairpersons' posts - for SC/ST proportionate to their population and for women not less than one-third of the Members/Chairpersons posts. Women's minimum one-third reservation to be not only in total seats of a Panchayat or total number of Chairpersons at a level but also among those reserved for SC/ ST separately. With the 1996 law, all Chairpersons to Panchayat in Schedule V areas have to be tribals and their members to have fifty per cent tribal members.

Inherent in these essential provisions is a vision of vibrant, active Panchayats with more inclusive membership across caste, class and gender, respective and responsible to the local community, with resources and with powers to raise resources to fulfill their responsibilities and to meet the needs and aspirations of the local population. Functioning of the Panchayat bodies is expected to be not as mere agencies implementing state structured programmes/ schemes, but to be responsive and responsible local government institutions.

There are also certain permissible features which have been left to the discretion of the state legislature. This, they can give reservation to other Backward Classes. As exceptions to the general prescription for only elected members in Panchayats, the state Panchayat laws can include MPs, MLAs and MLCs as ex-officio members of the Panchayats at the district and intermediate levels. The Chairpersons of the Panchayats at the village and intermediate levels can be made ex-officio members of the next higher level Panchayat body to provide an organic link among them for their functions.

The 1996 law, extending the Panchayat Provisions to Schedule V areas adds certain essential for Panchayats in areas of tribal concentration in the states of Bihar, Jharkhand, Gujarat, MP, Chhattisgarh, Maharashtra, Orissa and Rajasthan. These include leadership positions of all Panchayats at all levels to be with tribals only, fifty per cent of their members to be tribals only, fifty per cent of their members to be tribals, over-reaching role of the Gram Sabha, preservation of tribal customs and traditions, control over natural resources, minor forest produce and minor minerals which are crucial for tribal livelihood, control over social sector institutions and functionaries in the area to manage them in the interest of tribals' special needs. This law is focusing more on the Gram Sabha and also provides for a Gram Sabha in every village or habitation instead of a Gram Sabha for the whole village Panchayat area. However, it also leaves a number of matters relating to allocation of specific powers to appropriate level Panchayats to the state legislatures.

Gaps between Theory and Practice: Frequent Violations by States

The philosophy of 'power' to the people at the grassroots was the guiding principle of the 73rd Constitional Amendment. Their main objective was to strengthen the PRIs throughout the country and make them 'institutions of self-government' with responsibility of promoting economic development and ensuring social justice. Therefore, the Amendment provided for devolution of powers, functions and finances, access to weaker sections in society to power at the grassroots level and making the PRIs financially strong so that they can perform meaningful role in overall development. The experience of implementation of various provisions and the situation that has emerged over the last few years of working of the PRIs in the revised set-up in different states raises certain questions regarding the expectations and ground realities. The extent of success in achieving devolution of powers, functions and finances, in empowerment of weaker sections in the society in general and women's empowerment I particular need to be seen, besides the functioning of newly established organs like the State Election Commissions and the State Finance Commissions and the overall attitude of the political leadership and bureaucracy towards these changes.

The provisions in the 73rd Constitutional Amendment Act, 1992 include mandatory items and some discretionary items. Although most of the mandatory items contained in the 73rd Amendment have been accepted and implemented by the State Governments, there are "deviations" or infirmities while implementing various provisions mandatory as well as discretionary, which go against the spirit of democratic decentralisation inherent in this Amendment. We look at these infirmities in the context of the core features of the Amendment and the 1996 law extending these provisions to the Schedule Areas. We also see them with reference to Panchayats' organisation, representations.

Electoral Process, The Loopholes and Wide Diversities

All the states have legislated to provide for organisation of Panchayats at three (or two in states with up to 20 lakh population) levels and for direct elections to their membership with reservations as mandated in the Amendment. However, there are deviations and additions which are against the letter as well as the spirit of the Amendment. No membership is possible now by co-option or nomination except the ex-officio membership of MLAs/MPs/MLCs in district and intermediate level Panchayats and Chairpersons of lower level Panchayat in the next higher level panchayat bodies.

But in Andhra Pradesh, Section 149 of the state law includes co-option of one person from the minority community in the Mandal Panchayat and Section 171 includes co-option of two members of the minority community in the Zilla Parishad. The legal validity of these co-options does not seem to have been questioned in any courts so far but these clearly violate Article 243C(2) that all panchayat members will be directly elected from territorial constituencies. The Panjab State Panchayat Act of 1994 as originally enacted stipulated that 40 per cent of the members of the Panchayat Samithies were to be elected directly by the voters and 60 per cent indirectly by and from amongst the Sarpanchs of the Samithi area. It has been changed recently, but only to make it 50 per cent direct and 50 per cent indirect election. This is again a clear violation in letter as well as in spirit of the provisions of Article 243C introduced by the 73rd Constitutional Amendment. Further, Gram Sabha areas have been constituted for village panchayats, but wards in the Gram Sabha area have not been demarcated. So, in case of re-election of Panchs to vacant seats irrespective of the reason, the total voters of Gram Sabha area will have to vote again for a Panch seat. This is against the clear provisions of Article 243C(2) that the members have to be elected from individual territorial constituencies.

Another deviation is in West Bengal Panchayat Act in respect of ex-officio membership of members of Panchayat Samithies and Zilla Parishads in Gram Panchayats and Panchayat Samithies, respectively, located within their individual constituencies. A popular view on the subject is that even though the constitutional validity of this provision is doubtful, it is a harmless one, and it contributes towards strengthening integration of different tiers. Andhra Pradesh also has made a provision that members of the Mandal Parishad territorial constitutency of the area will be permanent invitees in the Gram Panchayat with right to speak though having no right to vote (Section 7(2) in the Andhra Pradesh Act 1994).

In Madhya Pradesh, the Panchayat, law as initially enacted in 1993 provided for co-options of representatives of SCs/STs and co-operative societies in the Gram Panchayats, ex-officio membership of Chairpersons of district co-operative bodies and district co-operative banks and co-option of director of co-operative marketing society or of a co-operative bank and of members of SCs/STs in Janpad Panchayats and Zilla Panchayats. These, of course, were removed by an amending ordinance during the first Panchayat elections in 1994 and hence, rectified. Another feature added by the MP Panchayat Act is to permit the MPs and MLAs to send their representatives if they cannot attend the meetings of district or block level Panchayats of which they are ex-officio members.

Frequent Change of Chairpersons of PRIs

While the reservation in case of members as well as of Chairpersons of any PRI is for their full term i.e. five years in all the states, it has been changed to a shorter duration in the case of Chairperson's office in some states. For example, in Maharashtra in the case of Chairpersons of Zilla Parishad, though the term of office is five years, the Chairmanship was effectively changed to one year as it was rotated every year among all reserved categories. As it was a very short tenure, it has been changed later to two and half years. In Karnataka, it has been changed to 20 months, so the Chairmanship is rotated after this period and one tenure of five years will see three Chairpersons. The Amendment stipulated mandatory rotation of reservations of Chairpersons' posts in a manner prescribed. It is this reference to "prescribed manner" that these states have used to ensure that there is no evolution of new leadership from the new entrants from the social groups who have entered these posts in significant number though reservations for the first time at this level.

Negligence of SCs and STs in PRIs

The 73rd Amendment provides for reservation of SCs/STs in proportion to their population as far as the membership is concerned and in the total for Chairmanship. Article 243D (1) reads as follows: "The number of seats so reserved shall bear as nearly as may be, the same proportion to the total number of seats to be filled by direct election in that Panchayat as the population of the Scheduled Castes in that Panchayat area or of the Scheduled Tribes in that Panchayat area bears to the total population of that area... "243D(4). About Chairpersons, it says: "The number of offices of Chairpersons reserved for the Scheduled Castes and the Scheduled Tribes in the Panchayats at each level in any state shall bear, as nearly as may be, the same proportion to the total number of such offices in the Panchayats at each level as the population of the Scheduled Castes in the State or of the Scheduled Tribes in the State bears to the total population of the State."

In the Madhya Pradesh Panchayat Law, posts of Sarpanchs of Gram Panchayats are to be reserved for SC/ST in proportion to their population to their population in the district. Only in the Zilla Panchayats, these are to be reserved in proportion to their population in the state [Section 17(2) for Gram Panchayat, 25(2) for Janpad Panchayat and 32(2) for Zilla Panchayats].This has resulted in giving reservations to SC/ST in the posts of Presidents of Janpad and Zilla Panchayats differently than what would be permissible when based on the proportionate population in the state.

Some of the states have also given additional reservations, which is in line with the intent of the amendment. Thus, M.P. law provides that if the President of a Zilla Panchayat or Janpad Panchayat or Sarpanch of a Gram Panchayat is not SC / ST or OBC, then the Vice-President of Zilla Panchayat [Section 32 (4)], the Vice-President of Janpad Panchayat [Section 25(4)] and Up-sarpanch of Gram Panchayat (Section 17(6)] has to be from SC/ST/OBC categories. In West Bengal and Orissa, reservations have given to women among Vice-Presidents of the Panchayats. These are positive additions in accordance with the spirit and expectations of the 73rd Amendment. However, combining the SC/ST/OBC in the case of MP State is a combination of unequals and is skewed in favour of OBC as against SC/ST who are more disadvantaged politically, socially and economically.

Another deviation from the 73rd Amendment in respect of representation is in Himachal Pradesh where the law provided for direct election of the Up-Sarpanch of Gram Panchayat from the whole Panchayat area. As he is neither a simple member who could be from a territorial constituency nor a chairperson who can be from the whole Panchayat area, this is a questionable provision. Himachal Pradesh provides another deviation in the quorum of the Gram Sabha. The spirit and philosophy of the Panchayat law and practice as well as for other democratic institutions is for representation of individual voters in various fora. But by a recent amendment in the Himachal Pradesh Act in 2000, the quorum in the Gram Sabha can be "one-third of the total number of families represented by one or more members of the Gram Sabha area" and for the adjourned meeting it will be 'one-fifth of the total number of families represented by one or more members of the Gram Sabha." The family is defined here as a 'joint family of all persons descended from common ancestor including adoption, who live and worship together permanently as shown in the Gram Panchayat." This definition of the family is a questionable concept as it may exclude some voters and particularly women whose other responsibilities and constraints affect their ability to come for various meetings.

Violation of 2 Child Norm in Elections

In terms of representations, another deviation is seen in the various disqualifications provided for election to the Panchayats, as these would debar a large number of persons who would be entering Panchayats for the first time after the reservations given there. These deviations against the spirit of the 73rd Amendment include the eligibility criterion of "two child norm" that anyone having more than two children after a specified date cannot contest or continue as a representative in the Panchayat at any level. Andhra Pradesh, Haryana, Rajasthan and Orissa included this disqualification in their laws enacted in 1993. The states of Mandhya Pradesh (undivided) and Himachal Pradesh have introduced it in 2000 Recent studies of this experience have shown how this law adversely affects the new young entrants to Panchayats, especially women and weaker sections whom the 73rd Amendment has sought to bring in Panchayat through the reservations across caste, class and gender.

Irregular Elections of PRIs

Irregular elections despite the clear tenure of five years from the first meeting of a Panchayat stipulated in the Amendment has been attempted in a number of states and the matter had to go to the High Courts and Supreme Court before the second set of Panchayat elections were organised in these states. Thus, Karnataka and Andhra Pradesh delayed their elections with AP raising the issue of the three/two upper levels of Panchayats and the direct/indirect elections of their members. Karnataka suddenly felt the need to review the delimitation of constitutions rather late when the elections were to be organised again. In Madhya Pradesh, the whole matter of reservation was taken, of course, by an individual petitioner to the High Court, questioning the high percentage of reservations, especially for tribals in the tribal areas. The High Court stayed the elections but vacated the stay after six months. So the elections were held in January - February 2000, instead of June 1999. The local perception was that the whole process to delay the elections by using the legal proceeding was because it did not suit the political parties in the state to have the elections before the Parliament elections suddenly called in 1999.

In Orissa, when the ruling party changed in the elections to the state legislature, the Panchayats were dissolved through a resolution in the state legislature, using the powers in Article 243N introduced by the 73rd Amendment but then the elections were postponed again and again on various grounds including the ground of drought condition in the state. The elections were then held only after continuous civil society pressure. In Punjab, a tenure of five years for all the three-tiers of the Panchayati Raj system has been enacted in the Punjab Panchayat Act in accordance with the Constitutional Amendment. So, the elections to Panchayat Samithies and Zilla Parishads were due in October 1999. But these have been postpones time and again.

Independent Election Mechanism Lacking in Several States

Another deviation in practice, though not stipulated in any enactment, relates to the elections to the Chairpersons of district and intermediate levels. In some of the states, these elections are not conducted by State Election Commissions. These are conducted by the government machinery. Madhya Pradesh, Maharashtra and Karnataka come in this category, while in the states of Orissa and UP, these elections are organised by the State Election Commissions. The argument in the former group of states is that the direct elections of Chairpersons are indirect elections by the members of these bodies, these will be organised by the State Governments. If this argument is accepted, then the Rajya Sabha elections will not be organised by the Election Commission of India. This position, therefore, needs to be corrected and all states must have elections to Panchayats, of their members as well as Chairpersons, whether direct or indirect, organised only by the State Election Commissions.

Delimitation of Constituency : A Chronic Problem

The constitional amendment speaks of the delimitation of constituencies and also makes it clear that the validity of a law relating to this subject cannot be questioned by any court of law (Article 243 O). Delimitation of constituencies has, therefore, been done by the executive governments from time-to-time and has not always been seen as fair and objective. The case of Uttar Pradesh had to go the High Court and Supreme Court before the first Panchayat elections could take place in 1995. It would be desirable if the delimitation of the constituencies is entrusted to a Delimitation Commission or given to the State Election Commissions instead of leaving it to the executive authority of the concerned states where politics of the political leaders at higher levels influence various decisions.

Let us Look Back

Thus, while reading between the lines, in spite of several innovative features introduced for the election of PRIs in order to empower them considerably in the arena of implementation, although some states have followed the letter and spirit of the 73rd Amendment, many more have turned out to be deviators/violators of the basic objectives. The rational behind such as slip-slot follow up measure seems to be as follows. First, the state leaders in different corners of the country, consider any dictates or impositions (even under the garb of a constitutional amendment) from the centre as a sort of infringement on this autonomy. Even, on the issue of recognising the PRIs, these state leaders would not like to be dictated by New Delhi. Second, as both caste and class factors dominate in the state politics of India, very often one funds that the minority voice which includes that of the women, SCs & STs, get suppressed or bypassed by the power brokers in some states.

In order to rectify such shortcomings relating to election of PRIs, the Union Government need to follow a proactive policy of keeping a watchful eye on the implementation of various provisions relating of PRIs in all the states and UTs and try to punish the erring states through withdrawal/reduction of grants. These states can also be side lined/exposed by other states in India for their gross neglect of PRIs.

SELECTED REFERENCES

Asha Ramesh and Bharati Ali, Reservation Towards Political Empowerment, Bangalore, Books or Change, 2001.

Bharati Tekchandani, Jyothi Kiran and Priti Sharma (Eds.), *They Call me Member Saab : Women in Haryana Panchayati Raj*, New Delhi, MAARG, 2000.

Gender Issues in Panchayats in Uttar Pradesh: A Report by Sahbhagi Kendra, Lucknow.

Institutes of Social Studies, *Status of Panchayati Raj in the State and Union Territories of India 2000,* New Delhi, Institutes of Social Studies, 2000.

Jos Chathukulam and M.S. John, Empowerment of Women Panchayat Members: Learning from Kerala, *Asian Journal of Women's Studies,* Vol. 6, No. 4, 2000.

KR Shastry, "Panchayats Raj in Andhra Pradesh: Recent Developments", Kurushetra, April 1999.

Kumud Sharma, Transformative Politics : Dimensions of Women's Participation in Panchayati Raj, *Indian Journal of Gender Studies,* Vol. 5, No.1, March 1998.

Mahila Chetna Manch, *Panchayati Raj* and the *"Two Child Norm', Implications and Consequences,* (A summary of the Preliminary Findings of Exploratory Studies in Andhra Pradesh, Haryana, Madhya Pradesh, Orissa and Rajasthan – Mahila Chetna Manch, Bhopal, January 2003).

Nirmala Buch, "Let the Sun Shine on the Grassroorts Too : 73rd Constitutional Amendment : Story of Implementation and Deviations" in D. Bandyapadhyay and A. Mukherjee (Eds.) *New Issues on Panchayati Raj,* New Delhi, Task Force on Panchayati Raj, Rajiv Gandhi Foundation & Concept, 2004.

Poornima Vyasulu and Vinod Vyasulu, Women in Panchayati Raj : Grassroots Democracy in Malgudi, *Economic and Political Weekly,* December 25, 1999.

Vina Mazumdar, Historical Soundings, *Seminar,* 457, September, 1997.

16

Total Sanitation Campaign and Nirmal Gram Puraskar: Role of Panchayats in Four Indian States

JOS CHATHUKULAM AND K. GIREESAN

Background

Mahatma Gandhi included the issue of sanitation as a major component of his constructive programme formulated for attaining independence. Promotion of sanitation was very close to his heart and he advocated that 'Cleanliness is next to godliness'. Gandhiji spoke and wrote extensively on topics related to sanitation, hygiene and environment. Through his articles, essays and letters, Gandhiji offered detailed comments on cleanliness and good habits, and its relationship with good health. He squarely blamed the unclean and unhygienic conditions for the emergence of communicable diseases in the country. Many times, he appealed to educated Indians to become missionaries in hygiene and sanitation. Perhaps he is the greatest leader of any country who realised the significance of sanitation and hygiene in the overall development of a nation. The comments of that great visionary, "If we do not keep our backyards clean, our swaraj will have a foul stench", remains poignantly relevant even now.

However, the sanitation coverage in rural areas of India remained very low in the early 1980's. It is estimated that about three crore persons in rural areas suffer from sanitation-related diseases. An annual loss of 18 crores man-days and Rs. 1200 crore to the economy is estimated to sanitation related diseases alone.[1] According to a baseline survey on water and sanitation in 1997, only 20 per cent households reported having private latrines and most people defecate in open space in most of the states.[2] Census reports 2001 indicates that the overall sanitation coverage in India is 37 per cent and the sanitation coverage in the rural areas is further less, i.e., 22 per cent only. While analysing the sanitation coverage in South Asia, India (22%) lags far behind most of the neighbouring countries like Sri Lanka (80%), Bhutan (70%), Bangladesh (44%), Maldives (41%) and Myanmar (39%).[3]

Government of India launched the first-ever structured programme for promoting rural sanitation in 1986 – Central Rural Sanitation Programme (CRSP). In 1999, CRSP was restructured from allocation mode to a demand driven and community based programme as Total Sanitation Campaign (TSC). From 2003, an award (Nirmal Gram Puraskar) has been instituted by the Ministry of Rural Development, Government of India to recognise the role of PRIs and motivate them in the sanitation movement across the country.

Total Sanitation Campaign

TSC is the most comprehensive programme on rural sanitation ever launched in the country, which involves the Central Government, State Government, civil society organisations and community as partners. Introduction of TSC has resulted in generating a major shift in the approach and strategies adopted in the implementation of conventional sanitation programmes. The campaign provided space for each district to submit its proposal, keeping in view the specific sanitation situation prevailing in its area of jurisdiction. In addition, TSC provided ample scope for meeting the local-specific needs and demands during the operationalisation of the campaign. Its thrust on 'demand driven approach' and emphasis on Information, Education and Communication (IEC) activities to increase awareness among the population regarding health and hygiene, good sanitation practices, etc. with beneficiary participation has been a paradigm shift from the 'allocation based' sanitation programmes. Various components of TSC include Individual Household Latrine (IHHL), School Sanitation and Hygiene Education (SSHE), Anganawadi sanitation, Community Sanitary Complex (CSC) and Alternate delivery mechanisms like Rural Sanitary Marts/Production Centres (RSM/PC).

TSC is implemented in a decentralised mode and the role and involvement of Panchayati Raj Institutions (PRIs) is very prominent. PRIs have a major say in the all the phases during the operationalisation of the programme like planning, implementation and monitoring, with major thrust on awareness building and social mobilisation of all segments of the society. In addition, this has also provided lot of scope for people-centred and community-led initiatives, local interventions, and adoption of a technology according to customer preferences. In general, TSC resulted in a holistic and integrated approach to sanitation programmes.

Civil society organisations like Non-Governmental Organisations (NGO) and Community Based Organisations (CBO) also play an important role in awareness generation, advocacy and educative campaigns to spread the message of 'Total sanitation' in the rural areas. However, the involvement of civil society organisations depends upon their acceptability, approach, credibility, professionalism, willingness and many other aspects.

Nirmal Gram Puraskar (NGP)

Recognising the role of PRIs and towards motivating them for promoting rural sanitation, an incentive scheme called Nirmal Gram Puraskar (NGP) was initiated on 2nd October, 2003. The concept of NGP is to reward those GPs, blocks and districts that have achieved full sanitation coverage. It is an award instituted by the Department of Drinking Water Supply (DDWS) in the Ministry of Rural Development (MoRD), Government of India (GoI) under TSC for bringing dignity and quality in life.

The cash incentive based on population criteria at the time of inception of NGP is given below:

Table-1
NGP: Incentive Pattern

	GP		*Block*		*District*	
Population criteria	Upto 5,000	5,001 and above	Up to 50,000	50,001 and above	Up to 10 lakhs	Above 10 lakhs
Cash incentive (Rs. in lakhs)	2.0	4.0	10.0	20.0	30.0	50.0

Source: Website of Department of Drinking Water Supply, MoRD, GoI.

The Union Ministry of Rural Development has changed the criteria for awarding NGP to GPs at the conference of State Ministers for drinking water and sanitation. This was borne out of the arguments that the states where the GPs have less population were receiving more money when compared to the States with larger population in each GP. The slab in respect of the GP was revised based on classification of population and amount of award money as given in Table 2.

Table-2
NGP—Revised Incentive Pattern*

	GP				
Population criteria	Less than 1,000	1000 to 1999	3,000 to 4999	5000 to 9999	10,000 and above
Cash incentive (Rs. in lakhs)	0.5	1.0	2.0	4.0	5.0

Source: Website of DDWS, MoRD, GoI.

Note: * The criteria for Block and District remained the same as in Table 1.

The cash incentive for PRIs can be utilised for improving and maintaining the sanitation facilities in their respective areas, with more focus on solid and liquid waste management and maintenance of the sanitation standards. It is expected that such incentives will give a positive boost to the sanitation drive across the country and will play a major role in making India *open defecation free* by 2012.

Four aspects are considered for scrutiny while selecting the PRIs for NGP. They are: *(a)* All households should have access to toilets with full use. There is no practice of open defecation and no place for open defecation in the respective PRI; *(b)* All schools should have sanitation facilities, which are also put to use. All co-educational schools must have separate toilets for boys and girls; *(c)* All anganawadis should have access to sanitation facilities; and *(d)* General cleanliness is prevailing in the village.

For the first award, applications from 481 PRIs from 10 states were received. Out of which, 360 applications were forwarded to District Level Monitoring (DLM) agencies for verification of the claims. Based on the reports, 38 GPs were selected for the award by NGP Committee headed by the Secretary, DDWS, MoRD, GoI. The first award ceremony of NGP was held on February 24, 2005, in which the President of India gave away the awards to the Presidents/Pradhans of PRIs.

A close look at the trend of NGP applications awarded since its inception will bring out some interesting features.

Table–3
NGP – Number of Awardees Year-wise

State	*No. of GPs Awarded in*		
	Year 2005	*Year 2006*	*Year 2007*
Andhra Pradesh	–	10	143
Arunahcal Pradesh	–	–	2
Assam	–	1	3
Bihar	–	4	40
Chhattisgarh	–	12	90
Gujarat	1	4	576
Haryana	–	–	60
Himachal Pradesh	–	–	22
Jharkhand	–	–	12
Karnataka	–	–	121
Kerala	1	6	220
Madhya Pradesh	–	1	190
Maharashtra	13	380	1974
Mizoram	–	–	3
Orissa	–	8	33
Rajasthan	–	–	23
Sikkim	–	–	27
Tamil Nadu	12	119	296
Tripura	1	36	46
Uttar Pradesh	–	40	488
Uttaranchal/Uttarkhand	–	13	109
West Bengal	10	126	468
Total	**38**	**760**	**4946**

Source : Website of DDWS, MoRD, GoI.

NGP can be used as a 'Proxy variable' to ascertain the progress of TSC implementation in different states, though no direct relation could be yet established. It is observed that the achievement in terms of NGP awardees in each state match with the corresponding progress it has made during TSC. From Table 3, we can see that the States like Gujarat, Kerala, Maharashtra, Tamil Nadu, Uttar

Pradesh and West Bengal have made significant achievement over the period. And the states like Andhra Pradesh, Haryana, Karnataka and Tripura have achieved moderate progress. However, the states like Bihar, Chhattisghar, Jharkhand, Madhya Pradesh, Orissa and Rajasthan could not make the desired progress. We can see that Kerala and Uttar Pradesh had a giant leap in terms of number of NGP awardees over the period, whereas a steady progression could be seen in the case of Tamil Nadu and West Bengal. In this context, one may see a correlation between the progress made by each State in the field of TSC and the number of NGP awardees in each passing year.

Even among the States with high achievement, distribution of progress in the districts has not been even, which depends upon several factors. Table 3 also indicates the need for classification of the states based on their performance into categories like Low, Medium and High with necessary policy level interventions and strategies for each category separately. It is seen that among the North-Eastern States, only Tripura could perform relatively better. A separate approach and strategy is needed in those states to improve the sanitation situation.

There is an increasing urge for submitting the applications for NGP by the PRIs by each year. It is also observed that the number of awardees in each state has been on the rise in the subsequent years. This shows that initiation of NGP acts like a real incentive to the PRIs, thereby giving a positive boost to the sanitation drive across the country.

Objective

The broad objective of this paper is to highlight the growing importance and significance of Nirmal Gram Puraskar during the Total Sanitation Campaign and to portray the reflections gathered during the field visits through four states – West Bengal, Uttar Pradesh, Tamil Nadu and Kerala. Efforts were made to study the significant aspects of the scheme execution in different states and to analyse them from a close range. The reflections have been gathered during the discussions with the elected members of PRIs, field level officials involved with the scheme execution, representatives of CBOs functioning in the area and a cross-section of the society. They were gathered from the extensive field visits made by the DLM team through these states for the verification of claims by the PRIs for the award during the last three years.

Methodology

Methodology adopted during the NGP evaluation by our team has been indicated in this section and the same has been incorporated for the analysis of this paper as well. For verification of claim submitted by PRIs, a detailed questionnaire was provided by the DDWS, MoRD, GoI to the verification agencies. It aims at assessing the overall sanitation and hygiene situation in the area by commenting on the sanitation situation in the sample households as per the population of PRIs and its use by the population, method of disposal of child faces, sanitation conditions prevalent in the schools and anganwadis in the village area, hygiene education provided to students and children, verification of open defecation menace in the traditional places, general cleanliness in the village, method of waste disposal, and awareness among the sample population regarding hygiene and clean environment.

A strategic approach to the evaluation exercise was adopted by our team. Understanding the significance and considering the seriousness of the exercise, senior members from our organisation were assigned with the task. This helped in many ways, as the team member has to interact with a wide range of persons like members of the three-tier PRIs, senior district/block officials, political party leaders, media persons and even illiterate villagers. In addition, this gave a clear message to the hosts as to the seriousness of the evaluation exercise undertaken. In areas where the language of communication was the major issue, necessary support was obtained from the CBOs/NGOs and post-graduate students from Universities and Colleges, but no sub-contracting of the assignment was done.

The evaluation exercise was carried out keeping its motivational aspect in view. During the field visits, every effort was made to make a small address to the children, students and the villagers highlighting the significance of TSC and NGP. In all the areas, 'Bastis' (Colonies) of marginalised sections like SCs/STs were invariably visited to confirm the veracity of the claim.

During the presentations, NGP has been presented as the 'most prestigious award' presented by the President of India to a

GP. During the interactions with the community and elected members, it is mentioned that the award is presented to the 'whole village' and the President of GP would be representing the village to receive the same.

During the interactions with the elected members and officials of the PRIs, the style of communication and body language of an evaluator was never assumed by the team members. Instead, they were asked to present their claim for the award by narrating the activities carried out by them. In this regard, our view is that it is better for an evaluator to assume the features, vigour and enthusiasm of a TSC activist, in addition to a pro-active body language. Each evaluator should internalise the philosophy, processes and the dynamics of TSC and the politico-administrative environmental settings. After the field visits, the team members used to conduct a debriefing session at the Panchayat also. Appreciation of the significant efforts taken up, suggestions for overcoming the shortfalls during the execution and long-term perspective for addressing the issues of sustainability are conveyed through the session. Number of TSC district officials and UNICEF consultants accompanied the team members during the field visits commented that they gained lot of insights by exchange of experiences and information with our team members.[4]

In some places, press conferences were organised, which provided occasions to sensitise the media about NGP. During such sessions, media persons posed several questions to the evaluation team as well, which helped to fine tune the exercise in many ways. In brief, NGP evaluation was used by the team as an exercise for strengthening the TSC activities taken up in different states. In some parts, the evaluation exercise assumed the mode of a 'social audit' or even 'Jan Sunwayi' by the team members. All our exercises in the NGP evaluation could succeed to generate enormous data from different levels without any difficulties. In short, the methodology we applied for NGP evaluation worked out to be the methodology for this paper also.

Study Area

NGP evaluation was undertaken by the team in several PRIs from the four states. Number of GPs visited in each state during the period 2004-07 is indicated in the following table:

Table-4
PRIs Visited for NGP Evaluation

Name of the State	*No. of PRIs Visited by CRM Team*
West Bengal	337
Uttar Pradesh	305
Tamil Nadu	113
Kerala	11
Total	766

Source: NGP records of CRM.

Reflections from Different States in India

In this section, reflections gathered from the four states, in connection with the verification of claims for the award (Nirmal Gram Puraskar), have been presented.

(a) West Bengal

Some of the reflections gathered from the field visits through five districts of West Bengal have been mentioned in the following paragraphs:

Field visits and interactions with the party functionaries at different levels revealed that TSC has been in the political agenda of all major political parties at the local level.[5] Discussions with the party functionaries at the local level indicated that this resulted in minimising corruption in the selection of beneficiaries and provision of scheme benefits to deserving persons. The local leaders are well aware of the guidelines, principle and programmes of the TSC. It is known that progress of the scheme implementation by the PRIs is one of the major agendas of discussion during the meetings of the parties. TSC has been programatised in the agenda of all political parties at the local levels. Interactions with some of the officials in charge of the scheme implementation indicated that 'Politicising TSC' has benefitted by cutting down the expenses in Information, Education and Communication (IEC) activities.[6] Discussions with the some of elected members revealed that even minor punishments were given to some persons for violating the norms/instructions about hygiene and sanitation with the concurrence of party.[7] And some kind of consensus has been noted among all the political parties while dealing with sanitation programmes.[8]

Interactions with number of officials in-charge of the programme indicated that they have given their option to the TSC assignment, fully aware of it as a 'hard option'. A genuine spirit towards the programme has been noted in many of them. Presence of a healthy competition among the officials of different districts has also been observed during the visits. It is seen that wide use of Participatory Rural Appraisal (PRA) techniques during the programme execution has resulted in making them more people-friendly also. Discussions with them indicated that they employed a liberal approach towards the target group of beneficiaries, in providing the scheme benefits. And the continuous rule of 30 years of Left Front government in the state has resulted in tuning the officials to the left ideology, agenda and programmes. As a result in certain cases, the local bureaucracy assumes the role of a 'Corrective force' in the administration of the scheme in 'Party villages', of course within the permissible limits set by the political party.[9] In addition, a close and constant interface has been noted between the officials and local party functionaries during the scheme execution, mainly due to 'Politicising TSC'. A kind of synergy resulting in flow of information from the offices to the party circles and vice versa also has been observed. We came across ample examples of officials taking support of party functionaries in the scheme implementation in some difficult zones/pockets/areas. All these aspects seemingly resulted in the emergence of a committed bureaucracy during the scheme execution in the state. This assessment was based on the interactions with the officials of the state during the visits on three consecutive years.

Number of organisations like Ramakrishna Mission, Siksha Niketan, Atma Sakthi Sangh, Tubgram Grammyak Unnayan Samity, Kshithu Kanu Gram Unnayan Samithi, etc., are playing an important role in the TSC by actively involving in IEC activities, managing Rural Sanitary Marts (RSM) and in various other capacities. It is significant to note that many of them are nurtured and promoted by the left front. A recent development in the state is that with the permission of the political parties, local leaders from different class and mass organisations have floated several NGOs and are actively functioning in the sanitation sector.[10] However, it is noted that most of them are functioning at Block and GP levels only.

It is noted that RSMs function as the hub of sanitation activities at the field level. Most of the RSMs are managed by the CBOs and NGOs. The activities of RSM in the state is undergoing a sea change from construction of sanitary toilets to construction of hollow bricks and other construction materials, low cost housing, water quality testing, purification of water, etc.

A large segment of the schools (especially primary schools) in the rural areas have very poor infrastructure facilities. The status of school toilets in some of the areas visited has been at low ebb. During the field visits, it is observed that the condition of rural pans in many houses has been pitiable. The possibility of deterioration of a rural pan over a period of time is quite high when compared to a ceramic pan. It is viewed that adoption of rural pans in the state has been driven more by ideological moorings than by a pragmatic approach. There is a need for a revisit to the ideologically loaded position of using only rural pans. Absence of appropriate research on the technology and design aspects concerning production of pans and construction of sanitary facilities has been noted in the state.

There is a high degree of exhaustion of ideas and programmes noted among the campaign managers in the some of the districts.[11] It may be because of the inability to sustain the campaign for such a long period. Every effort be made to achieve the targets at the earliest and to bring in diverse programmes and activities towards achieving 'Total sanitation'.

A Critic of Midnapore Model

Adoption of 'Midnapore model' played a prime role in achieving the targets of sanitation in many parts of West Bengal. The strategic approach in that model is to provide a small incentive to the poor to construct a low cost sanitation structure and to cultivate a habit of using toilets. It used to be at par with his/her living conditions. It visualises that when the socio-economic status of the poor goes up, there is a natural graduation to the sanitary facility constructed in his/her home as well. It goes without saying that when there is a natural progression to the living conditions of the poor, a corresponding improvement will be made in the sanitary facilities as well, without any further support from the state. However, the field visits through different parts of the state revealed that about 10 per cent of the population who adopted low cost toilets could not achieve the expected economic growth or their growth remained stagnant or deteriorated further. This resulted in the inability to improve the sanitary facilities as expected in the 'Model'. As the durability of low cost type sanitary facilities have been deteriorated over a period, they started feeling discomfort, which resulted in leading to open defecation again.[12]

A certain degree of manifestation of self-complacency over what has been achieved earlier has been largely visible among the campaign managers in Purba Midnapore and Paschim Midnapore Districts. In addition, this has also resulted in a large degree of intolerance towards criticism.[13] Though this cannot be construed as the failure of 'Midnapore Model', but points to the need for some changes to be adopted in the strategic approach. It is further suggested that a serious review of 'Midnapore Model' by an external agency need to be taken up as most of the functionaries in-charge of the movement have a large degree of sentimental attachment with it and unlikely to make an objective assessment.

(b) Uttar Pradesh

Some of the reflections gathered from the field visits through 21 districts of Uttar Pradesh have been mentioned below:

Interactions with the campaign managers and officials at different levels indicated that the direction of thrust of campaign in the State is given more towards schools than households. This is a strategy to penetrate to the family members (with several illiterate persons) by taking the support of children, as habit formation among them is quite easier. This strategy has been adopted as children can influence other family members, especially the aged people to wean away from open defecation.

During the field verifications, better performance in achieving the targets of TSC has been noted in some GPs where both the Pradhan and the Secretary are women.[14] Interactions with them revealed that provision of sanitation facilities being one of the prime needs of women, they are able to communicate the message of sanitation to the village population especially among women, and work together comfortably.

During the field visits through the villages of UP, it is noted that two types of social exclusion generally prevalent in certain areas have come down owing to TSC interventions. 'Intra-village' type of social exclusion is practised against certain households who practise 'manual scavenging' by different communities within the village. 'Inter-village' type of social exclusion is practised with a village where the concentration of such households who practise 'manual scavenging' is more by the nearby villages. It is observed that such issues of social exclusion could be tackled successfully up to a certain extent during the implementation of TSC in the state.[15] With the introduction of sanitary toilets, manual scavengers have moved to alternate avenues like farming, rearing non-milch animals, cleaning the streets, etc. It is felt that construction of toilets can be used as a powerful tool for inclusion of the excluded communities which leads to an 'all-inclusive village life'.

Dalit mobilisation and assertion in the villages of UP has successfully resulted in generating the demand for sanitation facilities by the marginalised sections of the society during the campaign. Demand for sanitation facilities exerted on the village panchayats have resulted in enabling distributive justice to them as both numerical strength and political equations favours them. It is observed that this has resulted in improving the sanitation conditions of the households in SC/ST colonies.

During the field verifications through some of the villages, it is noted that enabling environment in the area like the active role of number of ex-servicemen has been very much visible during the scheme execution. It is observed that active participation of several former soldiers in the village has given impetus to the implementation of scheme.[16] Even in many remote villages, where no support or intervention from the Block/District officials are available due to terror leashed by the dacoits, the construction activities have progressed well.[17]

During the campaign, number of consultants with specialisation in civil engineering, mass communication, social engineering, etc. were engaged at the State/Division/District levels. A rapid appraisal of the campaign through different parts of the State indicated that this has resulted in a positive impact on its execution.

During the field verifications, it is observed that several nominations of GPs with even less than 50 per cent of sanitation coverage at the households have been forwarded for the award.

These nominations may have been forwarded in the pretext that the targets would be achieved before the evaluation.

Interactions with the elected members, party activists and officials indicated that TSC has been given a prominent role at the State level meetings by the Chief Minister. However, this has not been in the agenda of political parties at the local level. However, of late the young leadership in the villages have started taking more interest in TSC, when compared to the traditional leadership.

During the field visits, it is observed that separate toilets for boys and girls have been made at the schools. However, in some places, it is seen that the construction was not made properly assimilating the philosophy behind this. It is observed that there is only one entrance to the toilet complex so constructed, though there are separate toilets available for boys and girls.[18]

It is observed that most of the efforts made during the campaign by the campaign managers have been more Pradhan-centric or Pradhan-Pati-centric. Hardly any effort was made to involve members of the GP in the planning and execution of the activities. It is also observed that most of the elected members of GPs were not sensitised during the campaign.

It is noted that provision of TSC assistance is not based on a rationalistic formula, but based on the demand from the Pradhan, his/her initiative in the campaign, interest shown by the GP Secretary, proximity to National Highway, demonstrative effect, personal preferences of TSC staff, etc. Influence of district/state level political leaders and chances of patronage distribution also could find their place in providing funds to the PRIs.

During the NGP evaluation exercise, it is noted that political and caste differences between the Pradhan and his/her opponents led to washing of dirty linen in the public at some places. This is mainly due to the reason that in case selected, the award will be received by the Pradhan from the President of India, against the wishes of his/her opponents.[19] It is felt that such attempts were made at number of places when the Pradhan does not belong to a majority community though there are exceptions also.[20] It would be better to address this aspect in such a way that the award is presented to the Pradhan of a GP on behalf of the whole village.

In the State, a specific scheme for achieving total sanitation coverage was initiated in five selected GPs of the State with increased financial support by providing Rs. 5200 as the financial assistance for an IHHL.[21] Due to economic reasons, it is known that such a scheme can never be replicated in other parts of the State. It is viewed that mere announcement of the scheme in some GPs itself has been a de-motivating factor for many other GPs in the same region. It is observed that they have slowed down their activities during the campaign, expecting a quantum jump in the allocations in the subsequent year. And the end-result is that mere announcement of the scheme has been proved to be counter-productive to the cause of TSC.

(c) Tamil Nadu

Some of the reflections gathered from the field visits through seven districts of Tamil Nadu have been indicated in the following paragraphs:

Involvement of NGOs in the construction of IHHLs has been an innovative approach introduced in the State. After an IHHL is constructed, an incentive of Rs. 50 is permitted to the NGOs on the submission of its photograph with the members of the household. In addition, services of Self-Help Groups, youth clubs, churches and other religious bodies in their respective areas have been utilised for ensuring maximum outreach of the activities. It is also seen that political parties did not take any active role in the scheme execution.[22]

Government of Tamil Nadu and UNICEF collaborated on scaling up the SSHE programme in the State in December 2006. The strategy was to use monitoring and the collection of data as a tool for planning and managing the scaling up of SSHE by involving the officials from key departments like education, health and rural development at the block level. A survey was initiated in each school in four districts of the state to assess the presence of five basic indicators like drinking water supply, toilet availability, water supply to toilets, hand-washing facilities and training on SSHE. The assessment rated each school on a '10 star scale' and about one-third of the schools achieved 10 star status or came close with 9 stars. The study found that more successful school programmes tended to have trained teachers, active Parent Teacher's Association (PTA) and Village Education Committees (VEC), vibrant student hygiene clubs, effective NGO partnership and a system of mobilisation of financial contribution from communities.

Tamil Nadu has earned wide acclaim for its spectacular performance in improving the sanitation coverage of the rural population from 15 per cent in 2001 to 57 per cent in 2005. A special thrust on Integrated Sanitary Complexes for women have been built in all village panchayats. A total 13062 such complexes were built at a cost of Rs. 278 crore.[23]

Initiation of Child Friendly Toilets (CFT) is one of the innovations in sanitation movement in the State under the interventions of a NGO. The CFTs were constructed under Water Aid Urban Slums Health and Sanitation Improvement Programme in Tiruchirappalli. As they are constructed adjacent to the community toilets, maintenance is easy. No money is charged from the children for using it and the community pays for soap and other cleaning materials from the income raised from pay and use toilets managed by the women groups. The caretaker of the community toilet teaches hand-washing and its importance to the children and also keeps an eye on the hygienic behaviour of the children after defecation.

Number of technological innovations in the design of sanitation pans was initiated in the State as in 'Kuthambakkam model'. This has resulted in developing cost-effective models of bathroom-cum-toilet, which is generally preferred by women. Designs of mobile sanitation units were also created in the Kuthambakkam village, with most of the items produced by the small scale industrial units in the village itself, which gave further boost to the local economy.[24]

During the visits through the villages, it is noted that the implementation of the scheme in Tamil Nadu is generally bureaucratic-centred. The District Collector and the District Rural Development Agency (DRDA) play the key role in operationalisation of the scheme. At regular intervals, meetings of Village Panchayat Presidents and Block Panchayat Chairpersons have been conducted by the District Collector.[25] It is seen that the scheme has resulted in reinforcement of bureaucracy in the State, as in the *Periyar Model*.[26] One of the IAS officers from the State on deputation to UNICEF, P. Amudha, was honoured with a special award for outstanding contribution to the promotion of rural sanitation on 15 August 2005, by the Government of Tamil Nadu.

Gandhigram Rural University (GRU), Dindigul has organised number of training sessions for elected members, district officials, and other stakeholders from within the State and outside. It is known that Government of Kerala requested GRI to set up Sanitary Science Parks for State Institute of Rural Development (SIRD).

Number of nominations from the GPs with even less than 50 per cent of sanitation coverage at the households has been forwarded to the Government of India for Nirmal Gram Puraskar. It is known that such nominations are forwarded with the assumption that they will be able to meet the targets at the time of evaluation.

(d) Kerala

Some of the reflections gathered from the field visits through six districts of Kerala have been mentioned below:

According to Census 2001, sanitation coverage of households in the State with latrines is 84 per cent, which is the best available figure among all Indian states. However, there is a difference of more than 10 per cent in the rural and urban settings in the State, favourable to urban. Out of 65.95 lakh households in the State, 55.4 lakh households have sanitary latrines.[27] A recent modest estimate in this sector indicates the sanitation coverage in the State touches 90 per cent. No doubt, the above data on households may include those with unhygienic and unacceptable standard of latrines. Number of latrines without sub-structures (to collect excreta from falling into water) is functioning in the canals, backwater and other inland water ways. Number of field studies are available on the data in the sanitation sector contrary to the aggregate figures at the State level.[28]

PRIs are very much involved in the overall process of TSC in the State—from the selection of beneficiaries to the completion of facilities. It is noted that three-tier PRIs earmarked additional provisions from their Plan funds to the central share of TSC, especially in IHHLs and CSCs.[29] PRIs have made provisions in their plan fund itself towards realising the physical targets set during the campaign. It is viewed that the active involvement of PRIs during the campaign has led to enhancing the sanitation coverage. However, it has also resulted in dilution of the demand driven approach to a subsidy driven one as in CRSP.

Sanitation is one of the subjects transferred to the PRIs as part of the decentralisation process and this has paved the way for improving the sanitation scenario in the State.[30] Provision of a significant portion of plan funds to the Panchayats initiated during PPC has resulted in achieving a quantum jump in the sanitation sector in the State. In the Ninth and Tenth Plans, about 600 Grama Panchayats have given top priority to sanitation and more than 100 of them achieved the goal of 90 per cent sanitation coverage. During the period, PRIs initiated several projects for construction of household toilets, school toilets and community complexes during the PPC, as a forerunner to the TSC activities in the State.

SHGs and Kudumbasree units played a significant role in the implementation of TSC at different parts of the State. They were mainly used for creating awareness among the population regarding sanitation aspects. In some places, they were involved in carrying out the base line survey also. Selected members of SHGs/Kudumbasree units received masonry training during the scheme. It is noted that they have constructed number of sanitary toilets resulting in saving money in selected areas. Majority of the Community Sanitary Complexes in the State are managed by SHGs. It is noted that management of RSM/PC was entrusted to the SHGs in many places.

During the field visits through the State, it is noted that the role of NGOs/third sector organisations during the operationalisation of the campaign has been very limited. In some places, they were used for environment creation and organising capacity building sessions during the campaign. In some places, they were entrusted with the responsibility of running CSC also. However, it is noted that the existing potentials of third sector organisations have not been properly tapped, incorporated and utilised during the campaign.

In the recent times, number of PRIs have started giving more attention to solid waste management in their activities. Government of Kerala brought out an order in 2006 instructing PRIs to prepare a 'sanitation approach document' as part of *Malinyamuktha Keralam* (Clean Kerala) project which special attention to solid and liquid waste management in their functional areas.

A sanitation park has been set up at Kerala Institute of Local Administration (KILA) campus as a tool for demonstration of different models and types of sanitary units during the training sessions to elected members and officials of PRIs. This demo park was set up with the financial support from UNICEF, Chennai. However, it is observed that the facility is not utilised on the expected lines during the capacity building sessions for the elected members from PRIs.

Significant strides the state has made in the fields of literacy, health and sanitation, and the 'boast of a relatively high personal hygiene of an average *Malayalee*' have not been adequately reflected in improving the community hygienic standards in the State. This may be a great paradox, which needs further analysis.

The officials/staff involved in the implementation of TSC at different levels were primarily drawn from the Rural Development Department (RDD) of the State Government. Generally it is seen that the assignment with the TSC is treated as a 'soft option' by the RDD officials, which may have its own inherent limitations.[31]

Due to high density of population and land fragmentation issues, a significant section of families dwell in small and even tiny lands, with no space or inadequate space for construction of toilets. In many cases, construction of toilet has been an area of conflict with neighbours whose water sources fall within the distance limits. Panchayat had to intervene during the past for finding out the solution while dealing with such cases. In many cases, scientific and technological options available are limited and not cost-effective. Political expediency may be the deciding factor in settling such issues, either in favour of protecting the water source or permitting the construction of toilet. And it is seen that in majority cases, the decision is taken at the cost of 'total sanitation'.

Procedural issues stand in the way of enabling the benefits of TSC by the people in the State. In Kerala, a potential beneficiary needs to produce various documents (Title deed, land tax receipt, ration card of the family which includes the name of the beneficiary and BPL certificate) to become eligible for the scheme assistance. In case of non-availability of title deed, he/she is required to produce a certificate from the Village Officer of Revenue Department stating that he/she is a permanent resident of the area for the last 12 years.[32]

By keeping the system for sanctioning of the scheme assistance highly rigid and cumbersome, many potential beneficiaries could not avail the assistance. In such cases, he/she has no other option than to go for open defecation, until a facility is available. Hence, the target of achieving the remaining families cannot be achieved easily. The practice of fixing criteria for a potential beneficiary of TSC seems to have been adopted from housing and other welfare programmes. And the criteria may have little relevance while addressing the issues of health and hygiene sectors. Only by taking a liberal approach in dealing with the issues of sanitary sector, the scheme benefits will reach a certain segment of population living in *Poromboke* lands, slum areas, and other common places.

During the field monitoring through the Districts, it is noted that operationalisation of the programme has not been practised as a 'concerted campaign' in most of the places. The synergy expected among various departments/agencies in a campaign approach could not be realised in the field. It is being implemented as another centrally sponsored programme of the RDD in which the existing officials themselves are involved in the implementation. No functional linkages could be seen with the different sectors like health, water supply, women's welfare, SC/ST development, etc., during the execution.

No doubt, sanitation and water supply should go hand in hand. However in Kerala, the Department of Rural Development is implementing the TSC and the Public Health Division of Kerala Water Authority under the Department of Water Resources is implementing the Swajaldhara in most of the districts. It is revealed from the field that the overall impact of both the schemes could not achieve the expected results, since these schemes are implemented independently, without any functional linkages and co-ordination between them.

No active linkage/collaboration with other centrally sponsored programmes could be noted during the campaign in the State. By developing appropriate linkages with those programmes and without losing the identity/ownership of TSC, the overall benefits/impact would have been much more as a result of co-production.

The campaign activities were also fund inadequate, with no specific proposal to address the sanitation issues at hotels, hospitals, water bodies, etc. during the programme. The totality of approach required for achieving tangible results in the sanitation scenario has not been adequately reflected in the programme.

Some level of insentivity to women has been noted during the campaign in the state. For example, certain illustrations in the IEC materials reiterate the traditional practices adopted in the families like woman cleaning the toilets, woman cleaning the surrounding areas, etc. There is hardly any hint available in the IEC materials as to the need for participation of men during such activities. The traditional division of labour between men and women in hygiene and sanitation tends to be reinforced due to such illustrations in the IEC materials. However, it is noted that a two-day workshop on 'Towards a more women-friendly and child friendly approach' was organised by the Kerala Total Sanitation and Health Mission, Thiruvananthapuram and TSC District Office, Thrissur at KILA. Elected members and officials from Panchayats, representatives from professional organisations and officials from different development departments of Government of Kerala participated in the workshop. The workshop led to wide deliberations regarding the gender and child sensitive approaches and to bring out appropriate strategies, tools, techniques and operational guidelines to overcome the lacunae.

No specific thrust was provided to address the attention of marginalized sections like Scheduled Tribes during the implementation in the State. This has been largely noted during the preparation of IEC materials. Absence of specific thrust on tribals in the IEC activities may have resulted in not sufficiently translating the efforts into tangible results in the selected areas.

The scheme assistance provided in the state Rs. 2000, includes contribution from plan funds of three-tier PRIs as well, in addition to the central funds. It is viewed that this has been an attractive amount for ineligible beneficiaries as well and several such cases were spotted during the field visits. At the same time, rent seeking behaviour of certain RDD officials is also noted from different parts, especially in geographically vulnerable areas of the State.

Highlights from the States

A scan undertaken through the scheme execution in four states show that there is hardly any common aspect present in them. However, an attempt has been made to derive some of the salient features to make a model out of their experiences. Politicising TSC, support to the campaign by the bureaucracy and active role of NGOs during the campaign could be taken out of West Bengal context. Support offered by consultants from diverse fields like civil engineering, communication and social engineering and the thrust on school sanitation has been noteworthy in Uttar Pradesh. Incentive offered to NGOs for promoting total sanitation and use of diverse technological options have been significant in Tamil Nadu. Pro-active role of three-tier PRIs, a recent movement for incorporating waste management into the campaign and the need for a flexible approach towards the target group have been taken out of Kerala context. A convergence of the salient features of these States may lead to the emergence of an ideal approach in other parts of India. At the same time, there is a need to provide ample space for local initiatives and flexibility in approach in diverse settings while operationalising a scheme like this.

'Allegations' Against NGP

Number of 'allegations' about the process and efficacy of selection of PRIs could be heard from different sides, when its pitch was largely heard with the declaration of recent NGP awards. In this direction, a serious debate on NGP experiences from different parts of India was undertaken under the auspices of UN initiative of Solution Exchange for Environment/Water Community and Decentralisation Community.[33] During the session, 26 responses were posted by the campaign managers, social activists and academic scholars about the issues, concerns, and experiences related to the NGP. Some of the major allegations are listed here. *(a)* Some villages had received awards on considerations not entirely based on their sanitation status; *(b)* Many deserving villages were excluded; *(c)* Transparency in the selection process is very low; *(d)* Emphasis seemed to be on getting the award rather than achieving total sanitation; and *(e)* Evaluation in NGP found the emphasis on toilet construction more than its usage.

It is noted that there is some substance in the negative comments cited above. However, we would like to put forward our views in this regard. The very process of NGP award starts with the self-declaration by the Pradhan/President of PRI in the application indicating that cent percent coverage has been achieved in the area. This would be verified, countersigned and routed through Block administration, District office of TSC, District Magistrate/Collector and State office of TSC. Only then, the nomination is available to the Government of India for verification. This seems to be a manifestation of larger ethical issues in governance rather than the shortcomings in the selection process alone. MoRD has taken due precautions towards addressing the weak areas by taking several steps. Assigning the role of verifying agency outside the state of its functioning, taking strict action against the agencies involved in wrong selection process and ordering of re-verification of the claim of PRIs by another agency are some of the steps taken in the direction. However, the practice of re-verification has its shortcomings too. The process of re-verification has given rise to several claims coming up and in some cases, it is being used as a strategy to get as many awards as possible by staking claims (including several undeserving ones). In addition, it also gave sufficient time to improve the situations after the first visit and then seek for re-verification.

The motivational value of NGP has been widely accepted. The evaluation exercise itself can be used as a powerful tool for motivating the different stakeholders for strengthening the campaign. And it cannot be forgotten that the award money is again invested for the same cause in the same area, for improving the existing facilities or initiating unique activities. We would like to argue that there is no limit to the hygiene and sanitation practices and the concept is ever-evolving. Hygiene practices of yesterday, today and tomorrow would be different, and that will depend upon socio-economic aspects and technological advancements.

From our experiences, we can say with full confidence that at no point of time there was external pressure exerted on us from any side - either from the campaign managers at different levels or from political leaders. In this regard, we would like to specially mention the role of UNICEF consultants, as they have supported us in the exercise by presentation of facts and figures, without seeking any undue favour. And the enthusiasm about sanitation in the rural areas has been definitely increased, which helped to move towards achieving 'total sanitation' in their area by adopting multiple pathways.

'E' and 'F' errors are commonly occurred either while fixing targets or giving awards. 'E' error occurs due to 'Excessive coverage including coverage of non-eligible'; 'F' error is due to 'Failure to include all eligible' in the process of selection; and 'S' is the 'Share of non-eligible in the total award winning cases'. By considering the volume and cumbersome nature of work involved in the selection process and number of PRIs applied for the award, both 'E' and 'F' errors are quite negligible. And we admit that in this context, 'E' error has been relatively on the higher side. However, there is an in-built mechanism to correct both the errors in the process. The very logic of investing the award amount in the sanitation sector itself is an in-built measure to check 'E' error. As the award is presented on a yearly basis, 'F' error occurring in one year can be corrected in the subsequent years. However, in this regard, when we compute 'S', it is very less.

Suggestions

Number of suggestions are put forward to improve the implementation of TSC and to make the selection process of NGP foolproof, up to a great extent.

- Training sessions on various technological options be organised for rural masons on a regular basis.
- By making minor structural variations, two-in-one toilets may be constructed which will be a major point of attraction for women. Sociologically, open defecation is not viewed as a great sin in our country; but open bathing is. Towards catering to both these issues, cost-effective designs of two-in-one toilets are suggested, which will be a great relief to women.
- Generally elders carry out open defecation as they are accustomed with the old practice. In addition, joint pains and difficulty to get up after defecation generally found in aged people, discourage them from using it. This point to the need for a focussed approach to attract elders by creating additional support systems within the toilet and sessions for behavioural changes.
- There is an urgent need for internalising and

operationalising the concept of having 'child-friendly toilets' at the anganawadis.

- Efforts must be made for carrying out an Open Defecation Mapping (ODM) in a participatory method and through which appropriate remedial measures can be taken to check the menace.[34]
- Focussed attempts must be made during the campaign to involve all elected members of the GP towards increasing the programme coverage.
- Necessary efforts be made to actively involve CBOs, business community, retired persons, ex-servicemen, etc. during the scheme execution towards improving the programme output.
- The eligibility criteria for a beneficiary for receiving assistance for construction of IHHL shall be made liberal and flexible. This needs to be treated differently from housing and other welfare programmes, as non-availability of sanitation facilities in one family can lead to far-reaching implications in the health and hygiene of the community.
- Necessary efforts be made to bring TSC to the agenda of the political parties functioning at the local levels.
- Necessary support for Research and Design (R & D) activities be provided towards bringing out cost effective technological alternatives subjected to geographical variations.
- There is a need for scrutinising the nominations for NGP, by a process of graduation from the block, district and state levels. Even an independent verification of the claim can be initiated at District/State levels.
- It needs to be ensured that after achieving cent percent sanitary coverage, minimum six months may be completed before forwarding the nominations for NGP.
- The MoRD can think of inviting applications for NGP from the PRIs on a regular basis and to carry out the verification of the claim round the year to prevent the rushed process of selection for the award.
- The process of re-verification of claims must be used very judiciously. A liberal approach in the re-verification of the claims will send out a wrong message.
- The campaign managers must make the message loud and

clear to all that the NGP award is for the whole village and not to a single individual.

- During field visits through the UP villages, it is felt that some of the GPs need a focussed attention during the TSC and in the preparation for NGP. Presence of a number of habitations spread over a vast area, drought-affected areas, difficult terrains, dacoit-infested regions, availability of railway lines, national or state highways, presence of river bed, etc. may create number of impediments in the nomination for NGP. Hence a uniform approach is not feasible and practical here and a selective approach can also be thought of during the run up to NGP.
- NGP awardee GPs must be used as resource persons to motivate at least five more GPs in the subsequent years. In this line, some kind of assurance may be sought after the award ceremony. In addition, the Presidents/Pradhans of NGP awarded GPs can be included in the District Sanitation Committees as well.
- Need for a revisit of NGP awarded GPs to analyse the sustainability of the sanitation situation after a period.
- An extensive survey similar to the one undertaken by the Indian Institution of Mass Communication (IIMC) in 1997 as the baseline work for TSC needs to be initiated. Undertaking an extensive study with focus on the specific strategies and activities for High, Medium and Low performing States/Districts can bring further momentum to the campaign towards achieving 'total sanitation coverage' in all parts of the country.

Conclusion

Scanning through different IEC materials, interactions with the campaign managers and analysing the activities carried out, it is realised that Mahatma's perspectives and comments on sanitation have not been properly taken into account during the implementation at different States, though he can be called as 'the greatest proponent' of sanitation and hygiene. It is dismal to note that Gandhian activists and academicians did not give the desired attention to the campaign.

It is expected that the achievement in sanitation sector will lead to a better Human Development Index (HDI) for India. And the initiation of Nirmal Gram Puraskar for the PRIs has definitely given a positive boost to the sanitation drive at every nook and corner of the country. It is believed that this is a crucial move to make India open defecation free by 2012, much ahead of the UN timeframe for achieving the Milliennium Development Goal target for drinking water and sanitation. Only then we can hope to make a 'Swaraj without foul stench' as visualised by Gandhiji.

(Acknowledgements : Apart from the NGP visits, the authors are benefited by an exposure visit of elected Panchayat members from four districts of Kerala undertaken to Khejuri-1 Panchayat Samithy, Kamarda Grama Panchayat and Lakhi Grama Panchayat of Purba Midnapore District in West Bengal during 21-25 July, 2007 with the support of SDC-CapDecK, Thiruvananthapuram)

NOTES AND REFERENCES

1. www.ddws.nic.in (Website of Department of Drinking Water Supply (DDWS), Ministry of Rural Development (MoRD), Government of India).
2. A nation-wide baseline survey was conducted by the Indian Institute of Mass Communication (IIMC) on drinking and sanitation aspects. Details of the study is available in the consolidated report titled 'Water and Sanitation – A Baseline Survey' brought out by IIMC in January 1998.
3. This data on Sanitation coverage in South Asia was taken from the presentation by the DDWS to the Minister for Rural Development, in May 2004 (Downloaded from www.ddws.nic.in).
4 Discussions with Shibashish Banerjee, District Co-ordinator (TSC), Burdwan and Sakthisadhan Maiti, District Co-ordinator (TSC), Midnapore East in West Bengal. Similar comments were made by Wakkeel Ahmed, State Level Consultant (TSC), Dr. RK Shukla, Divisional Quality Control Co-ordinator and Pratima Verma, Divisional Co-ordinator (TSC) of Uttar Pradesh.
5. Role of party machinery during TSC was highlighted in a paper on 'Panchayat-Party Interface' presented by Rabiul Hussain, Local Committee Secretary of CPI(M), Khejuri-1, Purba Midnapore District during the Discussion Meet/Dialogue Session on West Bengal and Kerala Panchayat Raj Systems organised as part of the exposure visit to elected Panchayat members from Kerala by SDC-CapDecK and CRM initiative on 23 July 2007. Similar comment was made by Sushantha Mandal, Block Committee President of Indian National Congress (INC), Khejuri-1 and Prashanto Maiti, Zonal Committee Secretary of CPI (M), Khejuri-1 on 24 July 2007.

6. Interview with Shibashish Banerjee, District Co-ordinator (TSC) of Burdwan District in West Bengal on February 24, 2006.
7. This aspect was realised during the discussions with the elected members and political party leaders of number of GPs in Burdwan and Purba Midnapore Districts in West Bengal. Similar comment was made by Himangshu Das, Savapati, Khejuri-1 Panchayat Samithi of Purba Midnapore District in West Bengal and Member of CPI (M) District Committee.
8. Discussions with Sushantha Mandal, Block Committee President, INC, Khejuri-1 Block of Purba Midnapore District in West Bengal on March 9, 2006.
9. Discussions with Shibashish Banerjee, District Co-ordinator (TSC), Burdwan District on 24 Feb 2006 and KC Das, Joint BDO, Khejuri-1 Panchayat Samithy of Purba Midnapore District on 22 July, 2007. These two officials were very vocal on the corrective role of the bureaucrats. Many other local officials also expressed similar comments on the issue in a lighter vein.
10. Discussions with Prasun Kanti Das, Savapati of Shaheed Matangini Block in Purba Midnapore, West Bengal revealed that he is the major functionary of an NGO, 'Aamra Susama Jalaprapat', Demarihat, Tamluk, Purba Medinipur, West Bengal. He indicated that the NGO was constituted in 2003 after taking necessary permission from the CPI (M) District Committee. The NGO was instrumental in awareness building activities, preparation of IEC materials and organising training sessions during the sanitation campaign. On similar lines, many NGOs have been floated by party functionaries in West Bengal.
11. This was noted during the field visits through different parts of Purba Midnapore and Paschim Midnapore Districts in West Bengal during April 2007 along with Kumar Alok from Ministry of Rural Development. We have not shared this point with Kumar Alok. However, he is fully aware of the problems of rural pan.
12. This aspect was noted during the interactions with the officials and representatives of Ramakrishna Mission.
13. This issue was realised during the discussions with the campaign managers of Purba Midnapore and Paschim Midnapore Districts in West Bengal.
14. It is known that the understanding and team work displayed by the Pradhan and Secretary (Both women) in Lama GP of Banda District in Uttar Pradesh has been an important factor for the smooth execution of scheme in the area.
15. During the field visits through Hardua Aima GP of Kanpur Dehat District in Uttar Pradesh, it is noted that manual scavenging could be completely eradicated from the area during the campaign.
16. In Badpura GP of Etawah District in Uttar Pradesh, a group of 30

to 35 ex-servicemen were in the forefront of the TSC execution.

17. In Mavai GP of Kamasin Block, Tera-B GP of Naraini Block and many other dacoit-infested villages of Banda District in Uttar Pradesh, the construction activities in the field of sanitation have been done admirably.
18. This aspect was noted during the field visits through number of schools in Etawah District of Uttar Pradesh.
19. In Sadi Madanpur GP of Tindwari Block at Banda District in Uttar Pradesh, the former Pradhan, who forwarded the last year's nomination for NGP (2006) was in the forefront arguing that the requirements for NGP in the GP area could not be achieved now (2007). Analysing the issue, it is known that he lost the election in the last panchayat elections and now wishes that the present Pradhan should not receive the prestigious award.
20. During the field visits through Rampur Maghila GP in Umarda Block of Kannauj District in Uttar Pradesh, it is noted that the Pradhan belongs to a community which has only two families in the whole village area. However, during the discussions with the villagers, it is felt that they are quite happy with her approach, honesty, efficiency, leadership qualities and functioning.
21. The pilot scheme was introduced in Saifai GP, the home village of former Chief Minister of Uttar Pradesh, Mulayam Singh Yadav and 4 other Grama Panchayats in 2006.
22. During the discussions with Dr. Ponnuraj of Gandhigram Rural University (GRU), Dindigul, Tamil Nadu on the administration of sanitation activities in Tamil Nadu, this aspect was highlighted.
23. Excerpts from Tamil Nadu State Budget 2006-07.
24. Discussions with Elango, former President of Kuthambakkam GP and a Gandhian activist from Tamil Nadu on July 5, 2007.
25. This was revealed during the discussions with Dr. Ponnuraj of GRU, Dindigul, Tamil Nadu on July 3, 2007.
26. Details of Periyar Model are available in the book 'Environmental Sanitation, Health and Panchayati Raj' by Bakshi D. Sinha and PSK Menon, published by Institute of Social Sciences, New Delhi in 1996.
27. *Economic Review-2004*, Thiruvananthapuram: State Planning Board (SPB), Government of Kerala (GOK), p.185.
28. Details are available in the DLM reports on TSC in Kerala (2006-07) by Centre for Rural Management, Kottayam, Kerala and Draft Annual Report (2006-07) and Work Plan (2007-08) by the Research Unit on Local Self-Government, Centre for Development Studies, Thiruvananthapuram, Kerala.
29. More than two times of the central assistance on IHHL has been supplemented by three-tier PRIs in Kerala from their plan funds.
30. *Economic Review-2004*, Thiruvananthapuram: SPB, GOK, p.186.

31. This point was indicated in District Level Monitoring Report of TSC (January-March 2007) undertaken in 13 districts of Kerala by Centre for Rural Management, Kottayam, Kerala.
32. These issues were highlighted by Rajmohanan Nair, Member Kumaranalloor GP, Kottayam District, Kerala during the discussions on February 26, 2007. Similar comments were expressed by KP Sugunan, President, District Panchayat, Kottayam during one of the meetings of District Sanitation Committee.
33. www.solutionexchange-un.net.in (Website of Solution Exchange, a UN Initiative).
34. An effort was initiated by the Pradhan and Sanitation Team at Dingwahi GP of Banda District in Uttar Pradesh to eradicate on defecation and it found success.

17

Decentralisation of Panchayati Raj Institutions and Good Governance in Andhra Pradesh: A Vision of the Future

M. GOPINATH REDDY

Background

Democratic Decentralisation is viewed to be vital for overall development. It is argued that decentralisation leads to improved governance and better delivery and hence improving the livelihoods and alleviate poverty. The relationship between decentralisation and governance are manifold. Decentralisation leads to transparency in policies, responsiveness of the policy makers, accountability of implementers, openness and enhanced flow of information and hence reduces corruption. All these aspects are indicators of good governance. Decentralisation of governance is often argued to be more effective and efficient framework for delivering pro-poor programmes. The perceived benefits of decentralisation range from stimulation of economic growth, alleviation of rural poverty, strengthening the civil society and reducing the responsibilities of the centre (Manor, 1999). For, political accountability is often greater at the local level (Seabright, 1996). It was observed that project costs are four times higher in centralised systems when compared to decentralised systems. Besides, asset maintenance is much better in the decentralised systems (Bardhan, 1996). Decentralisation with its potential benefits coupled with the declining legitimacy of centralised systems has attracted support from a diverse range of ideological schools. However, it is cautioned that decentralisation is not effective or efficient in all situations. Under conditions of greater inequality decentralisation may result in political and elite captures and nexus formation between interest groups (Bardhan, 2002). While decentralised systems are found to be superior in terms of intra-regional targeting efficiency, their delivery systems target better in low poverty regions and worse in high poverty regions (Bardhan and Mookherjee, 2000).

In recent times, the issue of governance has emerged at the forefront of the agenda for sustainable human development. Experience from many countries shows that while good governance can help secure human well being and sustained development, it is equally important to recognize that poor governance could erode the individual capabilities as well as institutions and community capabilities to meet even the basic needs of sustenance for large segments of the population. This is particularly so for the poor, the disadvantaged and the marginalized section of the society. There is general acceptance now that human deprivation and inequalities are not merely for economic reasons rather they go hand in hand with social and political factors rooted in poor governance (HDR, 2001). Despite the diversity in the definition and paradigms of governance, there seems to be a consensus on the characteristics of good governance (see Box 1).

Box 1: Conceptualising Governance—Some Approaches

The World Bank

Governance is defined as the manner is which power is exercised in the management of a country's economic and social resources. The World Bank has identified three district aspects of governance (1) the form of political regime; (2) the process by which authority is exercised in the management of a country's economic and social resources for development; and (3) the capacity of governments to design, formulate and implement policies and discharge functions.

United Nations Development Programme

Governance is viewed as the exercise of political, economic and administrative authority in the management of a country's affairs at all levels. It comprises mechanisms, processes and institutions through which citizens and groups articulate their interests, exercise their legal rights, meet their obligations, and mediate their differences.

Organization for Economic Cooperation and Development

The concept of governance denotes the use of political authority and exercise of control in a society in relation to the management of its resources for social and economic development. This broad definition encompasses the role

(Contd..)

of public authorities in establishing the environment in which economic operators function and in determining the distribution of benefits, as well as the nature of the relationship between the ruler and the ruled.

Commission on Global Governance

Governance is the sum of the many ways individuals and institutions, public and private, manage their common affairs. It is a continuing process through which conflicting or diverse interests may be accommodated and cooperative action may be taken. It includes formal institutions and regimes empowered to enforce compliance, as well as informal arrangements that people and institutions either have agreed to or perceive to be in their interest.

Mahbub-ul-Haq Human Development Centre

Humane Governance is governance dedicated to securing human development. It must enable the State, civil society and the private sector to help build capacities, which will meet the basic needs of all people, particularly women, children and the poor. It requires effective participation of people in state, civil society and private sector activities that are conducive to human development.

Source: Adapted from Human Development in South Asia, 1999 — The Crisis of Governance, Oxford, p. 29.

Decentralised governance relies on the local institutional structures for delivery of pro-poor programmes. In India, decentralisation is often understood as devolution of powers to the locally (district and village) elected constitutional bodies i.e., the *panchayti raj institutions.* While these democratic institutions had an effective role in the early decades of independence, they experienced erosion of powers during the later years. This is mainly due to the absence of constitutional mandate for these institutions and leaving their fate to the whims and fancy of the state governments. Over the years state governments curtailed their powers in order to centralise the Governance structures. The 73rd Constitutional Amendment in 1993 was an attempt to resurrect these institutions. While the amendment helped in strengthening and systematising these institutions in terms of conducting regular elections, constituting the state finance commissions, etc., the option of devolution of powers, crucial for their vibrancy, is still in the hands of the State Governments. Despite the fact that the 73rd Amendment requires devolution of functions (29 in total), functionaries and funds, as per the 11th schedule, most of the state governments have not done so.

On the other hand, some states like Andhra Pradesh have adopted different institutional arrangements in the name of participatory institutions as decentralised delivery systems. These institutions effectively by-passed the democratic institutions and are also known as Parallel Institutions (PIs) or Community Based Organisations (CBOs) or User Committees (UCs). Financially these institutions are much stronger when compared to the PRIs. The rationale for promoting these institutions include: *(a)* user groups understand the day-to-day problems better than the elected and political representatives, *(b)* panchayati raj institutions (PRIs) failed to deliver the benefits over the last five decades, and *(c)* PRIs are known for elite capture and political patronage. However, divergent views are held on the role of these institutions regarding their effectiveness and their linkages with the PRIs (GoI, 1998; Sastry, 2000; Manor, 2001; Sitaram, 2002). Manor (2000 and 2001) argues that these institutions have not only weakened the PRI bodies but are also potentially damaging to the development. He calls for the integration of the user committees with the elected committees. The arguments favouring the convergence between PRIs and CBOs include: *(a)* improves the accountability, *(b)* address the inadequacy of powers and funds of the PRIs, *(c)* improves the sustainability of the programmes, as PRIs are permanent constitutional bodies. On the other hand, it was observed in a comparative study of AP and MP the participatory institutions like Development of Women and Children in Rural Areas (DWACRA) have delivered better pro-poor benefits. The authors argued "that MP's decentralisation process failed to challenge the well-entrenched power of the village chiefs, the *sarpanches*. By contrast, we make the case that 'political manipulation' on the part of bureaucrats and user committee members in AP provided tangible benefits to the rural poor, particularly in the form of low interest credit and subsidised grains" (Johnson, *et. al.*, 2003). However, these arguments need to be validated across other programmes in order to assess the general performance of the two types of local institutions.

It is often argued that these CBOs insulate development from politics. Manor (2001) counters: "This notion is a myth-and a dangerous myth at that. 'Politics—that is, the interplay of interests and forces in pursuit of power, resources, status, etc.—is pervasive." Elite capture was found to be a serious problem even in the case of community-driven development in West Africa (Platteau, 2004). How far these participatory institutions function above political interest and class interests (elite capture) and deliver pro-poor benefits is a moot point?

Decentralisation and Institutional Set-up in Andhra Pradesh

One way to look at the promotion of parallel institutions is the rationality of politics. That is, these parallel institutions are created by the state in 'top down' manner. Majority of the PRIs are occupied by the socially disadvantaged people due to the reservations for PRIs. There still exists an invisible wall between the village elite and other communities, more so in the backward regions. As per the reservation policy seats in PR bodies and their president posts are reserved as per the quota system. This leaves out less than 30 per cent of the seats (including women) for the forward (elite) classes resulting in a big drawback for the elite who previously held a majority of seats in the PRIs. The 'opportunity vacuum' created by the reservation policy seems to have been filled by the parallel bodies where there are no reservations for any group. Studies have shown that the higher positions of president/ chairman are disproportionately held by forward castes and economically strong households in the participatory institutions like watershed committees, water user associations, vana samarakshna samithis, etc. Therefore, the main argument that participatory institutions serve the interests of the users and the poor is not tenable. Similarly, there is no evidence to say that these parallel institutions are apolitical. In fact, studies revealed that political interference is widespread and positions are often shared/contested on political grounds and hence these institutions are equally politicised. These bodies often form nexus with political functionaries in PRIs or at higher levels of political system.

Structure, Purpose, Rationale, Roles and Responsibilities of Panchayati Raj Institutions (PRIs)

The Grama Panchayats (GP) stand at the base of the three-tier structure of local governance with the Zilla Parishad (ZP) at the district level and the Mandal Parishad (MP) at the intermediate level (Fig. 1). Along with 22 ZPs and 1095 MPs, there are 21943 GPs in AP covering a population of more than 55 million people. It is necessary to highlight the lack of a clear definition of what a

GP is in AP. Population of GPs varies from 300 to more than 30,000. This does raise questions on the economic viability of smaller GPs. In the case of Notified/Major Gram Panchayats there will be exclusive Executive Officers and in the case of Non-Notified/Minor Gram Panchayats, the Sarpanch himself is the Executive Authority. There will be a Village Development Officer for a group of five to six villages to look after the developmental works. At the intermediate level, i.e., MP Development Officers are not only the Executive Authorities for the Mandal Parishads, but are also the Executive Agencies for various other Departments/ Organizations which do not have executive agencies of their own. At the District level, ZP is the apex body as far as developmental works are concerned. It has several wings such as General Administration, Engineering, Education, Accounts, etc.

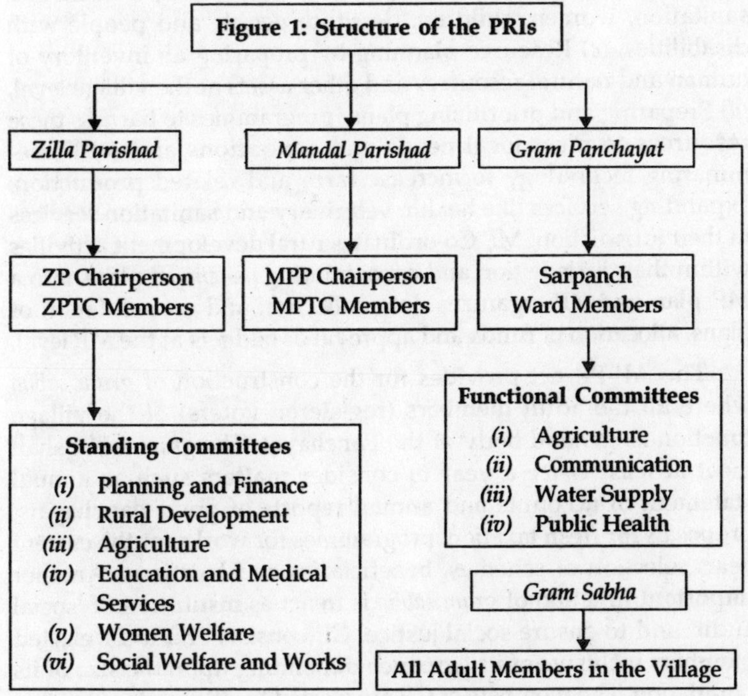

The departmental organisation at the district level consists of four levels–first the executive officers of Panchayats at the village level, second at the erstwhile block level which is headed by an Extension Officer (Panchayats), at the divisional level headed by a Divisional Panchayat Officer and at the district level headed by the District Panchayat Officer. All the above said officers deal with the subjects relating to GP only. The Commissioner, Panchayat Raj, by notification declares any revenue village or hamlet thereof or any part of a Mandal to be a GP. This excludes the following areas: Municipal Corporations, Municipalities, Mining Settlements, Cantonment areas, Nagarapalika Areas, Township Areas.

The responsibilities of GP include: *(a)* Implementing land reform measures, including consolidation of land holdings and cooperative management of community lands., *(b)* Implementing programmes related to agriculture, animal husbandry, cottage industry, pre-primary and primary education, health and sanitation, women, children, destitute people and people with disabilities, *(c)* Resource planning by preparing an inventory of human and natural resources and other assets at the village level, *(d)* Preparing and prioritizing plans/programmes to harness these resources to meet local needs and aspirations and *(e)* Disseminating technology to increase farm and related production; expanding services like health, veterinary and sanitation services in their jurisdiction. MP Co-ordinates rural development activities within their jurisdiction and consolidating *panchayat* plans into a MP plan and ZP organizes data collection and consolidation of plans, allocation of funds and approval of budgets at the MP level.

The AP PR act provides for the construction of *gram sabha* where all the adult members (registered voters) of the village function as general body of the Panchayat. The *gram sabha* shall meet at least twice a year to consider matters such as annual statement of accounts and annual reports of gram panchayats, proposals for fresh taxation, programmes for works for the current year, selection of schemes, beneficiaries and locations. Another important function of *gram sabha* is to act as institution of 'social audit' and to ensure social justice. GP consists of 5 to 21 elected members inclusive of its sarpanch depending upon the size of its population. The members of GP are elected by all registered voters from wards while all registered voters of the GP elect the sarpanch directly who continues in office for a period of five years unless otherwise removed from office. However, the elected members of the GP elect the *upa-sarpanch*. GPs are classified into *(a)* notified and *(b)* non-notified on the basis of their annual income. The notified *gram panchayat's* are again classified into *(a)* Group I notified gram panchayats (with an annual income of over Rs. 60, 000 and *(b)* Group II notified gram panchayats (with an annual income of more than Rs. 40,000 but less than Rs. 60, 000). Administratively, the notified gram panchayats are headed by an executive officer and assisted by clerks-cum-bill collectors, bill collectors, sanitary inspector, etc. The staffing pattern of non-notified gram panchayats comprises part-time bill collectors and part-time sweepers only. They are controlled by the executive officer. The salaries of these staff are to be met by panchayats' own resources.

For the purpose of election of members for MP from territorial constituencies, each constituency consists of population between 3,000 and 4,000. The elected members of MP are eligible either to contest or vote in the election to the offices of president/vice-president of the MP. At district level, the act provides for the constitution of ZP consisting of *(i)* members elected from territorial constituencies which obviously is a mandal, *(ii)* member of the legislative assembly of the state representing constituencies which form part or whole of the district, *(iii)* member of the house of the people representing constituency, *(iv)* member of the council of states who is a registered voter in the district, *(v)* two members belonging to minorities and co-opted by the elected members of the ZP. The staff of the ZP consists of Chief Executive Officer (CEO) to over see the administration of the ZP supported by the deputy CEO, parishad education officer, executive engineers, besides a few administrative personnel. The staff at MP consists of the Development Officer (MPDO), who is the overall in-charge of administration, supported by mandal engineering officer, mandal education officer, extension officer (rural development), village development officer (men), village development officer (women), etc. The striking feature in AP is that the administrative line of control of gram panchayat is direct and is different from that exercised at the MP and ZP level. The gram panchayats are under the control of the District Panchayat Officer (DPO). The executive officer of the gram panchayat works under the Extension Officer (EO), Divisional Panchayat Officer and District Panchayat Officer who are answerable to the collector. The other two bodies, i.e., MP and ZP are administered by the CEO. This arrangement is peculiar to AP alone.

According to the act, the ZP will be having seven standing committees. The chairman of ZP will be the chairman of four committees, the vice-chairman of ZP for one committee and two women members for two committees. In the present mandal system there is no provision for formation of standing committees whereas under earlier Panchayati Samities (PS) there was provision for 7 standing committees. The Act, provides for the constitution of 'beneficiary committees' for the execution of works of the GP and 'functional committees' for agriculture, public health, water supply, sanitation, family planning, education and communication at the GP level. However, in practice there is no evidence of such committees having been formed by the GPs (Reddy, 2003).

The present status of functional devolution in AP shows that its position is lowest among a few important states. It transferred functions in respect of sixteen (16) subjects of which five are with funds (agriculture, drinking water supply, minor irrigation tanks, social forestry, primary and secondary education and khadi and village industries) and only two are with functionaries (drinking water supply and minor irrigation tanks). Number of functions yet to be transferred remain thirteen; with funds twenty-four (24); and with functionaries twenty-seven (27) subjects; whereas in Karnataka state all the 29 subjects/departments have been transferred to panchayats with funds, functions and functionaries. Next comes Kerala followed by West Bengal and Madhya Pradesh (Report of the Tenth Five-Year Plan Working Group, 2001). In the recent years the Ministry of Panchayati Raj under UPA Government is showing considerable momentum to take forward PR reforms. As a part of this, activity mapping in various states and UTs is undertaken.

Status of Activity Mapping in States and UTs

The key objective of Article 243 G is to ensure that panchayats at all levels function as institutions of self-government. To this end, an essential step is to undertake activity mapping relating to developed functions with a view to attributing each activity to the appropriate level of Panchayat, keeping in mind the principle of subsidiarity. It was agreed during the first Round Table in Kolkata that all States and UTs would undertake activity mapping by the end of 2004-05, using the activity mapping model as evolved by the Union Ministry of Rural Development. It was also recommended

Table–1
Status of Devolution of Departments/Subjects with Functions, Funds and Functionaries to Panchayat Raj Institution in Selected States

State	*No of Department/Subjects Transferred of Panchayats*			*No of Department/Subjects Yet to Trasferred to Panchayats*		
	Functions	*Funds*	*Funct-ionaries*	*Functions*	*Funds*	*Funct-ionaries*
Andhra Pradesh	16	05	02	13	24	27
Karnataka	29	29	29	–	–	–
Kerala	29	15	15	–	14	14
West Bengal	29	12	12	–	17	17
Madhya Pradesh	23	10	09	06	19	20

Source: Ministry of Rural Development, Government of India.

that a measure of irrevocability could bear on devolution through legislative measure or, alternatively, by providing a strong legislative framework for devolution through executive orders. The progress of Activity Mapping, as on March 2006, indicates that AP is at the lower end of the spectrum as for as devolution and activity mapping is concerned (Table 2). AP is also among the 11 states that signed a MoU with the centre for completing the activity mapping in a specified time frame.

Participatory Institutions

Andhra Pradesh has had a long history of informal financial services purely as a local initiative, the women's savings and credit movement gathered momentum in 1993, in the Nellore district. Social mobilization enables the poor to build their organizations at grassroots level, in which they participate fully and directly and take decisions on all developmental issues. These emerging participatory groups are known as community based organizations (CBOs) or user groups (UGs) or parallel institutions (PIs) or sometimes also put under the generic term of Self-Help Groups (SHGs). The development of these groups or institutions has been phenomenal in Andhra Pradesh representing 60 per cent of the groups in India. These groups have become almost integral part in the programme design for the entire spectrum of development efforts in the State since late nineties. While the PRIs provide only limited scope for creating user or functional groups,

Table–2

Status of Activity Mapping (AM) Across States as on 16-3-2006

State/ UT	Subjects Trans ferred	AM Under Taken	Notes	State/ UT	Subjects Transferred	AM Undertaken	Notes
Andhra Pradesh	17	9	AM for critical subjects like housing not done. Only 8 departments have passed orders for Transfer of funds and Functions.	Orissa	25	7	Fiscal transfer yet To be made Draft AM prepared AM done for agriculture, soil conservation, PHED, elementary and secondary education, health and family welfare, irrigation, forest, industry, food, tourism, PWD, energy, technical education
Arunachal Pradesh	-	29					
Assam	29	29					
Bihar	25	-					
Chhattisgarh	29	27	Executive orders not issued	Sikkim	28	-	
				Tamil Nadu	29	-	
Goa	6	18	18 functions devolved to GPs, 6 to ZPs				Instructions issued for devolving all subjects to panchayats, but no actual devolution
Gujarat	15	14	Only 5 subjects partially devolved.				
Haryana	-	10	Subjects yet to be transferred	Tripura	29	21	Orders were issued for devolution of 21 subjects in 1994.
Himachal Pradesh	26	-	15 departments have issued orders delegating powers to panchayats	Uttar Pradesh	14	9	AM completed in respect of 32 departments. Implementation yet to take place.
Karnataka	29	29	AM implemented through fiscal devolution in 2005-06 budget with regard to 26 subjects.	Uttaranchal	14	9	Orders for devolution of 3 departments issued
Kerala	26	26	119 activities relating to 19 functions devolved. AM has been revised with complete details.	West Bengal	29	15	Orders issued in respect of 15 subjects for which AM has been completed
Madhya Pradesh	23	7	AM prepared by an NGO, Samarthan. Yet to be considered by government.	A & N Islands D&N Haveli Lakshadweep Chandigarh	3 - -	- -	AM in progress AM completed

Source: Ministry of Panchayati Raj, Government of India.

there is more number of groups than ever before. Each village now has 7 to 10 groups on an average and each group has 10 to 15 members. As a result, at least 150 people would have their own identity as a group member: in case of PRIs it is limited to 7 to 15 people (ward members). Regular meetings of these groups facilitate opportunities for people to interact and discuss various issues.[1]

Based on their activity profile the groups are organized under three categories viz., *(a)* Natural resource based (Water Users' Association —WUA; Watershed Development Committees—WDC; and Vana Samrakshana Samithis—VSS); *(b)* Employment generation (Women and Children in Rural Areas—DWCRA; Development of Women and Children in Urban Areas—DWCUA and Chief Minister's Empowerment of Youth—CMEY), and *(c)* Human resources development (Mothers' Committee and School Education Committees).

Need for Synergy: Strategy/Framework for Synergy

The argument has always been how to bring these parallel institutions under the purview of PRIs. These linkages are expected to increase the accountability of participatory institutions. According to one study which looked in to legal aspects of PRIs involvement in Natural Resource Management in the three Indian States namely Maharashtra, Madhya Pradesh and Rajasthan, the existing legal framework provides the requisite room for inter-relationship of the Panchayats with the user groups. The advantages of the user groups as smaller and specialized entities can be explored within the Panchayat Raj framework by the mechanism of committees. However, the efficacy of the Panchayat Raj institutions and the associated user-groups can be assessed with relation to their conduciveness in realization of the rights at the local level. This is particularly important when widespread emphasis is being attached to the rights of the local people in the discourse of participatory natural resource management (Upadhya, 2005).

Decentralization is being actively considered by the GoAP by interfacing between the PRIs and CBOs. The various CBOs that the government has created have resulted in spurting of many parallel structures, thus weakening the panchayats. The multiplicity of organizations has created confusion and has also resulted in conflict/s. The interface has become an important part of the GoAPs agenda in order to help make the numerous CBOs become more effective, sustainable and to strengthen the PRIs. A word of caution here is to accept that the inter-linkages would have limited role and effect in the process of decentralization and good governance unless definitive measures are taken up by the Government to devolve functions, funds and functionaries to the PRIs, ensuring decentralized planning and convergence. Empowering the PRIs would necessitate the higher authorities to disempower themselves. Devolution of power and authority from the State Government to the three-tiered PRIs would create space and opportunity to ensure closer measures of accountability.

Interface between the PRIs and the CBOs would usher in better mechanisms of accountability. Linkages are necessary to sustain and strengthen the CBOs and make them accountable to "all" the stakeholders at the Gram Sabha. The linkages already created and established by the various acts and other mechanisms have helped in creating only a token representation to the PRI members. The non-voting powers bestowed on the ward members and the Sarpanches has diluted their presence and participation. Also, the Gram Sabha's are used, if at all, for beneficiary selection. Gram Sabha should become an important forum in micro-planning where the different stakeholders meet to plan for the resources that are available to achieve convergence. Convergence cannot take place through a government order, (Sitaram, 2002).

Institutional and Functional Linkages

As of now, there are no Standing or Functional Committees at the Mandal. It is necessary to create committees at the MP on lines more or less similar to the ones prescribed at the ZP, viz., *(a)* Standing Committee for Planning, Finance and Works, *(b)* Rural Development, *(c)* Agriculture, *(d)* Women and Social welfare and *(e)* Education and Medical Services. The Chairperson of the ZP now heads four of the Standing Committees; this should be reduced to two.—Planning and Finance Works. The fee allowance, etc., are already in vogue and can be followed by adding on representation of the CBOs.

The Standing Committees at the Mandal can perform the role of *(a)* monitoring and *(b)* arbitration. Monitoring cannot only be regulatory also if incentive, encouraging the CBOs to perform better by arranging for monetary incentive, the Committees at the MP arbitrate when there is dispute between different GPs due to overlapping of function and jurisdiction (watershed area). The Functional Committee of the GP should be into planning and implementation, for those activities at the MP that also involves implementation, the fund release options similar to the ones described for the GP can be followed.

"APPR Act, 1994, provides for six functional standing committees at the Gram Panchayat (GP) level (Fig. 6). The seven to ten self-help Groups operating at the village level also represent more or less the same or similar types of activities. The gram sabhas shall co-opt one or more representatives of the SHGs into the respective standing committees of the Gram Panchayat. For instance, members of the Village Education Committee will be co-opted as members of the Standing Committee on education at the Gram Panchayat level. From amongst the co-opted members on the Standing Committees on education in all the Gram Panchayats, in a mandal, the Mandal Panchayat will co-opt in an open meeting of the Mandal Panchayat Samiti, a member/members onto the Standing Committee on education of the Mandal Panchayat. The Zilla Parishad in turn will co-opt, in an open meeting of the Zilla Parishad from amongst the co-opted members of Standing Committees on education of all the mandal panchayats in the district. The mechanism for selecting members in the other standing committees from the SHGs will be similar, starting from the Gram Panchayat level to the Zilla Parishad level".

The success of the benefits flowing from attaining the symbiosis between SHGs and PRIs will depend to a large on three things: *(i)* Strengthening of the PR institutions themselves, *(ii)* Bringing convergence of development programmes and institutions being implemented in the state by different agencies and line departments and *(iii)* Building the capacity of the Self-Help groups (Report of the Task Force of GoAP, 2002).

The Core/basic functions such as drinking water supply, health, sanitation including primary health centres and dispensaries, education including primary and secondary, roads, bridges and other amenities, etc., are the functions PRIs have been given mandate from its inception. The CBOs handling such activities such as Education Committees, Health Committees which are going to be integrated into the standing committees of PRIs are late entries in this arena of operation. In this scenario PRIs, given their long experience in handling these schemes would be the dominant bodies in terms of planning, implementation and monitoring of these functions (strong linkage). Members of the CBOs representing Standing Committees will act as pressure groups for efficient implementation and equitable distribution of the benefits.

The second arena of the discharging welfare functions such as poverty alleviation programmes, women and child development, social welfare of weaker sections such as SC/ST and physically challenged persons and other functions (Rural Housing and

Managing Public Distribution System) require that PRIs take slightly higher responsibility of course working in tandem with CBOs looking after some of these functions (moderate linkage). Mention may be made of DPIP (Velugu) SHGs, Mothers Committees and Disabled Groups etc. In this scenario, medium interface between PRIs and CBOs is desirable.

In the third arena i.e., Natural Resource Management (NRM) activities such as water, watersheds, water, forests, agriculture, etc., PRIs interface with CBOs is expected to be weak, which means that CBOs that are formed to manage water resource such as Watershed Committees (WCs), Water Users Associations (WUAs) and Forest resources (VSS/FPCS) need to be given larger role as they are found very effective in managing such resources. Most of the functions require technical skills and deep knowledge of the management of the resource. These CBOs formed around such resources found to have high stakes and PRIs which are governance institutions are found wanting in handling such resources and their capacities are found in adequate. At the most, PRIs can be monitoring institutions whereby accountability of the CBOs can be ensured to the constitutionally elected bodies. In this arena of managing NRM activities low interface between PRIs and CBOs is envisaged. In NRM arena PRIs can function mainly as watch dog.

The picture which is visualized at village level may be replicated at mandal and district levels. At district level apex agencies such as District Water Management Agencies (DWMA) looking after watersheds and District Rural Development Agencies (DRDA), District Forest Agency and Drinking Water and Sanitation bodies (looking after Swajaladhara Programme that is in the offing) need to be synergised with varying degrees of responsibilities with zilla parishads. Thus the bottom-up approach of the planning process synergising PRIs and CBOs is complete.

Conclusion

While the impact of the parallel institutions on the human resource development is unequivocal, the impact is very much limited. The main reason being that 'elite capture' is widespread among these parallel institutions. Number of studies has revealed that parallel institutions are mostly captured by the village elite (Reddy and Prakash, 2003; Reddy and Jenkins, 2004; Reddy and

Reddy, 2005; Reddy, *et. al.*, 2005). In fact, it is argued that parallel institutions are used to accommodate the elite who lost their positions in PRIs due to reservations (Reddy and Jenkins, 2004). This is more so in the case of NRM institutions, which have greater allocation of funds. Even in the case of self-help groups which are mainly meant for the poor, the coverage of the poor is only 56 per cent (Reddy and Prakash, 2003). One way of dealing with this is to integrate these institutions with the PRIs. Given their constitutional validity and reservation system, PRIs are likely to ensure greater involvement of poor in these institutions. Besides, bring these CBOs under the PRI umbrella ensures accountability as PRI acts as a monitoring agency/watch dog. The model suggested in this paper advocates three levels of linkages between PRIs and the parallel institutions. PRIs presently lack the skills and capacities to implement the NRM initiatives, where PRIs can act as a monitoring agent. On the other hand, PRI should be handed with full responsibility (implementing, monitoring, etc) in the case of core functions like drinking water, education, health, etc. In the case of welfare activities it should be given the intermediary responsibilities with partial involvement in the implementation. Such a division of responsibilities between PRIs and CBOs while avoiding the over burdening of PRIs, would ensure proper governance mechanisms on the part of both PRIs and CBOs.

REFERENCES

C. Johnson, P. Deshingkar and D. Start, 'Grounding the State: Poverty, Enquality and the Politics of Governance in India', Panchayats, ODI, Working Paper. 226, Overseas Development Institute, London, 2003.

C.S. Reddy and L.B. Prakash 'Status of SHG Federations in Andhra Pradesh: APMAS Assessment Findings', APMAS, Hyderabad, 2003.

Government of Andhra Pradesh, 'Report of the Task Force Committee on Convergence of Programmes', by Empowering Self-Help Groups (SHGs) and Panchayati Raj Institutions, Hyderabad, 2002.

Government of India, *National Human Development Report 2001*, Planning Commission, Government of India, Delhi: Oxford University Press, 2002.

Government of India, Report of the Working Group on 'Decentralised Planning and Panchayati Raj Institutions', for the Tenth Five-year Plan, Ministry of Rural Development, Government of India, New Delhi, 2001.

J. Manor, (1999), *The Political Economy of Democratic Decentralisation, in* Directions in Development Series, Washington DC, World Bank, 1999.

J. Manor, 'Democratic Decentralisation in Two Indian States: Past and Present',

Unpublished Mimeo, Livelihood Options Project, Overseas Development Institute, 2000.

J. Manor, 'Madhya Pradesh Experiments with Direct Democracy', *Economic and Political Weekly*, 3 March, 2001.

K.R. Sastry, C. P. Vithal, and G. Ramachandraiah, *Panchayati Raj in Andhra Pradesh in Panchayat Raj Institutions in Select States: An Analytical Study,'* Hyderabad, NIRD, 1995.

M. Gopinath Reddy, 'Status of Decentralised Local Bodies: Post 73rd Amendment Scenario', *Economic and Political Weekly*, Vol. XXXVIII, No. 12 and 13 March, 2003, pp. 22-29.

Pramab Bardhan, and Dilip Mookherjee, 'Capture and Governance at Local and National Levels', *American Economic Review*, Vol. 90 (2), 2000, pp. 135-39.

Pranab Bardhan, 'Decentralisation of Government and Development', *Journal of Economic Perspectives* 16(4), 2002, pp. 185-205.

Pranab Bardhan, 'Decentralised Development', *Indian Economic Review*, Vol. XXXI, No. 2, 1996, pp. 139-156.

Seabright Paul, 'Accountability and Decentralization in Government: An Incomplete Contracts Model', *European Economic Review*, 40, 61-89.

Shashikala Sitaram, 'Interface of PRIs and Community Based Organisations in Andhra Pradesh', Rural Poverty Reduction Project, Report Submitted to Society for Elimination of Rural Poverty (SERP), Hyderabad, April, 2002.

V. Ratna Reddy and Jenkins, 'Decentralisation, Participatory Institutions and Elite Capture (A Case of Watershed Development Programme in Andhra Pradesh, India)', Unpublished Paper, Centre for Economic and Social Studies, Hyderabad, 2004.

Videh Upadhya, *Panchayats, Water User Groups and Law in India: With Specific Studies on Participatory Irrigation Management, Rural Water Supply, and Watershed Development*, CSLG Working Paper Series (CSLG/WP/05-06), Centre for the Study of Law and Governance, Jawaharlal Nehru University, New Delhi, 2005.

18

Karnataka Panchayati Raj System: A Step Towards Good Governance

N. SIVANNA

Introduction

Decentralisation has been a key concept in progressive reform strategies in developing countries for promoting qualitative governance (Villadsen, 1999). It is also seen as a process of empowerment and a way for depressed class to reach mainstream social, economic and political life (Aziz, 1996; Mathew, 1995). Empowerment of decentralised units towards achieving good governance is one of the important development agenda items of the many developing countries. In the Indian context, the empowerment of rural local self-governments—Panchayati Raj Institutions (PRIs)—has been a priority area of the both Central and State Governments ever since their establishment in our federal polity. So far, several important and constructive efforts have been being made, especially by the Central Government (recent meeting of writers and thinkers, and earlier round-table meetings) and some state governments for empowering these grassroots level institutions in terms of political, administrative and financial decentralization. Falling in this line is the Government of Karnataka, which has put in some efforts to empower the panchayats through certain policy initiatives and amendments to its Panchayat Raj Act, 1993. As a consequence of these initiatives and amendments, there are some apparent improvements especially in the delivery of services and in ensuring transparency and accountability in the governance.

Set in the above framework, this paper closely examines the implication of these amendments and administrative initiatives for ensuring participatory governance, transparency and accountability in panchayat governance in particular, and decentralized planning and development, in general. This chapter is organised in to three sections: Section I gives in brief the *structural and functional aspects of Karnataka Panchayat Raj Act of 1993;* Section II analyses the *policy initiatives and the amendments for strengthening panchayat raj system and its process;* and Section III provides *concluding remarks.*

SECTION–I

Keeping in view of the broad framework of the 73rd Amendment, the Government of Karnataka redesigned the structure and pattern of PRIs. It is significant to note that Karnataka was the first State to pass a new legislation in 1993, namely, The Karnataka Panchayat Raj Act, 1993. The new act provides for a three-tier structure of Panchayat Raj with Zilla Panchayats (at the district level) Taluk Panchayats (at the Taluk level) and Gram Panchayats (at the village level). The Bill for constituting panchayats, which was introduced on 1, April 1993, came into force from 18, May 1993.

All the three panchayats are directly elected bodies. In its preamble, the 1993 Act resolves for promoting greater participation of the people and ensuring more effective implementation of rural development programmes. It also recognises panchayats as 'Units of Local Self- Government'. In conformity with the Eleventh Schedule of the Constitution, the 1993 Act has entrusted a wide range of functions (Schedules I, II & III) to panchayats. To carry out these functions, the Gram Panchayats, at present, receives Rs. 5 lakhs as annual grant and has powers to levy tax on buildings and lands, levy water rate, tax on entertainment, vehicles, advertisement and hoarding, market fee, fee on bus-stands and on grazing cattle. Both the Taluk Panchayat and the Zilla Panchayat are allowed to-charge fee on their property used by others but do not have powers to levy taxes. In addition, both the Grama Panchayats and the Taluk Panchayats obtain proceeds from cess on land revenue, surcharge on stamp duty levied by the State Government. Except for these, the panchayats have to depend solely on the resources transferred from the Government (for details see, Sivanna, 1998).

Karnataka comprises 5,652 Gram Panchayats, 176 Taluk Panchayats and 27 Zilla Panchayats. It has to its credit for entrusting major responsibilities and devolving all the 29 functions (a first State to do so in the country as a whole) as enlisted under the Eleventh Schedule of the Constitution 73rd Amendment. Karnataka is one of the few States that allotted more than the stipulated percentage of budget funds to its PRIs. It has allotted 28 per cent of its non-plan expenditure and 34 per cent of its total expenditure to PRIs.

SECTION-II

In recent years, the Karnataka Governement has been taking a procative stance to strengthen rural decentralisation governance and has introduced many administrative innovations, through policy measures and amendments, which have significant implications for promoting and operationalising the principles of good governance. They are as follows:

- The responsibility of plan formulation and implementation have been devolved to the panchayats by transferring the functions, functionaries and finances, and the Deparment of Rural Development and Panchayat Raj (RD&PR) has issued guidelines to prepare district perspective plan.
- Allocations to panchayats have been increased by 123 per cent, that is, from Rs. 1595 crore in 2004-05 to Rs. 3561 crore in 2005-06.
- Introduction of social auditing in the form of Jamabandhi to ensure transparency in the system; Grama Panchayats are empowered to call for tenders for all works with an estimated cost of Rs. 10,000 and above and for procuring materials worth Rs. 5000 and above.
- Computerisation of Grama Panchayats, taluk panchyayats and zilla panchayats; currently all the 27 Zilla Panchayats, 150 Taluk Panchayats and 1,270 Grama Panchayats have been computerised and some with broadband facility.
- Grama Panchayats Secretaries draw their salaries from the Grama Panchyat's account, thereby are more accountable to their panchayats.
- Capacity building programmes such as-certificate course for panchayat members, conducted by the University of Kuvempu, imparting functional literacy to around 2,1000 illiterated Grama Panchayat members, training through

satellite networks to all 93,000 plus elected panchayats functionaries at ANSSIRD, Mysore.

- to involve panchayats actively in the provision of public services, the department of RD&PR has initiated many new programmes like the *Kugrama-Suvarna* Grama Programme in 212 most backward villages, construction of water harvesting structures in 54 taluks; and *Namma Bhoomi Nammaa Thota* for improving the living standards of the landless in rural areas, construction of 51 lakh toilets for Below Poverty Line (BPL) and Above Poverty Line (APL) families under Total Sanitation Programme (for details, see Sekher *et al.*, 2006).

In addition to above policy initiatives, the Government of Karnataka, based on the suggestions of the Working Group, constituted in the year 2001, has evolved a detailed range of 'Activity Mapping' for all the three panchayats. Complying with the suggestions, the Cabinet Sub-committee had cleared an 'Activity Mapping Framework' in August 2003. Broadly, the activity mapping visualises both Zilla Panchayats and Taluk Panchayats as planners, facilitators and owners of common executive machinery, Grama Panchayats as the cutting edge of local service provision, and Grama Sabha and Ward Sabhas as instruments of downward accountability. The new activity mapping framework devolving functions has to be accompanied by adequate devolution of finances and functionaries. Government and Panchayat activities are to be separated through appropriate delegation of administrative functions and powers along with schemes to the appropriate levels. To translate this into reality, the department of RD&PR is in the process of coordinating with other departments to devolve functions, functionaries and finances.

Another step in the above direction is the simplification and rationalisation of schemes. Accordingly, the number of line items in the Panchayat Sector of the Budget is now reduced from 658 to about 330, thus simplifying the District Sector fund transfer mechanism. Minor schemes have been merged into larger ones, giving greater flexibility to panchayats to address their priorities. All State Sector schemes and funds dealing with functions devolved to panchayats are now transferred to the District Sector, with effect from the 2005-06 budget. With this, it is expected that the average budget for a gram panchayat in Karnataka would increase to Rs. 35 lakh.

One of the significant policy measures implemented by the State Government is the arrangement for direct release of funds through banks to gram panchayats thereby protecting them from treasury bans. The arrangement involves six nationalized and 12 grameena banks, in which all Grama Panchayats hold accounts. As a result, the maximum time taken for funds to reach panchayats has come down from 2 months to 12 days. Because the entire process is automatic, corruption in fund transfers has been eliminated. Other equally important policy initiatives are as follows:

- Karnataka's Right to Information Act empowers people to seek information. Additionally, detailed instructions have been issued to all panchayats for suo moto disclosure of information pertaining to 34 areas of functioning, including details of works undertaken, estimates and so on.
- Department of RD&PR publish a newsletter, *Karnataka Vikasa,* which reaches all panchayats in the State. This publication, which carries all departments' recent circulars, has prevented the officials keeping elected members in the dark by not divulging circulars and instructions. This has become handy for the members to insist the concerned officials to read out at each meeting, so that they can keep abreast of the latest developments.
- As an innovative exercise, the Grama Panchayats were entrusted with the responsibility of conducting multipurpose household survey by re-conceptualising BPL survey format. Through this, the Grama Panchayats are now having their own datasets, which are found to be highly reliable and accurate. The survey, being supervised and managed by the Grama Panchayat members, was found to be of immediate use to ward and grama sabha for selecting beneficiaries and also to the Grama Panchayat.
- With an increase in the budgetary allocations to Grama Panchayats, there has been a growing need for necessary technical support and assistance. This has to be provided by the line agencies like Public Health Engineering and

Public Works Department (PWD). To facilitate this requirement the Act has been amended to provide for gram panchayats to outsource engineers from a panel maintained by the State University of Engineering. In addition, all the engineers of the Rural Engineering Department and the junior engineers with the Taluk Panchayat have been merged into one division, namely, the Panchayat Engineering Division. The engineers, who are re-deployed, are specifically assigned to the gram panchayats. Now three to four gram panchayats would share the services of an engineer, who would be accountable to them for his works.

- 'Jamabandhi', an innovative administrative mechanism introduced by the State Government in 2000 for inspection of the functioning of the Grama Panchayats, has had a significant impact. The programme has ensured openness in the governance of grama panchayats, and made Presidents and Secretaries of grama panchayats more responsible and accountable. There is a vast improvement in the dissemination of information and the attitudes of grama panchayat functionaries after the introduction of *Jamabandhi* (*Hindu,* 2003, *Sivanna and Babu,* 2004). However, there were few shortcomings in the implementation of the programme. As revealed from the field study (Sivanna and Babu, 2004), in many instances, the guidelines were not properly followed, lack of awareness among the members of grama panchayats, in particular and people in general, and more importantly, spot inspection of works executed was hardly undertaken by the officials concerned.

As referred to, in June 2001, the Government of Karnataka constituted a Working Group on Decentralisation, with the Development Commissioner as Chairperson. The working group, which submitted its report in March 2002, suggested a good number of changes to strengthen the working of panchayats that included legislative amendments, a framework for activity mapping, for rationalizing budget line items and transferring them to the district sector of the budget. By taking note of the above recommendations, the Government amended the Act 1993. The Karnataka Panchayat Raj (Amendment) Act, 2002 contains a good number of amendments that were brought in to the act for strengthening the panchayats in terms of political, administrative and financial. While recognising the importance of people's participation, the act states in its preamble that the panchayats have been established for promoting greater participation of the people and more effective implementation of rural development programs. To facilitate for the meaningful and responsive participation of the local people in the panchayat governance, the amended act provides for constituting "Ward or Vasathi Sabhas" in all the Grama Panchayat member's constituencies. The sole purpose is to give more opportunities to local people to participate in panchayat activities, thereby ensuring transparency and accountability in governance.

The amended Section 2 (16) of Chapter I of the Act describes grama sabha as a body consisting of persons registered in the voters list of a Grama Panchayat. Section 3-A of Chapter II describes about composition, powers and functions of the grama sabha. One of the important powers assigned to grama sabha is about identifying, selecting and preparing the list of beneficiaries for beneficiary oriented programmes (the list so prepared is binding on the concerned panchayat). But, unfortunately, these mandatory powers have been withdrawn through a recent amendment which authorizes a committee headed by the local M.L.A. to select the beneficiaries. This has been severely criticized by the public, intellectuals and more significantly, the functionaries of the panchayats, along with the support of NGOs and other like minded associations and groups, led strong protest movements against the highly undemocratic move of the government. Encouragingly, all this has resulted in a victory as the amendment bill was returned by the Governor back to the government to have a re-look at it.

There are also many significant amendments that are in practice, such as requiring the elected taluk and zilla panchayat members to declare their assets within three months from the date of commencement of his term of office and until the expiry of his term, in every calendar year, file a declaration of assets owned by him and any member of his family before the State Election Commission or Competent Authority. Further, candidates contesting elections to submit their election-related accounts in detail regarding the expenditure incurred by them from the date of filing their nomination till the declaration of results to the Returning Officer. Any failure on the part of a candidate will result in disqualification. In fact, this process was observed during the recent elections to taluk and zilla panchayats. However, as per the information available, the State Election Commission is yet to have complete information on the assets declared. Seen in the backdrop of electoral reforms, this could be seen as a good beginning and may have implications also for the macro-level electoral process.

Some of the other amendments aimed at strengthening the participatory aspects of panchayat's governance. By making general body meetings of the panchayats at all the three levels to be held every month (with a quorum of one-half instead of one-third), an opportunity is provided to members to voice their views quite frequently. Furthermore, to protect the sanctity and for ensuring accountability and transparency in the deliberations of the meetings, some radical amendments have been brought in to the Act. For instances, panchayats have to display the proceedings of the meetings, within three days of the meeting, on the notice board of the respective panchayat, along with the details of the names of the members voted respectively for or against the resolutions passed in the meetings. For ensuring the vertical accountability such as in dealing with boundaries and election-related activities, the Government has once again reposed its faith with State Election Commission and its officers by reverting back the responsibilities given to Assistant Commissioner, Deputy Commissioner, Commissioner and the Government.

SECTION-III

The above analysis of policy initiatives and amendments, undertaken by the Government of Karnataka, has been in a way to streamline, rejuvenate and reinvigorate the working of panchayats at all the three levels of Karnataka panchayat raj system. However, these policy initiatives and amendments are still in the process of evolving. At the same time, there are also apprehensions that these structural and functional changes may strengthen the hands of the bureaucracy in the absence of regulatory powers with the political executives (Sivanna, 2003). For instance, Section 234 authorises the Government on behalf of zilla panchayat and the Chief Executive Officer in respect of taluk panchayat and Grama Panchayat to call for proceedings or documents, call for explanations, whenever, the lower panchayats commit any irregularities and fix a period for a specified work. Also, Section 232 authorises an officer, designated by the Governemnt, in respect of zilla panchayat, the Chief Executive Officer in respect of taluk panchayat and the Executive Officer in respect of Grama Panchayat to exercise the powers of inspecting and supervising the works carried out by the respective panchayats, and examine the books of accounts and any other related documents.

Although, the above mentioned interventions uphold the role of the government and the officers in the activities of the panchayats, the Karnataka Panchyat Raj Act is known for balancing the powers between the officials and the elected members. The act has provided sufficient 'checks and balances' to control the arbitrary functioning of either the officials or the elected members. It is important to note in this regard that, every member of the panchayat and every officer coming under all the three panchyats—grama panchayat, taluk panchayat and zilla panchayat—is deemed to be a "public servant" (Section 286). As a consequence, every member and officer comes under Section 21 of the Indian Penel Code and the Prevention of Corruption Act, 1988 (Central Act of 1988). Both policy initiatives and the amendments intend to ensure autonomy to all the three-tiers, by giving them certain independent powers.

Notwithstanding the above, the current phase of reform, Karnataka's approach has been one of sustained incrementalism (http://Panchayat.nic.in). This was achieved through commitment to a strong theoretical framework, followed by persistence and timing in pushing reform. A slowdown and downslide seems less likely this time around, for the following reasons:

- Strong lobby bodies for devolution have been organised, particularly amongst Panchayat members. A non-partisan Elected Womens' Representative federation has been formed. *Karachuma* has been conducting voters' education campaigns, petitioning local legislators and networking among elected women representatives on panchayat-related issues.
- MLAs committed to Panchayats keep a vigil on any retrograde administrative or legislative action and seek and get assurances from the Government in the legislature that the thrust towards devolution would continue.

- The satellite communication system enables quick and widespread publicity for favourable developments. This creates expectations among Panchayats and reduces the possibility of the government backtracking.
- The media is very positive, with considerable space devoted to good news from Panchayats. Editorial comments have been universally in favour of Panchayats.
- There is a sustained effort at working closely with other line departments ensuring that their objectives are met and optimised through Panchayati Raj Institutions.

It is evident from the above description of policy initiatives and amendments that Karnataka State is certainly moving towards a 'progressive state' as far as promoting decentralised planning and development is concerned. As a corollary to this, recently, the Ministry of Panchayat Raj, Government of India, adjudged Karnataka as the "Second Best State" in the country after Kerala for its commitment shown for empowering PRIs. It is significant to note in this context that this achievement is being made possible irrespective of political regimes governing at the state level. The subject of decentralised governance has never been neglected, but the quantum of reforms depended on politico-administrative dynamics at a given point of time. Many of the recent reforms for empowering panchayats, no doubt, are taking time. But efforts are being made that the appropriate messages reach the common man in rural areas, development administration and panchayats. On the whole, the Government of Karnataka has made sincere efforts to move towards the attainment of the spirit of Article 243-G of the 73rd Amendment for making its panchayats as real centres of institutions of self-government engaged in promoting economic development in the rural areas and also to ensure social justice in distributing the benefits of development to all the sections of society, including the vulnerable ones.

REFERENCES

Abdul Aziz (Ed.), *Decentralised Governance in Asian Countries*, New Delhi: Sage Publications, 1996.

George Mathew (Ed.), *Status of Panchayati Raj in the States of India*, New Delhi, Concept Publishing Company, 1995.

Government of Karnataka, 'Institutional Reforms for Human Development: Panchayat Raj'(Abdul Aziz) in Karnataka *Human Development Report 2005*, Bangalore, Department of Planning and Statistics, 2006.

http// Panchayat.nic.in/ *Panchayats in Karnataka best practices*.doc.

M. John Cohen and B. Stephen Peterson, *Administrative Decentralisation: Strategies for Developing Countries*, London, Kumarian Press, 1999.

Madhushree Sekher *et al.*, *'Making Decentralisation and Local Governance Work for the Rural Poor'*, Draft Report, Bangalore, ISEC, 2006.

N. Sivanna, 'Amendments to the Panchayati Raj Act', *Deccan Herald*, September 28, 1997.

N. Sivanna, 'Decentralised Governance and Planning in Karnataka: A Historical Perspective', *Social Change*, Vol. 28, No. 1, March 1998.

N. Sivanna, 'The Karnataka Panchayat Raj Amendment Bill: A Critique', *Panchayati Raj Update*, August, 2003.

N. Sivanna, and M. Devendra Babu, *Panchayat Jamabandhi in Karnataka: A Case of Transparency and Accountability in Good Governance, Working Paper 142*, Bangalore, Institute for Social and Economic Change, 2004.

Prabhu Nagesh, 'Jamabandhi Improves Functioning of GPs', Bangalore, *The Hindu*, April 17, 2003.

Soren Villadsen, *Good Governance and Decentralisation, Public Sector Reforms in Developing Countries*, Copenhagen, 1999.

The Karnataka Panchayat Raj Act, 1993, Bangalore, Karnataka Law Journal Publications, 2004.

19

Social Marketing: A Case Study of Drinking Water Supply and Sanitation in Karnataka State

VEERASHEKHARAPPA

Introduction

In India, the local governments have conceived as an instrument for providing of services at the village level, because of the responsibility and closeness to the people. The local governance is also proved to be competitive in management of services like promotion of education, health care, and poverty elimination programmes etc. (Slater and Watson, 1993; Singh, 1999; Crook and Manor, 1998). Since introduction of reforms, the governments considering greater roles for the private sector, NGO's and community in social marketing of services, including water supply and sanitation. This approach has been making inroads due to change in demand for the quality of services, further the social market is being achieved through participatory management, by giving chance to stakeholders to raise their voice and choice (Rao and Veerashekharappa, 1989; Harmeyer and Mody, 1997; Pushpangdan and Muragan, 1998) this minimizes the role of bureaucrats and pave the way for stakeholder (Saleth and Dinar, 1999) and will have a positive correlation between participation and delivery of services (Prokopy, 2004). Thus, studies strongly support that the replacement of state monopoly (water supplies and sanitation) and bringing them under social marketing mechanism will have efficiency in provision of services. Other scholars have shown reservation, according to them this will have unfair burden on poor (Oakley, 1991), and participate against their will (USAID, 1993), benefits skew in favour of affluent section of society (Veerashekharappa, 2002).

In India, presently an attempt is being made for social marketing services through various models through reform projects[1] including bilateral and multilateral. In fact, the water and environmental sanitation services are being marketed under quality of life concept. The community is made part of whole process the results are mixed (Veerashekharappa, 2006). Given this background, this paper examines social marketing under 73rd Constitutional Amendment, with the following objectives:

- To identify the mandated functions of the local government in service provision.
- To assess the different dimension of social marketing of services and effective delivery.
- To identify constraints in social marketing the services.

The required material for this chapter is drawn from published secondary data (annual reports, sectoral reports, etc.) based on various acts, government legislations and studies carried out by the scholars and practitioners.

Drinking Water Supply

Introduction

Providing potable drinking water and sanitation is a state subject and central government supports through budgetary allocation[2] and policy directions. But, now the government wants market through new programmes, such as Swajaldhara. Under this, service providers have to market the concept that the water is commodity and it has price. To market this concept, the community, including vulnerable section has been included, assuring them that through cross subsidy there interested is protected.

Situation in the State

In Karnataka, both center and state government have been making all efforts to provide safe drinking water and sanitation services in rural areas. The Karnataka State's vision is to provide accessibility of potable water to entire rural population (GoK, 2003), which is ahead of Million Development Goals (MDG). The Government of Karnataka carried out activity mapping under panchayat raj system among its three-tiers institution. The funds required for investment was drawn from, in addition to budgetary allocation, from donor agencies in the form of grant and aid. Thus, the source of funds so far is from government and aid from other agencies Table 1. However, funds received from other agencies are channeled through ministry of Rural Development and Panchayati Raj but sometime by passing local governments.

Table-1

Source of Finance for Water Supply and Sanitation Projects

Central Government	*State Government*	*External Aided*
Accelerated Rural Water Supply (ARWS).[1] National Drinking Water Mission (renamed as Rajiv Gandhi National Drinking Water Mission[2]) Sector Reforms Programme[3], Swajaladhar[4] a Total Sanitation campaign MP Funds.	Minimum Needs Programme[5] (MNP) & other Programme's[6] (Drought Relief Programme. MP and MLA Development Fund, etc.), resources from panchayat (local tax and tariff). Nirmal Grama Yojana, Swacha Grama Yojane and Legislature Fund.	World Bank[7], Dania[8] and Netherlands[9], etc.

1. DANIDA, KFW, DfiD, World Bank, UNICEF, UNDP and European Union and sector reforms programme introduced with Tenth Five Year Plan.
2. Under the ARWS, the grants and funds considered for schematic were provided to the state governments for provisioning safe drinking water.
3 Under this programme five sub-missions were constituted focusing on—water quality, drying up sources, construction of water conservation and recharge structures and other measures that can be state specific.
4. The programme was implemented in 64 district across country in Karnataka is implemented in Bellary, Mysore and Dakshina Kannada districts.
5. This programme is being implemented since 2002.
6. Government of Karnataka provides funds under budgetary allocation.
7. Funds provided for Gram Panchayat resources mobilized through, water tariff, local tax on property, in addition to grants to maintain assets.
8. Bangalore Ruaral, Kolar, Mandya, Mysore, Shimoga, Hassan Dashina Kannada, Bidar, Gulbarga, Raichur Bellary and Tumkur.
9. Kolar, Bijapur, Bagalkot and Chitradurga.

Activity Mapping

According to activity mapping, the functions of three-tiers are specified. Zilla Panchayat is the top-tier body of the PRI system and receives funds from central and state governments to perform activities. Similarly, the Taluk and Gram Panchayat do perform functions specified under activity mapping. It is anticipated that involvement of PRIs was to help correct the imbalance in provision of water and sanitation services. For this, each tier is specified particular function in provision of potable drinking water and sanitation services. However, in recent years these bodies are outsourcing some functions under pretext of reforms. The outsourcing is done through social marketing.

Table-2
Drinking Water Supply by Responsibility at Different Tiers

Activity	*Distribution of Functions*		
	Zilla Panchayat	*Taluk*	*Gram Panchayat*
Development of Water Supply System	Formulating major water supply schemes. Technically appraising and approve schemes proposed by TPs and GPs. Awarding contracts for the execution of major schemes outside TP and GP plans. Estalishing water testing laboratories for the control of chemical and biogenic impurities.	Formulating Projects and seek technical approval from ZP. Construct schemes within the prescribed cost limits for TPs.	Identifying schemes and locations, estimate cost & formulate projects through the involvement of Gram Sabha. Constructing wells, tanks and village water supply schemes of its own or as assigned by the ZP or TP Periodically chlorinating open wells and treat water. Ensure proper distribution of water to all households in its villages. Collecting water sample for testing.
Monitoring rural water supply schemes	Monitor and supervise the progress, quality of work and target achievement	Monitor and Supervise progress and quality of works	Monitoring scheme implementation and report progress
Maintenance of Water supply system			Maintain drinking water schemes, collect water charges and appoint operators wherever necessary

Source: State Gazetteer, August 22, 2003.

Under the reforms, the government proposes gradually withdraw from provision of services and assigning to an agency for social marketing. Under this approach, the community not only owns the responsibility of meeting the total cost of O & M but also shares partial capital cost. For instance, in World Bank assisted Integrated Water Supply and Sanitation (IRWSS) project, 30 per cent of capital cost of sanitation services is borne by community through social marketing. But, sharing capital cost through social marketing remained a myth rather than reality (Veerashekharappa, 2006).

Household Coverage

In Karnatata, 20 per cent of households do not have access to potable drinking water in rural areas (Table 2). And the accessibility indicates only the capacity but not the actual quantities of water being supplied. To cover both partially covered and not covered households, the type of schemes required are, 7,749 Piped water supply systems (PWS), 8086 Mini Water Supply (MWS) systems 8,086 and 48, 020 Bore Wells with Hand pumps (BWH). Thus, the total number of schemes required is 63, 855, on an average more than one scheme per habitation (GoK, 2003).

Table-3
Per cent of Households by Principal Source of Drinking Water (2001)

Sources of	*Karnataka*			*All India*		
Drinking Water	*Total*	*Rural*	*Urban*	*Total*	*Rural*	*Urban*
Tap	58.89	48	78.43	36.7	24.3	68.7
Hand pump	17.11	23	6.19	35.7	43.2	16.2
Tube well	8.56	9	7.51	5.6	5.7	5.1
Well	12.40	16	6.48	18.2	22.2	7.7
Others	3.04	4	1.4	3.9	4.5	2.2
Per cent of Households with Safe Drinking Water Supply.						
Potable Sources	84.56	80.00	92.13	78.00	73.20	90.00

Note: Others include Tank, Pond, River, Canal, springs and any other.
Source: Census, 2001.

As most of the villages are depending on ground water, the quality of water varies from place to place. The government has identified 37 per cent of habitations as facing problems of chemical contamination in excess of prescribed limit, indicating the poor quality of drinking water (GoK, RDPR, 2003). The studies have revealed that lack of skilled persons and the resource crunch that the GPs are unable to operate and maintenance services (Rajsekhar and Veerashekharappa, 2003) and made about 20 per cent of households depend regularly on old sources (Veerashekharappa, 1999). The study by High Power Committee reveals that 13 per cent of BWH, 15 per cent of MWS and 19 per cent of PWS schemes had irregular water supply (GoK, 2002).

Operation and Maintenance of Sources

The provision of potable water is a mandatory function of gram panchayat. However, maintenance is done by GP and TP. The cost of the maintenance depends largely on type of systems. As the cost of each system varies, for instance, a piped water supply scheme cost between Rs. 10 and 15 lakh, depending on location, population covered, distance of water source and distribution network. Similarly, a mini water supply scheme cost between Rs. 1 lakh and 2 lakh and a bore well with a hand pump cost between Rs. 30, 000 and Rs. 40,000. The annual maintenance cost of these schemes is between 5 and 10 per cent of their capital cost, but the government provided financial support for maintaining them at Rs. 8000 for each PWS, similarly, Rs. 3500 for MWS and Rs. 600 BWP scheme. This grant did not match 1/4th of total expenditure incurred in a year to maintain each scheme. To fill the gap, GPs were to generate own revenue to meet the operation and maintenance costs. To meet this cost, the social marketing has become inevitable. The household connection have been priced.

Table-4
Expected Cost in Provision of Different Services

Costs	*PWS Scheme*	*MWS Scheme*	*BWH Scheme*
Per capita investment costs	10-15 lakh	1-2 lakh	30-40 thousand
Cost of operation and maintenance	5-10 per cent	5-10 per cent	5-10 per cent
Per annum maintenance cost in Rs. (Approx)	1-1.5 lakh	10 to 15 thousand	3 to 4 thousand
Amount provided by government	8000	3500	600

Presently, the GPs collect user charges against the provision of drinking water to the household. But, 20 per cent of GPs do not levy any user charges, followed by 42 per cent of them were levied a mere amount between Rs. 5 and 10 only. Even this was paid by as part of property tax. The reasons was many households are still under impression that GP should provide water free of cost. To overcome this problem, the Karnatka Government issued an order to all GPs fixing a minimum of Rs. 25 per Private Household Connection (PHC) and Rs. 5 per household drawing water from stand post (SP). But, many GPs could not put it in practice lack of political will and inefficiency in provision of services.

The sponsored projects had assigned the responsibility of operation and maintenance to Village Water Supply Committee (VWSC), for social marketing of services. But, these committee have become defunct. For instance in Gulbarga district out of 102 schemes, two are functioning and in remained villages the schemes transferred to GPs.

Sanitation Services

Introduction

As mentioned earlier, the Government of India introduced reforms in Central Rural Sanitation Programme (CRSP) and restructured it as Total Sanitation Campaign (TSC, 1999) which was a step towards realizing the suggested reforms in the sanitation sector. This approach was based on 'demand driven' intended to bring efficiency in the delivery system and sustain the programme by involving the beneficiaries in the implementation of the programme by making them contribute a part of the capital cost (GoI, 2002). In fact, this new approach was based on the findings of a comprehensive Baseline Survey on Knowledge, Attitudes and Practices in rural water supply and sanitation by Indian Institute of Mass Communication, (1996-97), which showed that 55 per cent of those with private latrines were self-motivated. The TSC was involving all tiers of local government, at a district level the Zilla Panchayats, similarly, at Block and village levels, the TPs and GPs responsibility in the implementing programme.

Sanitation in the State

Since independence, the Karnataka state is having policy to provide sanitation services to all the villages including construction of individual latrines. The 20-point CRSP programme have facilitated to address the issue in a systematic and organised manner. However, the CRSP had the weakness of ignoring the households Above Poverty Line (APL) and covering only Below Poverty Line (BPL), households, for which it was not always a priority (GoK, 2000). The Mysore Zilla Parishad addressed this weakness by extending subsidy to all the households and named the programme Nirmal Grama Yojana (NGY). The outcome was very positive and encouraged by this; the State modified the scheme marginally and extended to the entire state on October 2nd, 1995.

Nirmal Grama Yojana (NGY)

As mentioned above, the programme was made accessible to all habitations and households in the state and required funds were made available under the Minimum Needs Programme (MNP). A cash subsidy of Rs. 2,000 and 1,200 was paid per latrines for households Below Poverty Line (BPL) and Above Poverty Line (APL) respectively. The programme was executed by GPs under the guidance of the NGY committee at village level, consisting of GP members, teachers and health workers. Of the total funds allocated 10 per cent was earmarked to create awareness and to train local persons for construction of latrines. To popularize NGY latrines among the elected member's an amendment was brought to the Karnataka Panchayati Raj Act 1993 in 1997. Accordingly, the elected Member of the GP was required to construct an Individual Household Latrine (IHL) for the use of the family, failing which the member would forego the membership. Thus, construction of latrine becomes mandatory among elected members. This amendment helped to construct 45,000 latrines in two months time, but later this circular was withdrawn on high court order. Despite all these efforts, the set targets had not been achieved and many villages did not have a single latrine though the village was covered under NGY (GoK, 2001). As this programme was not catching up in villages (in addition to it), a comprehensive Swachcha Grama Yojana programme, based on demand driven approach, was introduced with the financial assistance from HUDCO.

Swachcha Grama Yojana

The Swachcha Grama Yojana (SGY), is an integrated approach for Total Sanitation consisting of five important elements, viz., *(a)* paving of internal roads and streets of the village, *(b)* construction of sullage and storm water drains, *(c)* removal of manure pits from residential areas to community compost yards, *(d)* providing smokeless chullas and *(e)* construction of household, community and school latrines (Table 5). Thus, the programme is considered a comprehensive package to keep the village clean. HUDCO, the State Government and Community share the total capital cost in a ratio of 80:20 respectively. The Grama Panchayats will empower user groups through Village Water and Sanitation Committee (VWSC) and all households, which have a minimum space, shall construct household latrine. Houses constructed with financial assistance of the government such as 'Ashraya' and other housing schemes will have household latrines.

Table–5

Components of Swachcha Grama Yojana (Rs. in lakhs)

Services Provided	*Amount (in lakhs)*
Paving of internal roads and construction of efficient sullage and storm water drainage.	10.0
Provision of community compost yards and removal of manure pits from dwelling area.	1.25
Provision of smokeless Chulhas for all the households.	0.75
Construction of household Latrines and Community latrines.	6.00
Construction of school toilets.	2.00
Total	20.00

Source. GoK, RDPR, 2002.

Integrated Rural Water Supply and Sanitation (IRWSS)

This programme was implemented through community participation, by forming stakeholders committees, such as VWSC.

* The Karnataka Panchayat Raj Act, 1993 lists "maintenance of general sanitation, cleaning of public roads, drains, tanks, wells and other public places, and construction and maintenance of public latrines" among the functions of the Gram Panchayat (Section 58 and Schedule I, Entry XVIII). "Implementation of Rural Sanitation Schemes" and "Promotion of Drinking Water and Rural Sanitation programmes" are also listed among the functions of Taluk and Zilla Panchayats espectively (Schedule II, Entry IX, and Schedule III Entry X) Under XVIII. Rural Sanitation: Maintenance of general sanitation. cleaning of public roads-drains, tanks, wells and other public places; Maintenance and regulation of burning and burial grounds, construction and maintenance of public latrines disposal of unclaimed corpses and carcasses. Management and control of washing and bathing ghats.

This provided a platform to empower the SCs/STs and women to interact with various persons and raise their voice and choice in a selection of technology. The by-laws of VWSC provided an opportunity to the committee members to take all decisions related to water supply and sanitation services to be provided and installed. The IRWSS integrated the construction of latrines along with water supply, habitation component and sanitation. The village community shares 30 per cent of capital cost for sanitation and participates in all stage of implementation. In this context the VWSC meetings had to be held at least bi-monthly to discuss the progress and follow up action. But, according to minutes of meeting, 43 per cent of the meetings were held as per schedule, though these meetings were crucial for the follow-up actions. The meetings were called at short notice, which was made difficult to participate weaker section and women, as most of them were wage earners. Thus, the programme has given an opportunity to the weaker section and women for participation, but the village system as such did not encourage them. The IRWSS programme was in operation in 22 districts, approximately 2, 000 habitations, with the support of the World Bank, DANIDA and Netherlands (Table 6).

Table–6
Details of Programme Under IRWSS

Indicators	*World Bank*	*DANIDA*	*Netherland*
Districts	Bangalore Ruaral, Kolar, Mandya, Mysore, Shimoga, Hassan, Dashina Kannada, Bidar, Gulbarga, Raichur Bellary and Tumkur	Kolar, Bijapur, Bagalkot and Chitradurga	Dharwad, Haveri, Gadag, Bijapur and Bagalkot
Villages Covered	1104	201	719*

Note: * Schemes.
Source: Annual Report, 2002-03 GoK.

A NGO was hired in each district to create sufficient awareness on the need of environmental sanitation by posting required staff at the village level including health facilitator. The community development expert, health and hygienic expert and gender specialist guided the health facilitator. The 'health facilitator', creates awareness for construction of latrines in general, particularly among the women by explaining the relation between sanitation and health profile of household members, for creating demand for project.

Role of Panchayati Raj Institutions

Table 7, presents the responsibilities of PRIs in the provision of sanitation services based on activity mapping. Accordingly, the Zilla Panchayat act as planner and adviser in the promotion of the programme at the district level, whereas the Taluk panchayat was assigned the supervisory role with obligatory functions such as formulation planes for assisting in the construction of sanitary latrines. The Grama Panchayat had been assigned various functions, including execution supervision and assisting in implementation. From the table, it can be observed that it was obligatory on the part of the Gram Panchayat to perform functions.

Coverage

In spite of all the above policies and strategies, the coverage was not much encouraging. According to latest data, 22 per cent of the households had access to latrines (NSS, 1998; Census, 2001), thus, more than 78 per cent of the households had no access to safe and hygienic latrines. In Karnataka, in spite of all these efforts, still it was not on par with the all-India average (Table 7). The Table also gives an impression that, in Karnataka, urban areas had been provided better sanitation services compared to rural areas. The households not covered with any type of toilets were 82 per cent in

Table–7
Role of PRIs in Sanitation in Karnataka

Functions	Approaches suggested (Under section 184).
Health infrastructure	Establishment of health centres including maternity centres to cover the entire population within 5 years.
Provision of water Supply	Construction of underground water recharge structure to ensure availability of water in the wells. Prevention of drilling of irrigation borewells in the vicinity of drinking water wells to ensure adequate supply of water.
TALUK PANCHAYAT	
Tasks related to public health and sanitation	Approaches suggested (Under Section 145).

(Contd.)

Provision of water Supply	Construction and augmentation of water supply works facilitate not less than 40 liters per capita.
Water supply and sanitation in primary school's	Providing adequate water supply and promoting sanitation maintenance of water supply and sanitation.
Waste management	Acquiring land for locating manure pits away from dwelling houses.
Health related tasks	Water supply works. Households and community latrine. Progress of immunisation. Strengthening of public health units. Establishment of sub centres. School health programmes. Equipment and linen supply. Promotion of health and family welfare. Health and sanitation at fairs and festivals.
GRAM PANCHAYAT	
Task reated to sanitation	Approaches suggested (Under Sections 68, 69, 75, 77, 82, 85 to 92, 99, etc.). Not less than 10 per cent of the households to be covered by latrines in a year. Construction and maintenance of adequate number of community latrines for men and women.
Provision of sanitation	Notifies owners for improving the sanitary condition or keeping clean drainage or Constructing of drainage if the place is insanitary conditions affecting health. Carry out drainage, sewer, conduit, tunnel, culvert, pipe or water course. Maintaining, deepen or improving of the drainage. Constructing of new drains. Inspection of drains.
Provision of waste management	Earmarking places for dumping waste and manure.
Provision for promoting health	Facilitating activities that are likely to promote health, safety etc. Prevention and remedial measures against epidemics

(Contd.)

Disposal of corpses	Disposing of corpses by burning or burial, licensing of place for burial.
Control of infectious diseases	Inspecting the places where infectious disease is reported or suspected, cleansing or disinfecting building or premises.
Regulation and licensing	Strict vigil and inspection of hotel, resturant, eating house, sweet meat shop, bakery, slaughter houses for maintaining hygiene and cleanliness, impose penalty.

Source: The Karnataka Panchayat Raj Act, 1993 (Amended in 2002).

rural areas whereas at all India level it was 78.1 per cent. Thus, in Karnataka, despite several programmes implemented by the Government of India, State and bilateral and multilateral agencies, the number of household covered by latrines was not much impressive (World Bank, aide memoir 1998).

Table–8

Per Cent of Households with Sanitation Facilities (2001)

Sanitation Services	*Karnataka*			*All India*		
	Total	*Rural*	*Urban*	*Total*	*Rural*	*Urban*
Type of latrine withing the house						
Pit latrine	13.38	9.48	20.70	11.5	10.3	14.6
Water closet	18.64	4.67	44.86	18.0	7.1	46.1
Other latrine	5.48	3.25	9.67	6.9	4.5	13.0
No latrine	62.50	82.60	24.77	63.6	78.1	26.3
Type of connectivity for waste water outlet						
No drainage	48.77	64.61	19.03	53.6	65.8	22.1

Source: Census 2001.

The reasons attributed for low coverage were religious belief and culture. For instance, an early civilization in the Indus River valley had sophisticated sewerage systems and was among the oldest known toilets (Pathak, 2001). But, development of Hinduism and its caste system in later centuries changed the attitudes and practices concerning defecation and disposal of human waste (Cooper, 1997). In addition, the attitude of the traditional Indian society and cultural value towards personal hygiene, but gone little importance to a clean and healthy community environment. The accessibility of hygienic latrines regarded as a matter of individual initiative and not as a collective obligation of the community. In

Karnataka, the village physical structure and insufficient motivation/awareness by people and lack of affordable sanitation technology (Veerashekharappa, 2002) and the constraints are:

1. lack of space because of closely built houses.
2. non-affordability among poorest of the poor.
3. Unsuitability of the site due to rocky strata or water logging.
4. reluctance of people to have latrines located next to or within their houses.
5. low priority to the IHL.

Apart poor performance in the construction of latrines, the latrines were either not utilised or misused; the percentage of households misusing latrines was 69 in Bijapur 56, Gulbarga 51 in Raichur; most of the households used them to store fuelwood or for bathing purpose (GoK, 1998). The other reason for not using constructed latrines was scarcity of water and difficulty in cleaning. (STEM, 2001). The finding of the research team in Tumkur and Raichur district supports this. Further it was observed that NGY was not much successful. People participation in SGY is relatively less because of monetary contribution to meet partial capital cost. In Raichur district a typical type of community latrines, unhygienic 'pig type' latrines are being constructed, where pigs are the scavengers. Nevertheless, villagers expressed the unhealthy tendency of creating parallel structure of governance for implementing/monitoring specific projects (such forest user committees, irrigation water user committees), which were otherwise under the jurisdiction of the PRIs. This was generally done in the name of ensuring community participation. However, this neglected the forum of community participation provided under the Panchayati Raj i.e. Gram Sabha or Ward meeting in which all the adult residents of the community were eligible to participate. This tendency to create separate user groups by independent agencies should be avoided and efforts should be made to strengthen the forum provided under Panchyati Raj Act.

Conclusions and Suggestions

The above analysis brings out two factors, what functions are to be under taken by the PRIs under social marketing. Based on the experience, it can be stated that the GPs are unable effectively involve themselves in social marketing due to non-availability of funds and required manpower. The bilateral and multilateral agencies approach for social marketing by community participation neither helped to save public expenditure nor social marketing sustained. Thus, both the approaches have their own limitation in the effective delivery of services. In the process, the household economy is affected due to increased health expenditure.

The GP can take up the governance function rather then owning the burden the delivery of services, as the jobs are conflicting nature. If the GP finds it difficult to govern the delivery of services on its own. Under Sections 100 and 106 the Grama Panchayats or anyone appointed by them is empowered to inspect any sewer, drain, privy, water closet, house-gully or cesspool. Considering this legal support, the GP can compel households to construct sanitary latrines. Thus, GP can become the local pubic health-enforcing agency with power to take penal action for contravention of laws. TP may be appellate authority against decision of the GP.

Considering the legal support, the grama panchayat can market the concept or appoint any dedicated organisation to do it. Now in each village the Self-Help Groups are coming forward to take social activities and they have been proved successful in managing sanitary complexes in Andhra and Tamil Nadu. Such organizations can be entrusted with social marketing of water supply and sanitation services. Some of the messages such as washing hands; safe storage and handling of water; are universal and marketable in all the areas. Such messages can be developed at the state level and can be propagated through national/state level media. However, local health promotional schemes should also be prepared by the district health agencies on water sources, contamination of water (such as high flouride content, etc) for social marketing. Such plans should be put before ZP and approval by TPs and GPs. GPs using its quasi-judicial powers may make some local rules forbidding defecation in open places or near the sources of drinking water.

Annex A : Percentage of Households Covered by Toilets Across States

States	*1991*		*2001*	
	Total	*Rural*	*Total*	*Rural*
Andhra Pradesh	18.40	6.62	32.99	18.15
Assam	37.43	30.53	64.64	59.57

(Contd...)

States	*1991*		*2001*	
	Total	*Rural*	*Total*	*Rural*
Bihar	11.75	4.96	19.19	13.91
Chhattisgarh	–	–	14.20	5.18
Delhi	63.38	29.60	77.96	62.89
Gujarat	30.69	11.16	44.60	21.65
Haryana	22.45	6.53	44.50	28.66
Jharkhand	–	–	19.67	6.57
Karnataka	24.13	6.85	37.50	17.40
Kerala	51.28	44.07	84.01	81.33
Madhya Pradesh	15.07	3.64	23.99	8.94
Maharashtra	29.56	6.64	35.09	18.21
Orissa	9.81	3.58	14.89	7.71
Punjab	33.18	15.79	56.84	40.91
Rajasthan	19.57	6.65	29.00	14.61
Tamil Nadu	23.13	7.17	35.16	14.36
Uttar Pradesh	18.02	6.44	31.43	19.23
Uttaranchal	–	–	45.20	31.60
West Bengal	31.51	12.31	43.71	26.93
Total	**23.70**	**9.48**	**36.41**	**21.92**

Sources: Census of India, 2001. Series 1, Tables on Houses, Household.

Census of India 1991 series 1 Part VII, Tables.

Borban – A 'Hagandari Mukt Gaon'

Borban is a small community of about 185 households in Sangamner Taluka of Ahmednagar district in Maharashtra. This village ranked second prize at the district level competition. Every household has constructed a household toilet. Under the leadership of the village Sarpanch, guarantee for the material was provided and the district administration made available low cost technology to them, has contributed to achieve this. In fact, the village now imposes a fine if anyone is seen to continue the traditional practice. The community solidarity and status has become a model for the entire district.

Source: Notes from field visits by ISEC Team under the Project on Restructuring Local Environment Management in Karnataka, January 2004.

Privatisation of Sanitation Services

The Rural Sanitary Marts Programme, in Uttar Pradesh aimed specifically to shift from a subsidy-based programme to a privatized one. Over the years, it has been noted that offering a much lower subsidy actually increased the sanitation coverage. This idea was replicated in several other States. In Allahabad, the RSMs went further to 'no subsidy'. Between 1993 and 1998 they sold over 35,000 latrines sets. Under the traditional subsidy system, this would have cost the Government $ 17.5 million. Under the new system, it only cost $ 60,000 of external support plus managerial support for one and a half years.

Source: UNICEF, Vision 21 : Water supply and Sanitation collaborative Council.

REFERENCES

1. Bindeshwar Pathak, 'Sulabha Sanitation Technologies for Sustainable Urbanisation Strategies', Paper presented at *International Conference on Sustainable Urbanisation Strategies,* Organised by United Nations Human Settlements Programme, Nairobi, 2003 and Ministry of Construction of the People's Republic of China and Weihai Municipality, 2003. *www.sulabhinternational.org*
2. S. Cairncross, Sanitation in the Developing World: Current Status and Future Solutions, *International Journal of Environmental Health Research,* 13 (June), 2003, pp. S123-S131.
3. J. Cooper Kenneth, Human Waste Overwhelms India's War on Disease". *Washington Post,* Foreign Service, Monday, February 17, 1997.
4. Richard, C. Crook and James Manor, *Democracy and Decentralisation in South Asia and West Africa,* London, Cambridge University Press, 1998.
5. Monica Dasgupta *et al.,* Governance of Communicable Disease Control Services: A Case Study and Lessons from India, 2003, *Background Paper for WDR 2004* (unpublished).
6. Government of India, *54th Round. Drinking Water, Sanitation and Hygiene in India. New Delhi:* National Sample Survey Organisation, New Delhi, 1999.
7. Government of India, *Towards Total Sanitation and Hygiene: A Challenge for India,* New Delhi: *Ministry of Rural Development,* New Delhi, 2003. Website: *www.ddws. nic. in*
8. Government of Karnataka, *Evaluation Study on Water Supply and Sanitation,* Directorate of Economics and Statistics, Bangalore,1998.
9. Government of India, *National Health Policy – 2002.* New Delhi, MoHFW, 2002.
10. Government of Karnataka, *Strategy Paper on Rural Water Supply and*

Sanitation, 2000-05, Bangalore, Department of Rural Development and Panchyat Raj, 2000.

11. Government of Karnataka (1993). *The Karnataka Panchayat Raj Act,* 1993, Bangalore: Ameya Publications.
12. Government of Karnataka, *Report of the Working Group on Decentralisation,* Bangalore, Department of Rural Development and Panchayati Raj, 2002.
13. F. Elledge Myles, *International Water and Sanitation,* Reviewed by Roland Schertnlib (SANDEL), IRC International and Sanitation, 2003.
14. K. Pushpangdan, G. Murgan, 'User Financing and Collective Action: Relevance for Sustainable Rural water Supply in India", *Economic and Political Weekly,* April 4, 1998.
15. David Harmeyer and Ashok Mody, 'Private Capital in Water and Sanitation', *Finance and Development,* March 1997.
16. P. Oakley, *Projects with People: The Practice of Participation in Rural Development,* Geneva, International Labour Office, 1991.
17. L.S. Prokopy, Women's Participation in Rural Water Supply Project in India: Is it Moving Beyond Tokenism and Does It Matter? Water Policy, No. 6, 2004.
18. Radhika Ramasubban, Public Health and Medical Research in India,. Saree Report (4): Stockholom: *Swedish Agency for Research Cooperation with Developing Countries,* 1982.
19. D. Rajasekhar and Veerashekharappa, '*Role of Local Organisations in Water Supply and Sanitation Sector: A Study in Karnataka and Uttaranchal States,* India, Bamgalore, Institute for Social and Economic Change, 2003.
20. K.V. Raju,Veerashekharappa and S. Manasi, '*RWS in Karnataka – Moving Towards Organized Complexity' – A Ecological: Governance Approach,* Bangalore, Institute for Social and Economic Change, 2004.
21. Nageshwar Rap and Veerashekharappa, Rural Community Water Supply Systems: Some Observations, *Kurukshetra* (Special issue on Water Supply) June, 1989.
22. Maria, R. Saleth and Dinar Ariel, Water Challenge and Institutional Response: A cross-country perspective, *Policy Working Paper No. 2045.* Washington D.C., The World Bank,1999.
23. M.L. Santhanam, Community Participation in Rural Water Supply and Sanitation Programmes. *Social Change,* 19 (1), 1989, pp. 53-58.
24. S.K. Singh, Panchayat Udyogs in Uttar Pradesh: A Democratic Experiment in Micro Enterprise Development, *The Journal of Entrepreneurship,* 8(2),1999, pp. 207-17.
25. R.P. Slater, and J. R. Watson, Decentralised Planning and the Anti-Poverty Programmes: Some Possible New Direction, in Rakesh Hooja and B. Yerram Raju (eds.) *Decentralised Planning in Multilevel Framework,* New Delhi, Rawat Publications, 1993.

26. STEM, *Sanitation and Hygiene Promotion. Part I – Strategy*. Bangalore: Centre for Symbiosis of Technology, Environment and Management, 2003.
27. *The Hindu*, Finance Minister Statement in Public Function, Government of Karnatka, Bangalore, October 5, 2005.
28. United States Agency for International Development (USAID), Lessons Learned in Water, Sanitation and Health: Thirteen Years of Experience in Developing Countries, *Water and Sanitation for Health Project*, Washington, DC, 1993.
29. Veerashekharappa, Karnataka Integrated Rural Water and Environmental Sanitation: Impact: An Evaluation Study, Bangalore, *Institute for Social and Economic Change*, 1999.
30. Veerashekharappa, Reforms in Rural Drinking Water Supply: Perspective and Problems (Discussion), *Economic and Political Weekly*, Vol 35(7), February, 12-18, 2000.
31. Veerashekharappa, Community Participation in Rural Drinking Water Supply and Sanitation: A Case Study of Karnataka' *Journal of Indian Water Works Association*, Vol XXXIV (1) , Jan-March, 2000.
32. Veerashekharappa, K.V. Raju and S. Manasi, Financing Rural Water Supply: A Case Study of Karnataka, *Working Paper 168*, Bangalore: Institute for Social and Economic Change, 2006.
33. Veerashekharappa, Community Contribution for Environmental Sanitation: Myth or Reality, *Working Paper 171*, Bangalore, Institute for Social and Economic Change, 2006.
34. World Bank, Rural Water Supply and Sanitation. Washington, D.C. Allied Publishers, The World Bank, 1999.
35. Robert Woods, Public Health Service Delivery: The Historical Experience of the developed countries (especially the United Kingdom, France and the United States in the nineteenth and twentieth centuries), in Monica Das Gupta and Peyvand, 2003.

20

Guarding the Commons in India: Panchayats and Globalisation

V. RAGHUPATHY

Aspiration for social liberation and empowerment at the grassroots has been triggered by the 73rd Constitutional Amendment Act and the Policy of Reservation of positions for SC, ST and women in panchayats. In a feudal rural society where inequity is institutionalized, democratic decentralization has little meaning without affirmative action. Some of the social revolutionaries like B.R. Ambedkar considered empowering panchayats without social leveling as a threat to marginalized groups.[1] The Gandhian concept of Gram Swaraj was opposed by Ambedkar and others who considered the village as a sink of localism, a den of ignorance, narrow mindedness and exploitation.[2] More power to panchayat means more power to high caste, majority community and dominant groups in the villages and it may result in more exploitation of poor minority groups and socially deprived classes.[3] Against this background, 73rd Constitutional Amendment included social justice as one of its main objectives of the Panchayati Raj system. Development without equity does not mean anything to poor. Reservation for women, SC and ST in panchayats is an important step in the direction of ensuring social justice and equity. Democracy has it's own strength and it gives power to the poor to bargain. Reservation for SC and ST has opened the scope for bringing fundamental change in the power structure by providing right to scheduled caste people to participate in decision-making and governance at the grassroots.

But legislation alone cannot bring social transformation. Many legislations for social transformations could not bring much changes in the society. Numerous laws to improve the status of

SC, ST and women have not been properly implemented. According to legal sociologist Upendra Baxi there are two laws in India i.e..[4] One enacted by the state and the other: societal law. The laws enacted by the legislatures alone could not bring much impact in the society. Sometimes societal laws are more powerful than the laws of the state. The empowerment of scheduled caste people is a long process of struggle and there are number of stages in it.[5] Empowerment is enhancing an Individual's or groups capacity to make decisions and transform their choices into desired actions and outcomes. Empowerment has to give the capacity to use the available choices and it must bring the desired results. Empowerment also means redressing unbalances of power between those who have it and those who don't.[6] Occupying formal position by a SC person in Panchayats is not sufficient. It necessarily does not empower him. Mere providing positions to SC people in Panchayats is not the end of the empowerment process and it may be only a beginning.[7] There is a need for close study of the process of empowerment of SC people in Panchayat.

Reservation for SC people in Panchayats is a policy of the state and enactment of a law is a step in the legal domain. But implementation of the policy and the process of empowerment takes place in political, social and economic domains. As Upendra Baxi points out the societal and customary laws sometimes are more powerful in the social domain than the laws of the legislature. It is possible for SC people to contest in elections and occupy positions in Panchayats. But it is still very difficult for them to execute their power. Positions in Panchayats do not bring much changes in the position of the elected representatives in the social and economic domain.

Panchayat is one of the major formal institution in a village. But there are many informal institutions in a village which affect the process of empowerment. In villages cultural practices, traditions and norms play a critical role and economic relationships between different social groups influences the power relationship.

The lower level bureaucracy plays a significant role in the functioning of Panchayats and they have their own unofficial institutional arrangements in their dealings with Panchayats. Empowerment of SC is very much affected by the lower level administration.

Empowerment is the capacity to make choices and transform these choices in to desired actions and outcomes. Reservation alone does not give this capacity. But state does not take sufficient steps to build the capacity of the elected leaders.[9] There is no powerful civil society working for to building the capacity of SC people to use the policy of reservation effectively. In many places the SC people are locked into a cultural framework in which they accept their disempowerment.[10] Very few efforts have been taken to liberate them from this cultural and psychological bondage.

Where they are free from the disempowering psychological lock, social institutions do not allow them to enjoy their equal status. When SC leaders are ready to function on their own, they have to face the challenges of the existing rural social institutions.

Economic status of SC representatives plays a very significant role in the process of empowerment. Assets give them the capacity to aspire and struggle. Asset less people find it very difficult to struggle for their empowerment.

Reservation policy must be followed by building the capacity of the SC people and efforts to bring a favourable change in the existing social and administrative institutional structures at the grassroots in the absence of such efforts empowerment will not deliver the desired outcomes.[11]

Empowerment Process in Panchayats in Tamil Nadu

Against this backdrop the status of the process of empowerment of scheduled caste people in Panchayats in Tamil Nadu is discussed. Tamil Nadu is considered as a progressive state with a long history of struggle for social liberation. Non-Brahmin movement since 1920 worked for reservation policy in legislature and government offices. The Anti-brahminical movement in Tamil Nadu headed by E.V. Ramasamy Periyar contributed significantly for the development of non-Brahmins and backward communities. Many social legislations have been passed in Tamil Nadu for the social and economic upliftment of backward communities. Compared to many states Tamil Nadu has made significant achievements in the areas of social development. Powerful civil society organisations are functioning and working for the empowerment of weaker sections. But few scholars think non-Brahmin movement could not bring any significant changes in the status of SC people in Tamil Nadu, it gave more power to backward communities and it did not ensure the upward mobility of SC people.[12]

Struggle for Social Justice

The policy of reservation for SC and ST in Panchayats has brought changes in the rural power-structure in Tamil Nadu. The positions reserved for SC people in panchayats have been filled as per the law in the 2006 elections. Nearly one-third of the positions in Village Panchayats have been occupied by SC/ST elected representatives.

In Tamil Nadu out of 12,593 Village Panchayats Presidents 3,810 presidents are from SC and 237 presidents are from ST.[13] The numerical strength of SC elected representatives in panchayats is very impressive. It is possible for such a strong group of SC Panchayat representatives to bring social justice at the grassroots. They have the critical mass to bring a social transformation.

But the experiences of SC representatives in panchayats reveal that the process of empowerment of SC people through panchayats has to face many challenges difficulties and hurdles. Even though SC people form about 19 per cent of the population in Tamil Nadu, they have not still emerged as a political force. SC population is thinly spread all over Tamil Nadu and only in few pockets they are numerically strong. They are everywhere but everywhere they are minority. They are also disintegrated in to many caste groups. There is no unity among different SC caste groups. Each caste group has it's own political outfit and they are in conflict with each other.

Even in reserved panchayats, SC people are not able to influence the electoral outcome. Other caste groups normally unite together and prevent the ascendancy of SC power in villages. In most cases the other backward castes put puppet SC candidates.

In Tamil Nadu, village panchayat elections are not contested on party basis. In the absence of political parties caste play the determining role in the outcome of elections and formation of power structure. Caste, clan and hamlet are the vital elements in the electoral process in panchayats.

In 1996, Panchayat elections it was reported in three village panchayats of Madurai district the reservation policy of the constitutional amendment was sabotaged. In three Village

Panchayats, where President's office was reserved for SC no one was allowed to contest by local community. From 1996 to 2005 in spite of the repeated attempts by state election commission the process of election in the three Panchayats were not permitted to complete. It was reported that in many districts of Tamil Nadu elected SC leaders were not permited to function by the dominant local community.[14] After the first panchayat elections few SC elected panchayat representatives were brutally murdered. In this context the need for deeper understanding of the process of empowerment of SC in panchayats is very much required.[15]

Empowerment in Practice

Process of empowerment is not one quantum jump. As Baviskar argues one does not jump from a zero power situation to all power situation.[16] Bavishkar argues that empowerment has several stages and it is a long journey. But it is not necessary that every individual or group should pass through all these stages. Depending upon the existing situation the empowerment process takes place. Stage here means the situation in which an elected representative has to operate. Based on the experience in Tamil Nadu five stages could be identified in the process of empowerment of Scheduled Caste Presidents in Panchayats. In few villages of Tamil Nadu SC people were prevented from using legitimate right to contest in panchayat elections for reserved positions. Even elected Presidents are prevented from using symbolic powers. Particularly in certain pockets of Madurai, and Virudhunagar district this situation was noticed. In villages where SC people are very few and caste discriminations are very high. SC people find it very difficult to contest in Panchayat elections. So they do not contest in elections. The five identified stages are discussed here.[17]

Table–1

Sl. No.	*Stages of Empowerment*
1.	Rejection
2.	Tokenism
3.	Compromise
4.	Struggle
5.	Empowerment

Rejection

The powerful middle and upper caste groups are not able to accept the policy of reservation. For these groups their caste and customary norms are superior than the laws of the state. Low level of awareness is one reason for this status. These groups generally try to sabotage any measures for social transformation in rural areas. Powerful caste groups do not allow the SC people to rear the benefit of the policy of reservation. SC people are threatened and prevented from contesting elections. Even if they are elected they are forced to resign. In some cases even elected representatives are murdered. The SC elected leaders are prevented from attending their official duties. They are humiliated. They are forced to follow the directions of the majority community.[18]

Particularly in Panchayats where the non-SC caste groups are in majority they feel that they have the natural right to occupy positions in panchayats and the policy of reservation of seats for SC is a violation of natural justice. Absence of the role of civil society organisations in convincing these groups on the intentions of the policy of social justice is another reason for this state of affair. In Tamil Nadu major political parties also do not come forward to take any bold steps to challenge and correct this dangerous trend. Because in villages the dominant caste groups have very big vote bank major political parties are not ready to come forward to support the cause of scheduled caste people in Panchayats. Even though this is a problem related only to so few Panchayats, there is scope for the problem to spread to other areas.

Tokenism

Tokenism is doing something in insincere way so as to be seen to be obeying the law or satisfying a particular group of people. Tokenism is more dangerous than rejection. In rejection it is openly declared that the reservation policy is not acceptable. But in tokenism the reservation policy is manipulated to satisfy the needs of the powerful groups.[19] In majority of the reserved panchayats in Tamil Nadu the policy of Tokenism is practiced. Caste groups and powerful individuals manipulate the electoral process and elect reliable candidates as Presidents and members. They control Panchayats by proxy. The elected leaders are powerless and helpless. Any work related to Panchayats and all their powers are enjoyed by somebody else.

Tokenism is practiced generally where SC people are in minority and organisations working for SC people are not active. Particularly where powerful caste groups are not able to reject the policy of reservation they try to practice tokenism. It allows them to enjoy power without responsibility. In this situation the SC leaders are not in a position to bring any changes in the existing social structure. They could not improve the status of Schedule Caste people in their Panchayats.

Compromise

When tokenism is not possible, powerful caste groups try to accommodate SC leaders in the Panchayats. When SC people have reasonable awareness and considerable population in the Panchayat area powerful caste groups want to come to an understanding with SC leaders. In many places the SC candidates for the election are nominated after due consultation with majority caste groups. Particularly when SC people are disunited powerful caste groups use the opportunity to accommodate SC candidates of their choice in Panchayats. Independent SC candidates are defeated by the powerful caste groups by using this method. Even though elected SC leaders are not the puppets, they are dominated by the powerful caste groups. The SC panchayat leaders cannot take decisions on their own. Social reality compels the SC Presidents and members to practice this as a method of compromise.[20] Most of the SC presidents are economically and socially marginalized and they find it very difficult to fight with powerful groups. Instead they take a position of compromise. Such leaders are not able to bring any change in the existing social structure.[21] But sometimes they may be effective in implementing welfare schemes for the benefit of the Scheduled Caste people.

Struggle

Struggle is a very significant stage in the process of empowerment. When SC people are economically and politically well placed they are in a position to assert and struggle for their legitimate rights. Particularly in panchayats, where SC people are in numerically strong there is a tendency to assert their rights. The political parties, NGOs and dalit organisations play a critical role in the process of struggle. Once SC are elected, they try to assert their legal rights to use the power to make decisions. In this process there are opportunities to antagonize the powerful caste groups in the village. They are abused and attacked. Most of the Presidents have a non SC Vice-Presidents. Majority of the members are from other communities. There is no reservation in the appointment of Panchayat Clerks in Tamil Nadu. Panchayat clerk, a key person in the Panchayat Administration, normally does not facilitate an SC President to function independently. A SC Panchayat President has to convince and get the support of all these forces for effective management of Panchayat. In many cases it leads to violent struggle also. But few SC Panchayat Presidents are able to convince the local community and mobilise support for their activities. In this stage NGOs, civil society organisations and government agencies must give support to SC leaders. Training, networking and consultancy are very critical in helping the struggling leaders.

Empowerment

In rare cases in Panchayats empowerment of SC elected leaders has been accepted and SC leaders are able to function freely and independently. SC leaders at this stage are able to make decisions affecting the entire community.[22] In this stage, they are able to get the support of other communities for their activities for the development of the Panchayat. It is found that acceptance is possible only under certain conditions. Numerical strength of SC people, level of social development, influence of NGOs and political parties, support structures and leadership play critical role in facilitating acceptance. Particularly in states like Kerala, where social development is high, political parties play a positive role and civil society is active acceptance of SC empowerment in grassroots is very effective and smooth. In Tamil Nadu in rural areas still there is no favourable climate for the empowerment of SC leaders in Panchayats. Panchayat President requires constant support of the members of Village Panchayat and Gram Sabha for effective functioning. Particularly a SC President finds it difficult to get the support of the other groups.

Case Studies on the Stages of Empowerment

Rajiv Gandhi Chair for Panchayati Raj Studies undertook extensive field research in Tamil Nadu to understand the process of empowerment of women and SC elected presidents of village Panchayat.[23] About 200 cases have been studied and analysed.[24] Based on these case studies, five stages in the process of empowerment have been identified. Five cases representing each stage are illustrated and discussed.[25]

Pappapatti Syndrome – A Case of Rejection

Usilampatti Taluk in Madurai District is known for female infanticide and sabotage of reservation in Panchayats. The three village panchayats of Pappati, Keeripatti and Nattarmangalam are not able to function since 1996 because of the problem of reservation of the office of the Panchayat President for SC. Between 1996-2001 and 2001-05 as per the constitutional requirement elections were announced every six months. But in first-five years no SC candidate came forward to contest in elections. In the second-five years, candidate contested in elections, but the elected individuals resigned immediately after their elections.

The villages are dominated by one single Most Backward Caste (MBC), the 'Kallar' community. This caste was notified as a criminal tribe during the British rule. These village panchayats are dominated by caste panchayats and traditional practices. The caste panchayats are bound by stringent community rules. Most of the members of Kallar community are poor and educationally backward. Due to the effects of the Christian Missionary activities, around fifty years back, education was introduced among them. Kallar community is considered as a sub-group of Thevar community, a pre-dominant community in South and East Tamil Nadu. The overall electoral out come, in around 8 districts of Tamil Nadu is determined by the vote banks of Thevar community.

SC people are minorities in these three Village Panchayats where 80 per cent of the population belong to the Kallar community. These single caste dominant villages have local traditional Panchayats which decide the affairs of the village. Pappapatti has a temple which is considered as very sacred for the Kallar community of the district. This village is considered as the head village for the entire Kallar community of the region.

Against this background when office of President is these three panchayats were reserved for SC, there were protests from the Kallars of the region. Kallars considered that reservation of Pappapatti for SC was a challenge to their honour and as a first step to damage their traditional practices. First-five years no one was permitted to contest in elections. In the second-five years due to pressure from NGOs elections were permitted and few candidates contested in elections. But immediately after elections they resigned.

In spite of efforts by NGOs the process of elections were not allowed to complete and elected presidents were not ready to function. Major political parties AIADMK and DMK are not ready to take any serious steps to arrest this problem because of electoral compulsion. They do not want to damage their relationship with the Thevar community. Minor political parties like communist parties and Dalit political parties tried their level best to solve this problem, but they could not achieve anything. NGOs are not able to change the mindsets of the majority community. In 2007 DMK government took many steps to facilitate.

Pappapatti syndrome is very dangerous because it may spread to other regions of Tamil Nadu. It is a open challenge to the Constitution of India and the concept of social justice. Because of the vote bank politics major political parties are not ready to take clear stand on this issues. State Government has no clear policy to stop this trend. Some of the NGOs and political leaders suggested stringent measures like stopping of government schemes in these three villages. But government is still not ready to do so. Because of Pappapatti syndrome many Dalit parties demand changes in the electoral system of India. They demand caste based proportional representation to SC people. Only such a system could help SC people to elect representatives of their choice.

Participation of political parties in Village Panchayat election is another demand from NGOs and Leftist organizations. Party based elections may play a positive role in situations like this.

Rejection of reservation requires serious study of the problem from constitutional, legal, administrative, social and cultural angles.

Uthapuram – A Case of Tokenism

Uthapuram is a Village Panchayat in Sedapatti Block of Madurai District. A block official says "Most of the SC Panchayat Presidents are only puppets of the dominant caste organisations of the village. Sedapatti is well-known for atrocities against women and scheduled caste people. Uthapuram Village Panchayat has a population of 1800. The Kallar is the majority caste group with 1100 population and there are 350 scheduled caste people in the Panchayat. Rain fed agriculture is the main source of livelihood.

The village has only small and marginal farmers and no individual in the village owns more than 10 acres. The majority Kallar community is classified as the Most Backward Class. Once Kallars were notified as a criminal tribe by the British Government. The village has a community Panchayat dominated by the Kallar community. The community panchayat plays a key role in the affairs of the village, particularly on issues related to the management of common property resources, village temples, festivals and common fund.

When the Uthapuram Village Panchayat President position was reserved for SC women in 1991, a community Panchayat meeting was organised to discuss the issues related to the election. In the meeting it was decided to nominate Chinnu, 45 years old SC widow as the common candidate. She is a landless labourer and uneducated. She has three female children. Her husband was once elected to the office of the President as the common candidate of the village. Her husband was very cooperative and loyal to the community panchayat.

Chinnu did not know anything related to Panchayat. She was asked to put her signature in the nomination form. The community panchayats also put two more SC candidates to show the Panchayat elections in the village was free and fair. In three corner contest Chinnu was elected as Panchayat President. But Chinnu was never allowed to sit in the Chair of Panchayat Presidents. The Vice-President, a man from Kallar community was recognized as the real acting President by the community Panchayat. He functioned as the de-facto President of the village. Chinnu never visited the Panchayat office. She was never permitted to attend the meetings of the Village Panchayat. Letters and other correspondences related to Panchayats were not shown to Chinnu. In the cheques she was forced to put her signature and no details were given to her.

She was never allowed to go to Block Office or Collectors Office. She was not permitted to attend training programmes organised by the Government, Chinnu attended farm work to earn her livelihood. She did not have any chance to think about the affairs of the Panchayat. Only benefit she got was the fixed traveling allowance and the sitting fees for attending the Panchayat meetings. Once in a month she went to the house of Panchayat clerk to receive Rs. 400.

Chinnu is a typical case of Tokenism. According to a block official of Sedapatti block most of the SC women Panchayat Presidents are like Chinnu. SC women were used to fulfill the constitutional requirements by the dominant groups.

Presidents like Chinnu are not capable of using their offices because of their social and economic background. They do not have strength to assert their right as elected leaders. Wherever SC are minorities and without economic independence, dominant caste groups never permit them to take their legal role in Panchayati Raj Institutions. They do not have any support structure to facilitate their empowerment. In large number of villages of Tamil Nadu such practices are going on. The constitutional provision of reservation has been.

Nuthulapuram Ms. Kala – A Case of Compromise

Nuthulapuram Village Panchayat is located 60 km away from Madurai city in Dindigul District. It is in an industrially backward area and with limited scope for agriculture because of the scarcity of water for irrigation. The population of the village is around 5000. Nearly one-third of the population belong to SC people.

Nuthulapuram village is known for conflicts between SC people and non-SC communities. Non-SC communities are dominating the public affairs of the village, particularly in the management of village temples and common property resources. SC people are not permitted to take part in many of the rituals in temple festivals. They have to stand outside, they are not permitted to enter in to the temple. Every year temple festival only created further scopes for conflicts between SC and other communities.

The Presidents position was reserved for SC women when the new system was introduced in 1996. The Village Panchayat has it hamlets and Nuthulapuram is the biggest among them. When election was announced in 1996 three SC women candidates contested in election. Ms. Kala, a 10th passed SC women came forward to contest in election. She is a trained health worker. Before election she was working as a field health organizer with Association of Sarva Seva Farms (ASEFA) a leading Gandhian Non-Governmental Organisation in Tamil Nadu. She was also associated with Congress Party. Her husband is an ex-service man and a taxi operator. Her family has good reputation in the village.

Kala could get non-SC votes also. Because of the support of the non-SC voters Kala could win the election.

She was known as a moderate leader and could get the support of other Backward Class voters also. Kala was considered as a candidate of compromise by non-SC communities. The SC youths of the village were very much against the influence of the upper castes in Panchayat administration. But Kala did not want any violent conflict in the village. She wanted to bring peace in the village. Understanding between Kala and dominant community leaders became inevitable. In this process Kala got the displeasure of the SC youths. SC youths considered Kala as the agent of upper caste. But an objective observation reveals that Kala took a pragmatic stand to avoid conflict and violence in the village. Most of the members of the Village Panchayat are from non-SC communities, Vice-President is from the dominant community. In this situation Kala has no option but to come to an understanding with the powerful leaders of various caste groups. There was no unity among the members of the SC community and so Kala could not depend only on them.

But Kala is very particular that all the funds allocated for the development SC people must be properly used for the benefit of the SC people. She could get all basic facilities to the SC colonies of the Village Panchayat. At the same time, she also took all the required steps to fulfill the needs of the other communities. She took pain to convince the non-SC people about the activities of the Panchayat.

Kala is case of accommodation. The dominant caste groups found Kala as a candidate of compromise. She was not a proxy Panchayat President. But at the same time, she was also not independent. She did not question the authority of the dominant community leaders in some significant areas like temple management and management of common property resources. Because of this she got the displeasure of the SC youths. But at the same time Kala sincerely took all efforts for the development of SC people of the Panchayats.

Pottulpatti Mani – A Case of Struggle

Pottulppatti is a Village Panchayat in Usilampatti Panchayat Union of Madurai District. Usilampatti is known for the practice of female infanticide and violence against SC people. Pottulppatti village Panchayat has a population of 2,300. The Village Panchayat has 1,108 voters. Out of them 356 are SC voters. There are six ward members in the Panchayat. Two ward members are from SC. Pottulppatti village panchayat president position was reserved for SC women as per the rules in 2001 Panchayat elections.

In 2001, elections two SC women candidates contested for the post of Village Panchayat President. They were from two different hamlets of the village panchayat and got the support of community of their respective hamlets. Mani, aged 37 contested in the election for the first time with the support of the dominant caste group of her hamlet. Mani was educated upto forth standard and she was an agricultural labouer. In Panchayat elections candidates have to spend money. Local community leaders gave voluntary contributions to Mani for the election purpose. About Rs.16,000 was spent on election by Mani and the electoral expenses were managed by one Mr. Jeyaraj belonging to a dominant caste. Mani could win the election. With the support of the local community leaders. One of the ward members Mr. Ravi Chandran was elected as the Vice-President by the ward members of the Village Panchayat. He was from the dominant community. He wanted to control the panchayat using Mani as a Proxy president. As per the rules of the Tamil Nadu Panchayat Act, Vice-President plays a critical role in the functioning of village panchayat. Bank accounts are jointly operated by the President and Vice-President.

As Mani had studied only upto fourth standard initially she could not understand the administrative procedures of the Village Panchayat. She was influenced by the Vice-President in Panchayat administration. She consulted the village elders of all communities. The village panchayat got Rs. 1,00,000 for the repair of houses affected by floods. Using the ignorance of the president, the Vice-President and Panchayat Clerk got her signature in the cheque and took Rs. 30,000 from the amount sanctioned for the repair of houses of SC people. But Block Development Officer could understand the problem and instructed Mani to be careful in future. He instructed the Vice-President and Panchayat Clerk to distribute the sanctioned amount to the real beneficiaries without any future delay.

After this, Mani could understand the intention of the Vice-President and tried to assert her power. She wanted to function independently. She activated the village panchayat council and gram sabha. Few of the dominant community leaders did not like the change in the behaviour of the Panchayat President. They insisted that she should function as per the instruction of the Vice-President and dominant community leaders. But Mani conducted village panchayat ward members meetings and took decisions – she could get the support of four members out of the six ward members. The Vice-President and the another member did not cooperate with the President.

One day when Mani and her family members went to the nearby town, her hut was looted and her thatched hut was burnt by the henchmen of the Vice-President and few of the dominant community leaders. Mani made a complaint in the police. But the police did not arrest the culprits. After a week, few of the dominant caste group attacked Mani and prevented her from entering into the panchayat office. She could not enter into the office for few days. Again she made a complaint to the police, with the help of the police, she could enter the panchayat office.

One day when she was conducting the Panchayat meeting, a supporter of the Vice-President from the dominant caste entered into the office and disturbed the meeting. He verbally accused the President. He pulled the saree and the blouse of the President. He physically attacked her. But few of the public came to the rescue of the Panchayat President and protected her.

She went to the District Collector and gave a written complaint against the culprits. She asked for the police protection. Collector ordered from the BDO and the local police to give her enough protection and helped her to discharge her responsibilities without any fear.

Mani went to every family in the village and explained her problems. She asked their help to run a honest and efficient administration in the village panchayat. In the next Gram Sabha meeting she discussed the problems and many of the gram sabha members expressed their support to Mani. A village Panchayat council meeting was called and a resolution to dismiss the Vice-President was passed. The district administration facilitated the implementation of the resolution as per the procedure and the Vice-President was dismissed. With support of the four ward members she could manage the affairs of the Panchayat smoothly. But she did not feel secure and afraid of some of the supporters of the former Vice-President. Mani could fulfil all the basic municipal requirements of the people and took steps to improve the facilitates in the SC colonies. New houses for SC people were constructed. Roads, water and sanitation facilities were provided to SC colonies.

She also undertook programmes for the development of the entire village Panchayat. Water bodies, of the village panchayat were desilted with the active participation of local community. A threshing ground was constructed for the use of the farmers of the village. A child care centre was constructed. Group houses were constructed for SC and backward class people below poverty line.

In the beginning Mani could emerge as an independent leader only after great struggle. The village society could not accept a SC women as their president. But Mani could assert their legal rights and she suffered in the process. But she proved that after the struggle she could emerge as an independent leader.

Kuthambakkam Elango – A Case of Empowerment

Kuthambakkam Gram Panchayat is in Thiruvallur district. It is located about 40 kms away from Chennai city. The village is well connected with the city due to its large number of industries. The village is rich in agriculture and the lands are well irrigated. But 90 per cent of the land is owned by the upper caste people and most of the SC people are without land. Landless villagers are employed as agricultural labourers, construction workers and factory workers. Few of them are involved in illicit arrack trade and petty criminal activities.

In 1996, the Panchayat elections were announced and the office of the President was reserved for SC. Mr. Elango, an Engineer working with central government wanted to use the opportunity to serve the village. So he resigned his job and contested in the elections. During the election he mobilised SC youths behind him and he also could influence the upper caste voters of the village. His family is well respected even by the upper caste people. As the SC has the majority votes, the upper caste people were not in a position to influence the outcome of the election. Elango could win the elections with the support of the cross-section of the community.

Once Elango was elected he fully asserted his position. As he is well educated, experienced, well connected, no one could undermine his position. But at the same time Elango also wanted to gain the confidence of the non-SC people of the village. He took special interest in participation of all sections of the village in Gram Sabha meeting. He always consulted the village elders and youth groups on various issues related to the development programme of the village. He wanted to make his village Panchayat as a model Panchayat and bring integrated development to the entire community emerging as a leader of the all sections of the Village Panchayat. He was not identified as a SC Panchayat President. As a scientist he could use science and technology for the development of the village. He brought many model schemes and pilot projects of various government departments and organisations. He brought real change in the mind set of the village community in favour of social transformation. Panchayat has been used to bring many innovative social transformation initiative like Samathuvapuram (equality village scheme of Government of Tamil Nadu which helps people from all castes to live as a single community).

Elango was well-educated with rich administrative experience. He developed contacts with few key officials in government at the state level. He had a clear vision about development of the village. He used the confidence of various sections of the local community. He was identified by others as the leader of the entire village. His village had a strong population of SC people.

In this case the entire village community could accepted the leadership of Elango irrespective of his caste background. Elango is a fully empowered leader as he was able to take his own decision and implement them. He brought the desired results with the support of the cross-section of the community.

Key Determinants of Empowerment of SC in Panchayats

Based on the case studies discussed, few key determinants affecting the process of empowerment are identified.[26] Numerical strength of the SC population plays a critical role in effective implementation of reservation policy. In many reserved Panchayats SC are minorities. Their minority status do not allow them to enjoy real power. In such cases only Tokenism is practiced. Puppet SC leaders are elected and they are controlled by the dominant caste groups. Particularly in Gram Sabha meetings SC Presidents find it difficult to get the support of the members of the majority community. Where SC people have numerical strength and they are in majority, SC elected representatives are more powerful.

Table–2

Sl.No.	*Key Determinants of Empowerment of SC*
1.	Numerical strength
2.	Social Development of the panchayat
3.	Economical status of SC leaders
4.	Leadership among SC people
5.	Organizations of SC in the area
6.	Support from NGOs
7.	Role of political parties
8.	Unity among SC sub-groups
9.	Interest of government officials
10.	Affiliation of SC panchayat leaders (Associations Network)
11.	Capacity Building Programme

Unity among the SC people is another factor which influence the process of empowerment. In Tamil Nadu the different caste groups within SC people do not have unity and they are fragmented. The dominant caste groups are using this factor and try to divide and rule.

Economic and educational status of SC people also had a great influence in the process of empowerment. When the SC elected leaders are very poor and asset less, they are not in a position to effectively use the opportunities provided by the reservation policy. Poor SC leaders are used by the dominant caste groups. Educated, middle class SC leaders are able to assert their rights and function independently.

Social development facilitates empowerment of SC people. Villages with reasonable social development provide favourable climate for social change and equity.

NGOs also play a critical role in bringing a positive social climate favourable for SC empowerment. Social change and awareness cannot be brought by legislation alone. It needs powerful social movements. NGOs and civil society organizations play a critical role in bringing such movements for social change. SC Panchayat Presidents supported by NGOs are able to function independently.

Political parties also can play a significant role in the empowerment process. In states like Kerala, where Panchayat elections are contested on party basis SC leaders enjoy real power. But in Tamil Nadu major political parties do not show interest in empowering SC leaders at the grassroots level. Major political parties are not interested in the empowerment process and they are much worried about the votes of the majority community. In few districts of Tamil Nadu left parties support SC Panchayat Presidents and these leaders are more assertive.

When SC elected leaders are supported by political parties, NGOs, and associations, they are able to assert their powers. Leaders affiliated with political parties are more powerful than others. It is found that networks of SC leaders provide confidence and support to SC leaders. Members of such networks are in a better position.

Conclusion

Village Panchayat level elections are conducted not on party basis. Even though this policy has several advantages, this is not helpful in bringing a climate favourable for social change. In the absence of political parties caste is the main consideration in Panchayat elections. SC leaders elected on party basis have chances to get the support of their respective political parties in their functioning.

When SC people are not united because of the problems associated with sub-caste and inner conflicts they are exploited by the dominant groups in the villages. Horizontal and vertical integration of various sub-castes of SC community from grassroots to higher levels is required. Leadership play a key role in the success of reservation policy. Building leadership among SC is an essential requirement. Leadership schools or training institutions for SC leaders must be promoted by the NGOs.

Networking of SC Panchayat leaders from grassroots level to state level will be very much useful for strengthening SC Panchayat leaders. Network gives them self-confidence and self-reliance. Particularly block level networking of SC Panchayat leaders can facilitate them to emerge as an empowered group. The success of Self-Help Groups (SHGs) of women gives a clear picture of the strength of small groups of marginalized people. It promotes the concept of self-reliance.

Most of the SC Panchayat leaders are first generation leaders, they do not have any experience in governance. The rules of Panchayat administration are very complex. Rules and government orders are not available to them. They are not able to understand the complex language of administration. They need consultancy service in day-to-day administration. NGOs must come forward to establish such consultancy centers at district level.

Government has not taken any steps to strengthen the emerging SC Panchayat leaders. Government can establish help desks at the district level for Panchayats. An experienced official familiar with the problems faced by the SC Panchayat leaders must be posted for this desk.

Most of the SC Panchayat leaders are from poor economic background and without any assets. Many of them work in the fields of upper caste land lords. The poverty of SC leaders are used by the powerful groups to control the SC leaders. In Tamil Nadu, there is no salary for Panchayat leaders. Panchayat Presidents have to spend lot of their energy and time in attending works related to Panchayats. They do not have much time to take up any other employment. Particularly honest Panchayat leaders find it difficult to earn for their livelihood. A reasonable monthly salary must be given to SC leaders with poor economic background.

But Panchayats have opened up opportunities for empowerment at the grassroots. For effective use of these opportunities a powerful social movement is required. To certain extend Non-Governmental Organizations are able to mobilize women at the grassroots through Self-Help Groups. The Self-Help Groups experiments have revelled the capacity of the NGO sectors to organize women for social transformation. Government must come forward to use this capacity of NGOs to empower Scheduled Caste people in Panchayats.

Empowerment of SC in Panchayats much depend on the status of SC people in social and economic domain also. It is also found that SC representatives with capacity and assets occupy a stronger position and assert their legal rights. State should work to improve the status of SC people in the social and economic domain.

Government should take serious initiatives against discriminative practices at the grassroots Active involvement of civil society organization is very much required there. It should take place as a mass movement. In 1937, when Madras State enacted a law on the rights of Harijans (SC) for temple entry by the civil society it was easy for the state to implement the law and facilitate temple entry of Harijans in most of the sacred pilgrimage centers of Tamil Nadu.

Empowerment process is affected by the domains in which it takes place social and economic domains in rural areas are not still conducive for empowerment of SC leaders in Panchayats. In Tamil Nadu, state has not taken significant steps in bringing changes in the social and economic domains in Tamil Nadu. The status of SC Panchayat Presidents are much more better in Kerala and West Bengal because of the favourable climate in the political social and economic domains. State policies and powerful social and political movements for change have created such a climate in these states. In Tamil Nadu and in many other states, state and civil society have not taken effective steps in this direction. In the absence of such powerful social and political movement reservation policy cannot achieve desired outcomes.

NOTES AND REFERENCES

1. AVARD, Panchayati Raj as the Basics of Indian Polity, *AVARD*, New Delhi: 1962.
2. PRIA, *The State of Panchayats – A Participatory Perspective*, PRIA, New Delhi, p. 1, 2001.
3. S. Viswanathan, *Dalits in Dravidian Land,* Navayana Publishing House: Chennai, 2005.
4. Upendra Baxi, *The Crisis of Indian Legal System,* Vikas Publishing House, New Delhi, 1982.
5. Bavishkar, Stages in Empowerment of Marginalized Groups, paper presented in the National Seminar, *Panchayati Raj—An Institution of Development Organized* by Shri Ram Centre, New Delhi: March 2005.
6. R. Alsop, M. Bertelsen, and J. Holland, Empowerment in Practice from Analysis to Implementation, *The World Bank,* Washington DC, 2006.
7. Bavishkar, *op.cit.*
8. Baxi, *op.cit.*
9. G. Palanithurai, Dalit Leadership in Panchayats, Rajiv Gandhi Chair for Panchayati Raj Studies, Gandhigram, 2003.
10. SC (Schedule Caste) people are traditionally excluded from power

in Indian society. They were disempowered by the social system for thousands of years. Indian Constitution has given equal rights and freedom to all citizens. It has also facilitated affirmative actions like reservation in public offices for Schedule Castes and Schedule Tribes. Still because of historical reasons SC people are not able to assert their rights.

11. G. Palanithurai, *op.cit.*
12. Viswanathan, *op.cit.*
13. *State Election Commission,* Report on Elections for Local Governments in Tamil Nadu, 2006, Chennai.
14. V. Ragupathy, Working of Panchayati Raj System in Tamil Nadu, paper presented in *Institute of Development Studies,* Sussex, July 29th, 2003.
15. *The Hindu,* Melavalavu Murder, 25th July 1996.
16. Bavishkar, *op.cit.*
17. These stages are identified based on the field work of the Rajiv Gandhi Chair for Panchayati Raj Studies, *Gandhigram,* Tamil Nadu.
18. Viswanahan, *op.cit.*
19. V. Ragupathy, *op.cit.*
20. G. Palanithurai, *op.cit.*
21. V. Ragupathy, *op.cit.*
22. G. Palanithurai, *Evaluation of Process and Performance of Dalit Panchayat Leaders,* Concept Publishing Company, New Delhi, 2005.
23. *Ibid.*
24. Five cases are drawn from the reports of Rajiv Gandhi Chair for Panchayati Raj Studies, Gandhigram.

21

Role of Self-Help Groups in Panchayati Raj Administration: The Andhra Pradesh Experience

D. KRISHNAMOORTHY

India followed the policy of 'Trickle down in the first 20 years of economic planning. The practical experience of twenty years of development planning in India amply brought out that the 'Trickle down' theory had miserably failed and a larger segments of people (about 50%) continued to languish in abject poverty in early 1970s. Dandekar and Rath's analysis showed that in 1960-61 about 1/3rd of the rural people and half of the urban population lived on diet in adequate even in respect of calories. Along with the growth of population, the absolute number of poor people in the country continued to multiply. These statistics clearly indicated that the incidence of poverty both in absolute and in relative terms surged unabated. The Community Development Programme (1952), National Extension Scheme (1955), Intensive Agricultural Development Programme (1960) and such other programmes were all general in nature and the emphasis was on overall growth. The benefits of over all growth in the economy were cornered off by the affluent sections and better-endowed areas. The policy makers realised that unless a direct attack on poverty is launched by identifying the target groups and provide them with necessary credit, inputs, subsidies along with facilities for marketing, the development efforts are likely to by-pass the poor. Accordingly many target oriented self-employment and wage-employment anti-poverty programmes were devised and implemented. These anti-poverty programmes were suffering from a number of functional and administrative weaknesses. The major weakness of these programmes is that the coverage of women beneficiaries is highly inadequate at round 11.52 per cent and 9.67 per cent in self-employment and wage employment programmes respectively. This gender-bias in anti-poverty programmes assumes significance in the light of fact that 70 per cent of world's poor are women. All these necessitated the need for formulating gender specific programmes exclusively for women. National Policy on Empowerment of Women was adopted in 2001 with the objective of bringing about gender equality in India. In tune with the national policy, the Government of Andhra Pradesh also initiated several measures for the empowerment of women. It declared 1997 as the Year of Gender Equality with Social Justice. One-third of all vacancies in Government offices, local bodies and public sector undertakings including APSRTC are reserved for women. In the IRDP programme 40 per cent of financial and physical targets are earmarked for women and women headed households by the State Government. On the lines of National Commission for Women, State Women's Commission is also established with the objectives of probing atrocities on women, monitoring the implementation of laws framed for the protection of women. The tenth Janmabhoomi was devoted for women and it is termed as 'Mahila Janmabhoomi'.

DWCRA Programme

Much before the pronouncement of National Policy on Empowerment Women, an innovative programme known as "Development of Women and Children in Rural Areas"(DWCRA) was conceived and implemented. It aims to improve the socio-economic status of the poor in rural areas through the formation of self-help groups of women for collectively undertaking income generating activities on a self-sustaining basis. The DWCRA scheme was as a sub-programme of IRDP in 50 selected districts in 1982. By the end of the 7th Plan (1985-90), the programme was extended to 162 districts.

The Salient Features of DWCRA

The following are the salient features of DWCRA.

1. *Group action:* In DWCRA programme women are organised into groups to foster collective approach to their problems and improve their lot by enhancing their bargaining power and also resist exploitation.
2. *Participatory approach:* Women group members, Government functionaries and voluntary agencies are

expected to function shoulder to shoulder in implementing development programmes meant for women.

3. *Revolving fund:* Under DWCRA programme Rs. 10,00 to 25,000 is provided to the group as a *lump sum* grant. The members can use it collectively or share it on pro-rata basis and it can be used for any income-generating activity. This is a common fund, which is recouped and revolved periodically.
4. *Thrift and credit:* DWCRA members recognised that Thrift and Credit are essential for self-reliance. Within the group women are encouraged to save their own money (minimum of Rs. 30 per month) as a common fund. DWCRA helps to keep the women out of the grip of the money-lenders who often charge exorbitant interest rates and keep the poor as 'poor' for generations.
5. *Income generating activities:* Women's income is found to have a positive correlation with the nutritional and educational status of the family. It also enhances positive attitudes towards the status of women inside and outside the households. With the help of revolving fund, thrift amount and additional loans provided by agencies like DRDA, the DWCRA members undertake income-generating activities either collectively or individually.
7. *Training and awareness:* Unskilled and illiterate women have lesser employment opportunities and low wages. This makes women to be categorised as marginal workers or unpaid workers. Training in leadership, attitudinal changes, skills for income generation are an integral part of DWCRA scheme. Training provides an opportunity to teach their sisters who are better than those women.

Achievements Under DWCRA in Andhra Pradesh

Andhra Pradesh occupies a pride of place in the implementation of DWCRA Scheme. It has taken up the theme of Women's Empowerment through self-help groups. At present, there are 1.15 lakh DWCRA groups and 2.19 lakh SHG groups in Andhra Pradesh with a membership of 46 lakh women, having a savings of Rs. 300 crore. Government has given assistance to the tune of Rs. 383 crore, thus bringing the corpus fund to Rs. 683 crore.

Focus of the Present Study

The present study is a part of the larger project undertaken with ICSSR financial assistance in six districts, viz., Chittoor, Anantapur, Nellore, Guntur, Khammam and Medak districts of Andhra Pradesh. The major objectives of the study were to assess the impact of the DWCRA scheme on the achievement of economic empowerment of women and to evaluate their role in development activities like health, education and collective development of the society. As shown in Table-1, in Guntur district two mandals viz., Mangalagiri and Tadepalle were selected randomly and from each mandal two villages were selected.

Table- 1
Distribution of Sample Units by Village

Name of the Mandal	*Name of the Village*	*No. of Group Leaders*	*No. of DWCRA Members*
Mangalagiri	Nothakki	2	10
	Peddavadlapudi	2	10
Tadepalli	Tadepalle	2	10
	Peddakakani	2	10
	Total	**8**	**40**

Source: Field Data.

From each village two DWCRA groups were selected and from each group five DWCRA members were selected randomly. Pre-designed interview schedules were used to collect the required information from the Group leaders and the sample DWCRA members. The collected data were carefully analysed using simple tools and techniques to draw useful conclusions.

Socio-economic Profile of the Sample Groups and Members

The social class-wise distribution of sample group leaders and sample DWCRA members indicated that weaker sections of the society took minor role in DWCRA programme. As could be seen from Table –2, out of 8 group leaders, 12.5 per cent belonged to BCs and 12.5 per cent to SCs. OCs constituted a major proportion of 75.0 per cent of total group leaders in the District. This is in contrast to the trend observed in other mandals were the weaker sections of the society such as STs, SCs and BCs took active part in DWCRA programme.

Table-2
Social Group-wise Distribution of DWCRA Group Leaders

Caste	*Mangalagiri*	*Tadepalli*	*Total*	*%*
SC	0	1	1	12.50
ST	0	0	0	0
BC	0	1	1	12.50
OC	4	2	6	75.00
Minorities	0	0	0	0
Total	**4**	**4**	**8**	**100.00**

Source: Field Data.

The social group-wise distribution of sample DWCRA members also reiterates the same conclusion. As could be seen from Table-3, out of 40 sample members, about 12.5 per cent belonged SCs and 2.5 per cent to Minorities. About 12.5 per cent belonged to BCs. In other words, out of total members, 72.5 per cent was from Other Castes (OCs) indicating that poor people were also there among other caste groups of the society who have taken bold initiative to ameliorate their conditions through collective action.

Table-3
Social Group-wise Distribution of DWCRA Group Members

Caste	*Mangalagiri*	*Tadepalli*	*Total*	*%*
SC	0	5	5	12.50
ST	0	0	0	0
BC	2	3	5	12.50
OC	17	12	29	72.50
Minorities	1	0	1	0
Total	**20**	**20**	**40**	**100.00**

Source: Field Data.

Majority of the members of the DWCRA groups (about 77%) were literates. In fact 50 per cent of the DWCRA members got educated up to 10th class and about 10 per cent of DWCRA women have done their graduation. Even though about 22.5 per cent of DWCRA women were illiterates, most of them have learned to put their signature thanks to the adult education campaign undertaken by the educated members of the DWCRA. Illiteracy was widely seen among all caste groups as could be observed from the Table-4.

Table-4
Educational Levels of Sample DWCRA Group Members

Caste Group/ Level of Education		*Mangalagiri*	*Tadepalli*	*Total*	*%*
ST	Illiterate	0	0	0	05
	Primary	0	0	0	0
	Secondary	0	0	0	0
	College	0	0	0	0
SC	Illiterate	0	2	2	5.0
	Primary	0	0	0	0
	Secondary	0	3	3	7.5
	College	0	0	0	0
BC	Illiterate	1	2	3	7.5
	Primary	1	0	1	2.5
	Secondary	0	1	1	2.5
	College	0	0	0	0
OC	Illiterate	2	2	4	10.0
	Primary	3	2	5	12.5
	Secondary	9	7	16	40.0
	College	3.	1	4	10.0
Min-orities	Illiterate	0	0	0	0
	Primary	1	0	1	2.5
	Secondary	0	0	0	0
	College	0	0	0	0
Total	Illiterate	3	6	9	22.5
	Primary	5	2	7	17.5
	Secondary	9	11	20	50.0
	College	3	1	4	10.0
Grand Total		20	20	40	100.0

Occupational Pattern

The members of the DWCRA groups utilised the DWCRA assistance and additional financial facilities extended by banks through the NABARD programme of Bank–SHG linkage to undertake income-generating activities either collectively or individually. The findings of the study indicated that out of 8 groups surveyed two groups seemed to have undertaken productive activity collectively. The leaders of the both the groups belonged to OC community. Similarly both groups belonged to Tadepalli Mandal. The Krushi Mahila Podupu Group in Tadepalli village of Tadepalli mandal was involved in making dolls out of Chinese clay.

Table-5

Nature of Economic Activity Undertaken by the DWCRA Groups

Caste	*Nature*	*Mangalagiri*	*Tadepalli*	*Total*	*%*
SC	Group	0	0	0	0
	Individual	0	1	1	12.5
ST	Group	0	0	0	0
	Individual	0	0	0	0
BC	Group	0	0	0	0
	Individual	0	1	1	12.5
OC	Group	0	2	2	25
	Individual	4	0	4	50
Total	Group	0	2	2	25
	Individual	4	2	6	75
	Grand Total	**4**	**4**	**48**	**100**

The other six groups carried out the production activity individually. Out of the six groups who carried out the production activity individually, the leaders of 4 groups belonged to OC community. While one belonged to the SC community, the other belonged to the BC community. In short, majority of the groups in the district carried out the production activity individually and most of them belonged to OC community. Photos—1 and 2 display the attractive dolls made by the Krushi Mahila Group in Tadepalli Mandal of Guntur district, Andhra Pradesh. She has displayed the attractive dolls in many district, state and nation level DWCRA Bazars and won many awards at district and state levels. She also obtained additional loan under Chief Minister Empowerment of Youth (CMEY) programme.

The other group viz., Lakshmi Bogeswara Group in Peddakakani village of Tadepalli mandal was involved in making plastic bushes used to the legs of chairs and tables. Photo—3 displays the involvement of these DWCRA women in the manufacture of plastic bushes. These women get raw material from Vijayawada city and they sell the output in the retail market in Vijayawada town itself. The major problem reported by the members was inadequate power supply especially in summer. This being the village the power supply is highly inadequate and erratic. There was also problem of voltage fluctuations in power.

Photo–1
The DWCRA Group Member in Tadepalli Village of Tadepalli Mandal in Guntur District Involving in Doll Making

Photo-2
The Attractive Dolls Manufactured by the DWCRA Group Member in Tadepalli Village of Tadepalli Mandal in Guntur District of Andhra Pradesh

Photo-3
The Lakshmi Bhogeswara Bhavani group in Peddakakani Village of Tadepalli Mandal of Guntur District Involving in the Manufacture of Plastic Bushes

As could be seen from Table-6, before they came in to the DWCRA fold, all the members of the groups who carried out the production activity either collectively or individually were housewives with no remunerative work. Out of them 29 members (72.5%) belonged to OC, 5 members (12.5%) each belonged to SC and BC. The sole member belonged to minority caste.

After becoming the members of DWCRA, these women undertook many productive activities. The diversified structure of activities undertaken by these enterprising groups indicated many interesting insights. (Table-7). A close perusal of the table clearly indicates that out of 40 members, 11 members (27.5%) still continued to be agricultural labourers. 6 members (15%) undertook tailoring and embroidery as their economic activity. Five members each pursued rubber bush making or dairy with buffalo rearing as their activity. Doll making as group activity was pursued by three members of the group. Another three members were either Anganwadi worker or involved in the preparation of midday meal in Anganwadi centers. Two members were teachers in private schools. Some members continued to involve in agriculture, painting, clothe business or running petty shops. The category of housewives that formed overwhelming proportion in the pre-DWCRA

Table-6
Occupational Pattern of the Members Before DWCRA

Caste	*Nature*	*Mangalagiri*	*Tadepalli*	*Total*	*%*
SC	House Wife	0	5	5	12.5
	Agri. Cooli	0	0	0	0
	Other Cooli	0	0	0	0
ST	House Wife	C	0	0	0
	Agri. Cooli	0	0	0	0
	Other Cooli	0	0	0	0
BC	House Wife	2	3	5	12.5
	Agri. Cooli	0	0	0	0
	Other Cooli	0	0	0	0
OC	House Wife	17	12	29	72.5
	Agri. Cooli	0	0	0	0
	Other Cooli	0	0	0	0
Min-orities	House Wife	1	0	1	2.5
	Agri. Cooli	0	0	0	0
	Other Cooli	0	0	0	0
Total	House Wife	**20**	**20**	**40**	**100**
	Agri. Cooli	**0**	**0**	**0**	**0**
	Other Cooli	**0**	**0**	**0**	**0**
	Grand Total	**20**	**20**	**40**	**100**

Source: Field Data.

Table-7
Activities Undertaken by the Members of the DWCRA Group Members

Activity	*Mangalagiri*	*Tadepalli*	*Total*	*%*
Agriculture	0	1	1	2.5
Agri. cooli	5	6	11	27.5
Anganwadi worker/aya	2	1	3	7.5
Art designing painting	1	0	1	2.5
Bush making	0	5	5	12.5
Cloth business	0	1	1	2.5
Dairying	5	0	5	12.5

(Contd.)

Activity	*Mangalagiri*	*Tadepalli*	*Total*	%
Doll making	0	3	3	7.5
Embroidery/ tailoring	6	0	6	15
Hotel	1	0	1	2.5
Petty shop	0	1	1	2.5
Teacher	0	2	2	5.0
Total	**20**	**20**	**40**	**100**

Source: Field Survey.

period virtually vanished. The few who were pursuing traditional occupations have moved to higher occupational structures or have improved their business prospects.

Income Generation

The pursuit of independent occupation by the DWCRA members enabled them to earn income and thereby to gain economic independence. Since the entire sample DWCRA members were housewives earlier with zero transfer earnings, the entire incremental income was a real gain to them. On the average, the sample DWCRA members in the two mandals earned Rs.1026 per month. The average income of DWCRA members in Mangalagiri mandal worked at Rs.1139 that was higher than that of Tadepalli mandal (Rs. 912.45). The average income of DWCRA member who pursued hotel business seemed to have earned highest income at Rs. 2500 per month. Those who pursued dairy as the economic activity earned the next highest income. These members earned Rs. 1686 per month. Those who pursued agricultural cooli as the occupation earned the lowest income of Rs. 686 per month.

The caste-group-wise income levels earned by the members of DWCRA groups also yielded interesting inferences as could be noticed from Table-9.

The average income of a SC member and the sole minority member was Rs. 600 per month. Similarly, the average income of a BC member turned out to be at Rs. 880 per month. The average income of these three groups was less than the overall average of Rs. 1026 and also that of an OC member (Rs. 1139). The entire incremental income was the transfer earnings for the members of the group.

Table-8
Monthly Average Income of the Members of the DWCRA Groups

Activity	*Mangalagiri*		*Tadepalli*		*Total*	
	No.	*Avg. Income*	*No.*	*Avg. Income*	*No.*	*Avg. Income*
Agriculture	0	0	1	800	1	800
Agri. Cooli	5	750	6	633	11	686
Anganwadi Worker/aya	2	1200	1	500	3	967
Art designing Painting	1	1000	0	0	1	1000
Bush making	0	0	5	1200	5	1200
Cloth business	0	0	1	1000	1	1000
Dairying	5	1686	0	0	5	1686
Doll making	0	0	3	1067	3	1067
Embroidery/ tailoring	6	783	0	0	6	783
Hotel	1	2500	0	0	1	2500
Petty shop	0	0	1	1000	1	1000
Teacher	0	0	2	975	2	975
Average Income	**20**	**1138.9**	**20**	**912.45**	**40**	**1025.68**

Source: Field Survey.

Table-9
Monthly Average Income of DWCRA Members by

Caste Group	*Mangalagiri*		*Tadepalli*		*Total*	
	No.	*Avg. Income*	*No.*	*Avg. Income*	*No.*	*Avg. Income*
SC	0	0	5	600	5	600
ST	0	0	0	0	0	0
BC	2	1050	3	767	5	880
OC	17	1181	12	1079	29	1139
Minorities	1	600	0	0	1	600
Total	**20**	**1138.9**	**20**	**912.45**	**40**	**1026**

Source: Field Survey.

Another important achievement of the members of the DWCRA groups in the study area was increase in the level of savings for the groups. As could be seen from Table-10, in the study area, an amount of Rs. 25, 440 was being saved per year and their cumulative savings up to 31st March, 2003 amounted to Rs. 1,12, 200. Total savings per year and the cumulative savings were relatively higher in Mangalagiri mandal (Rs.15, 000 and Rs. 72,000) when compared to that in Tadepalli mandal (Rs. 10, 400 and Rs. 40,200 respectively). The caste group-wise analysis of savings levels indicated that SC Groups saved Rs. 7,200 and the minorities saved Rs. 2400 in total. In fact out of all the caste groups, the savings levels of OCs were very high at Rs. 88,800. BCs could save Rs. 13,800 during the period.

Table-10

Yearly and Total Savings of the DWCRA Groups

	Magalagiri		*Tadepalli*		*Total*		
Caste Group	*Per Year*	*Upto March 2003*	*Per Year*	*Upto March 2003*	*Per Year*	*Upto March 2003*	*Average per member per year*
SC	0	0	1440	7200	1440	7200	1440
ST	0	0	0	0	0	0	0
BC	1,200	4,800	1,800	9000	3000	13,800	2760
OC	13,200	64,800	7,200	24,000	20,400	88,800	3062
Minorities	600	2,400	0	0	600	24,00	2400
Total	15,000	72,000	10,440	40,200	25,440	1,12,200	2805
Average	750	3600	522	2010	636	2803	–

Source: Field Survey.

The total amount of savings depends upon the starting year of the group as well as the number of members in the group. Hence, in order to neutralize these two factors, the average amount of savings per member per year was computed and the information is provided in the last column of the table. As could be seen from the table the average level of savings per member per annum was very high among OCs followed by that of BCs, minorities and SCs. Nevertheless, the pooling of small amounts to become a lump sum is really the remarkable achievement as the total amount of savings in the two mandals for the eight groups amounted to Rs. 1,12,200.

Concluding Remarks

Women empowerment is a multifaceted concept. It seeks to bring about the advancement, development and empowerment of women. The policy encourages active participation of all stakeholders for achieving its goals. The DWCRA programme is one of the means to achieve the ultimate objective of women empowerment. The foregoing discussion clearly reveals that the DWCRA women in the two study mandals have performed extremely well by fostering savings, by pursuing a diversified structure of occupations, by earning income to achieve economic independence. The study also made it clear that a substantial number of stakeholders in the programme were women belonged to weaker sections of the society who were socially and economically oppressed by the society at large. These women now do not depend on their husbands or sons or wards for their needs. They do not also depend on the local money-lenders whenever they need any money to meet the education, medical or other emergency expenditures in the family or to meet their personal needs. They simply use their pooled savings or SHG loans from banks. This according to them is a remarkable achievement of DWCRA programme.

22

Decentralised Planning in India: Are the Panchayati Raj Institutions Really Empowered?

M. DEVENDRA BABU

Introduction

When India attained independence in the year 1947, a vast majority of population was living in pathetic conditions. Low-income (GDP) growth, poverty, unemployment, inequalities and a host of other problems were afflicting India. The leaders of free India felt the need for urgent measures to overcome the above problems. The most important policy decision the Central Government took in this direction was to adopt economic planning. Consequently, five-year plans have been launched from 1951. For a systematic and continuity to planning the centre constituted an institution called 'Planning Commission' through an Act of Parliament in the year 1950. The functions entrusted to this body among others are – the preparation of annual and five-year plans; determination of priorities; allocation of plan resources among the states; reviewing the progress of plan targets and achievements. Planning for economic and social development is in the concurrent list (List III) of subjects in the Constitution and hence the states are also made to shoulder the responsibility of planning and development.

The Planning Commission prepares the blueprint of economic plans in consultation with the states and in accordance with the guidelines provided by the National Development Council (NDC). Thus, fixing of the priorities and plan formulation were done at the state and the Central level. Broadly, this kind of planning is termed as centralised (top-down approach) planning.

Each five-year plan, beginning with the second one, stressed the need for peoples' participation in planning and implementation.

In the latter part of 1950s a Study Team on the Working of 'Community Development Programmes and Extension Services' recommended the need for local democratic bodies (PRIs) for the success of rural community development programmes/schemes (Mehta, 1957). However, no concrete measures were initiated either at the central level or at the states' level as far as decentralised planning is concerned except establishment of PRIs in certain states in the year 1959. When the country could not overcome the problems of poverty, social and economic inequalities even after decades of planning, a shift in the plan approach was initiated in the Fourth Plan (1969) with a focus on sectoral and area specific development programmes. In this direction, a large number of sectoral development programmes such as MFDL, SFDL, IADP and area programmes like DPAP, DDP, ITDP were launched throughout the country. Funds relating to these programmes were transferred directly to the district administration. This shift of policy was intended mainly to have plans prepared at the district level.

However, in spite of these changes in the plan perspective not much change was seen from the previous plan practices. The Report of the Working Group on District Planning observes that "real planning functions have not percolated to the district levels and only a limited job of assembling departmental schemes within the district frame is now being attempted" (Planning Commission, 1984). The main reasons for not achieving the desired results in district/local planning among others were lack of freedom in fixing priorities, dominance of bureaucracy in planning and implementation, lack of peoples' participation and absence of sustainable local self-governments.

The above Working Group cites lack of prerequisites for failure of the effort at decentralised district planning in the 1970s. It was of the view that the decentralised plan will succeed only if some essential prerequisites are created and with the active involvement of panchayati raj institutions. The essential prerequisites according to it are:

1. existence of political will and commitment;
2. setting up a district planning body;
3. setting up a suitable machinery for planning;
4. demarcation of planning functions;
5. devolution of financial resources;

6. delegation of administrative powers;
7. evolution of new patterns of political and administrative behaviour;
8. ensuring public participation at all stages in the planning process; and
9. training and re-training of personnel.

Though the Working Group made the above suggestions in the year 1984 no concrete measures were taken by the Central Government until 1991. However, a paradigm shift in the governance structure occurred in India in the year 1992, with amendments to the Constitution (73rd and 74th) which made mandatory on the part of states to establish elected local bodies both in rural and urban areas. The above Amendment Acts ensured the establishment of local bodies by all the states and broad guidelines for transfer of powers, functions, finances to them by the respective states. One of the principal objectives of decentralisation reform was to enable the country to switch from centralised planning to decentralised planning.

The 74th Amendment Act has gone a step forward as far as decentralised planning is concerned. Article 243(ZD) of the above Act provides for the constitution of a District Planning Committee (DPC) at the district level in every state. The main objective of DPC is to consolidate the plans prepared by panchayats and municipalities in the district and to prepare a draft development plan for the district as a whole. Further, the provision states that while preparing the draft development plan by the DPC it should have regard to:

1. *(i)* matters of common interest between panchayats and municipalities including spatial planning, sharing of water and other physical and natural resources, the integrated development of infrastructure and environmental conservation;

   (ii) the extent and type of available resources whether financial or otherwise;
2. consult such institutions and organisations as the governor may, by order, specify.

Thus, Article 243(ZD) of CAA has set a trend for comprehensive and integrated district plan covering both rural and urban areas.

Mere establishment of local democratic institutions doesn't ensure that the plans are prepared and implemented by the local bodies with active participation 0f people. The success of local planning depends on certain essential conditions/requisites as highlighted by the Working Group.

Objectives of the Study

In the above background this paper makes an attempt to analyse the status of district planning in the post-73rd amendment period in India. The specific objectives are:

(a) to sketch the status of district planning in the various states;
(b) to evaluate the extent of prerequisites (functions, functionaries and resources) created at the local governmental level; and
(c) to suggest policy measures for making DPCs functional.

The analysis made in the paper mainly pertains to rural local bodies. Further, only the major states are considered for the study. It is based on quantitative information and within this it is relied upon secondary sources of data.

Status of DPCs

It is 15 years now since 73rd and 74th Constitutional Amendments were effected to the Indian Constitution and almost all the states have compiled with the mandate and have enacted their own new Legislative Acts to establish local democratic institutions in the middle of 1990s. With regard to DPCs, the states were supposed to make a provision with respect to:

(a) the composition of the DPCs;
(b) the manner in which the seats in such committees to be filled;
(c) the functions relating to district planning which may be assigned to DPC; and
(d) the manner in which the Chairpersons of such Committees is chosen.

Thus, the 74th CAA has given broad guidelines for the states to follow while constituting DPCs and to make them operational (Government of India, 1992). In this connection, it is important here to look at the status of DPCs in different states, which, in turn, reflect the direction in which they are moving, their functional status and other related issues. The state-wise information on DPCs has been presented in Table 1. It can be seen from the table that as on 2006, out of 18 major states, 7 states (in one state elections to PRIs was not held) had not yet constituted DPCs and in two states DPCs had not been constituted in all the districts. This implies that half of the states were not for DPCs. The states, which had compiled with the Constitutional mandate and set up DPCs, three states had appointed the minister in-charge of the district as Chairperson of DPC and in the remaining six states the Chairperson of Zilla/District Panchayat had been made Chairpersons. No information on this matter was available for Haryana state. About the progress made on the constitution and operationalising DPC, the 10th Plan document has observed that "State Governments had not given adequate attention to the DPCs and the Government of India's

Table–1
Status of District Planning Committees in Major States

State	*Status*	*Chairperson of DPC*
Andhra Pradesh	Not yet constituted	–
Assam	Not yet constituted	–
Bihar	Constituted	Chairperson of ZP
Chhattisgarh	Constituted	District in-charge Minister
Gujarat	Not yet constituted	–
Haryana	Constituted	No information
Karnataka	Constituted	Chairperson of ZP
Kerala	Constituted	Chairperson of DP
Madhya Pradesh	Constituted	District in-charge Minister
Jharkhand	*	Not applicable
Maharashtra	Not yet constituted	District in-charge Minister
Orissa	Partially (in 26 distrits)	District in-charge Minister
Punjab	Not yet constituted	–
Rajasthan	Constituted	Chairperson of ZP
Tamil Nadu	Constituted	Chairperson of ZP
Uttar Pradesh	Not yet constituted	–
Uttaranchal	Not yet constituted	–
West Bengal	Constituted	Chairperson of DP

Note : * Elections to PRIs are yet to be held.
Source : Website of *Ministry of Panchayati Raj*, Government of India.

guidelines on district planning had not been fully operationalised (Planning Commission, 2003). It is significant to note that though the states had constituted DPCs they were yet to be made functional. Only Kerala had made DPCs functional with having drafted the Ninth and Tenth Plans through panchayats/DPCs.

On the working of DPCs, it is observed that "looking back, one can firmly maintain that decentralised planning has been virtually abandoned by a majority of the states with impunity..... although all states have constituted SFCs, the Commission's task will remain incomplete without reference to the DPCs. In fact, DPCs are alive and kicking only in Kerala" (Oomen, 2002). This is one part of the picture on the status of district planning. The other and the most fundamental question is—are the decentralised bodies have embarked upon planning in the real sense of the term? In other words, have the states provided the requisites, which are *sine-quo-non* for the initiation of planning by local bodies? The following paragraphs unearth the position on this in different states.

Requisites for Decentralised Planning

The success of grassroots level planning depends not merely on the working of DPCs but largely on the provision of supportive facilities to decentralised bodies. This, as mentioned in the beginning, results in empowering people, promoting public participation and increasing efficiency. The prerequisites such as powers, responsibilities, functionaries, finances, space for public participation are crucial for the success of local democratic institutions and the plans they prepare and implement. In this regard, if we observe the extent of requisites created by different states, the position is very unsatisfactory. Table 2 shows the extent of provision of important requisites to PRIs in different states. It can be seen from the table that the states are more liberal in transferring functions than functionaries and funds to PRIs. As against the 29 subjects mentioned in Article 243(G) of 11th Schedule of the Constitution to be transferred to PRIs by the states, 12 out of 18 major states have not fully implemented. About eight states have transferred more than 15 but less than 29 subjects.

In the matter of functionaries and funds, only eight states have done some justice. To be precise, only Karnataka state has transferred all the 29 subjects along with functionaries and funds followed by Maharashtra, Kerala, Gujarat, West Bengal, Chhattisgarh and

Table–2
Status of Devolution of Funds, Functions and Functionaries to Panchayat Raj Institutions in Major States as on 1-4-2004. (in No.)

State	*Number of Departments/ Subjects Transferred to Panchayats with*			*Number of Departments/ Subjects yet to be Transferred to Panchayats with*		
	Funds	*Functions*	*Functionaries*	*Funds*	*Functions*	*Functionaries*
Andhra Pradesh	5	17	2	24	12	27
Assam	0	29	0	29	0	29
Bihar	25	5	*	4	23	29
Jharkhand	*	*	*	29	29	29
Gujarat	15	15	15	14	14	14
Haryana	0	16	0	29	13	29
Karnataka	29	29	29	0	0	0
Kerala	26	26	26	3	3	3
Madhya Pradesh	10	23	9	19	6	20
Chhattisgarh	10	29	9	19	0	20
Maharashtra	18	18	18	11	11	11
Orissa	9	25	21	20	4	8
Punjab	0	7	0	29	22	29
Rajasthan	18	29	18	11	0	11
Tamil Nadu	0	29	0	29	0	29
Uttar Pradesh	4	12	6	25	17	23
Uttaranchal	0	11	11	29	18	18
West Bengal	12	29	12	17	0	17

Note: * Only functional control; ** Elections to PRIs have not yet been held
Source: Same as in Table 1.

Madhya Pradesh. However, the real strength of PRIs will be known only if their actual resource and expenditure levels are studied. The information on per capita revenues and expenditures of PRIs of major states has been given in Table 3. It can be seen from the table that the per capita revenue and expenditure of PRIs in four states out of 15 states exceeded Rs. 500 per annum during 1997-98. In another six states, the same varied between Rs. 100 and Rs. 500. However, if we take a cut-off point, i.e., the average of all states, then, only in seven states their income and expenditures exceeded the average of all states. Almost same situation is noticeable during 2002-03.

Table–3
Revenues of PRIs (all the Three-Tiers) in Major States During 1997-98 and 2002-03 (Rs. Crore)

	1997-98				*2002-03*			
States	*PRIs Revenue*	*Net State Domestic Product**	*Per State Revenue*** *(Rs.)*	*PRIs Share in NSDP (%)*	*PRIs Revenue*	*Net State Domestic Product**	*Per Capita Revenue** *(Rs.)*	*PRIs Share in . NSDP · (%)*
Andhra Pradesh	2511.59	85791	517	2.93	4579.15	145198	827	31.5
Assam	15.50	20211	8	0.08	7.61	32583	3	0.02
Bihar	365.96	30307	49	1.21	295.93	51325	40	0.58
Gujarat	2232.54	77266	825	2.89	3302.37	118513	1042	2.79
Haryana	85	33909	69	0.25	376.37	58655	251	0.64
Karnataka	3768.07	64757	1213	5.82	4303.03	1004406	1233	4.29
Kerala	982.77	44883	451	2.19	960.69	71064	407	1.35
Madhya Pradesh	1779.01	53141	350	3.35	478.52	71646	108	0.67
Maharashtra	3307.47	172530	683	1.92	5337.02	259042	956	2.06
Orissa	640.02	28000	233	2.29	187.84	38737	60	0.48
Punjab	135.41	43099	95	0.31	178.55	64094	111	0.28
Rajasthan	1520.41	56912	448	2.67	1811.63	75048	418	2.41
Tamil Nadu	422.16	92689	115	0.46	890.58	135252	255	0.66
Uttar Pradesh	883.24	120125	79	0.74	623.61	176076	47	0.35
West Bengal	487.75	89595	99	0.54	177.23	153781	. 31	0.12
TOTAL	19136.93	1013215	308	1.89	23509.91	1551420	349	1.52

Notes: * At current prices; ** calculated on the basis of projected rural population for the year 1997-98; * Based on 2001 rural population.

Sources: 1. Government of India, *'Report of the Finance Commission'*, 1996 and 2005.

2. Ministry of Finance, *Indian Public Finance Statistics*, 2005.

Another measure, i.e., the ratio of revenue to the state domestic product also unfolds the level of fiscal decentralisation that has been carried out in different states. From the same table it can be seen that the share of PRIs revenue of seven states out of 15 states had less than one per cent in their respective state domestic product. Karnataka is far ahead of other states in terms of both per capita and ratio to NSDP (Net State Domestic Product). Similar is the status with regard to expenditures.

As far as composition of revenues of PRIs is concerned, in almost all the states the own revenues (tax and non-tax) in their total revenues was very negligible. For instance, the calculations made reveal that at the all states level the share of own revenues of PRIs in their total revenues was 5.60 per cent in 1990-91, 3.62 per cent in 1997-98 and 6.84 per cent in 2002-03 (Government of India, 2000: 227-31; 2004: 436). That means the PRIs depend largely on the transfers from the higher level governments for their needs. Further, a cursory look at the recommendations of various State Finance Commissions (SFCs) (Table-4) unfolds the piecemeal treatment and assignment of tax powers and transfer of resources to PRIs. The main reasons for this kind of recommendations by many SFCs are limited expenditure assignment to the local bodies, lack of clarity on the roles of different tiers of panchayats. Besides and the most important aspect is that the grants-in-aid made to the PRIs in almost all the states are specific in nature (tied) and as such it is impossible for them to initiate planning as envisaged in the Constitution. Another relevant issue as far as planning is concerned at the local level is that there should be administrative decentralisation. In most of the states adequate and responsible personnel were not provided at the local level and in particular the planning personnel.

Another aspect, which has a bearing on planning and development at the local level, is the status of DRDA (District Rural Development Agency). It may be noted that DRDAs were established in every district of the country in mid-1970s to implement anti-poverty and rural development programmes. A large amount of money was channeled through this agency to plan and manage the above programmes. It was expected that the states would merge the DRDA along with personnel and funds with the respective Zilla/ District panchayats soon after their establishment. Contrary to this, many states had not only retained their separate identity but also made the bureaucracy as implementing authorities. It is significant

Table-4
Major Recommendations of First State Finance Commissions of Major States

State	*Recommendations*	*Status*
Andhra Pradesh	9.14% of the tax and non-tax revenue of the state PRIs	Accepted
	Increase of per capita grant to GPs from Rs. 1 to 4, and to MPs Rs. 5 to 8	Accepted
	Rs. 2 to Rs. for ZPs	Accepted
Bihar	SFC constituted	Details not available
Gujarat	SFC constituted	—do—
Karnataka	Transferring 36% of State's non-lona gross revenue receipts	Accepted
	85% to PRIs and 15% to Urban local bodies	Accepted
Kerala	25% of net motor vehicle tax colletion to local bodies	Accepted
	Proceeds of building tax to village panchayats and municipalities	Accepted
	Earmarking a portion of the income form the sale of court fee stamps to LBs	Accepted
Madhya Pradesh	Grants to GPs to discharge their functions	Accepted
	Agency fee to Janpad and ZPs for carrying out Agency functions	Accepted
	For providing tied and untied grants	Not accepted
	A lump sum non-recurring grant	Accepted
		Details not available
Maha-rashtra	Total 129 recommendations (12 accepted)	
	And records by each local body	Accepted
	Share of state taxes for transfer to local bodies to be 2 % in each year	Accepted
	Transfer of 10% of net proceeds of MVT	Accepted
Orissa	Massive external assistance to local bodies to upgrade basic services	Unknown
	Surcharge on stamp duty for transfer of properties in rural areas	Unknown
Punjab	Assignment of land revenue to GPs	Accepted
	Sharing of 20% of the net proceeds of the stamp duties, MVT, electricity	Accpeted
	Duty and entertainment tax with PRIs and municiplaities	—do—
Rajasthan	To devolve 2.18% of the net proceeds of the state's own tax revenue to PRIs	Accpeted
	To provide 50% matching grant	—do—

(Contd.)

State	*Recommedations*	*Status*
Tamil Nadu	Assigning local cess surcharge on stamp duty to PRIs	Accepted
	90% of entertainment tax to PRIS	Accepted
	8% of total state tax revenues	Accepted
U.P.	SFC constituted	Details not available
West Bengal	Sharing of 16% of the net proceeds of all taxes collected by state with PRIs and municipalities	Accepted

Source: Rajiv Gandhi Foundation, *Panchayati Raj in India: Status Report 1999*, New Delhi, 2000, pp. 268-71.

to note from Table 5 that the DRDAs were merged with their respective Zilla/District panchayats in only 8 states out of 18 major states. Thus, quite a significant number of local development programmes and funds have been kept away from the purview of PRIs.

Table–5
State-wise Status of District Rural Development Agency

State	*Status of DRDA*
Andhra Pradesh	Not merged with ZP
Assam	Not merged with ZP
Bihar	Not merged with ZP
Jharkhand	Elections to PRIs not yet held
Gujarat	Not merged with ZP
Haryana	Not merged with ZP
Karnataka	Merged with ZP
Kerala	Merged with ZP
Madhya Pradesh	Merged with ZP
Chhattisgarh	Merged with ZP
Maharashtra	Not merged with ZP
Orissa	Merged with ZP
Punjab	Not merged with ZP
Rajasthan	Merged with ZP
Tamil Nadu	Not merged with ZP
Uttar Pradesh	Merged with ZP
Uttaranchal	No information
West Bengal	Merged with ZP

Source: Planning Commission, *Five Year Plan – 2002-07'*, Vol. III, Appendix 5.1, Government of India.

Another important requirement for the success of decentralised planning is peoples' participation right from decision-making to implementation and monitoring of plans. All the states in their Panchayat Raj (PR) Acts provided for Grama Sabha (Village Assembly consisting of all the adult people of the village whose names are enrolled in the voter list). This is a grassroot level platform available for public to participate in the local governance and planning. But the experience of its working so far leaves much to be desired. Only in a few states such as Kerala, West Bengal and to some extent in Karnataka Grama Sabhas are functioning satisfactorily (Webster, 1992: 154; Aziz, 1994; Bhargava and Raphael, 1994: 152-6; Aziz, *et. al.*, 1999; Muraleedharan, 2000; Jagajeevan and Ramakantan, 2000; 344-45; Mathew, 2000:14; Sebastin, 2001; Babu, 2002; Mohanty and Kumar, 2002).

The above information on the strengths of PRIs in India is self-revealing. They are far from becoming self-governing institutions. With very few functions and resources at their disposal, decentralised planning as envisioned under the constitutional amendments is far away from reality. With these weaknesses afflicting the PRIs in a majority of states how can one expect the DPCs to function even if they are made operational?

Overview

The foregoing analysis of the working of DPCs and the enabling inputs provided to PRIs to undertake what may be called bottom-up planning still remains a mirage. It is of no use in talking and analysing the working of the DPCs without the provision of powers, functions, finances and functionaries to PRIs. The states, by and large, have shown interest only in transferring some functions but it should be complemented by the devolution of funds and functionaries to implement those functions. This should get precedence before the setting up of DPCs and making them functional.

Many states are yet to fulfill their obligation to constitute DPCs in accordance with the procedures set out in the Constitution. The states in the first instance are required to lay down the necessary guidelines for composition and powers of DPCs and then proceed to constitute DPCs. After fulfilling these basic requirements the local bodies must be asked to undertake decentralised planning in an integrated framework model.

In certain states the minister in-charge of the district is made the Chairperson of the DPC. The practice of appointing ministers as Chairpersons of DPCs results in converting them into parallel bodies and imposition of state priorities on the local bodies. To avoid such ill treatment of democratically elected local government, the Chairmanship of the DPC should invariably be vested with the ZP/DP Chairperson.

Besides, there is need for activation of the defunct Grama Sabhas in various states. Unless the Grama Sabha is made active and vibrant, peoples' participation in the local development, in general and in decentralised planning, in particular, will be a myth. Mere making a provision for Grama Sabha and laying down its functions in the state PR Acts will not serve the purpose unless the needed powers and legal status of the decisions taken are specified in the act itself.

Another related issue is that the states are more interested in fulfilling the mandate of Constitution in constituting SFC. But, in a majority of the states scant regard has been shown to their important recommendations. Unless there is a continuous flow of funds from above and stability over a period of time, planning and development from below would be a distant dream. The CAA doesn't say anything on the part of a state to accept the recommendations of SFC. In this respect, Constitutional safeguard is required to implement the recommendations of the SFC. Over and above this, the SFCs in a number of states could not do justice because of non-transfer of functions to PRIs. Confusion also prevailed in certain cases where some functions were shown as panchayat functions but, in reality, the planning and implementation were vested with other state agencies/parallel bodies. Thus, before assigning SFCs the task of distribution of resources between the state and the local bodies, the concerned state must transfer all those functions which are local in nature to the respective local body tier.

Again, in many of the states, the funds transferred to PRIs are tied to the schemes. If this is the reality, how can the grassroots level planning be need based, flexible, and what sort of integration can be established in planning? Hence, the funds given to PRIs should be free from conditions and they should have their own resource raising powers which lessen the dependency level on the higher level governments for resources. Further, the transferred grants should be of different kinds like block, incentive, equalisation, specific to meet different objectives

In many of the states, the much needed planning personnel and machinery were not provided at the village and intermediate level panchayats. Thus, for undertaking meaningful planning, technical and planning personnel need to be provided at all the three level panchayats.

Another serious problem the panchayats have been facing in many of the states is lack of own administrative personnel. In most cases the panchayats have inadequate personnel and are deputed from various state departments. They are more loyal to the heads of parent departments and to the local MLAs. The panchayats have no control over them either to transfer or to initiate any disciplinary action. This comes in the way of mobilisation of local people, proper plan formulation and implementation of programmes. Hence there is need for administrative decentralisation in true spirit. Alternatively, the panchayats should be empowered to initiate action on the personnel for any misconduct or for not carrying out the resolutions they passed which are within the legal frame.

Above all the elected representatives of PRIs are new to the system and lack knowledge on various aspects such as administration, functions and finances. Plan formulation is not a simple job. It requires lot of ground works such as inventory of resources, collection of statistics, identifying the local experts who can lend their services, enlisting the services of voluntary and non-governmental organisations, mobilisation of people, conduct of grama sabha regularly etc. Hence, capacity building of non-officials including the officials working in panchayats through periodic training programmes enhances the success of decentalised plans they initiate.

REFERENCES

Abdul Aziz, *Decentralisation: Mandal Panchayat System in Karnataka,* National Institute of Rural Development, Hyderabad,1994.

Abdul Aziz, N. Sivanna, M. Devendra Babu, Madushree Sekher, Charles Nelson, *'Utilisation of Ford-Foundation Untied Grants by the Selected Grama Panchayats in Karnataka: A Concurrent Evaluation,* Institute for Social and Economic Change, Bangalore, 1999 (mimeo).

B.S. Bhargava, and Raphael C. Jos, 'Working of Gram Sabhas in Karnataka: A Study at Micro Level', *Journal of Rural Development,* Vol.13, No.2, 1994.

Balwantrai Mehta., *Study Team on Community Development Programmes and Extension Services*, Ministry of Rural Development, Government of India, 1957.

Bidyut Mohanty, and Girish Kumar (Eds.), *Women and Political Empowerment 2000 – Womens Political Empowerment Day Celebrations on Gram Sabha and Women*, Institute of Social Sciences, New Delhi, 2002.

George Mathew, *Panchayati Raj in India – An Overview*, Institute of Social Sciences, New Delhi, 2000; *Status of Panchayati Raj in the States of and Union Territories of India*, Institute of Social Sciences and Concept Publications, New Delhi, 2000.

Government of India, *Report of the Eleventh Finance Commission–2000-05'* 2000.

Government of India, *Report of the Twelfth Finance Commission–2005-10*, 2004.

K. Muraleedharan,'Women's Participation in Development: A Study of Dynamics of Women's Participation in the Local Level Planning of Kerala, *Asian Economic Review*, Vol. 42, No. 2, 2000.

M.A. Oommen,'Rationalising Fiscal Federalism vis-à-vis Rural Local Governments', *Panchayat Raj Update*, Institute of Social Sciences, New Delhi, September, 2002.

M.Devendra Babu, 'Working of Gram Sabhas in Andhra Pradesh: Problems and Prospects', *Working Paper 113*, Institute for Social and Economic Change, Bangalore, 2002.

Mary Sebastin, 'Gram Sabha and Women: The Kerala Experience', in K Subha and B. S. Bhargava (eds.), *Women Empowerment: Gram Sabha and Women*, Institute of Social Sciences, Bangalore, 2001.

N. Jagajeevan and N. Ramakanthan,'Grama Sabhas: A Democratic Structure for Development Planning', in Conference on *Democratic Decentralisation*, 23-27 May, State Planning Board, Thiruvananthapuram, 2000.

Neil Webster, 'Panchayati Raj in West Bengal: Popular Participation for the People or the Party?', *Development and Change*, Vol. 23, No. 4, December, 1992.

Planning Commission, *Report of the Working Group on District Planning*, Government of India, 1984.

Planning Commission, *Tenth Five Year Plan–2002-07*, Government of India, 2003.

23

Emerging Women Leadership at the Grassroots: A Micro-Level Study in Andhra Pradesh

K.C. SMITHA

Ever since the enactment of 73rd Amendment Act (1993) to the Constitution of India, *Women Leadership* at the grassroots has become an important theme, though with different meanings and contexts. Particularly the women constituting important actors affecting the national development and also form half of the population (Bhargava and Subha, 1994: 42).

Indeed the reservation of not less than one-third of seats in all categories and at all levels of the grassroots institutions for women has raised the expectations among all sections of the community that this group would create a 'critical mass' at the Pachayat Raj Institutions (PRIs). It is hoped that a new paradigm of political participation would emerge and the new situation would witness a drastic change in the distributive system of benefits (Buch, 1998). But women as such were caught quite unprepared by this development (Poornima and Vinod Vyasulu, 1999). Even though the amendment made the 'space' for both these to enter the PRIs, the alacrity with which they take to the new role will vary (*Ibid*, 1999: 30). No wonder, women's leadership and political participation at grassroot democracy have come to be duly recognized and widely acknowledged. Against this backdrop, the present study aims to examine the question of emerging women leadership in PRIs and their leadership potentials with special reference to the Chittoor district of Andhra Pradesh (AP).

Women and Political Leadership

'One who leads is a leader' is the general definition of a leader. (Bhargava and Sivanna, 1990: 3). A leader is 'an individual whose rationalization, judgement, feelings are accepted by the group a base of belief and action'. A similar emphasis 'any person who is more than ordinarily efficient in carrying psychological attitude to others and is thus effective in conditioning collective responses may be called a leader'. Some studies mention about three main components of leadership, the leader, the follower, and the situation. If these components are brought together leadership is defined as the interaction between leaders and followers in a particular situation (*Ibid.*, 1990: 3).

The term 'leadership' is defined as the persons who are elected for political positions in the PR (Panchayati Raj System). Leaders are those persons who have been elected as members and presidents for the PR system that include the village level, taluk level and district level leaders. These three levels of leadership is considered to be the 'Rural leadership' since these leaders are said to have constant interaction and face to face contact with rural mass (Sirsikar, 1969). Thus, the assumed criterion of a leader in our context, is that he/she is an elected member of one or more of the institutions of PR system. In other words, the very fact that a person who is an elected member of PRIs makes him/her an institutional leader (Dube, 1965: 10). Consequently, the years that followed adult franchise and PR, the old leadership structure started to undergo subtle changes, slowly giving way to the emergence of a 'New Pattern of Leadership'.

Importance of Women Leadership

The quintessence of leadership is felt in every walk of organized social life that needs no explanation. With the introduction of PRIs there has been a corresponding change in the attitudes and behaviour of rural leaders giving birth to different patterns in the emerging leadership in these institutions. While emphasizing the importance of leadership in PRIs, it has been observed: "Leadership is more important in the context of PRIs because explicitly one of the significant objectives in instituting them was to develop proper leadership suited to development needs of the countryside (Bhargava, 1977: 7). When women achieve an equal share of political power, many things besides politics would have changed profoundly.

Thus, leadership has a pivotal role in the working of PRIs. It is through the leaders, that the wishes and aspirations of the rural people are met. In this sense, they are the 'eyes' and 'ears' of the rural people. It is the uppermost responsibility of every leader to work for the welfare of the people. Leadership should have the capacity to influence people to cooperate towards 'common end' and also to create conditions of collective response. Thus the effective functioning of PRIs depends mainly on the quality of leader available at the grassroot. Moreover, it is widely believed that leadership plays significant role in promoting political development and democratic growth (Bhargava and Sivanna 1990). Thus, women's leadership and empowerment is one of the major objectives of the third generation of Panchayats in India. Particularly, women leadership in PRIs involves women as (1) voters, (2) members of political parties, (3) candidates, (4) elected members of the PRIs taking part in decision-making, planning, implementation and evaluation, and (5) as members of Mahila Mandals and their association with voluntary organizations (Bhargava, B.S and Vidya K.C., 1992: 603).

It is a matter of national pride that India is the only country in the world today, that has not only paved the way for the creation of institutions of PRIs, but also has reserved not less than one-third of the seats for women by passing constitutional amendment (73rd). Though there is many hurdles for making this reservation provision a reality, even at the Panchayat level, as there persists mass illiteracy of women and the social discrimination, exploitation and oppression are encountered in the society (Kaur and Ushvinder, 2000: 80). Indeed, 1/3 of reservation of seats for women in the local bodies is intended for

(*a*) political empowerment,
(*b*) removal of the idea of or non-participation or isolation of women in village political system, and
(*c*) changing the quality of women leadership at village level.

The political empowerment and assumption of leadership role resulting from the Amendment Act (1993), therefore, has had impact in two socio-political areas. There is, first of all, a visible improvement in the administration and delivery of services at GP (Gram Panchayat) level mainly, or of greater focus on the felt needs of the people, transparency, greater reliance on horizontal linkages and greater participation of people particularly women members of the village community (Palanithurai, 2002). Secondly, the amendment has made possible the creation of political space, which has enabled women to gain social status, confidence and to shake of age-old strong hold of repressive tradition.

Women and Panchayati Raj Institutions in AP

Andhra Pradesh was one of the first-two states in India to establish the PRIs in the year 1959. The state legislature created a three-tier PR set-up under Andhra Pradesh Praja Samiti and Zilla Parishad Act (APPSZP), 1959, this act has provided for co-option of two women. The Andhra Pradesh Gram Panchayat Act (APGP), 1964, governed the composition and functions of the Gram Panchayat (GP) in Andhra Pradesh. This act provided for reservation of two seats for women if the total strength of the GP is 9 or less, 3 seats if the strength is between 10 and 15 and 4 seats if the strength is more than 15 (Mishra, and Singh, 1993: 39). It is clear that the act ensured between 22 per cent to 25 per cent of representation of women in these bodies. In the middle level bodies, till, 1986, women representation was governed by the Andhra Pradesh Praja Samiti and Zilla Parishad Act of 1959, which provided for co-option of two women for each samiti in addition to the possibility of women members finding membership in PS through the electoral process. Based on the recommendations of Ashok Mehta Committee Report (1978), the Mandal Praja Parishad, Zilla Praja Parishad Abhivrudhi Mandal Bill was introduced in legislative Assembly in July 1986. This bill completely altered the PRIs set-up in AP and in 1987, a new reservation set-up was introduced for BCs and Women, i.e., 9 per cent. Thus, women got further encourage-ment to share in the democratic decision-making process of PRIs.

Keeping in view the Amendment Act of 1993, State Government of Andhra Pradesh has enacted a new law thereby making the previous PR system in-operative. In this new arrangement, after the first elections, the representation of women at Gram Panchayat (GP) level was 33.84 per cent, at Mandal Panchayat (MP) level it was 37.01 per cent, and at Zilla Parishad (ZP) level it was 33.38 per cent. This has contributed for the enhancement of women leadership especially in PRIs to get access to decision-making process concerning to vital problems of economic development, social reconstruction and distribution of scarce resources.

As the amendment opened new avenues for women to political empowerment in PRIs, which enabled them to improve their socio-economic conditions, participatory abilities and leadership competencies and hence the focus of the study on the women leadership in PRIs. The problem comes to the forefront to examine how far women at the grassroot democracy of Chittoor district (Andhra Pradesh—India) are availing the opportunities of reservation in the panchayat and performing their political roles effectively. The interrelated objectives of the study are:

1. Has the political background of women leaders of PRIs and their families enabled them to emerge as effective women leaders at local governance?
2. Are the women in present PRIs positions are capable of implementing development policies successfully?
3. Does the capacity of women leaders successfully influence other women to join politics?
4. Has reservation really succeed in promoting political empowerment of women and thereby contribute for emerging women leadership?
5. Are present women leaders willing to continue in the political positions?

Sample Size and Area of the Study

The area selected for the present study includes Panchayats coming under Yadamarri Mandal Parishad (MP), Pichattoor MP and Madanapalli MP of Chittoor district in Andhra Pradesh.

The unit of inquiry is three-tier system of Panchayati Raj (PR), which include Zilla Parishad (ZP), Mandal Parishad (MP) and Gram Panchayat (GP). Both qualitative and quantitative methods were used for the collection of data. As regards to sample strategy (Table 1), a census survey was adopted covering 16 elected women ZPTC members, 12 elected women members at MP level this include one president of the MP from each of the three selected MPs and 9 MPTC members, three from each of the selected MPs and finally at Gram Panchayat level, 9 sarpanchs, three from each of the selected MPs and 27 ward members, three from each of the three selected GPs, total 36 (*see* Table 1).

Keeping in view the mentioned criteria, the Gram Panchayats selected are:, Ramapuram, Appambattu and Karoor GPs from Pichattoor MP (Tirupathi—Revenue Division), Thelarapalli, Dalavaipalli and Dasarapalli GPs from Yadamuri MP (Chittoor Revenue Division) and Chinnathippasamudram, Kothavaripalli and Kondamarripalli GPs from Madanapalli MP (Madanapalli Revenue Division).

Table-1
Sample Selected

Respondents	*Presidents*	*ZPTC Members*	*MPTC Members*	*Ward Members*
Zilla Panchayat (GP)	1	16	–	–
Mandal Panchayat (MP)	3	–	9	–
Gram Panchayat (GP)	9	–	–	27
Total	13	16	9	27

Collection of Data

The data collected primarily consists of the following aspects:

1. Awareness and the attitude of the elected women representatives at various levels in PRIs.
2. Separate pre-tested schedules were personally canvassed to a sample of respondents such as elected women representatives at the Zilla Parishad, Mandal Parishad and Gram Panchayat to obtain their views and opinions. In addition to this personal discussion was also held.

The secondary data was collected through review of literature, books, magazines, periodicals, journals and official documents on PRIs including various reports of committees, and the Acts relating to PRIs in AP. In addition to this, information was gathered from journals like Kurukshetra, Yojana, Indian Journal of Public Administration etc. Similarly, data was also collected from the office of ZP Chittoor and the offices of the three selected MPs and GPs in Chittoor district.

Women Leaders and Political Awareness

The political awareness is a prerequisite for a person's effective political participation. The efficacy of leadership depends upon the level of political awareness in the leaders. Political awareness once attained may stimulate political interest and hence motivate any individual to enter politics. Besides, reservations created a space for women's needs within the structural framework of politics and has 'legitimatized' women's issues, but women have to be aware of their new role of political power (Buch, 2000). This section mainly focuses on assessing the responses of the elected women leaders and the relevant reasons to enable us to examine their views on women leadership issues in PRIs. In this chapter, unless stated otherwise the percentage of responses shown in the tables are of those who indicated the correct answer. The purpose of presenting the data in this way is to provide a picture of the political efficacy of respondents to understand and explain the different aspects of women leadership.

Respondents Attendance in Gram Sabha (GS) Meetings

Successful functioning and responsiveness of PRIs is judged by the holding of GS (Gram Sabha) meetings at respective village panchayats. It is worthy to examine the level of participation and general awareness about GS. In this context, the respondents were asked whether they attended the meetings if any organized by the GS ?

Table–2
Reasons for not Attending Gram Sabha Meetings

Responses	*MP Level**	*ZP Level*	*Total*
No information on GS meetings	14 (24.10)*	02 (20.0)	16 (23.5)
Not interested to attend the GS meetings	10 (17.20)	03 (30.0)	13 (19.10)
GS meeting are not regularly conducted	9 (15.50)	02 (20.0)	11 (16.20)
GS meetings is conducted at a very distance so could not atted	11 (19.00)	01 (10.0)	12 (17.60)
Public are not given opportunity to speak so not interested to attend	10 (17.20)	02 (20.0)	12 (17.60)
DK/NR	04 (6.90)	-	04 (5.90)
Total	**58 (100)**	**10 (100)**	**68 (100)**

* For the convenience of analysis the sample of Gram Panchayat and Mandal Panchayat has been combined and this continuous for rest of the tables as well.

* Figures in the Parenthesis represent percentage. This is applicable to rest of the tables.

For this majority of the total respondents –13/16 at the ZP level and 30/48 at the MP level said they were attending the meetings organized by the Gram Sabha. This indicates that at MP level women representatives are more irregular in attending the meetings than the women representatives at ZP level. This shows that at ZP level the participation is high compared to the MP level participation.

Nearly 32.20 per cent of respondents of both ZP level and MP level have not attended the Gram Sabha meetings. The reasons indicated by the respondents those who did not attend the GS meetings are provided in the Table-2.

Table-3

Respondents Awareness about Gram Sabha Meetings

Responses	*MP Level*	*ZP Level*	*Total*
Twice	38 (79.20)	13 (81.30)	51 (79.70)
Thrice	01 (2.10)	-	01 (1.60)
Fourt Times	01 (2.10)	-	01 (1.60)
DK/NR	8 (16.70)	3 (18.80)	11 (17.20)
Total	**48 (100)**	**16 (100)**	**64 (100)**

In the Table-3 more than 81 per cent at ZP level and 79 per cent at MP level said that Gram Sabha meetings are conducted twice in a year. Only 18.80 per cent at ZP level and 8/48 (16.7%) at MP level did not provide information on GS meetings. This indicates that only 17.20 per cent of respondents at both ZP level and MP level have not participated actively.

Leadership Position Held Previously in PRIs

The Table-4 shows that many women representatives did not hold any leadership position previously in PRIs. To this only 17.29 per cent of the total representatives 3.13 per cent at ZP level and 14.06 per cent at MP level respondents held leadership position previously in PRIs. This amply shows that present women leaders experience in political leadership positions is weak.

Table-4

Leadership Position Held Previously in PRIs by the Respondents

Responses	*MP Level*	*ZP Level*	*Total*
Yes	09 (14.06)	02 (3.13)	11 (17.19)
No	39 (60.94)	14 (21.88)	53 (82.81)
Total	**48 (100.00)**	**16 (100.00)**	**64 (100.00)**

The respondents those who held the leadership position previously in PRIs were only at GP level as a Sarpanch all the ZP level respondents and one respondent at MP level. The remaining eight respondents at MP level held the position of ward member. All the ZP level respondents worked as a Sarpanch during 1995-2000, while the MP level respondent held the leadership position during 1990-2003. However, the remaining respondents (7/8) held the ward member position in different years. It is clear that of those who had experience in PRIs as leaders (90.9%) have served as ward members, which shows that the present women leaders have very less experience as leaders in political positions.

A majority (48.40%) of the total women leaders belong to Congress-I party, it is highest (56.30%) among ZP level and 45.80 per cent at MP level. It is then followed by the TDP (Telugu Desam Party) 45.30 per cent of the total respondents. They constitute almost equal at both levels (*see* Table-5).

Table-5
Political Parties Represented by the Respondents

Responses	*MP Level*	*ZP Level*	*Total*
TDP	22 (45.80)	07 (43.80)	29 (45.30)
CONG-1	22 (45.80)	09 (56.30)	31 (48.40)
Others	04 (8.30)	-	4 (6.30)
Total	**48 (100)**	**16 (100)**	**64 (100)**

This shows that 93.70 per cent of both at ZP and at MP levels have support of political party and in general the emergence of leadership in any political system is made easily by the political party interference and support.

One of the interesting points is that all the respondents have affiliation with the political party as outside supporter only and are not actively involved in the party activities. This also proves that respondents are only sympathetic for a political party, which is an important indicator for the person's political career. It is clear that the leaders of political parties must come forward to enroll women as members or office bearers by making special reservation, which will change the situation favourably.

Leadership Position Held by the Family Members of the Respondents

Women generally in Indian polity have less interest in affiliation with any political party because of their pr-eoccupation with domestic functions. Political affiliation and subscription to certain political ideology will definitely influence the leadership involvement and efficacy of political leaders. Hence the affiliations of the respondents have to be studied in the light of the political affiliation of their families.

Table-6
Leadership Position Held by the Family Members of the Respondents

Responses	*MP Level*	*ZP Level*	*Total*
Yes	07 (14.60)	0.5 (31.30)	12 (18.80)
No	41 (85.40)	11 (68.80)	52 (81.30)
Total	**48 (100)**	**16 (100)**	**64 (100)**

It is evident from the Table-6 that more than 31 per cent at ZP level, and nearly 15 per cent at MP level the family members of the respondents have held leadership positions. However, it is also very interesting to note that more than 81 per cent of the total respondent's family members have not held leadership positions previously. They constitute almost equal at both levels (Table- 6). This shows that family members of the women representatives are not active in local politics.

More than 58 per cent - 2 at the ZP level and 5 at the MP level—belong to TDP. Only 41.67 per cent of the family members of the respondents are from Congress-I party, of which 3 are at the ZP level and 2 are at the MP level. Further, the respondent relationship with leaders of their family members is husband; constitute nearly 67 per cent. The remaining 4 respondent's relationship with their family members is son-in-law and son. One important point to note here is that, these family members were only supporters or sympathizers of political party and not the members or office bearers of any political party.

In general, the emergence of leadership in any political system is made easier by the political association and subsequent political activities of the individuals. However, it is evident that only 18.80

per cent of family members have political party affiliation, this shows that respondents have achieved their status of leadership despite their non-political status. This phenomenon may be attributed to the reservation provision adopted in the PRIs even before the adoption of the Amendment (73rd) in AP, on non-party basis.

Respondents Probable Reasons to Join Politics

The decision of women to participate in political activities in general and to contest the elections in particular is very much influenced by the perception of their family. Nevertheless, the introduction of Mandal System, the corresponding changes in the PRIs, legislation providing 1/3 mandatory reservation for women has paved the way for greater political participation. Despite the facilitating provision of reservation, women have to be motivated and encouraged towards political participation by the members of the society. When the respondents were asked to give the 'probable reasons to join the politics, 62.50 per cent of the total respondents at both levels say that due to the interest of their family members interest they joined politics. However, for this the responses are almost equally divided (Table-7).

Table-7
Probable Reasons for Joining the Politics

Response	*MP Level*	*ZP Level*	*Total*
Own interest	14 (29.17)	05 (31.25)	19 (29.69)
Persuasion	01 (2.08)	01 (6.25)	02 (3.13)
Family support	30 (62.50)	10 (62.50)	40 (62.50)
Initiative by people	02 (4.17)	-	02 (3.13)
Pressurized by political party	01 (2.08)	-	01 (1.56)
Total	**48 (100)**	**16 (100)**	**64 (100)**

It is also evident from the above Table-7 that their own interest has been source of inspiration for political interest in respect of 30 per cent of the respondents. The responses of the respondents at both levels, however, have slight variations. Similar findings can be accounted in the study of Panda (Panda, 1997: 664) that concluded that women entered politics due to the persuasion of their family members or a pressure from political party etc. But nearly 30 per cent of the total respondents have participated in politics due to their personal interest which is an indicator of prospective emergence of women leadership in Chittoor district.

Views of the Respondents on the Participation of Political Parties in PRI Elections

Majority of the respondents (84.40%) at both levels (all respondents at ZP level and 80 per cent at MP level) have conceded for interference of political parties in PRI elections. This shows that political party involvement plays a major role in the emergence of women leadership. The influence of political parties in PRIs elections as it provides validity of candidates for political positions especially at local levels. This justifies the argument that political party involvement plays a major role in the emergence of leadership of the respondents (Table-8).

Table–8
Views on the Participation of Political Parties in PRI Elections

Responses	*MP Level*	*ZP Level*	*Total*
Yes	38 (79.20)	16 (100)	54 (84.40)
No	01 (2.10)	–	12 (1.60)
DK/NR	09 (18.80)	–	09 (14.10)
Total	**48 (100)**	**16 (100)**	**64 (100)**

The respondents who *Agreed* about the participation of the political parties in PRIs elections advanced the following reasons:

1. Majority of the respondents have a view that due to the support offered by the political parties in the PRIs elections, the general public quickly recognizes the candidate that leads to wider publicity.
2. Some said that due to the participation of political parties especially in the canvassing the acquaintance with the general mass becomes easier.
3. More than 10 per cent of both levels say that people will support the candidates based on the party's recognition of the candidate.
4. Very few feel that political party participation is inevitable for any election including the PRIs elections.
5. More than 10 per cent of the respondents only at MP level say that political party provides coherence and exposure

to the candidates and this will provide them recognition in the public.

Respondents Views Regarding Women Entry into Politics

The women in India at local levels are still confined mostly to domestic functions. The heads of the families, is the males, have more opportunities than the women in associating themselves with politics. In this context, women representatives have attributed different opinions, as regards to women entering into politics. The opinions are presented in the form of percentages (Table-9). It also reveals that whatever may be the reason for entering politics; it is certain that the below-mentioned reasons do have impact on the women leadership at PRIs.

Table-9
Views on Women Entry into Politics

Responses	*MP Level**	*ZP Level*	*Total*
Provide opportunity to be independent and exposure	09 (18.80)	03 (18.80)	12 (18.80)
Exposure to wide range of development activities	08 (16.70)	03 (18.80)	11 (17.20)
Role model to future generation women	03 (6.30)	02 (12.50)	05 (7.80)
Leads to mobilisation of women	09 (18.80)	02 (12.50)	11 (17.20)
Increase responsibilities towards women's empowerment	10 (20.80)	02 (12.50)	12 (18.80)
Concentrate on community development	06 (12.50)	03 (18.80)	09 (14.10)
Broadens political elite structure	02 (4.20)	01 (6.30)	03 (4.70)
Women promotes unbiased development of village	01 (2.10)	0 (0)	1 (1.60)
Total	**48 (100)**	**16 (100)**	**64 (100)**

Are Women Given Equal Opportunities in Politics?

The revolution in the status of women, for which constitutional equality was to be only the instrument, still remains a very distant objective. Leadership is influenced by the degree of equality and freedom enjoyed by women in the shaping and sharing political position of power and value given by the society. In Indian society there exist a wide gap between men and women in all spheres of life namely, literacy, education, employment, and political representation, indicating inequality in status (Kaur and Ushvinder, 2000: 55; Kaushik, 1993). Despite reservation of women through Constitutional Amendment (73rd), politics is a male dominated domain, which refuses to provide political space for women. The fact that mere entrance of women in local governance does ensure greater representation in politics but solution is sought with alternative discourse to authority and actual power sharing that would enable effective participation of women (Vijalakshmi, 2007:457).

In this context, analysis of present women leaders in PRIs provides an opportunity to understand the situation and they were asked to express their views relating to 'whether women are given equal opportunities in politics or not?'

Table–10

Are Women Given Equal Opportunities in Politics or not?

Responses	*MP Level*	*ZP Level*	*Total*
Yes	30 (62.50)	10 (62.50)	40 (62.50)
No	14 (29.20)	6 (37.50)	20 (31.30)
DNK	04 (8.30)	–	04 (6.30)
Total	**48 (100)**	**16 (100)**	**64 (100)**

More than 62 per cent of the total respondents at both levels agree that the women are given equal opportunities in politics. However, it is also important to note that more than 31 per cent of the total respondent's with a small difference of opinion do not agree (Table-10).

This result can be attributed to the changed scenario, due to few legislations that meant to enhance the women status such as Committee on the Status of Women in India in 1977, establishment of National Commission for Women in 1992 and the National Perspective Plan for Women (1988-2000) and of course, the Historic Act (73rd-1993), which provided an opportunity to improve the socio-economic status along with political status especially in PRIs. This provides further impetus to change in the gender composition to PRIs, and further inspire more women to enter politics and to represent and articulate women interests.

Among those who *Agree* that women leaders are treated equally, attribute to the following reasons:

1. Since the present women leaders belong to the local areas and they have prior acquaintance with the people and previous leaders. So they are not prone to discrimination and inequality.
2. Those who already have previous experience in political positions do not face any problem of inequality.
3. As people have voted for their present political positions men in general support them.
4. Women especially from dominant castes and affluent family background are treated with high esteem.

The respondents who (31.30%) *Do Not Agree* that women are treated fairly, give the following reasons:

1. Women lack political knowledge, especially at MP level, and men of their family interfere either to help or decide on the important matters relating to PRIs.
2. Indifference attitude towards women as leaders.
3. Women sometimes find politics unattractive.

Difficulties Faced by the Respondents as Women Leaders

Women experience as leaders of PRIs has provided both political opportunities and challenges in the form of difficulties. This can be attributed to various reasons, which is examined by asking the respondents that 'Are you facing difficulties as women leaders of PRIs?' A majority of the respondents (80%) both at ZP and MP level opine that they have faced difficulty as women leaders of PRIs. This constitutes 87.50 per cent at ZP level and 77.10 per cent at MP level. The respondents who said that they do not face any difficulty constitute about 13 per cent at the ZP level and 23 per cent at MP level. The responses of the women respondents are indicated in Table-11.

So at both the levels particularly those who have joined after 2000 PRIs elections (as they are new entrants in politics) have faced problems. Those who have not faced difficulties constitute very less (only 20%) at both levels. This is because of previous experience and support extended by the family members especially

Table-11

Difficulties Faced by the Respondents as Women Leaders

Responses	*MP Level*	*ZP Level*	*Total*
Yes	37 (77.10)	10 (62.50)	40 (62.50)
No	11 (22.90)	6 (37.50)	20 (31.30)
Total	**48 (100)**	**16 (100)**	**64 (100)**

to those who held previous political position. Number of reasons provided for facing problems is:

1. After they are elected to present leadership position, they feel very much handicapped by inability to read and write.
2. Especially those who are engaged in livelihood activities like agriculture and daily-wage labour attending to the leadership responsibilities was difficult.
3. Mostly male members do not recognize capacity of women as leaders to manage the institution as such male members of family usually interfere in the functioning aspects of PRIs.
4. Further, the women leaders themselves have been oriented to believe that they have been elected to the PRIs only because of the influence of their family members such as husband or male members of their family.
5. The family burden, along with the workload at PRIs, made the elected women leaders tired of the activities in public affairs. Their capability could not be fully utilized, as they had no time to engage in public activity effectively and
6. Women especially at MP level complained that they have no experience of sharing their views on issues and matters with men.

Problems Encountered by the Women Leaders while Implementing Rural Development Programmes

The elected women leaders of PRIs were interviewed to respond to the question,' personally speaking could you kindly narrate some of the problems encountered by you in implementation of the RDP while performing your duties? The responses are *(a)* Problems, *(b)* No Problems, and *(c)* DK/NR. If problematic how do you overcome the problems? More than 46 per cent of the respondents i.e., 62.50 per cent at the ZP level and 41.67 per cent at the MP level respondents think that they have encountered some 'problems' in implementation of RDP (Rural Development Programme) while performing their duties. However, nearly 38 per cent of the women respondents have considered that they had no problems in implementing the RDP in performance of their duties, but these respondents are equally divided at both levels (Table-12).

Table-12
Problems Encountered by the Women Leaders While Implementing RDP

Responses	*MP Level*	*ZP Level*	*Total*
Problems	20 (41.67)	10 (62.50)	30 (46.87)
No Problems	18 (37.50)	06 (37.50)	24 (37.50)
DK/NR	10 (20.83)	–	10 (15.36)
Total	**48 (100)**	**16 (100)**	**64 (100**

Women leaders considered the following problems, which they face while implementing the RDP are:

1. There is demand and pressure for allocation of funds for the respective MPs and GPs by the MPTC members and GP presidents.
2. Nearly 11 per cent of total respondents felt that as there is general shortage of water source in the constituencies, generally they demand to drill bore wells and provide water sources to up-lift the livelihood of the people.
3. Some of the members at the MP level and GP level (Ward members) do not know about the allocation of funds to the RDP.
4. Lack of political experience among new entrants of women leaders at MP level and ZP level adds to their woes.
5. Sometimes it happens that at MP level works are started but in between funds become insufficient to complete, as such works will be stopped till additional funds are sanctioned.
6. Nearly 10 per cent of respondents (inclusive of ZP level and MP level) are irregular to the activities of PRIs and lack interest in political positions, which also contributes to the problems.

From this it is clear that lack of political experience hinders effective political participation of women leaders. When requested to suggest measures to overcome the problems encountered while implementing RDP, only 17/20 at the MP level and 7/10 at the ZP level have provided the reasons to overcome the problems in the form of following suggestions:

(a) While allotting the funds some adjustments are made through consultations and discussions.

(b) Basic needs of the local areas are met if sufficient funds are available.

(c) Sometimes male members help is taken to resolve their issues.

(d) They wait patiently for the release of sufficient funds for the successful implementation of development programmes.

Respondents Interest in Continuing in the Present Position of Leadership

The political leadership of women after constitutional the Amendment (73rd), constitutes a milestone in involving women in leadership who were otherwise left powerless to influence governance that effect them. But it must be remembered that a change cannot be brought about over-night and by legislation alone. So in this context, it is pertinent to know whether present women leaders would wish to continue in the present position of leadership and to know whether they accept higher political positions if offered. All the respondents at both levels are interested to continue in the present position of leadership. This offers a positive sign that amendment made big dent in eliciting participation of women as leaders in PRIs.

Majority of them gave some reasons for continuing in the present position:

1. Some of the women leaders opined that the present position would provide an opportunity to influence and mobilize other fellow women towards political empowerment.
2. Some of the women leaders said that the present positions would give an opportunity to improve the socio-economic conditions of their local areas, since they understand better the local needs and priorities.
3. Some of them said let them just complete the present leadership term, and think about other term later.

Attendance at Meetings by Women Leaders

The nature of women leaders in the decision-making process at all the levels of PRIs, depends on the nature of attendance in the meetings which is very significant. In this background we asked the respondents 'how often you attended in the meetings organized at your GP, MP and ZP level', a majority of the respondents are 'Often' attended the meetings. They range from 62.50 per cent at ZP level to 69.45 per cent at GP level. This indicates that higher the tier lower the attendance and lower the tier higher the attendance. The respondents who 'rarely' attended the meetings i.e., nearly 38 per cent to ZP meetings, 25 per cent to MP and 22.22 per cent to GP meetings (Table-13).

Table–13
Attending the Meetings of PRIs at Different Levels by the Women Leaders

Responses	*Often Present*	*Rarely Present*	*Never Present*	*Total*
ZP level	10 (62.50)	06 (37.50)	–	16 (100)
MP level	08 (66.67)	03 (25)	01 (8.33)	12 (100)
GP level	25 (69.45)	08 (22.22)	03 (8.33)	36 (100)

This suggests a healthy trend in the working of democratic institutions, which has been decentralized in the form of PRIs, for which people are very close and they elect their representatives to deal with the present developmental issues.

Problems Faced by Women Leaders in Presenting the Issues

Many studies on active work among the women especially at rural areas demonstrated faith in women and trust in their leadership. In this context, problems faced, if any, by the PRIs women leadership can be examined from the following Table-14.

Table–14
Problems Faced by Women Leaders in Presenting the Issues

Responses	*MP Level*	*ZP Level*	*Total*
Problems	19 (39.60)	10 (62.50)	29 (45.30)
No Problems	06 (12.50)	06 (37.50)	12 (18.80)
DK/NR	23 (47.90)	–	23 (35.90)
Total	**48 (100)**	**16 (100)**	**64 (100**

It is very clear that more than 45 per cent of the total respondents faced some problems while presenting the issues. But the responses of the respondents at ZP level are very high (Table-14). But it is also very clear that more than 37 per cent at the ZP level and 12 per cent at the MP level respondents have not faced any problem in presenting the issues in meetings. The respondents those who come under the category of DK/NR constitute less than 50 per cent only at the MP level, which means that they have not participated in the presentation of issues in the meetings of the GP. This shows that adequate training must be provided to the present women leaders in order to see that they also fulfill the hopes and aspirations of many other women who have an overwhelming faith in their leadership.

Those who faced problems have the following reasons: *(i)* Language barrier, *(ii)* Lack of political experience, *(iii)* Busy in livelihood, and *(iv)* Lack of communication skills and consequent poor management.

Performance of Women Leaders in Comparison to then Male Counterpart

Generally it believed that women leaders are less competent to take up the task of political positions. In rural areas, women are basically attached to household cores and domestic activities evincing less interest and inclination to the political activities. As such eliciting their views on the performance in comparison to their male counterparts becomes more relevant. Then the respondents were asked 'How do you rate your performance in comparison to your male counterpart? The responses of the respondents were categorized as (1) Better, (2) Equal, and (3) Poor. Nearly 60 per cent of the total respondents considered that their performance is almost equal to their male counterparts. However, it is very high (87.50%) at ZP level and only 50 per cent at the MP level (Table-15). It is also very clear that their performance is very poor when compared to the male leaders, which is about 48 per cent at the MP level. One thing can be noted here is that lower the tier there is a low performance.

The reasons for the *Poor Performance* in comparison to the male leaders particularly at the MP level are indicated below:

1. Few lack communication skills and have less exposure to political experience.

Table-15
Performance of Women Leaders in Comparison to Male

Responses	*MP Level*	*ZP Level*	*Total*
Better	01 (2.10)	02 (12.50)	03 (4.70)
Equal	24 (50.00)	14 (87.50)	12 (59.40)
Poor	23 (47.90)	–	23 (35.90)
Total	**48 (100)**	**16 (100)**	**64 (100**

2. Lack of effective interaction with men and in public life.
3. Incompetence leading male interference.
4. Caste difference.
5. Interference of local political leaders.

Frequency of Visit to Their Constituency

After coming to the leadership positions the efficacy of their political participation depends upon the frequency of visiting their constituency to understand and fulfill the needs of their people. In fact, the essence of the democracy and political leadership positions vitally depends on the accessibility and frequent visiting of the constituency to meet the public by whom they are elected to the present leadership positions. This particularly was very significant for the representative institutions like the PRIs. In this context, the question posed was 'How frequently you visit your constituency'?

Table-16
Frequency of Visit Made by the Women Leaders to Their Constituency

Responses	*MP Level*	*ZP Level*	*Total*
Better	05 (10.40)	08 (50.00)	13 (20.30)
Equal	18 (37.50)	08 (50.00)	26 (40.60)
Poor	25 (52.10)	–	25 (35.90)
Total	**48 (100)**	**16 (100)**	**64 (100**

The responses were categorized as (1) *Regularly,* (2) *Rarely* and (3) *Do not visit* (Table – 16). If we consider 'Regularly' and 'Rarely' as positive and favourable into one category, we find that nearly 61 per cent of the total respondents have regular visits to their areas, but such respondents constitute 100 per cent at ZP level and nearly 48 per cent at MP level. The responses of the women leaders have wide gap if closely looked at the data relating to the ZP and MP level respondents.

This indicates the level of contacts with the people that often they are elected to the offices to serve them. But compared to ZP level it is clear that 39.10 per cent of respondents at MP level particularly at GP level do not visit constituency, this shows that they lack contacts with people.

When asked about the purpose of visiting to their constituencies the women respondents mentioned the following reasons:

(i) As causal visit.
(ii) To check whether the way their functioning is justifiable or not.
(iii) To implement the programmes and monitoring of the schemes.
(iv) For identification of beneficiaries for the various programmes and schemes.

When asked the respondents as to 'How they address the grievances of the electorate?' they gave the following reasons:

1. They direct the electorate to the proper officials/persons to get the things done.
2. Sometimes they take the help of male members to resolve the issues and clarify the matters.
3. Resolve the issues according to the rules and regulations laid down by the PRIs Act.

Do Respondents Discuss the Politics with Other Women?

The participation of women in the leadership positions particularly of the lower class and castes may be attributed to a higher level of awareness of value of the present leadership positions and to higher degree of mobilization of fellow women for further increase in the number of women leaders. Thus this awareness, in order to translate into political exercise like occupying leadership positions, needs a tremendous mobilization on the part the present women leaders. In this context, the frequency of present women leaders discussing the politics with the other women can be examined.

If we examine the Table-17 only 25 per cent of the total sample as well as 25 per cent at each level do discuss politics with other fellow women; but it is also significant to note that, majority (75 %) of the total sample do not discuss politics with other women. However, they also constitute 75 per cent at each level.

Table–17
Do Respondents Discuss the Politics with Other Women?

Responses	*MP Level*	*ZP Level*	*Total*
Yes	12 (25)	04 (25)	16 (25)
No	36 (75)	12 (75)	48 (75)
Total	**48 (100)**	**16 (100)**	**64 (100)**

The reasons for 'Not' discussing politics with other fellow women given by the respondents are:

1. Especially in the rural areas, owing to lack of interest in politics women do not discuss politics.
2. Women from lower caste and economic strata, as they are busy in the livelihood activities they evince less interest to discuss politics.
3. Lack of previous political experience constraints women to discuss politics with other women.
4. Women those who are not educated usually show less interest in discussing politics.
5. And lastly, de facto politics has adversely affected women furthering political interest among fellow women.

Need for Reservation for Women in PRIs

Women leadership and empowerment is one of the major objectives of the third generation of PRIs in India. Women leadership in PRIs is considered essential not only for ensuring their political positions in the democratic process but also for realizing the developmental goals of women. When respondents were asked 'whether present reservation pattern in PRIs is essential?' All the respondents at both the ZP and MP levels unanimously said yes and accepted its significance in mobilizing the women to political leadership positions. This situation is definitely an encouraging trend and further strengthening reservations for women would go a long way in adding momentum to the already existing encouraging trend. In this context, when respondents were asked 'explain the reasons for the need of reservation in PRIs for women?' The responses of the respondents are given in the Table-18.

Table–18
Views on the Need for Reservation for Women in PRIs

Responses	*MP Level*	*ZP Level*	*Total*
To uplift the position of women socially and economically	19 (39.60)	08 (50.00)	27 (42.20)
To provide exposure to various problems of rural society	21 (43.80)	08 (50.00)	29 (45.30)
Provide opportunities to women for political empowerment	08 (16.70)	–	08 (12.50)
Total	**48 (100)**	**16 (100)**	**64 (100)**

The Need for Empowerment of Women on Women Related Issues

Empowerment means the process of building capacities of creating an atmosphere, which enables people to fully realize their creative potentials in pursuance of a quality of life. Especially empowerment of women on women related issues gives them the capacity to influence decision-making process, planning, implementation and evaluation by integrating them into the political system. Here respondents were asked 'should women be empowered on women related issues?' All the respondents of both levels unanimously agreed that women must acquaint themselves on women related issues.

Reasons for '*Women Empowerment*' on Women Related Issues

Again respondents were asked to 'explain the reasons for women empowerment on women related issues' the respondents attribute the following reasons:

1. Nearly 32 per cent at the ZP level and 33 per cent at MP level said that women must be exposed to wide range of development issues.
2. 50 per cent of women leaders at ZP level and 30 per cent at MP level viewed that women must be provided compulsory training during their political positions.

3. 20 per cent at ZP and 38 per cent at MP level said that through means of empowerment women will be made self-sufficient and self-dependent.

Usefulness of Training Elected Women Leaders

To effectively address issues of gender equality in the service delivery of local governance, broad awareness, knowledge and political commitment need to be achieved. This can be achieved through training, particularly in the context of the rural people, especially of women. Poor women and women from low caste and lower economic strata, constitute a major section of rural women population. The struggle for survival as political leaders has immense potential for political training. The training thus aims to improve the capacity who are otherwise in despair and feel a sense of powerlessness. The training also helps essentially in bringing out hidden potentials, which seeks to convert 'the social failures and frustrations' into a 'political advantage' and seek to build political awareness on the basis of collectively, common interest and community development. Training then becomes an integral part of the mechanism that need to be adopted to enhance women's political participation within governance.

On the basis of information gathered through the schedule, it can be said that, on the whole, a majority (65.62%) of the non-officials (elected women representatives) both at the MP and ZP levels consider the training as useful to improve the women leadership qualities and for effective implementation of various community development programmes and also to create understanding between the women leaders and officials of PRIs at different levels. Of them (65.62%) at MP level respondents constitute the higher group i.e., 66.67 per cent than the ZP level respondents (Table-19). It is necessary at this stage to know that a majority (82.81%) of the total sample—40/48 at the MP level and 13/16 at ZP level—have attended the training programmes organized by the government or other organizations. But only 11-3 at ZP level and 8 at MP level have not attended the training programmes.

Those who *Agree* that the training is helpful in enhancing their general performance of their functions as leaders of PRIs, are indicated below:

- Training helps to improve the skills of women leaders and change their behavioural pattern to suit the organizational norms.
- Generally present women leaders have come from different backgrounds and their training will create an understanding between them and help them in the implementation of various developmental programmes.

Table–19
Views on Helpfulness of Training

Responses	*MP Level*	*ZP Level*	*Total*
Helpful	32 (66.67)	10 (62.50)	42 (20.30)
Not helpful	11 (22.92)	04 (25.00)	15 (23.44)
DK/NR	05 (10.41)	02 (12.50)	07 (10.94)
Total	**48 (100)**	**16 (100)**	**64 (100)**

- Training provides an opportunity to understand the present conditions, needs and necessities of people, which will be useful for framing developmental programmes.
- Training promotes awareness about their roles in the implementation of developmental programmes.
- Training brings a mutual understanding between women leaders and officials for successful implementation of developmental programmes.
- Training also helps in smooth functioning of the administration, enhance people's participation and schemes and works.
- Training is useful in solving local level problems at PRIs thus helping in betterment of rural people life. As a result of this cooperation, problems can be easily identified and solved with the help of the training.

Reasons advocated by those *Who Do Not Agree* are:

1. The training does not emphasis on the current and relevant aspects.
2. Due to lack of interest the training does not necessarily create understanding among the women leaders.
3. Training is not helpful in creating awareness and it does not enhance the capacity of women leaders for implementation of Rural Development Programmes.

Here an attempt is made to provide the details of the training undergone by the women leaders both at the ZP and MP level. The training was given by PR department, concerned Divisional Level Panchayat Officer (DLPO), District Panchayat Officer (DPO), District Collector (DC), Revenue Divisional Officer (RDO) and Mandal Parishad Development Officer (MPDO) of the concerned MP. This can be seen in detail in Table-20 on selected samples regarding the training information, relating to nature of the training, year of training, place of training, who has organized the training and the duration of the training undergone by the women leaders of PRIs in Chittoor district of Andhra Pradesh.

Table-20

Details of Training Undergone by the Women Leaders
Pichatur Mandal Parishad for Gram Panchayat Sarpanchs Only

Nature of Training	*Year of Training*	*Place of Training*	*Organized by*	*Duration of Training*
Administrative aspects of GP	2002	Satyavedu MPDOs Office	DPO	4 days
Administrative aspects of GP	2003	Pichatur MPDOs Office	DLPO	3 days
Record maintenance of GP	2004	Tirupati MPDOs Office	DPO	3 days
Drinking water	2004	Satyavedu MPDOs Office	DPO	2 days
On rural development activity	2004	Vijayapuram, MPDO Nindra MPDO and Pichatur MPDOs Office	Ex-MPDO	3 days
For MPTCs and ZPTCs only				
Rural Sanitation	2004	Pichatur MPDOs Office	MP Resource	2 days
Women & Child Welfare	May, 2004	Pichatur MPDOs Office	DWACWO	2 days
Yadamarri Mandal Parishad for Gram Panchayat Sarpanchs Only				
On GP administration	2002	Chittoor MPDOs Office	DLPO	3 days
On GP administration	Jan., 2004	Yadamuri MPDOs Office	DLPO	2 days

(Contd.)

Nature of Training	*Year of Training*	*Place of Training*	*Organized by*	*Duration of Training*
On GP administration	2004	Chittoor MPDOs Office	DLPO	2 days
Only of MPTCs				
On GP administration	2004	Chittoor MPDOs Office	DPO and MP Resource Persons SKT	3 days
Madanapalli Mandal Parishad for Gram Panchayat Sarpanchs, MPTCs and ZPTCs				
On GP Administration	2001	Madanapalli MPDOs Office	Collector and sub-Collector	3 days
On duties and activities of GP	2002	Madanapalli MPDOs Office	DLPO	2 days
Water scarcity and Sanitation	2003	Madanapalli MPDOs Office	DLPO	3 days
Utilization of Grants, Review of Functions, and GP Administration	2003	Madanapalli MPDOs Office	DLPO	2 days

Source: Mandal Panchayat Office, Chandragiri, 2004.

Major Findings and Suggestions

1. Provision of adequate post-electoral training should be imported to the newly elected women representative enabling them to effectively participate in the decision-making process of the panchayats. As taking an effective part in the law making procedure is not a laymen's work and as it needs some expertise as it involves some technical complexity, as it necessitates to know, some working knowledge about the matter, it is therefore, highly essential to provide a systematic training to women leaders about the scope of which must cover the factors like their rights, duties, how to deal with government officials how to handle the meetings in the gram panchayat and how to meet some unforeseen situation or problems in the meetings. Through the training programme, which should be imparted from time-to-time the women representatives should be informed about various rural development

schemes and programmes of government so that they can convey it to the women to take advantage of them for their empowerment.

2. Proxy attendance should be strictly prohibited and it should be made compulsory for every women representative to remain present in the gram panchayat meeting only excepting some reasonable situation.
3. The women representatives should from time-to-time consult with the elderly members of the gram sabha in order to know about the panchayati matters which will help them in effective participation in the meetings.
4. The women representatives should not be guided by partisan spirit after election is over. They should unitedly work for the development or empowerment of women as a whole.
5. Women organisation, Mahila Sangathans, NGOs and social activists should take efforts in mobilizing women at all levels. The above said organizations or activists by organizing seminars, meetings work shops can provide some kind of training to the women representatives regarding their rights, duties and provide information to them.
6. The women representatives should regularly attend the meetings and should raise the problems of their work and give suggestions in the meetings. The evolution of women participation in governance must be facilitated and fostered, and the decisions of mahila sabhas need to be honoured by gram sabhas. Equally significant is reservation for women in parallel systems—for example watershed development management bodies and others.
7. If they are not informed or ignored or if their suggestions are set aside they should complain the chairman of, the panchayati samiti or other higher officials or authorities.
8. The women representatives should keep themselves informed regarding the matters like income, expenditure and functions of the panchayats.
9. The presence of a vibrant and sensitive media is critical in providing visibility to struggles and helping to create pressure.

Concluding Observations

The strengthening of women's leadership has become a major issue in the discourse of economic and social development. Efforts must be onward to integrate multifaceted role of women including political role in the decision-making process.

This is time now to deal with the fundamental question of reservation and political leadership of women. In the final analysis, it can be concluded that political empowerment is not an end in itself. It is a means to achieve something, which is nothing but socio-economic empowerment. Another positive symptom of reservation is the growing political socialization of women. We can understand this by comparing the twin situations of pre-reservation and post-reservation period. In the former case the women had option to join or not to join the politics and as the socio-economic situation plays a decisive role in the participation, a few women entered into the arena of politics. But after reservation came into force, a lot of women are coming to politics notwithstanding the fact that women politics has been a thrust on them, because of the magnitude of pressure exerted over them for the purpose. By compulsorily coming to politics, the representatives are now creating an atmosphere where female mentality is getting socialized politically. Women are gradually learning how to articulate their demands, thus enabling them to act upon their visions of a better society and to make a meaningful contribution to national and societal development. This process will create a very congenial social atmosphere with the fading away of narrow and conservative ideas on women leadership in politics in the long run.

REFERENCES

B.S. Bhargava, Emerging Leadership in Panchayati Raj System, ISEC, Staff Paper, Bangalore, Institute for Social and Economic Change, 1977.

B.S. Bhargava, and N. Sivanna, Emerging Pattern of Leadership in Panchayati Raj System, Case Study of a Zilla Parishad in Karnataka. Working Paper No. 3, Bangalore, Institute for Social and Economic Change, 1990.

B.S. Bhargava and K.C. Vidya , Position of Women in Political Institutions, *Journal of Rural Development*, II (5), 1992.

B.S., Bhargava and K. Subha, Women in Panchayati Raj: Some Reflections on Karnataka's Experience, *Kurukshetra*, XLII (9), 1994.

Nirmala Buch, Decentralised Governance: Women's Participation and Poverty

Eradication, in Bidyut Mohanty and Saraswaty Haider (Editors), *Women and Political Empowerment*, New Delhi, Institute of Social Sciences, 1998.

Nirmala Buch, Panchayats and Women, in George Mathew (Ed.) *Status of Panchayati Raj in the States and Union Territories of India: 2000*, New Delhi, Institute of Social Sciences, Concept Publishing Company, 2000.

S.C. Dube, A Framework for the Study of Rural Leadership in Transitional Societies, in *Emerging Pattern of Rural Leadership*, Southern Asia, Hyderabad, National Institute of Rural Development, 1965. (Notes pages and Webpage).

Susheela Kaushik, *Women and Panchayati Raj*, New Delhi: Har-Anand Publications, Friedrich Ebert Stiftung, 1993.

Ushvinder Anand Kaur, Empowerment of Women at the Grassroots: An Effort through Panchayati Raj Institutions, *Contemporary Social Work*, XVIL, 2000.

Snehalata Panda, Political Empowerment of Women—A Case Study of Orissa, *Journal of Rural Development*, 16 (4), 1997, pp. 663-672.

S.N. Mishra, and S.S. Singh, *Roads to Models of Panchayati Raj*, New Delhi, Mittal Publications, 1993.

G. Palanthurai, *Dynamics of New Panchayati Raj System in India*, Vol. I: Selected States, New Delhi, Concept Publishing Company, 2002.

The AP, MPPs and ZPs Code (1986-87). Vol. I, Section 4, Hyderabad, Panchayat, Publications, 1987.

Poornima and Vinod Vyasulu, Women in Panchayati Raj: Grassroots Democracy in India, in *Indian Experience from Malgudi, Meeting on Women and Political Participation: 21st Century Challenges', Background Paper No. 4*, New Delhi, United Nations Development Programme, 1999.

V.M. Sirsikar, 'Rural Elite in a Developing Society—How and Why Grassroots Leadership becomes Important when Viewed in Wider Perspective (Indian Political System)', in B.S. Bhargava, *Training of Grassroots Leadership: A System Analysis Approach, Kurukshetra*, 18 (2), 1969, pp. 15-26.

V. Vijayalakshmi, Difference and Identities: Women and Political Participation, in T.M.Joseph (ed.) *Local Governance in India: Ideas, Challenges and Strategies*, New Delhi, Concept Publishing Company, 2007.

24

Dalit Women Panchayat Representatives: Tamil Nadu Experience

S. VISWANATHAN

Union Minister of Panchayati Raj Mani Shankar Aiyar in a thought-provoking article published by "The Hindu" in its (2007) Independence Day issue raises a very pertinent question: "Is rising India a just society? If not, what must be done?" He begins the article with a painful reference to the finding of the Arjun Sengupta Committee on the Unorganised Sector in its report released recently that "83.6 crores (836 million) Indians live on less than Rs. 20 a day, that is less than 50 cents a day, which is half way below the somewhat arbitrary 'poverty line' of a dollar a day drawn by the World Bank and other international institutions." The Minister then makes a pointed reference to a sarcastic observation of P. Sainath, the Magsaysay Award winner that the "phenomenal" spurt in GDP growth rate in recent years, which will see us breaking the magic 10 per cent barrier this year, has raised the *aam admi* on the UN Human Development Index from 127th position all the way to the 126th position. "So, around 20 crores (200 million) Indians go to bed hungry every night. This is injustice indeed," writes Mani Shankar Aiyar.

How can this injustice be undone? In the Union Minister's considered view, the hope for the suffering masses lies in the state. Writes he, "... [T]o make ours a truly just society, my plea is that we ally economic reforms to governance reforms through the panchayats so as to translate accelerated growth into 'inclusive growth' – the overarching objective of the Eleventh Five Year Plan."

The importance, and the relevance, of the Panchayati Raj Institutions and the need to hone it in order to meet the challenge thrown up by the distortions in economic growth cannot be better said. To counter economic inequity and social injustice there can be no better weapon than these institutions at the grassroots level. This is because the 73rd Amendment to the Constitution (1993) that gave birth to the PRIs of today made it mandatory to establish strong, decentralised, democratically elected local bodies in rural areas for the purpose of ensuring the twin objects of "economic development and social justice." The two defining features of the panchayati raj system that was put in place by the amendments are: (1) the provision that gram sabhas, of which all the electors are members, meet at regular intervals to involve the people in the planning process and (2) the reservation of posts for women as well as the Scheduled Castes and Scheduled Tribes in the elected local bodies.

These two important tools that can be of immense use in building up an "inclusive society" and ensuring an "inclusive growth" understandably generated a lot of hope among the marginalised sections across the country and Tamil Nadu was no exception. The State which did not have elected local bodies for many years welcomed the new legislation that ensured also regular, periodical free and fair elections to the local bodies. Three rounds of elections, the first in 1996, the second in 2001 and the third in 2006 have so far been held to fill over one lakh posts in 12,619 village panchayats, 385 panchayat unions and 29 district panchayats. Of the 12,619 village presidents' posts, 3,198 were reserved for women (general), 1104 of Scheduled Castes (women), 1,855 for Scheduled Castes (general), 66 for Scheduled Tribes (general) and 27 for Scheduled Tribes (women). By and large, the performance of the PRI system in Tamil Nadu in the last about 11 years has not been totally disappointing. Although the functioning of the Panchayati Raj Institutions has been badly affected by several inadequacies such as lack of power, paucity of funds and bureaucratic indifference, the political empowerment of women and dalits, has generated a great deal of enthusiasm in rural Tamil Nadu. However, these weaker sections, particularly dalits, have to submit themselves to countless acts of humiliation, before overcoming resistance from vested interests.

The most glaring flaw in the working of the system was the failure of the state machinery for 10 long years to conduct elections to four village panchayats in which the posts of president had been reserved for dalits, owing to resistance from caste forces. The four defiant villages were Pappapatti, Keerippatti, and Nattarmangalam in southern district of Madurai and Kottakachiyendal in the neighbouring Virudhunagar district. Sections of caste Hindu people, who had been enjoying power all along, were in no mood to yield to those at the bottom of or outside the caste hierarchy even on the basis of a system of rotation, as provided in the Act. The reason that the caste Hindu opponents of dalit empowerment gave out was that Dalits were in a "minority" in these villages, and so were not acceptable to them as panchayat presidents. "If dalits become presidents," they said, "we may have to show respect to them in village festivals and public functions. This we cannot do."

Dalits, who account for about 20 per cent of the population in the State, live scattered almost evenly all over the State, segregated from the rest of the population. This being the pattern of living thrust upon these victims of centuries-old prejudice, they need not necessarily constitute the majority in the villages in which the posts of panchayat presidents have been reserved for dalits. Perhaps that is why the Act has prescribed a system of rotation of the panchayat presidents' posts between dalits and non-dalits, by way of appeasing the caste Hindus. Another apparent purpose in following this system of rotation is to create in due course room for integrating the segregated with the mainstream. The idea is that within a period of 15 to 30 years, depending upon the number of five-year terms specified for altering the presidentship pattern under the rotation system, eligible dalits in all villages in the State would have the opportunity to get elected as panchayat presidents. By that time, one would only wish, the mindset of the large sections of people belonging to the so-called upper castes might change and they may get used to sharing power with the oppressed people and living in peace with them. "The system, therefore, should be given a fair trial," experts have pointed out.

Left political parties, dalit organisations and progressive sections of the civil society have all along been warning that any lenient state attitude to the caste Hindu resistance to Dalit empowerment would jeopardise its very objective of building a stronger and healthier democratic political and administrative structure at the grassroots level.

Right from the second half of 1996, when the Tamil Nadu Government identified about 2,250 of the 12,609 village panchayats, in which the posts of president would be reserved for dalits in proportion to their number in the population, the hostile caste Hindu groups started mounting protests in many parts of the State. The resistance was particularly more intense in the southern districts, the heartland of caste-related violence. The administration in the beginning sought to create an impression that though the electoral process was set in motion in these panchayats like in other areas with the necessary security arrangements. Dalits were mostly not willing to fight the elections ignoring the resentment among the caste Hindus, in whose lands they worked as agricultural workers. But the use of force by caste Hindus to prevent dalits from contesting the elections or campaigning or participating in the electoral process in any form and the helplessness of the administration could not be concealed for long.

In the four villages mentioned earlier no nominations were received and so no elections were held. At Melavalavu panchayat, reserved for dalits, in Madurai district, sections of caste Hindus let loose a reign of terror when two persons managed to file nominations with police protection as a result of which the election was countermanded. In the re-election held two months later Murugesan, who entered the fray again, came out successful. Caste Hindu opponents then began placing all sorts of hurdles to the functioning of Murugesan as the panchayat president. Murugesan braved these impediments with courage and conviction. This could not, however, go on for long. Murugesan's complaints to the police and the district administration about the activities of his caste Hindu oppressors and his appeal for protection were of no avail. He was brutally murdered along with five of his associates in less than a year.

Since then the "Melavalavu massacre" was used by the caste Hindu opponents of dalits to cow down the prospective dalit candidates. In several areas dalits are agricultural workers in lands owned by caste Hindu landlords and so are totally at the mercy of their masters. In such areas, the informal "oor panchayats" dominated by the predominant caste Hindu social group used to field somebody from among the dalits in the panchayat election as their own candidate, help them win and keep them under their control. At Pappapatti and Keerippatti also, a similar tactic was followed in the by-elections but with a difference: the elected dalits were forced to resign their posts as soon as they assumed charge. The only dalit president who refused to oblige had to lose the post-after he was fixed in a criminal case charged with misappropriation of public funds. Naattarmangalam, which had an elected dalit panchayat president during 1996-2001, joined the rebel panchayats in 2001.

Although a number of human rights organisations and political parties consistently pressed the state administration at various levels to bring to an end this kind of subvertive action against a statutory democratic process, no effective intervention resulted. The successive State Governments during 1906-2006, irrespective of the party in power, were reluctant to take any firm action against those blocking the electoral process, fearing erosion of their support base. This happened although there were enough provisions in the Scheduled Castes and Scheduled Tribes (Prevention of Atrocities) Act for taking severe action against such miscreants as well as the officials who refuse to prosecute them under the Act.

Studies have also revealed that dalits in the villages that come under the four rebel panchayats are landless agricultural workers, who depend totally on caste Hindu landholders for their livelihood and have been subjected to untouchability, banned by law, in its varied forms such as denial of access to public facilities, natural resources, social ostracism and sexual torture.

But then, Dalits in other parts of the State also suffer the same kind of treatment from caste Hindu social groups and, as most of them are agricultural workers, dependent on their "upper caste" or "intermediate caste" masters for their very survival. In these areas the electoral process in respect of village panchayats in which presidents' posts have been reserved for dalits, has never been resisted by the oppressive caste forces, or at least up to some level. In these places, dalits, however, had to face a different problem. The elected dalit panchayat presidents were never respected by caste Hindu people. In many places they were not even allowed to occupy the chairs meant for them in the panchayat office. The "upper caste" vice-presidents invariably refused to cooperate with the dalit presidents. It took several years for dalits to assert themselves under such adverse conditions. Despite all these, the elections were held without any hitch. On the other hand, the people of the rebel Madurai/Virudhunagar village panchayats were stubborn in their resistance to holding the elections. One of the reasons attributed to this united action by the caste Hindu majority is the rigidity of a traditional informal 'nadu' system (a kind of 'state within a state') still prevailing in the region under a president, who generally hails from a rich family of 'naattar', a powerful section of the majority caste. Be it what it may, it is, for 10 long years the resistance prevailed. The majority caste Hindu people in this region had been hoping that at the conclusion of two five-year terms the village panchayats would come under their control under the system of rotation. But this was not to be.

After the 2006 Assembly elections, when a new government led by Dravida Munnetra Kazhagam, which fought the elections in alliance with the Congress, the two Communist parties and a few other parties, a new situation developed. Pressure was mounted on the ruling DMK to retain the four rebel panchayats in the list of those reserved for dalits for 10 more years, because the electoral process was not allowed to have a full play in these villages. The DMK, which during its earlier stint in power during 1996-2001 did not do much to make the rebels fall in line was now successfully forced to intervene on dalits' behalf. Political and electoral compulsions played a key role in making the government accept the demand and as a result these four panchayats continued to remain in the reserved category. This firm action had the desired effect on the adamant caste Hindu people. They started realising the futility of further resistance and also began to fear that if they continued to be defiant they would not only lose development projects but also face prosecution by the Government which they thought would no more be a silent spectator. It became clear when Chief Minister M. Karunanidhi announced in the State Assembly his government's resolve to break the resistance to the empowerment of dalits. This political will on the part of the ruling class, which was conspicuously absent all these years, ultimately triggered a transformation.

The moment the Government made its stand clear, the district administration in Madurai and Virudhunagar started doing the spadework. The Collectors visited the villages repeatedly to infuse confidence in the minds of dalits and instill fears in caste Hindu minds about the consequences of any move to sabotage the electoral process. The administration adopted a policy of "carrot and stick" to make the majority group give up its resistance and come round to accepting dalit empowerment with grace. Assurances were given liberally to provide basic amenities and development projects specially prepared for these villages that had been left out in the past 10 years because of their unhelpful attitude and consequent failure to have an elected panchayat for them. Schemes costing Rs. 50 lakh in all were sanctioned for each panchayat. Self-Help Groups of women operating in these villages were provided loans to the tune of Rs. 35 lakh. These apart, polling booths were rearranged and the procedures governing the filing of nominations were simplified. There were also assurances that each of these villages would be developed as a model one, in addition to assurances that jobs would be created for the youth of all sections. Besides the government machinery political activists, functionaries of non-governmental organisations and progressive writers were also deployed in the villages to take the message of peaceful completion of the electoral process in these village panchayats.

The cumulative effect of these efforts could be seen on the day of polling. With absolute cooperation from all sections of the people the electoral process was completed in the four villages. The elected dalit panchayat presidents were congratulated by the caste Hindu leaders who also assured them of their continued cooperation. They were greeted and honoured by the Chief Minister himself at a gala function in Chennai. The successful conduct of the elections clearly proved that given the political will, sincere and swift ground work by committed officials and an active cooperation from the lovers of democracy and social justice, even seemingly impossible things could be accomplished.

Unless this momentum is maintained and the hopes that were kindled by the united effort of the administration and progressive sections of civil society are kept alive by planning for expanding their activities in several other areas, the gains of Madurai/ Virudhunagar campaign cannot be sustained for long. This has been proved by certain incidents involving newly elected dalit panchayat presidents reported from some parts of the State, hardly weeks after the Madurai/Virudhunagar success. A dalit panchayat president in Tirunelveli District was done to death for the simple reason that he refused to oblige his own deputy, belonging to the rival caste group, by agreeing to be a "dummy" president. Another Dalit president was found dead under mysterious circumstances in the same district. He had to confront caste Hindu hostility from the very beginning. Even in Madurai District a number of panchayat presidents have complained that they are not allowed to function independently either by their deputies in the panchayat boards or the majority caste Hindu elements, which include former panchayat presidents. This has been the position in many other places as well.

In the northern district of Villupuram, a dalit panchayat president, who began to show his talent in obtaining development projects for his village and mobilizing funds for certain works from the village public, cutting across caste lines, had to run for life from place to place following harassment. He complained of ill-treatment from a section of caste Hindu people including the supporters of the dethroned caste Hindu panchayat president. Yet another dalit panchayat president in Dindigul District had complained that he had to conduct panchayat meetings standing all along, because caste Hindu members did not allow him to sit in his official chair. His rivals reportedly even indulged in sabotage to harm the reputation of the new president for the good work he had initiated.

A common factor in all these incidents is the indifference of the bureaucrats to the complaints of the affected dalit panchayat presidents or their families and also their disinterestedness in setting things right. This is in total contrast to the way issues were addressed by the district administration in Madurai and Virudhunagar. This only highlights the need for the government not only to restrain the oppressive caste forces but also to sensitise the bureaucrats about the plight of a substantial section of the people who have been victims of prejudice and social injustice for long.

And now back to Union Panchayati Raj Minister Mani Shankar Aiyar's article mentioned in the beginning of this paper. He writes: "... for those 836 million Indians surviving on under Rs. 20 a day even six decades after Independence, the only hope of survival is the state. But not – above all, NOT, – the state intervening through an indifferent bureaucracy but a state reaching the people through the intermediation of elected panchayats." This will be possible when panchayats themselves are empowered fully through effective devolution of functions, finances and functionaries. The genuine empowerment of dalits through PRIs is also linked to the successful completion of efforts to "genuinely" empower the panchayats themselves. A genuine and total empowerment of PRIs has acquired importance today more than ever before in the context of the neo-liberal policies that have been taking the country on a disastrous path. It must also be noted that South American countries such as Venezuela, Bolivia and Brazil, which have wriggled themselves out of the neo-liberal path have shown to the world that local bodies are the most effective and dependable instruments in the task of rebuilding the lives of the people impoverished by the reforms regime.

25

Panchayati Raj Institutions After 60 Years of Independent India: Working Towards Decentralisation and Good Governance

D. SUNDAR RAM

The significance of decentralised governance was realised with Mahatma Gandhi's insistence for the establishment of village panchayats at the grassroots levels, as units of local self-government. Democratic decentralisation or Panchayati Raj, as it is popularly in our country, aims at making democracy real by bringing the millions in to the functioning of their representative government at the grassroots level.

For the first time by the 73rd Constitution Amendment Act, power was proposed to be transferred to the local bodies in 1992. The credit for reviving this grassroots democratic institutions goes to Shri Rajiv Gandhi, who introduced the 73rd Amendment to the Constitution, which made panchayat elections mandatory and in particular recognising Gram Sabha as a basic institution of the new panchayat raj system. The enactment of the 73rd Constitution Amendment has paved the way for the creation of statutory institutional structures for realising the goals of self-governance in India.

The explicit objective of this initiative for democratic decentralisation of governance is to accelerate the socio-economic development of the rural areas within a participatory framework at the grassroots level. The Amendment has given statutory recognition to a three-tier system of governance with Panchayati Raj Institutions (PRIs) at the District, Intermediary and Village levels. Although the PRI's provide a framework of decentralised rural development, the 14 years experience and experiments of the 73rd Constitution Amendment reveals that the many states—

barring a few states like Kerala, Karnataka, West Bengal—are not willing to devolution of powers to the Panchayati Raj Institutions in letter and spirit. What the states demand from the Union should also be made applicable to the Panchayati Raj Institutions from the State Governments in respect of the devolution of powers.

In recent times, the issue of devolution of powers to the Panchayati Raj Institutions has emerged at the forefront of the agenda for sustainable good governance. With the formation of the Ministry of Panchayati Raj, for the first time in Independent India by the UPA Government, a clear and dedicated action plan emerged, to secure the cooperation of State Governments in the implementation of the 73rd Constitutional Amendment in letter and spirit. In strengthening the Panchayati Raj Institutions in all respects, the Union Ministry of Panchyati Raj convened Seven Round Tables of State Ministers of Panchayati Raj between July 2004 and December 2004. At the Round Tables, about 150 points for action, touching 18 dimensions of Panchayati Raj were formulated by consensus. The first Round Table at Kolkata held on 23 and 24 July, 2004 considered the issue of strengthening Gram Sabhas and effectively devolving functions, functionaries and funds to panchayats. In addition, the Ministry of Panchayati Raj has also initiated the process of visiting each state of jointly review with the State Government, the progress achieved in operationalising the resolutions.

The issue to be examined is whether the 73rd Constitutional Amendment Act make the Panchayati Raj Institutions as constitutional bodies ? Will these institutions reflect the aspirations of the people at the grassroots ? Why is that Panchayati Raj Institutions do not receive the adequate powers to its potential, even after 14 years of the enactment of the 73rd Constitution Amendment? What are the factors contributing to the disempowerment of Panchayati Raj Institutions in contemporary India? The present paper provides answers to these questions.

The main objective of the article is to make an attempt to explore the initiatives of the various Union Governments towards the *power to the people* through Panchayati Raj Institutions in contemporary India. The article is divided into four parts. Part one examines the formulations and initiatives of the Panchayati Raj Institutions after Independence, under the leadership of Pandit

Jawaharlal Nehru. The second part deals with the reformatory changes in the Panchayati Raj system through 73rd Constitution Amendment Act. The third part explores the initiative taken by the UPA Government towards the devolution of powers to the PRI's. The final part of the chapter provides some solutions for *power to the people.*

I

Since Independence, lots of efforts have been made to offer decentralised governance both in rural and urban sectors. Mahatma Gandhi had been a champion of rural self-sufficiency in resource utilisation, governance and other aspects for the welfare of the rural community. Gandhiji believed that human happiness with mental and moral development should be the supreme goal of society and that this goal should be achieved decentralisation of political and economic powers. It is widely acknowledged that decentralised governance and local polity holds great potential for development and poverty alleviation. It can ensure more efficient allocation and utilisation of resources, enhance local resource mobilisation, facilitate participation of the people, ensure target group orientation in the planning and implementation of development programmes make monitoring and supervision over the implementation of the development more effective and improve local governance.[1] Thus, the democratic decentralisation became very important after Independence from the point of view of the twin objective of the Indian polity, namely, democracy and development. As a result of the general consensus in the debate in favour of decentralisation of power, village panchayat, as unit of local self-government was inserted into the Constitution of India under Article 40.[2] The amendment became Article 40 under Directive principles of the Constitution, reads:

> "The state shall take steps to organise village panchayats and endow them with such powers and authority as may be necessary to enable them to function as units of self-government".

The need for popular participation in development takes under the Five Year Plans prompted the Congress leaders now in government to look in the direction of strengthening the panchayat system. Accordingly, Balwantrai Mehta Committee was appointed in 1957 to enquire into, among other things, the lack of initiative, apathy and indifference on the part of the rural population. The committee, officially designated as the 'Team for the Study of Community Projects and National Extension Service', visited all the states and held extensive discussions with all those concerned. After the Balwantrai Mehta Committee recommendations, the term 'Panchayati Raj'[3] gained currency as a process of governance organically linking the will of the people from the Gram Sabha to the Lok Sabha.

It was in this context that Pandit Jawaharlal Nehru described panchayats as the 'foundations of democracy' in India. Speaking on the occasion of the Inauguration of Panchayati Raj in Rajasthan State on 2nd October, 1959, he expressed his faith in the capability of the people in managing their affair in the manner considered best by them. He said:

> "It is only by providing opportunity to the people that they can be trained to shoulder responsibilities. It became imperative that bold step be taken whereby more and more responsibility could be transferred to the people. People were not merely to be consulted but effective power was to be entrusted to them. Therefore, we decided that in every village there should be a village panchayat with more power as also a cooperative society which will help its economic efforts."[4]

Pandit Jawaharlal Nehru was of the opinion that panchayats should not be allowed to be officialised; that they should controlled and run by the people themselves and the role of officials should be strictly advisory in nature. Speaking at a meeting held in the Indian Institute of Public Administration on 25 April, 1959, he said:

> "We want to give far greater powers to panchayats and to the village cooperatives than they have today, knowing full well that they may misuse it, make mistakes and the like. The mistakes of the panchayats will not endanger the security of the country. We can survive it. But they will suffer for it, they will learn from it and the public will learn from it too."[5]

Whenever Pandit Nehru found that the functioning of the system was hampered by some impediments—financial, administrative or others—the government took remedial measures.

Speaking to the Conference of Ministers of Community Development at New Delhi on 1 August, 1963, he said :

> "We must give power to the people, even though it leads us to hell. We will certainly come out of the hell if we get there."[6]

It is apparent that with the demise of Pandit Jawaharlal Nehru and the formation of various coalition governments in states by different political parties, initial enthusiasm about the Panchayati Raj started waning.[7] In 1978, the Union Government led by the Janata Party, finding that the States had not managed the Panchayati Raj Institutions properly, set up a Committee with Shri Ashok Mehta as the Chairman to review the working of Panchayati Raj Institutions and in particular, among other things, to delineate their true role in the task of integrated rural development. The Ashoka Mehta Committee submitted its report in August 1978, making 123 recommendations to revitalise Panchayati Raj as a living and integral part of the democratic continuum.[8] However, the respective State Governments had not transferred substantial authority to the Panchayati Raj Institutions (PRI's). The state level authorities were neither prepared to part with their powers nor confident that the local elected bodies could carry out their designated functions effectively. This is reflected in the half hearted devolution of powers and the retention of tight control over the devolved functions. The result has been to restrict the autonomy of the local bodies and introduce checks and balances at all levels.

As G. Ram Reddy had put it :

> "Even the mild reforms envisaged by the Mehta Team have not been fully made. Structures of reforms are there, but not the substance."[9]

It is in this context that the ups and downs through which panchayati raj had gone through indicate that the multitude of goals—democratisation, economic development, social upliftment, decentralisation, etc., cannot be attained *ipso facto*. This is no less true of the reforms brought out by the Janata Government at the Centre.

II

The Panchayati Raj Institutions in India, popularly known as agents of rural transformation, are not merely a formal arrangement, with specific form and function but have a certain legitimacy and meaning by which they are identified. After Independence, there have been several attempts to make panchayats a more viable grassroots institutions and crystallise certain practices which are necessary for rural development.[10] Unfortunately, panchayat as institution failed to make its own identity. This prompted the young and dynamic Prime Minister Shri Rajiv Gandhi to find out the exact reasons for the failure of government efforts.[11] As Prime Minister, Shri Rajiv Gandhi was driven by a vision to provide the people with 'representative administration', as he repeatedly emphasised in his address to Nation in January, 1985 and included in the Revised Twenty-point Programme of 1986. To this end, Shri Rajiv Gandhi convened five Regional Workshops[12] of District Collectors / Magistrates in various regions of the country over a seven-month period in 1988 and concluded that the way forward lay in amending the Constitution to give Constitutional sanction and Constitutional sanctity to Panchayati Raj. Shri Rajiv Gandhi had direct interaction with the officers who are responsible for implementation of the development schemes in the districts in all the five regional workshops unmindful of the criticism of this event by Chief Ministers who harp on 'State Autonomy.'[13]

Change in the direction of a democratic decentralisation brings into sharp focus the power to the people in policy-making during the Rajiv Gandhi regime. Among the five regional workshops of District Collectors, the North-Eastern Regional Workshop held at Imphal in April, 1988 recommended that 'Democratic Decentralisation' was essential for the successful implementation of the Poverty Alleviation Programmes and Rural Development Programmes without which good success cannot be hoped for.[14] The land mark recommendation from the side of the bureaucracy of the country impressed the then Prime Minister Shri Rajiv Gandhi and he was all out to implement it. Subsequent efforts made by Shri Rajiv Gandhi lead to the passing of the Constitutional Amendment for incorporating Panchayati Raj as an integral part of the system of government of the Indian Republic by the Lok Sabha.[15] In May 1989, Prime Minister Shri Rajiv Gandhi himself introduced the Constitution (64th Amendment) Bill, saying:

> "Our Bill will ensure that Panchayati Raj has a democratic character similar to the Lok Sabha and the State

> Assemblies and Constitutional Protection for their functioning as representative institutions of the people."

Speaking on the occasion, Shri Rajiv Gandhi stressed that with the devolving functions, functionaries and funds to panchayats a new dimension was being added to the Panchayati Raj system in all respects. The following words of Shri Rajiv Gandhi further highlights his vision towards the devolution of powers to PRI's:

> "The single greatest danger we have to guard against is the devolution of powers to the panchayats being followed by the transfer of these powers out of the Panchayati Raj system into other bodies constituted outside the system... It is the purpose of our Bill to ensure that powers delegated to the panchayats remain with the panchayats and are not channeled outside the system. By the same token, our Bill is designed to ensure that all developmental agencies are brought within the framework of the Panchayati Raj Institutions and made responsive to the elected authority."[16]

The Constitution (64th Amendment) Bill was followed in July 1989 with the Constitution (65th Amendment) Bill that sought to endow urban local bodies, from town Panchayats and Municipalities to Metropolitan Councils, with powers similar to those that were sought to be devolved to the rural panchayats. Although both Bills received the required two-thirds majority with at least half the members present and voting in the Lok Sabha, on 13 October, 1989, the Bills failed by a handful votes[17] to muster the required Constitutional majority in the Rajya Sabha.

The National Front Government made another vain attempt to amend the Constitution in this regard. In September 1990, the V.P. Singh led National front Government introduced the Constitution (74th Amendment) Bill—a combined bill on panchayats and municipalities—but before this was taken up for discussion, there was a change of government at the centre.[18]

Being committed to decentralisation of power and authority rural development and revitalisation of Panchayati Raj Institutions, the P.V. Narasimha Rao Government introduced the 72nd (Panchayats) and 73rd (Nagarpalikas) Constitutional Amendment Bills, based substantially on the Bills moved in the Eighth Lok Sabha by Shri Rajiv Gandhi but also incorporating some of the changes wrought by the National Front Government. These two bills were referred to a Joint Select Committee on the Parliament, which effected some further changes but conformed in very considerable measure to the earlier 1989 initiative. The Lok Sabha and Rajya Sabha passed both bills on the 22nd and 23rd December, 1992 respectively. By the time, the Parliament passed the two bills their sequence changed to 73rd and 74th Constitution Amendments.[19] Following their ratification by more than half the State Assemblies as required under the Constitution, the President of India gave his assent, and then came into force as the Constitution (73rd Amendment) Act, 1992 on 24th April, 1993 and the Constitution (74th Amendment) Act, 1992 on 1 June, 1993, adding two new parts to the Constitution, namely Part IX titled 'The Panchayats' and Part IXA titled 'The Municipalities.' Thus democracy and devolution of powers to Panchayats have now become part of the Constitution of India. In the Eleventh Schedule, 29 subjects have been listed under Article 243G which stipulates that states may by law endow the panchayats with such powers and authority as may be required to enable them to function as Institutions of self-government.

In pursuance of its election manifesto called the National Agenda for Governance, the National Democratic Alliance (NDA) Government headed by Shri A.B. Vajpayee has appointed a 13-member National Commission to Review the Working of the Constitution (NCRWC) under the chairmanship of the former Chief Justice of India Shri Justice M.N. Venkatachaliah on 1st February, 2000. After considering the various viewpoints and recommendations to the Government of India through a comprehensive report submitted on 31st March, 2002 for reconstruction of the executive, legislative and judicial aspects of the Constitutional Provisions of Governance. There were 38 recommendations made by the NCRWC on the decenstralisation and devolution besides empowerment and strengthening of Panchayati Raj Institutions alone.[21] In addition, the NDA Government took keen interest in organising the All India Panchayat Adhyakhas Sammelan in New Delhi during 5-6 April, 2002 for formulating National Declaration for Local Self-governance, a text consisting of 15 point recommendations.[22] This resolution was at the Centre of the recommendations made by the 1,600 elected heads representing 3,40,000 Panchayats of India.

III

To improve the quality of life of the mass of the people of India, the National Common Minimum Programme (NCMP) of the United Progressive Alliance Government headed by Dr. Manmohan Singh placed at the core of its pro-poor strategy the devolution of powers to Panchayats. In respect of Panchayati Raj, the NCMP said :

> "The UPA Government will ensure that all funds given to States for implementation of poverty alleviation and rural development scheme by Panchayats are neither delayed nor diverted. Monitoring will be strict. In addition, after consultations with states, the UPA Government will consider crediting elected panchayats with funds directly. Devolution of funds will be accompanied by similar devolution of functions and functionaries as well. Regular elections to Panchayat bodies will be ensured and the amended act in respect of the Fifth and Sixth Schedule Areas will be implemented. The UPA Government will ensure that the Gram Sabha is empowered to emerge as the foundation of Panchayati Raj."[23]

In keeping with this commitment to the cause of empowering the poor, one of the first acts of the UPA Government after assuming office was the creation of the Union Ministry of Panchayati Raj on 27th May, 2004. The constitution of an independent Ministry of Panchayati Raj at the Centre was a significant move. For the first time in Independent India, a separate Central Ministry was constituted to oversee, facilitate and ensure that the 73rd Constitutional Amendment is observed in letter and spirit.[24] With the formation of the Ministry of Panchayati Raj a clear and dedicated action plan emerged, to secure the cooperation of State Governments in the implementation of the 73rd Constitutional Amendment in letter and spirit. The first step in defining the scope of the Ministry's work was taken when the Ministry, jointly with the Union Ministry of Rural Development, organised the Conference of Chief Ministers on Rural Poverty Alleviation and Prosperity through Panchayati Raj, at New Delhi on 29 and 30th June, 2004.

While inaugurating the Conference of Chief Ministers on Rural Poverty Alleviation, the Prime Minister Dr. Manmohan Singh stressed that effective and sustainable poverty alleviation could be achieved only by empowering Panchayati Raj Institutions (PRIs) in the letter and spirit of the Constitution. Set the tone for the task ahead, Dr. Manmohan Singh said:

> "The key instrument for integrating economic reforms with institutional reforms in the country side is Gandhiji's farsighted goal of Purna Swaraj through Gram Swaraj. This was given constitutional shape and sanction by late Shri Rajiv Gandhi vision of empowering Panchayati Raj Institutions to function as 'institutions of self-government', to plan and implement programmes of economic development and social justice... The key issue (here) is action on transfer of functions, functionaries and funds. Transfer of functions are has to be based on the principle of subsidiarity and any task that can be done by a lower level should not move to a higher level. Effective Panchayati Raj requires that functionaries of government work under elected leadership. As far as funds are concerned, the awards of the State Finance Commissions should be fully honoured."[25]

In pursuance of the decision taken at the conference of Chief Ministers in June 2004, the Ministry of Panchayati Raj organised a series of Seven Round Tables of State Ministers of Panchayati Raj at Kolkata, Mysore, Raipur, Chandigarh, Srinagar, Guwahati and Jaipur, for detailed deliberation on the blue print for future action. Within a period of 150 days, from 23 July, 2004 to 19 December 2004, consensus was achieved among all States/Union Territories on a Compendium of Action Points covering 18 jointly identified dimensions of Panchayati Raj and comprising 150 key steps on what remained to be done.[26] The Kolkata Round Table was resolved the States should be work towards devolving powers and responsibilities in respect of all matters listed in the Eleventh Schedule in the letter and spirit of Article 243 G of the Constitution. It was agreed that the devolution of functionaries to panchayats would be based on the mapping of activities related to the devolved functions, in all states by 1 April, 2005. Within three months it was clear that the compendium encompassed a time bound Action Plan and Agenda for the Ministry and the State Government for achieving devolution of functions, funds and functionaries to Panchayati Raj Institutions. Following the acceptance of the compendium document by all State Chief Ministers, the Union

Minister for Panchayati Raj has embarked upon a series of visits to States and Union Territories in order to interact with panchayats and review with the State/Union Territory authorities concerned the progress on the ground in implementing the recommendations of the Seven Round Tables. In this direction, the Union Minister for Panchayati Raj Shri Mani Shankar Aiyar has so far visited 18 States and 3 Union Territories during the period 2005 April to 2007 March.[27] During these visits, Shri Mani Shankar Aiyar attends nearly 150 Gram Sabhas and meets with the representatives of the Gram Panchayats, Intermediate Panchayats and District Panchayats all over the country.

At the end of each visit, a joint statement of conclusions is signed between the Union Minister of Panchayati Raj and the Chief Minister of the State or the appropriate authority in Union Territories. With persistent efforts of the Union Ministry of Panchayati Raj, some states, in accordance with Article 243G of the Constitution, have passed legislation devolving 29 subjects listed in the Eleventh Schedule, while others have devolved 6 and 18 subjects, for undertaking development programmes. Details in respect of the devolution of powers to PRI's by various State Governments by the end of October, 2006 may be seen at a glance in the Table-1 on page 398.

IV

The devolution of powers to the Panchayats in terms of Article 243G of the Constitution is essential for making decentralisation successful. The progress of devolution of function, functionaries and finances in respect of 29 subjects listed in the Eleventh Schedule is not uniform among the states. We note that only Kerala, Karnataka and West Bengal have competed activity mapping, as envisaged in the 73rd Constitution Amendment. With the experience of the status of devolution in respect of 29 subjects it can easily be realised that after more or less 15 years of the passage of the 73rd Constitution Amendment Act, the devolution of powers and authority to the Panchayats is minimal'.[28] However, conformity legislation is only the beginning of the process of devolution. It has to be operationalised through Government orders that specify which activity pertaining to which function is to be devolved to which level of the three-tier Panchayati Raj system. Activity Mapping is the instrumentalist argument for devolution,

Table–1

State	Transfer of Subjects through Legislation	Subjects Covered Under Activity Mapping
Andhra Pradesh	17 subjects	9 subjects
Assam	29 subjects	29 subjects
Arunachal Pradesh	–	3 subjects
Bihar	25 subjects	25 subjects
Chhattisgarh	29 subjects	27 subjects
Goa	6 subjects	18 subjects
Gujarat	15 subjects	14 subjects
Haryana	29 subjects	10 subjects
Himachal Pradesh	26 subjects	–
Karnataka	29 subjects	29 subjects
Madhya Pradesh	23 subjects	23 subjects
Maharashtra	18 subjects	–
Manipur	22 subjects	22 subjects
Osissa	25 subjects	7 subjects
Punjab	7 subjects	–
Rajasthan	29 subjects	12 subjects
Sikkim	28 subjects	–
Tamil Nadu	29 subjects	–
Tripura	29 subjects	21 subjects
Uttar Pradesh	12 subjects	–
Uttaranchal	14 subjects	9 subjects
West Bengal	29 subjects	15 subjects
Union Territory		
Dadra and Nagar Haveli	29 subjects	29 subjects
Daman and Diu	18 subjects	18 subjects
Abdaman & Nicobar Islands	8 subjects	8 subjects
Lakshadweep Islands	25 subjects	25 subjects

Source: The State of the Panchayats – A Mid-term Review and Appraisal 22 November 2006, New Delhi, Ministry of Panchayati Raj, Government of India, 2006.

and is grounded in the democratic ideal. It involves an identification of functions within a given sector and the disaggregation of these functions into tasks, activities and responsibilities for devolution to the three levels of Panchayats.

Indeed, two and a half years ago, when the Union Ministry of Panchayati Raj was constituted, very few states had detailed Activity Maps. It is perhaps worth noting in this context that the vision and intensive interaction over the last two and a half years between the Union Ministry of Panchayati Raj and State Governments, as many as 16 States and 3 Union Territories have released, are about to release or have reached a more or less advanced stage of preparation of Activity Maps. Thus, progress is being made, even though it remains imperative to accelerate its pace. It is true that the effective devolution requires not only the devolution of functions but also the devolution of functionaries and finances. Not until functions, functionaries and finances are all devolved can there be effective devolution? The number of subjects listed for devolution is less important than securing effective devolution of functions related to these subjects. States, may, therefore, prepare a road map for effective functionaries and finances accomplishing full devolution of functions, functionaries and finances for all devolved subjects in pre-determined annual stages within the eleventh Five-Year Plan Period (2007-2012).

Today, a need of the hour is to look at the devolution of powers to the Panchayati Raj Institutions to achieve vibrant development at the grassroots.[29] For this, the major issue of the devolution powers to PRI's is to reviewed, policies are to be redesigned and grassroots level realities are to be recognised. What is now needed, in this fifteenth anniversary year of Constitutionally obligated Panchayati Raj, is a stock-taking of the experience of all states which will enable us to review and appraisal for the time-bound implementation of the devolution of 3F's – Functions, Finances and Functionaries to the PRI's. It may be necessary to further consider the following suggestions for effective devolution of powers to the grassroots democratic institutions:

1. To introduce the Indian Panchayati Raj Service (IPRS) at all India level and minimise the supremacy of the Collector's Raj in the decision-making of local self-government institutions.
2. To strengthen the decentralised planning at the grassroots and provide an opportunity for more and more people to be involved in formulation of their own developmental plans through Gram Sabhas and other statutory bodies.

3. To re-define the role and responsibilities of MP's/MLA's in Panchayati Raj administration and re-statement of the distribution of work between the three-tiers of the governance.
4. To identify the real beneficiaries and disadvantaged sections of the society through Gram Sabha in a transparent way, while implementation of various welfare and development schemes.
5. To provide adequate training to the elected representatives of PRI's through Governmental as well as Non-Governmental Organisations for their capacity building in transforming the panchayats into real institutions of local self-governments.
6. To give incentives to the States which strengthen the Panchayati Raj Institutions in all respects, include the devolution of powers.

NOTE AND REFERENCES

1. Prabhat Datta, 'Local Politics, Decentralisation and Poverty Reduction: Analytical and Methodological Issues', *Socialist Perspective*, Vol. 32, No's : 3 & 4, December, 2004 - March 2005, p. 167.
2. While introducing the Draft Constitution, a large number of Members, including Shri Shibban Lal Saxena, Shri H.V. Kamath, Shri P.S. Deshmukh, Shri A.C. Guha, Shri T. Prakasam, Shri Alladi Krishna Swami Ayyar, Shri M. Ananthasayanam Ayyangar and Prof. N.G. Ranga argued forcibly in favour of Panchayat system. As a result of the general consensus in the debate in favour of decentralisation of power and Panchayati Raj Institutions, an amendment was moved by Shri K. Santhanam, proposing to insert an article in the chapter on Directive Principles of State Policy. For an elaborate debate, See. *Constituent Assembly Debates*, Vol. III.
3. The Balwantrai Mehta Team affirmed that 'rural development and rural welfare are possible only with local initiative and local discretion' and offered two broad directional thrusts : first, it argued that there should be administrative decentralisation for the effective implementation of the development programme and second the decentralised administrative system should be under the control of elected bodies. The Chairman of the Committee Shri Balwantrai Mehta said : 'Independence must begin at the bottom. Thus, every village will be a republic or panchayat having full powers. It follows, therefore, that every village has to be self-sustained and capable of managing its affairs'. See *Report of the Study Team on Community Projects and National Extension Service*, Vol. I (Chairman : Balwantrai G. Mehta), New Delhi, Government of India, 1957.

4. *Jawaharlal Nehru' Speeches*, Vol. IV, September 1957 - April 1963, New Delhi, Goverment of India, 1964, p. 93.
5. *Jawaharlal Nehru's and Public Administration*, New Delhi, Indian Institute of Public Administration, 1964, pp. 80-81.
6. Sarvepalli Gopal, *Jawaharlal Nehru – A Biography*, Vol. 3, 1956-1964, New Delhi, Oxford University Press, 1984, p. 242.
7. The story of Panchayati Raj in Independent India has been a story of ups and downs. According to Ashoka Mehta Committee, it seems to have passed through three phases : the phase of ascendancy (1959-1964); the phase of stagnation (1965-1969); and the phase of decline (1969-1977). Subsequent events have unequivocally shown that the 'phase of decline' was coming to an end and a new phase started about 1978 which may be called 'Panchayati Raj reforms phase'. For the critical analysis of the major developments in Panchayati Raj, See. *(i)* B.S.Bhargava, *Panchayati Raj System and Political Parties*, New Delhi, Ashish Publishging House, 1979; *(ii) Politico – Administrative Dynamics in Panchayati Raj*, New Delhi, Ashish Publishing House, 1979; *(iii) Panchayati Raj Institutions ; An Analyses of Issues, Problems and Recommendations of Ashok Mehta Committee*, New Delhi, Ashish Publishing House, 1979; *(iv)* George Mathew, *Panchayati Raj : From Legislation to Movement*, New Delhi, Concept Publishing Company, 1994; *(v)* B.S. Bhargava and V. Venkata-krishnan, 'Panchayati Raj Movement : An Analysis of its Phases, in G. Palanithurai (Ed.). *Empowering People – Issues and Solutions*, New Delhi, Kanishka Publishers, Distributors, 1996, pp. 31-60.
8. Balwantrai G. Mehta Committee recommended 'devolution of power to a body which when created will have the entire charge of all development work within its jurisdiction, the government reserving for itself the functions of guidance, supervision and higher planning and where necessary providing extra finance'. See. *The Report of the Study Team on Community Projects and National Extension Service*, Vol. I, New Delhi, Government of India, 1957.
9. G. Ram Reddy, 'Panchayati Raj and Rural Development in Andhra Pradesh (India)' Norman T. Uphofff (Ed.), *Rural Development and Local Organisation in Asia*, Vol. I, New Delhi, Macmillan, 1982, p. 83.
10. For a penetrating analyses, See. Subhash C. Kashyap, '*Institutionalisation of Grassroots Governance*', in D. Sundar Ram (Ed.), *Panchayati Raj Reforms in India : Power to the People at the Grassroots*, New Delhi, Academy of Grassroots Studies and Research of India and Kanishka Publishers, Distributors, 2007.
11. As Young Prime Minister of India, Shri Rajiv Gandhi constituted many important Committees, Working Groups and Sub-Committees with Panchayati Raj experts and specialists to identify the loopholes and drawbacks in the working of the Panchayati Raj System. In this

direction, Professor C.H. Hanumantha Rao Committee (1984); Dr. G.V.K. Rao Committee (1985); Dr. L.M. Singhvi Committee (1986); Sarkaria Commission (1988) and Shri P.K. Thungan Committee (1988) are notable ones.

12. The Five Regional Workshops of the District Collectors/Magistrate were held in Bhopal (December, 1987); Hyderabad (February, 1988); Imphal and Jaipur (April, 1988) and Coimbatore (June, 1988). After the completion of the five regional workshops, the youthful bureaucrats opted for renunciation of power by strongly recommending 'Democratic Decentralisation' at the district with emphasis on 'District Planning'.

13. While introducing the 73rd Constitutional Amendment Bill, the CPM Lok Sabha Members Shri Chitta Basu and Shri Somnath Chatterjee opposed the Bill, contrary to the violation of the devolution of power between the States and the Centre as determined by the Constitution of India. Participating in the debate on the Bill, Shri Chitta Basu said : '..... But may I know whether this kind of legislation should be sponsored in this House? I am going into the merits of the case. I would like to say that it falls within the purview of State List in item No. 5. It is violative of the basic principles of federalism and undermines the basic structure of the Constitution. The Sarkaria Commission is also contrary to that. I, therefore, oppose for leave to introduce the Bill'.

    Another CPM Senior leader Shri Somnath Chatterjee said : 'Sir, the trouble is that all the States are not having appropriate panchayat laws. The concept behind a Constitution Amendment is that all the states are either not making laws or are not implementing the laws. But in the name, if you try to encroach into the powers of the State Governments, we object to that. We objected last time also. We have to see whether still mischief is there or not. But at this stage, let it come'. For more discussion, See. *Lok Sabha Debates*, September 16, 1991.

14. V.A. Vasudevaraju, 'Panchayati Raj Democracy Vs. Parliamentary Democracy', in G. Palanithurai (Ed.), *Empowering People – Issues and Solutions*, New Delhi, Kanishka Publishers, Distributors, 1996, p. 75.

15. The 73rd Constitutional Amendment Act, 1992 provided Constitutional Status to the Panchayati Raj Institutions. The Amendment also institutionalised a three-tier system of panchayats (except for states with a population of less than 2 million), with panchayats at the village, block and district levels, but what is revolutionary in this Act is 'political empowerment of women'. See. *The Constitution (Seventy-Third Amendment) Act, 1992*, Gazette of India Extraordinary, Part-II, Section-I, New Delhi, Government of India, April 20, 1993.

16. For the Text of the Prime Minister Shri Rajiv Gandhi's Statement on 64th Constitution Amendment Bill, See. 'Power to the People', *Rajiv Gandhi's Speeches,* Vol. V, New Delhi, Ministry of Information & Broadcasting, Government of India, 1989.
17. It is interesting to note that the 64th & 65th Constitution Amendment Bills were lost in the Rajya Sabha by 3 votes only.
18. See. N.R. Inamdar, 'Panchayati Raj Leadership: Emerging Dimensions', *Journal of Rural Development,* Vol. 10, No. 3, September, 1991.
19. See *(i)* S.S. Singh and S.N. Mishra, *Legislature Framework of Panchayati Raj in India,* New Delhi, Intellectual Publishing House, 1993. *(ii)* Swetha Mishra, *Democratic Decentralisation in India : Study in Retrospect and Prospect,* New Delhi, Mittal Publications, 1994.
20. *The Hindu,* February 2, 2000. p. 1 & *Times of India,* February 2, 2000.
21. For more details, See. *Report of the National Commission to Review the Working of the Constitution* (Chairman: Shri Justice M.N. Venkatachaliah), New Delhi, Government of India, 2002.
22. See. The National Declaration for Local Self-Governance—Recommendation, *Kurukshetra,* April, 2002.
23. See. *The National Common Minimum Programme (NCMP)—A Document,* May 2004, New Delhi, Government of India, 2004.
24. For the first time in Independent India, the Ministry of Panchayati Raj at the Centre came into existence on 27 May, 2004, under the headship of Shri Mani Shankar Aiyar. No previous Government has had a separate Ministry or even Department of Panchayati Raj. The Ministry is a unique, first ever innovation of the UPA Government led by Dr. Manmohan Singh.
25. For a full Text of the Speech, See. *Chief Minister's Conference on Rural Prosperity and Poverty Eradication through Panchayati Raj,* Inaugural Address by Dr. Manmohan Singh, New Delhii, 29th June, 2004.
26. For a full Text of Compendium of Resolutions of the Seven Round-Tables of Ministers, In-Charge of Panchayati Raj in the State Government (July-December, 2004), See. *The State of the Panchayats—A Mid-term Review and Appraisal, 22 November 2006, Volume III,* New Delhi, Ministry of Panchayati Raj, Government of India, 2006, pp. 170-199.
27. As part of the State Visits, the Union Minister for Panchayati Raj, Shri Mani Shankar Aiyar visited the following states during 2005 April to 2007 March and reached the Memorandum of Understandings (MoUs) with the respective State Governments and Union Territories: (1) Karnataka (29, 30 April & 1 May, 2005); (2) West Bengal (13-15 May, 2005); (3) Uttaranchal (24 June, 2005); (4) Haryana (17-22, August, 2005); (5) Chhattisgarh (28 August, 2005); (6) Orissa (23-26 October, 2005); (7) Arunachal Pradesh (7-9

November, 2005); (8) Rajasthan (2-4 December, 2005); (9) Lakshadweep (23 January, 2006); (10) Sikkim (30 March, 1 & 2 April, 2006); (11) Goa (11-12 April, 2006); (12) Andhra Pradesh (19-22 April, 2006); (13) Punjab (25-26 April, 2006); (14) Himachal Pradesh (27-30 May, 2006); (15) Kerala (19-22 July, 2006); (16) Assam (9-12 September, 2006); (17) Manipur (4-5 October, 2006); (18) Madhya Pradesh (17 December, 2006); (19) Pondicherry (11 January, 2007); (20) Tripura (11 February, 2007); (21) Andaman & Nicobar Islands (19 March, 2007).

28. For a lucid debate, See. *(i)* D. Sundar Ram (Ed.), *Panchayati Raj and Empowering People – New Agenda for Rural India : Essays in Honour of Shri Mani Shankar Aiyar,* New Delhi, Academy of Grassroots Studies and Research of India and Kanishka Publishers & Distributors, 2007; *(ii)* D. Bandyopadhyay and Amitava Mukherjee (Eds), *New Issues in Panchayati Raj,* New Delhi, Concept Publishing Company, 2004; *(iii)* G. Palanithurai (Ed.) *Dynamics of New Panchayati Raj,* Vols. I, II, III, IV, V and VI, New Delhi, Concept Publishing Company, 2002, 2004, 2006, *(iv)* M. WAdhwani and S.N. Mishra, *Dreams and Relatives:Expectations from Panchyayati Raj,* New Delhi, Concept Publishing Company; *(v)* George Mathew (Ed.) *Status of Panchayati Raj in the State of India,* New Delhi, Concept Publishing Company, 1994; *(vi)* R.C. Chowdary & S.P. Jain (Eds.) *Patterns of Decentralised Governance in Rural India, Hyderabad, NIRD,* 1999,

29. For an elaborate discussion, See. *(i)* D. Sundar Ram (Ed.), *Dynamics of Grassroots Governance in India: Dreams and Realities,* Vols. I & II, New Delh, Academy of Grassroots Studies and Research of India and Kanishka Publishers, Distributors, 2007; *(ii)* S.S. Chahar, *Government at Grassroots Level in India,* New Delhi, Kanishka Publishers, Distributors, 2005.

APPENDIX–I

The Text of the 16 Point *Tirupati Panchayati Raj Declaration* for *Power to the People* at the Grassroots, Adpoted by the Academy of Grassroots Studies and Research of India at the National Conference Held During 19 and 20 August, 2007 at Tirupati, Andhra Pradesh

Tirupati

The Academy of Grassroots Studies and Research of India (AGRASRI), an autonomous, non-profit and Non-Governmental Professional Organisation, being headquartered at Tirupati, organised a two days National Conference on *Role of Panchayati Raj Institutions After 60 Years of Independent India – A Vision of the Future*, during 19 and 20 August, 2007, in collaboration with the Rajiv Rural Development Foundation, Tirupati. The National Conference was sponsored by the Ministry of Panchayati Raj, Government of India, New Delhi.

The National Conference was inaugurated by *Dr. A. Chakrapani*, Chairman of the Andhra Pradesh State Legislative Council, with *Shri Solipeta Ramachandra Reddy*, former Member of Parliament (Rajya Sabha) and Chairman, Andhra Pradesh Local Bodies Empowerment Forum, in the Chair. *Shri R. Dileep Reddy*, State Information Commissioner (RTI), Govt. of Andhra Pradesh, *Shri Manoranjan Bhakta*, Member of Parliament (Lok Sabha), Andaman & Nicobar Islands, *Professor Julian Swindell*, Royal Agricultural College, Cirincester, United Kingdom, participated in the Inaugural session of the Conference, as Guests of Honour and Special Invitees. On the second day, the Governor of Kerala *Shri R.L. Bhatia*, the former Speaker of Andhra Pradesh Legislative Assembly *Dr. Agarala Easwara Reddi*, participated in the deliberations as Chief Guest and Guest of Honour, with *Padma Bhushan Dr. R.A. Mashelkar*, President of the Indian National Science Academy and CSIR Bhatnagar Fellow, National Chemical Laboratory, Pune, as Main Speaker, who delivered the Sixth Bharat Ratna Rajiv Gandhi Memorial Lecture-2007.

The key document that emerged from the deliberations of the National Conference was the *'Tirupati Panchayati Raj Declaration'*. This resolution was at the centre of the recommendations made by the delegates, participants and elected representatives of PRIs, representing the states of Andhra Pradesh, Tamil Nadu, Karnataka, Kerala, Maharashtra, Orissa, Rajasthan, Haryana, Delhi and Union Territories of Pondicherry and Andaman & Nicobar Islands. The copies of the Tirupati Panchayati Raj Declaration is being forwarded to the policy makers at the helm of affairs, including the Union Minister for Panchayati Raj *Shri Mani Shankar Aiyar*, the Union Minister for Rural Development *Dr. Raghuvansh Prasad Singh*, the Chief Minister of Andhra Pradesh *Dr. Y.S. Rajashekhar Reddy*, and Chairman of the Second Administrative Reforms Commission *Shri M. Veerappa Moily*, for taking appropriate steps in strengthening the Panchayati Raj Institutions, as real Local Self-Government Institutions after 6 decades of India's Independence, for *Power to the People* at the grassroots.

The text of the 16-point Tirupati Panchayati Raj Declaration for *'Power to the People'* at the grassroots is as follows:

1. To provide equal status to the women in governance at the grassroots, the facility of reservation of seats for women should be increased from 33 per cent to 50 per cent in Panchayati Raj Institutions;
2. To scrap provisions of discretionary funds given to Members of Parliament and Members of Legislative Assemblies of various States under the Local Area Development Scheme or all these funds should be released through the Panchayati Raj Institutions only;
3. To instruct State Governments to abolish District Rural Development Agency (DRDA) and similar agencies and merge their assets, functions and functionaries with Zilla Parishads/ Zilla Panchayats, based on Karnataka model;
4. Creation of a separate District Panchayat Raj Services should be considered, as it is done in case of IAS, IPS, IFS and State Level Services etc.;
5. In order to make Gram Sabhas, which are the fulcrum of the Panchayati Raj system, more effective and efficient Ward Sabha could be created and all the developmental programmes should be implemented as per the decisions taken by the Gram Sabha only;
6. To widen the empowerment of women in our polity and governance as a whole, the Union Government should give top priority to the passage of the Constitution Amendment Bill as a first step towards 50 per cent reservation of seats for women in Indian Parliament and various State Legislatures;
7. The State Governments should be directed to study the existing Nyaya Panchayats and make recommendations accordingly, in

order to make 'Nyaya Panchayats' as an integral part of the Panchayati Raj System;

8. Action Taken Report (ATR) of the various State Governments in respect of the devolution of 3 F's – Functions, Functionaries and Finances – to the Panchayati Raj Institutions should be clearly published every year and distribute the same to all the Panchayati Raj Institutions, as fulfillment of the mandate of the 73rd Constitution Amendment Act, 1992;
9. Measures should be taken by the Union Government for including a 'Local Governments List', as we have Union List, State List and Concurrent List in the Constitution of India;
10. An enabling environment should be created, especially for the Rural Industries and Cottage Industries, to participate effectively in rural livelihood programmers and subsequent sustainability for enhancing the rural transformation;
11. Article 243 A of the 73rd Panchayati Raj Amendment Act, 1992 be reviewed with a view to remove the word 'may' (whereever it comes) and incorporate 'shall', for enlarging the scope of the Act;
12. The State Governments should bring the awareness on the Citizens Charter and Right to Information Act among the people and allocate special funds in the Budget for the purpose. These two should be incorporated in PR Acts of the States in the country;
13. To take steps to implement the reservation facilities to all categories in the Panchayati Raj Institutions for at least 2 terms or a period of 10 years;
14. The recommendations of the Grama Sabha in regard to developmental programmes should not be overlooked any further and the Grama Sabha recommendations must be implemented by the Gram Panchayats as mandatory;
15. To give emphasis to the training, field visits and exposure visits of Panchayati Raj elected representatives for enhacing the Capacity Building and Skills in delivery of services to the people and to this effect, the State Governments should consider the NGO's and Professional bodies also as training partners; and
16. To counteract the negative implications and consequences of globalisation, liberalisation and privatisation, Panchayat Raj Institutions should be strengthened appropriately.

APPENDIX–II

Draft of the Charter of the National Convention of the Presidents of District and Intermediate Panchayats, Presented the same to the Prime Minister Dr. Manmohan Singh on 24th April, 2008 at New Delhi

1.1. Gandhiji believed that democratic freedoms have to be founded in institutions of self-government in every village in India. He drew his inspiration from the traditional Panchayats; 'village republics', which he called Panchayati Raj. He based his vision of contemporary democracy in independent India on genuine peoples' participation in the development and welfare of their own habitats through elected Panchayats. Dr Bhimrao Ambedkar, the father of our Constitution, provided for Village Panchayats in the State List of the Seventh Schedule, but consistently stressed the need to incorporate reservations for the depressed segments of our society in the structure of Panchayati Raj. Rajiv Gandhi ensured this and added reservations for women of all said categories in Panchayats. His declared objective was 'Power to the People' through the Panchayats, thus making India not only the world's biggest democracy, but also the world's most representative democracy.

1.2. Today, more than 26 lakh representatives stand elected to the three levels of Panchayats. Of these, over 10 lakh are women, 5.2 lakh belong to the Scheduled Castes and 3.3 lakh to the Scheduled Tribes. The last fifteen years of Panchayati Raj have thus succeeded in empowering marginalized groups who have gained political representation and valuable experience. Many of them have successfully taken on the challenge of governance and brought about enduring social change through their close links with the community.

1.3. Speaking to the Chief Ministers less than a month after he assumed office, the Prime Minister said that Panchayati Raj is the medium to transform rural India into 700 million opportunities and the challenge is to institutionalize this system of local governance to make India the world's most representative and participatory democracy.

1.4. The 73rd Constitutional Amendment Act, 1993 ushered in a new era of democratic decentralization, in which both powers and responsibilities are devolved upon elected Panchayats at the District, Intermediate and Village levels. The Eleventh Five-Year Plan, which has identified Inclusive Growth as the overarching objective, seeks to 'substantially empower and use PRIs as the primary means of delivery of essential services that are critical to inclusive growth.' The Plan asserts that 'it is absolutely critical for the inclusiveness of our growth process that these large numbers of elected representatives in our PRIs are fully involved in planning, implementing and supervising the delivery of essential public services.' A detailed road map as to how this could be achieved has been elaborated in Chapter 10 of the 'Plan document entitled 'Governance', which recognizes decentralization and strengthening of PRIs as a major challenge. The stage is set for a new era of strong and effective local self-government.

1.5 Yet many obstacles to genuine empowerment of people through the Panchayats remain. Though States have enacted Panchayati Raj legislation, real devolution of powers and responsibilities so as to empower Panchayats as institutions of self-government is yet to happen. Progress in this respect has been uneven. In many States, Panchayats have not been able to become effective instruments of economic development and social justice as devolution of functions, funds and functionaries have remained largely on paper.

2. We, the elected representatives of the people of India, serving through the Panchayats at the village, intermediate and district levels, believe that we are on the threshold of a new dawn where the Panchayats will fully assume the mantle of vibrant local self- government as enshrined in the Constitution. To fulfill the high hopes and aspirations of the lakhs of Panchayat elected representatives we have drafted and adopted this Charter as our road map and seek the guidance and support of State and Central Governments, to fulfill the dreams of the Father of the Nation.

3. Functional Empowerment of Panchayats

3.1. By now Panchayats at the district, intermediate and village levels have experience of working for about 15 years as Local Governments. We are competent enough to shoulder the responsibility and exercise powers in respect of all the 29 matters listed in the Eleventh Schedule of the Constitution. Hence, all 29 matters listed must be devolved upon the Panchayats in all States.

3.2. All States have enacted Panchayati Raj laws that devolve some matters listed in the Eleventh Schedule of the Constitution to the Panchayats. However, formal legal provisions should be implemented in spirit through undertaking a detailed activity mapping to assign to each level of Panchayats activities relating to the particular functions devolved. Activity mapping should not merely give us powers of 'promotion' of programmes, but also substantive powers in local planning and implementation. To ensure clarity and sustainability in the devolution of activities to Panchayats, States should ideally route the activity mapping through legislative measures.

3.3. Various parallel Societies, Agencies, Committees and Missions which have been created by central and state level line ministries and departments to implement specific schemes that fall in the Panchayat domain, such as District Rural Development Agencies (DRDAs), Sarva Shiksha Abhiyan (SSA), National Rural Health Mission (NRHM) and National Horticultural Mission (NHM) societies etc., must be either abolished or merged or brought into a suitable institutional relationship with appropriate levels of Panchayati Raj Institutions so that Panchayats have full control over technical and non-technical manpower working under them.

3.4. In order that Panchayats function as institutions of self-government, their domain has to be widened. Judicial powers, Police, Revenue, Regulation and Development functions must be developed upon Panchayats.

3.5. In order to effectively implement the 73rd Amendment in letter and spirit, a uniform Panchayat Code should be prepared by the Ministry of Panchayati Raj. In order to facilitate this, efforts have to be made to bring the Panchayat subject from the State list to either the Concurrent list or the Central list.

3.6. In order to establish organic linkages between Panchayats at all levels and District Planning Committees (DPCs), elected representatives of village and intermediate tiers should also be given representation in the DPCs, in addition to the representation given to members of the Zilla Panchayats.

3.7. Administrative and financial procedures of the State and Central Governments must be simplified and redesigned to facilitate planning and implementation by Panchayati Raj Institutions.

Existing delegated legislation, codes, rules, and executive orders which were designed for an older hierarchical and centralized administrative system are no longer relevant for this new governance system.

3.8. Globalization and liberalization has thrown up both challenges and opportunities for all levels of the Government. The Panchayats cannot be hesitant any longer. We must look beyond higher level governments to design and implement programmes that meet local needs and promote the prosperity of our people. We will inculcate in ourselves the spirit of self-help and take up locally driven initiatives which need not necessarily be funded by the Central and State Governments.

4. Financial Empowerment of Panchayats

4.1. State and Central Governments must ensure that there is regularity and clarity in the flow of funds to Panchayats. To this end, it is essential to pattern the flow of finances to each tier of the Panchayati Raj system in strict conformity with the pattern of activity mapping for functions. It is only if functions and finances are matched that effective devolution of powers to the Panchayats will be ensured. With this in view, a panchayat sector window should be opened in the budgets of all line departments to ensure the flow of funds to each tier of the Panchayats to finance the functions devolved on them. These schemes may be consolidated into a single panchayat sector window, a practice followed by several States and some of the tribal areas covered by the Sixth Schedule.

4.2. Similar Activity Mapping for functions and finances is required for Centrally Sponsored Schemes (CSSs) and other Central Government funding streams such as Additional Central Assistance to enable local planning and implementation by Panchayats. The guidelines of those that pertain to the functional domain of Panchayats must be modified to ensure the centrality of Panchayats at all three levels in planning and implementation, as is the case with the Backward Regions Grant Fund, the Central Finance Commission grants and the Rashtriya Krishi Vikas Yojana. Priority must be given to modifying the guidelines of the National Rural Employment Guarantee Scheme (NREGS), National Rural Health Mission (NRHM), Sarva Shiksha Abhiyan (SSA), National Midday Meals Programme (MDM), Accelerated Rural Water Supply Programme (ARWSP), Total Sanitation Programme, Pradhan Mantri Gram Sadak Yojana, (PMGSY) Integrated Child Development Services (ICDS), Indira Awas Yojana (IAY) and Swarna Jayanti Gram Swarozgar Yojana

(SGSY). Compendia of all guidelines of flagship centrally sponsored schemes should be regularly published and distributed in local languages, so that Panchayats have up to date information on them.

4.3. Devolution of untied funds through block grant transfers by the Central and State Finance Commissions should substantially increase to keep pace with the increasing responsibilities entrusted to Panchayats for the maintenance and upkeep of local public services and infrastructure development. Central Finance Commission Grants must supplement the funds devolved to Panchayats, and must not be subsumed into funds transfers made by States to the Panchayats.

4.4. There must be a separate funding window in the Central Government to fund innovative proposals prepared by Panchayats, in the same manner as is available to NGOs.

4.5. Funds devolved to Panchayats by Central and State Governments ought to reach them directly with as few intermediate steps as is necessary. There should be uniform guidelines for funds flow applicable to all schemes across all Ministries and all States, with time limits fixed for funds to reach the Panchayats. Funds should reach each Panchayat promptly after it has submitted its utilization reports. Current initiatives in computerization of treasuries and transfer of funds electronically through banking channels should be adopted quickly by all fund transferring agencies.

4.6. The devolution of funds to Panchayats in Union Territories presents special problems, as there is no separate funding window in the Central budget to channelise funds to them for the implementation of Centrally Sponsored Schemes. Arrangements may be made in the Central budget to channelise funds to Panchayats in Union Territories directly, in accordance with the devolution of functions to them.

4.7. The proposed Central Scheme and Programme Monitoring System should enable the tracking of both release of funds and submission of progress reports and utilization certificates by each Panchayat. It should also function as a financial information system, so that all Panchayats are aware of when funds are released by Central and State Governments. All notifications regarding funds released to the States should be communicated to all levels of Panchayats to facilitate planning.

4.8. Panchayats currently underutilize the powers of taxation and user charge collection given to them. We will take earnest steps to mobilize our own revenue by undertaking systematic and timely assessments to fully survey our tax base and enforce tax collection, through a campaign mode approach.

4.9. There must be no conditionalities imposed by States on the expenditure and investments by Panchayats from their own revenues.

4.10. Panchayats should have access to bank credit to take up development projects such as universal housing for the poor, support to SHGs and their federations and construction of remunerative infrastructure assets. The Government of India should frame a policy framework in this regard.

5. Improving the Capacities of Panchayats through Devolution of Functionaries, Training, Panchayat Level Office Infrastructure and Provision of Technical Support

Provision of Staff for the Panchayats

5.1. Provision of staff for the Panchayats: Staff of the line departments relating to devolved matters should be placed under the control of Panchayats, through a separate cadre management system for such Panchayat staff. Functionaries relating to health, drinking water supply, education, public distribution system and livelihoods should be transferred immediately to the Gram Panchayats. Progressively, staff for performing functions devolved should be recruited by Panchayats. Zilla Panchayats should be permitted to select their CEOs through an open selection process, so that the best talent is available to them to head their administration. While still working under the overall supervision and control of the President of the Zilla Panchayat and the Council, enhanced powers may be given to the CEO of the Zilla Panchayats so that he can better coordinate with line departments. Clear powers of management and control must be given to the ZP Chairperson. All confidential reports of officials working under the Panchayats should be written by the Panchayat Presidents at the appropriate level.

5.2. ***Provision of adequate remuneration for elected Panchayat representatives at the District, Intermediate and Village levels:*** The elected representatives of Panchayats at all three levels shoulder the responsibility of preparation of plans for economic development and social justice and also carry out responsibilities of managing their Panchayat affairs. With the increasing emphasis on implementation of flagship schemes relating to rural service delivery at the Panchayat level, elected Panchayat ward members and sarpanches are working full time and receive only nominal honoraria and sitting fees for their efforts. Panchayat elected representatives at all three levels are executive authorities and beyond attending meetings of the Panchayats and standing committees, they also undertake field inspections, ward visits and attend meetings of line department offices. With increasing responsibilities being given to Panchayats at all three levels, there is a need to make adequate provision for Traveling Allowances, Daily Allowances and provide adequate remuneration to the Panchayat representatives at all three levels. This matter should be addressed by State and Central Governments.

5.3. *Training for Panchayat Elected Representatives and Officials*

5.3.1. Panchayat elected representatives and officials should be provided sustained and high quality training through a system that fulfils their own training needs. Training must also be flexible enough to meet specific requirements of Panchayats. Training materials should be easily accessible electronically and through help lines, call centers, interactive broadcasts and other modes of distance learning and replies to frequently asked questions, prepared in the local language.

To this end, we demand the acceptance and implementation of the Gairola Committee Report commissioned by the Union Ministry of Panchayati Raj, which has recommended an outlay of Rs. 7700 crore to ensure satellite and internet connectivity to every Panchayat level within the next three years. This will not only facilitate distance training of all elected Panchayat members and office bearers as well as Panchayat officials, but also facilitate transparency, accountability and vigilance.

5.3.2. Training and communication should not be viewed as a single one-time intervention but should be a continuous, ongoing process leading to an enhanced sense of self-esteem and confidence. Training should cover both the "before" and "after" election periods. Initial training and communication should reach all elected representatives within one year.

5.3.2. Panchayat training must promote a culture of oneness amongst Panchayats through exposure visits and interactions between districts. Peer to peer learning, both within and outside the state through regional or national tie-ups and visits to beacon Panchayats should be encouraged and supported, so as to spread innovations and best practices.

5.3.3. There must be specialised training programmes for different groups, such as for women Panchayat representatives, SC/ST members and young representatives. There should also be combined training of Panchayat representatives along with functionaries.

5.3.4. Special training programmes must be organized in areas covered by the Panchayats (Extension to Scheduled Areas) Act, 1996 so as to have regard to the cultural traditions and special needs of tribal people.

5.3.4. Semi-literate or illiterate PRI members should be given special training to enable them to achieve functional literacy within six months to a year.

5.3.5. Panchayat members should be actively involved in the preparation of training syllabi. Experienced Panchayat members and former members should be encouraged to become resource persons for further training of panchayat representatives.

5.3.6. Special efforts must be made to undertake training and awareness campaigns for Social Audit by Gram Sabhas. Adequate notice must be given for the conduct of Gram and Ward Sabha meetings so as to ensure that there is wider participation in them

5.3.7. Capacity building programmes must also be taken up in the 6th Schedule Areas and those areas that are not covered by the provisions of Panchayati Raj.

5.3.8. Education in local governance should be included in school syllabi so as to inculcate the spirit of participation in local self-governments amongst children.

5.3.9. Training should become a two way process so that feedback can help in reforming the content and process of training, as also result in systemic changes in panchayat and government functioning. Independent training impact assessment studies should be periodically undertaken to assess the outcomes of training and identify emerging needs for follow up.

5.4 ***Provision of Physical Infrastructure and Information Technology for Panchayats***

5.4.1. All panchayats must be provided adequate physical infrastructure in the form of adequate office space, meeting and waiting rooms, toilets, IT, telephone and road connectivity.

5.4.2. For effective performance, Panchayats should rely of state of the art technology, particularly on information technology and computerization of their operations. The Mission Mode Project on e-Panchayats under the National e-Governance Plan (NeGP) prepared by the Ministry of Panchayati Raj should be fully funded implemented in a time bound fashion within the next three years.

5.5. ***Extending the reservation cycle to three terms:*** In order to build and retain capacity and leadership among categories for whom seats are reserved in Panchayats, States shall consider favourably extending the reservation cycle to three five-year terms.

5.6. ***Removal of the two child norm:*** There must be no restrictions applied, such as the two child norm, which prevent talented and competent persons from standing for Panchayat level elections. This norm should be abolished as it also leads to undermining the position of women and has no effect on population control.

5.7. It is not in keeping with a strong local democracy that officers are given powers to dismiss Panchayats and assume powers as administrators of Panchayats. Such provisions should be removed from State Panchayat Raj laws.

6. Decentralized Planning and Implementation

6.1. Article 243G of the Constitution envisages that Panchayats would undertake planning for social justice and economic development. Decentralised planning constitutes an important part of the powers and responsibilities of the Panchayats. The Eleventh Plan has recognized that planning from the grassroots level upwards by the Panchayats is the most important step towards bringing Panchayats to the centre of local decision-making and service delivery. Considerable resources are available today through a host of central and state schemes and funding mechanisms for poverty alleviation, infrastructure development and improvement of service delivery such as the Rural Employment Guarantee Programme, the National Rural Health Mission, ICDS, Sarva Shiksha Abhiyan, Mid-Day Meal Programme, Drinking Water Supply and sanitation, Pradhan Mantri Gram Sadak Yojana, Irrigation Development and Rashtriya Krishi Vikas Yojana. All these schemes should be planned for in a coordinated manner and included in the comprehensive plan of the Panchayat level at which they are implemented. Own resources of Panchayats should also figure in their plans.

6.2. **Constitution of District Planning Committees by States in conformity with the provisions of Article 243ZD of the Constitution:** Article 243ZD of the Constitution provides that every state shall constitute at the district level a District Planning Committee to consolidate the plans prepared by the Panchayats and the Municipalities in the district and to prepare a draft development plan for the district as a whole. Of the 24 states covered by the Provisions of Parts IX and IX-A of the Constitution relating to Panchayats and Municipalities respectively, 18 states have constituted District Planning Committees in accordance with Article 243ZD. The remaining states must meet this constitutional mandate forthwith.

6.3. As provided for in the Constitution, each level of the Panchayati Raj system: Village, Intermediate and District—must prepare the perspective Five Year Plan and Annual Plans for their respective jurisdiction. The same exercise should be undertaken in the Municipalities of each district. The DPC should "consolidate" the plans prepared by the Panchayats and Municipalities, as provided for in the Constitution, rather than prepare the District Plan of its own accord or of its own volition. Plans prepared by Panchayats should be respected by higher levels of government and not changed.

6.4. High allocations to and implementation of MP and MLA Local Area Development Scheme, kills the spirit of participatory planning. Implementation of these programmes must be in convergence with the programmes taken up at the Panchayat levels.

6.5. Absence of line department officials during the planning process leads to disregard of plans and deliberate interference at higher levels. It must be made mandatory for officials to be present during the planning process by Panchayats.

6.6. Panchayats conduct Gram Sabhas to not only prepare a list of works, but also to fix priorities in implementation, as funds at the Panchayats level are limited. Line departments should not prepare their own priority lists for schemes such as MP and MLA Local Area Grants and take up works without the knowledge of the Panchayats. It must comply with the priority lists prepared by the Gram Sabhas.

6.7. In keeping with the recommendations of the Ramachandran Committee on grassroots level planning in areas not covered by the provisions of Parts IX and IX-A of the Constitution, suitable arrangements for district planning may be made in these areas.

6.8. Arranging technical support for DPCs to prepare district plans: Technical support and IT support must be provided to the DPCs to assist them in their task of consolidation of district plans.

6.9. Every State must have a State Development Council, which is comprised of all presidents of Zilla Panchayats, to deliberate upon issues relating to planning and implementation of programmes and policies by the Panchayats.

7. Panchayati Raj in Areas Covered by the Fifth Schedule of the Constitution

7.1. The Panchayats (Extension to Scheduled Areas) Act, 1996 (PESA) is a central legislation that extends the constitutional provisions of Panchayati Raj to Fifth Schedule Areas, subject to certain exceptions and modifications. Nine States, namely, Andhra Pradesh, Chhattisgarh, Gujarat, Himachal Pradesh, Jharkhand, Madhya Pradesh, Maharashtra, Orissa and Rajasthan have Fifth Schedule Areas. PESA lays down that every village will have a Gram Sabha which will be competent to safeguard and preserve the traditions and customs of the people, their cultural identity, community resources and customary mode of dispute resolution. PESA provides that in Panchayats in 5th Schedule areas, there must be a minimum of fifty per cent reservation of the total number of seats for the Scheduled Tribes. All Chairpersons' seats in Panchayats are also to be reserved for the Scheduled Tribes.

7.2. Gram Sabhas have been entrusted with the responsibilities of management of water bodies and licensing for the extraction of minor minerals. Gram Sabhas and Panchayats have to be consulted before any kind of land acquisition or resettlement and rehabilitation of displaced persons. Gram Sabhas and Panchayats at the appropriate level have been specifically given the powers and authority to enforce prohibition or to regulate or extract the sale and consumption of any intoxicant, ownership of minor forest produce, power to prevent alienation of land, powers to manage village markets, power to exercise control over money-lending, power to exercise control over institutions and functionaries in all social sectors. The recommendation of the Gram Sabha or the Panchayats at the appropriate level has been made mandatory prior to grant of prospecting licence or mining lease for minor minerals.

7.3. In PESA areas, the Gram Sabhas have been given executive powers and they can elect their traditional heads as the heads of the Gram Sabhas. There is a need to workout a harmonious relationship between the Gram Sabhas in PESA areas with the Gram Panchayats.

7.4. While all states have enacted requisite compliance legislations by amending the respective Panchayati Raj Acts, certain gaps continue to exist. Most states are yet to amend the subject laws, like those relating to money-lending, forest, excise etc., to bring these into conformity with PESA. Consequently, compliance with PESA remains incomplete and perfunctory in virtually all states.

Vital issues like the ownership of minor forest produce, planning and management of minor water bodies, prevention of alienation of tribal lands etc., which have been duly recognized in PESA as the traditional rights of tribals living in the Scheduled Areas have still not received the warranted attention and the necessary correctives remain unapplied. Central legislations such as the Indian Land Acquisition Act, the Forest Conservation Act, and the Indian Registration Act will also need to be harmonized with the provisions of PESA. States and relevant central ministries must take concrete steps to harmonize the provisions of the laws and policies concerned with the aims and objectives of PESA.

7.5. Powers statutorily devolved upon the Gram Sabha and the Panchayats are not being matched by concomitant transfer of funds and functionaries resulting in the non-exercise of such powers. Functionaries in the social sector should work under the overall supervision and control of the Gram Sabha as envisaged under PESA.

7.6. The concept of community ownership of resources in PESA areas should be integrated into the provisions of the Centrally Sponsored Schemes concerned. All community resource based schemes should involve Gram Sabhas in planning and implementation in PESA areas.

7.7. More than eleven years after its enactment there is little or no awareness about the provisions of PESA. Therefore, it is imperative that all persons in PESA areas are given in-depth training on the provisions of PESA through awareness campaigns. Officials concerned with the implementation of PESA should also be properly sensitized.

7.8. Physical infrastructure in interior areas should be strengthened in order to protect the life and property of tribals. Special attention should be paid to the construction of culverts, bridges, check dams, compound walls for schools, etc.

7.9. As of now, ownership of Minor Forest Produce does not vest with tribals. Steps should be taken to ensure that they get the best remunerative price for their Minor Forest Produce.

8. Decentralisation in Areas not Covered by the Provisions of Parts IX and IX-A of the Constitution

8.1. The entire philosophy of the Sixth Schedule of the Constitution is aimed at protection of tribal areas and interests, by constitutionally mandating district or regional local self-government institutions for them. These institutions are entrusted with the twin task of protecting tribal culture and customs and undertake development tasks for them. The provisions of the Sixth Schedule of the constitution should be operationalised in letter and spirit.

8.2. Areas that fall outside the purview of both Panchayati Raj and the Sixth Schedule must also provide for regular elections to local autonomous councils, so that the tribal people concerned can meet their aspirations for local democracy and decentralized and inclusive growth.

8.3. There is a significant degree of variation in the functions devolved to one Autonomous District as compared to another. The minimum extent of powers given to a District Council ought to be at least that enunciated in the Eleventh Schedule of the Constitution, which can be considered as an indicative list in this case also.

8.4. To make district planning in Sixth Schedule areas both inclusive and representative, Autonomous councils will need to live harmoniously with traditional arrangements. For this reason, these bodies should be given clear development functions, in addition to the regulatory, legislative and judicial powers bestowed upon them.

9. Activating Community Participation at the Grassroots

9.1. The Constitution defines Gram Sabha as a body consisting of voters relating to a village comprised within a Panchayat. The peoples' right to participate in local democracy must be interpreted in its widest sense. Therefore, the term 'Gram Sabha' must be understood in its holistic sense and not in a restrictive sense as an occasional meeting of voters. Since participation of people is most important, members of the Gram Sabha should be consulted even at their doorstep through surveys and ward and neighbourhood level meetings.

9.3. The legal framework and the practice of holding two levels of Gram Sabha meetings in some states, at the ward or habitation level and at the GP level should be universally implemented in all states.

9.4. Good Panchayat level practices such as the Kudumbashree programme of Kerala, which has fostered a vibrant participation between poor and marginalized members of the Gram Sabha, with the Gram Panchayats, should be promoted in all States.

9.5. There must be universal endowment of the Gram/Ward Sabha with meaningful empowerment through such measures as giving them powers to approve before implementation commences, plans and programmes (including budgets) for economic development and social justice prepared by the Gram Panchayat, to authorize the issuance of utilization certificates of funds allocated for the plans, projects or programmes of the Panchayat and to undertake the identification of beneficiaries.

9.5. Social audit is an important complement to formal audit and for the sound and healthy development of Panchayati Raj, it is essential to establish a symbiotic relationship between social and formal audit. Social audits must also be undertaken for Panchayats at the Intermediate and District level and line department offices.

9.6. For social audit to be effective and based on the best practices available in different States, consideration might be given to the preparation of Social Audit Policies for adoption by State Legislatures/Governments so as to provide a framework within which social audit is undertaken.

10. Rural Business Hubs

10.1. Panchayats need to be aware of the opportunities that exist for them to plan for economic development of their area and could promote rural non-farm enterprises, which utilise local skills and/or resources and generate/promote rural employment through Public-Private-Panchayat Partnership.

10.2. Artisan based clusters established under different schemes of the Central or State Governments and organisations such as the Khadi and Village Industries Commission, the NABARD and the Development Commissioner, Handicrafts must enable a clear role for Panchayats to be proactive in enabling convergence with existing schemes. The Panchayats could also actively promote local entrepreneurship through external facilitation, capacity building, access to credit etc., and thus play the lead role for rural development and economic empowerment, by acting as the gateway for central/state schemes and interventions of bank and other institutions.

11. Incentives for Panchayat Performance

11.1. Incentives must be provided to support States to devolve more functions, functionaries and finances to the Panchayats, encourage and facilitate States to restructure the system of self-government at the Panchayat level, motivate and assist Panchayats to use their newly enlarged responsibilities in a focused and productive fashion and ensure that Panchayats achieve standards that meet norms set out for public accountability.

11.2. Panchayats at all levels should be awarded for their annual improvement over the previous year in the achievement of the goals of transparency and accountability to their respective Gram Sabhas and efficiency in performing their roles and responsibilities.

12. Creating a National Network of Panchayat Representatives

12.1. In order to gain strength from each other, share experiences and best practices and gain a collective voice, we resolve to create a national network of Panchayat elected representatives. The specific objectives of the National network would be to enable Panchayats to *(a)* share best practices, *(b)* solve local problems with experience and support gained from other Panchayats, *(c)* be aware of and take preventive measures against malfunctioning of Panchayats, *(d)* bring to the notice of higher level governments, policy makers and commissions the problems encountered by Panchayats at all levels, *(e)* dissemination of policies, programmes and other Panchayats related information to the Panchayats, *(f)* organize training programmes, field visits and study tours, *(g)* undertake peer reviews and benchmark performances of member Panchayats at all levels and *(h)* network with similar institutions nationally and internationally.

12.2. Every elected representative of the Panchayats at the district, intermediate and village levels will be a primary member of the Association of elected members, which will be federated in the manner described below, so as to unite members across all levels of Panchayats and across states, upto the national level.

12.4. The composition of the federation from the grassroots level upwards will be as follows:

(a) There shall be an Intermediate level Association at each intermediate Panchayat level. The general body of the association shall be comprised of three members selected from each Gram Panchayats. The intermediate level association shall also provide adequate representation for elected representatives of intermediate Panchayats. For the areas under the fifth Schedule, one member shall be chosen from each Gram Sabha, to the Intermediate level Association.

(b) There shall be a District level Association for each District. The general body of the association shall be comprised of three members selected from each Intermediate level association. The District level association will also provide adequate representation for elected representatives of District Panchayats. It shall be ensured that there is adequate

representation for village Panchayat representatives in the District level Association.

12.5. There shall be a state level federation for each state, the general body of which shall be comprised of three members elected from each District level association. Each of the three members selected from the district will represent one level of Panchayat.

12.6. There shall be a national level federation of elected Panchayats representatives, the general body of which shall be comprised of three members elected from each state level association. Each of the three members selected from each state shall represent one level of Panchayat. Representation from states may be increased depending on the rural population of the state.

12.7. A minimum representation of 33 per cent for women and adequate representation for representatives belonging to the SCs and STs in the federations and associations at all levels shall be provided.

12.8. There will be an executive committee constituted for each Association and Federation, which will undertake the day-to-day activities of the body. A permanent office and requisite support system will be established for each Association and federation. Regular meetings of the associations and federations will be held at quarterly intervals upto district level, half-yearly at the state level, and annually at the national level.

12.9. Every Association and Federation will have its own fund, into which may flow contributions from the Panchayats, State and Central Government, the public, NGOs, banks and funding sources.

12.10. The federations and associations will sustain and promote their networking activities through the Internet, Video Conferencing and regular broadcasts over television and community radio on Panchayat programmes.

12.11. The Associations and Federations will be registered expeditiously. A Drafting Committee of Panchayat Representatives will be constituted to draft the model Memorandum of Association and the bye-laws of the Associations and the Federations. On this historic occasion of the fifteenth anniversary of the Seventy-third Amendment, which gave constitutional sanction, sanctity and status to Panchayati Raj, we, the elected representatives of over 80 crores of our rural brothers and sisters, rededicate ourselves to the cause of grassroots development through grassroots democracy and pledge to work tirelessly with compassion, social justice and equity for all, for inclusive growth through inclusive governance.

APPENDIX-III

The Text of the Prime Minister Dr. Manmohan Singh's Address at the National Convention of the Presidents of District and Intermediate Panchayats Held at New Delhi on 24th April, 2008 on the eve of the 15th Anniversary of the Gazetting and entry into Force of the 73rd Amendment Act (Part IX- The Panchayats) of the Constitution of India

Today is a historical day. We are celebrating the 15th anniversary of our Panchayati Raj. Thousands of elected Panchayati Raj leaders from all over the country have been invited to Delhi for the first time. I am happy to welcome all of you. Our aim is to take the voice of the common man from the Panchayat to the Prime Minister.

Mahatma Gandhi had a vision of an India where people of the villages would have self-government (Gram Swaraj). Shri Rajiv Gandhi gave shape to this idea of Gram Swaraj. He had a vision of according a prominent role to the Panchayati Raj in the process of social change. Rajivji gave a legal status to the vision of Mahatma Gandhi. Since the last 15 years, we have been strengthening the roots of democracy by following his footsteps.

During the last 4 years, the UPA Government has focused its attention towards rural India. The main objective of our Government is to build an inclusive society where there would be no discrimination between regions and society. We have to remove the gap between rural and urban India, between the rich and the poor, between educated and uneducated, and between strong and the weak. The struggle started by Pandit Jawaharlal Nehru after Independence to eradicate poverty, illiteracy and disease is continuing even today.

Since our Government has come to power, we have increased by four times the expenditure on village development and welfare and poverty alleviation programmes for the people living in rural areas.

We have started many programmes like—National Employment Guarantee Act, Bharat Nirman, National Rural Health Mission, etc. We must collectively ensure that the unprecedented quantum of money being spent on these programmes gives better results. It will be our endeavour to strengthen the role of Panchayati Raj Institutions in the programmes of the Central Government.

Panchayats have been empowered to implement the Rural Electrification Programme started through the Rajiv Gandhi Electrification Scheme. The Backward Region Grant Fund Programme provides for the Panchayats to evolve their own developmental schemes.

Panchayats play an important role in the management of local schools under the Education for All Campaign. Through these efforts, we have been able to open schools in almost all inhabited parts of the country. We have started the mid-day meal scheme across the country and the Panchayats are playing an important role in its implementation.

I believe that more attention needs to be given to the Nutritive Food Programme. We must also include local Panchayats in Integrated Child Development Scheme (ICDS).

In our Constitution system, each and every level has to play its role. These levels are—Centre, States and Panchayats. The implementation of programmes must be done at the level, which can effectively manage it. Most of our development works can be carried out in a better way at the local level.

That is why we are giving importance to the direct partnership of Panchayats in the management of our programmes of education, sanitation, health, etc.

The most historical decision the Government has ever taken in the field of rural development is the passing of the National Rural Employment Guarantee Act. Under the Act, rural workers have got the legal right to employment for the first time. The entire country has been covered under this programme from 1st April, 2008. This will increase food and employment security in villages.

Panchayats play a prominent role in works of the projects under this programme. The work of implementing this programme is in the hands of the Panchayat. The leaders of Panchayats have to implement as well as monitor the programmes. Rupees 10,000 crore have been spent through Panchayats within 2 years of implementation of this programme.

The Constitution clearly mentions that State Governments and State Legislatures are fully responsible for setting up of Panchayati Raj. States have their own circumstances and different ways to strengthen Panchayati Raj Institutions. There are some States that have implemented this to a large extent, while some States have to do much more in this regard. This matter needs discussion.

Today, we can assert it with a great sense of pride that there are approximately 2.5 lakhs local units in the country and we have sent a strong army of 32 lakhs representatives to it. Representatives from SC & ST communities enjoy an equal share of responsibility in their working.

Our great success in this field has been the number of women representatives that outnumber the sum total of elected women representatives all over the world. Political and Social Empowerment of Indian women is the greatest success of Panchayati Raj. It is unique in world history and in the modern era.

I am extremely happy today that on this historical occasion, Mrs. Sonia Gandhi ji is going to release an Experts Report on Women Empowerment in Panchayats.

As per the Right to Information Act, every common citizen is entitled to get information from the Government. To curb corruption the Gram Sabha should be given full information which should include information on resources deployed for works and their use.

Training is also needed. It is not an easy job to impart training to lakhs of representatives and keep them apprised of the information on a variety of matters. With the help of modern state of the art technology this can be made easy. Under the National E-governance Scheme, computer facilities should be provided to each Panchayat Ghar. I am happy that an Expert Report has been given to the Government to accomplish this work in a time bound manner. It is under consideration. We will soon embark on this new programme.

We will consider your recommendations on improvement of the Panchayati Raj system. We would like to assure you that the Union Cabinet would consider fully your suggestions. We would decide as to what type of changes can be made in the programmes of the Centre and states so that Panchayats could be involved fully in the progress of the nation. A primary objective of the Eleventh Five Year Plan is to involve every citizen in the development of the country. We would consider your recommendations in the Panchayat Ministers' Committee and the National Development Council (NDC).

Every citizen, whether he is poor or rich, should be given a chance to build his future through Panchayati Raj. This would make India not only the largest democracy of the world but also the most functioning democracy of the world.

This is the way that would make every citizen prosperous. When this prosperity reaches the home and heart of every Indian, only then the dream of Rajiv ji would come true.

Index